*Foundations for a Psychology
of Education*

Foundations for a Psychology of Education

edited by

Alan Lesgold
Robert Glaser

University of Pittsburgh

LEA LAWRENCE ERLBAUM ASSOCIATES, PUBLISHERS
1989 Hillsdale, New Jersey   Hove and London

Lawrence Erlbaum Associates, Inc., Publishers
365 Broadway
Hillsdale, New Jersey 07642

Production, interior, and cover
design: Robin Marks Weisberg

Library of Congress Cataloging in Publication Data
Foundations for a psychology of education / edited by Alan Lesgold,
  Robert Glaser.
      p.   cm.
   Includes indexes.
   ISBN 0-8058-0296-7
   1. Educational psychology.   I. Lesgold, Alan M.   II. Glaser,
Robert, 1921-   .
LB1051.F59 1989
370.15—dc19   88-24300
                                                                      CIP

Printed in the United States of America
10 9 8 7 6 5 4 3 2 1

Contents

Contributors

Lea T. Adams, Department of Educational Leadership, George Peabody College for Teachers, Vanderbilt University, Nashville, TN 37203

John D. Bransford, Department of Educational Leadership, George Peabody College for Teachers, Vanderbilt University, Nashville, TN 37203

John B. Carroll, 409 Elliott Road, Chapel Hill, NC 27514

Carol S. Dweck, Department of Psychology, University of Illinois, 603 East Daniel Street, Champaign, IL 61820

William K. Estes, Department of Psychology & Social Relations, Harvard University, 33 Kirkland Street, Cambridge, MA 02138

Gary M. Olson, Cognitive Science & Machine Intelligence Lab, University of Michigan, 904 Monroe Street, Ann Arbor, MI 48109

Greg A. Perfetto, Department of Educational Leadership, George Peabody College for Teachers, Vanderbilt University, Nashville, TN 37203

James F. Voss, Learning Research and Development Center, University of Pittsburgh, Pittsburgh, PA 15260

Nancy J. Vye, Department of Educational Leadership, George Peabody College for Teachers, Vanderbilt University, Nashville, TN 37203

Preface

The contributors to this volume provide richly informative and insightful views of the current state of knowledge in psychology and the study of cognition as it is relevant to understanding and improving the educational process. The authors of these chapters, some of the best scientists and scholars in their fields, review their disciplines with potential applicability to problems of education in mind. The fact that they agreed to do this represents a significant change in relationships between education and the disciplines that can contribute to it. It is still clear in our memories that 25 years ago the behavioral sciences and education were distant and reluctant relations. Despite the efforts of some outstanding pioneers, instructional practice and school learning were not salient concerns then in the work of scientists studying human behavior and cognition.

In recent years, social, professional, and scientific change have necessitated that these two worlds attend to each other more closely and recognize the value of each for the other. Educators interested in the contribution of modern advances to their profession have begun to unite knowledge of their subject matters with understanding of cognitive processes in learning, of the principles of human performance that underlie the design of teaching practices and materials, of variation in educational environments, and of attitudes and values that foster learning. They draw upon the knowledge of scientists who have taken on the educationally relevant areas of problem solving; motivation; the cognitive skills involved in reading, mathematics, and written communication; the structures of knowledge that facilitate reasoning and thinking; and the skills involved in self-learning and the ability to benefit from teaching and instruction.

The character of psychology has changed, partly because of this closer interaction. Until recently, the psychology that had been most useful to education was behavioral psychology. It brought a systematicity to education, including what we now call *management by objectives*. It introduced the general strategies of task analysis to education and stimulated our thinking about the effects of rewards and punishments. It also brought to education a scientific approach, in which ideas about how to teach were empirically tested. However, it had the weakness of assuming a generic learner who absorbs, in relatively passive fashion, microscopic and, for practical purposes, undifferentiated bits of facts and behaviors. It did not take account of the cognitive objectives of learning, because it avoided any direct treatment of mental activity.

The past few decades have been a period of rapid evolution of the psychology of thinking and learning. Cognitive psychology introduced a new focus on the mental processes whereby thinking occurs. At first it focused on general mental processes. More recently, it has come to deal with the specific content of thought and with specific subject matters. The new cognitive psychology is driven by specificity, of knowledge, of learner characteristics, and of thinking process. With this new emphasis, psychology in its forms relevant to education has changed dramatically, and it has come closer to explicating the grounds for some of the beliefs about education that reflective thinkers have held for centuries.

Here are some of the changes that we believe justify a deeper acquaintance with psychology for all educators:

- Psychologists now see the learner as a goal-oriented intelligence who constructs knowledge rather than absorbs it.

- Psychologists now see the knowledge-constructing capability of the learner as becoming richer in specifiable ways as a result of specific learning, general experience, and maturation.

- Psychological theory now reflects our beliefs that experiences in formal learning settings differ for different people, leading some to conclude that the goal of school work is acquisition of knowledge, whereas others come to focus more superficially on the performances that are rewarded in schooling situations.

- Psychology is starting to study how, and to what extent, aspects of learning ability are teachable, reflecting the view that intelligence is not so much a fixed trait but rather a person's current learning ability.

- Further, psychologists are beginning to learn what skills are required for learning various bodies of knowledge and how those partly domain-specific skills can be taught.

- Similarly, psychological theory is starting to reflect our realization that just as difficult athletic performances can be analyzed and coached, so too can problem-solving skills be coached and taught, that thinking hard is more than mere exertion of effort.

The courses and textbooks in psychology for education evolve like all other textbooks. Modifications are made as the field changes. However, because much of cognitive psychology has been developed outside of the disciplines of education, the knowledge acquired has not been quickly or completely absorbed into texts and courses. Part of this is, of course, a healthy conservatism. Not every theoretical proposal is a proven hypothesis, nor is every proven hypothesis immediately relevant. Nonetheless, there is now a core of stable, empirically supported theory in cognitive psychology that has major implications for education.

The importance of this theory can be seen by contrasting it with behavior theory. The principles of behavior theory rested on two general learning mechanisms—operant and classical conditioning. Learning was seen as involving some combination of reinforcement of existing behaviors that approximated target performances and highlighting of pattern relationships in the world by engineering temporal proximities for related events. The details of how to do this, the understanding of what specifically would be acquired, and the relationship between what a person already knew and what (and how) he or she would learn were left as "applied problems" to be engineered.

In a very real sense, what cognitive psychology has done for education is to put some science behind what formerly was, to the scientist, "mere engineering." It has not done this completely, and science is never complete for all time, but it has increased the extent to which the planning and conduct of instruction in complex subject matters can be grounded in principles. Equally important, it has changed the status of the learner and the teacher, giving both richer roles and responsibilities in the learning process.

We originally had in mind the creation of an encyclopedic handbook in which all the relevant areas of cognitive psychology were laid out, and each was presented in a definitive chapter. However, it rapidly became clear that cognitive instructional psychology is not yet ready for such codification. Although so much has been done that it is time to present it systematically to everyone who is entering the world of education, we keep learning more, and the categories of knowledge keep changing. So, we have asked some colleagues whose wisdom we particularly respect to summarize, from their own viewpoints, the parts of cognitive psychology that are likely to have enduring importance to education.

The chapters in this book show how concepts and principles now at hand can be viewed from the perspective of their value to thinking about the educational process. The authors do not provide specific prescriptions for educational problems. Rather, they have written deeply about the experimental and theoretical knowledge relevant to education that has accumulated in their fields: learning theory, cognitive development, motivation, intellectual abilities and attitudes, learning skills and the acquisition of knowledge, and problem solving—areas fundamental to teaching practice and the educational process.

The chapter on learning theory by William Estes is concerned primarily with the theoretical foundations of learning that underlie our ability to analyze the educational process. It describes the mental apparatus that enables learning in terms of contemporary theory, as structures and processes of the human information-processing system. Taking a long view of the history of learning theory, Estes distills concepts and principles of considerable generality from the accumulating scientific evidence. He first considers the basic mechanisms of human memory, including retention and forgetting, the failure of retrieval and loss of information. Then, he considers two kinds of learning: perceptual learning, basically a categorization process involving passive and relatively slow accumulation of recognition capability, and cognitive learning, which is more actively directed, selective, and relatively rapid. A final section on more complex learning considers the acquisition of concepts and the acquisition of knowledge and cognitive skill.

Estes concludes that there are two basic reasons why learning may be difficult. First, knowledge, although always acquired in some specific context, must be generalized in order for it to be available in other situations; that generalization requires carefully staged learning experiences. Second, even to understand material within a discipline requires some prior understanding of the discipline. In subject-matter learning, truly the rich get richer. As a result, careful "scaffolding" is required, with initial overview knowledge being taught to provide a basis for understanding more of a subject and becoming facile in the mental processes the subject requires. Estes notes that psychology still has much to learn about the ways in which the ability to learn more about a subject "take[s] form in the course of experience."

Recent approaches to the study of intellectual development are described in the chapter by Olson as a blend of (a) the traditions of Piaget, (b) psychometric approaches to intelligence, and (c) modern approaches to the underlying mental processes and structures that are responsible for intelligent behavior. His analysis of intellectual development is presented from the perspective of contemporary cognitive science, particularly in terms of underlying changes in the cognitive system that might provide the basis for intellectual development. Three broad classes of changes are described. The first has to do with changes in the basic characteristics of the cognitive system itself, including sensory and perceptual development, changes in the speed and efficiency of central processes, and motor development. A second category is knowledge modification, changes in the knowledge base. To develop intellectually is to know more and to know better, in the sense of having knowledge that is better organized and better represented in the mind. A third source of intellectual development is the development of specific and general cognitive skills upon which intellectual activity draws. These skills involve basic operations of memory (including association, recognition, and recall), skills of categorization and induction that derive general knowledge from experience, and skills that interrelate and combine existing knowledge, such as deduction and analogical reasoning.

Olson speculates on the mechanisms that might lead to the differences that are observed between children of different ages and points out that to date scholars have had more success in describing the properties of intellectual behavior at various stages of development than in describing the transition mechanisms that take children from one stage to the next. In this context he considers organismic and environmental factors and the spontaneous reorganizations of knowledge during the period of intense and disciplined environmental input that occurs in the school years.

The chapter on motivation by Carol Dweck considers achievement motivation, the striving toward cognitive competence. The chapter examines the factors, aside from the skills themselves, that affect the choice, pursuit, and performance of cognitive skills. Much of the research reviewed consists of empirical investigation of motivational variables that facilitate or impede learning, and the conditions that foster them. Dweck makes clear that children's adaptive patterns may change significantly in the course of educational experiences and that some well-intended instructional practices may not increase the probability that children will seek intellectual tasks and approach them with confidence and persistence. Further, both bright and less bright children are susceptible to debilitating motivational patterns.

The distinction is made between two kinds of achievement goals: learning goals, in which individuals strive to increase their competence, to understand or master something new; and performance goals, in which individuals strive to document or gain favorable judgments of their competence in order to avoid negative judgments. Although both learning and performance goals can promote active striving on challenging tasks, the research evidence suggests that these two goals are differentially associated with adaptive and maladaptive patterns. Learning goals predict the pursuit and mastery of challenging tasks more reliably than performance goals. Performance goals, in which the student views a situation as an occasion for being judged, as opposed to an opportunity for learning, may create a context that is less conducive to sustained efforts at mastery and understanding of new knowledge.

The kind of achievement goal that children adopt transforms the learning process in a great many ways, altering how they evaluate their own performances, what they expect of themselves, whether they have a sense of control over outcomes, how they respond to failure, whether they enjoy high-effort tasks, and what their attitude is toward teachers and peers. Dweck considers these aspects of motivation and also considers the profound changes in achievement motivation that can take place in early school years. She points out that while children are in school, relatively well-defined tasks present themselves automatically, along with fairly specific standards, deadlines, rewards, and punishments. However, after school, there is less structure given by the environment, and individuals often are called on to provide their own goals, spurs to action, and rewards for progress. Thus, skills that served children well in the structured school environment may no longer be sufficient, and long-term attainment may be better predicted by the presence of higher order motivational processes.

An overview of the past and the present views of intelligence is provided by John B. Carroll. In general, the measurement of intelligence has followed the rest of psychology in moving from a simple, generic view to a more context-specific and more detailed view. Carroll considers the accumulated findings on the multifactorial definition of intelligence together with more recent work that relates ability to knowledge bases, cognitive operations, and cognitive strategies involved in the performance of intellectual tasks. Carroll recommends that the most useful way of studying intelligence and intellectual abilities is to examine the detailed cognitive processes required by ability and aptitude test items. From that viewpoint, two people will have different test scores if they differ in their cognitive skills, knowledge, and processes and if the cognitive capabilities they do not share are required by some of the test items. The chapter elaborates a variety of methods and investigations that make it evident that intelligence is a term that refers to a composite of many abilities, some of which are quite general and widely applicable in character, and others of which have to do with more narrowly constrained domains of performance.

For Carroll, aptitude and achievement can be differentiated by a simple time relationship. An ability measurement taken before a learning task that predicts the learning is called an aptitude for that learning task. An ability measurement that indexes the accomplishment of a learning task is called an achievement measure for that task. Prominent in Carroll's analysis is the fact that psychologists have begun to take very seriously the possibility of improving and enhancing these predictive intellectual abilities through special programs of educational intervention.

A major contribution of the chapter is the formulation of the relationship between intellectual ability and task difficulty. This model offers a way of defining abilities and relating them to experimental studies and analyses of intellectual performances that have been conducted in cognitive psychology. This model proposes a criterion-referenced interpretation of scores on tests of intellectual ability. For example, a criterion-based score on a reasoning ability test "could indicate what kinds of reasoning problems an individual can easily master, and what kinds the individual has pronounced difficulty with." Such scores might indicate what mental operations the individual can easily perform, and what mental operations the individual is unlikely to perform at his or her stage of mental development. The possibility of developing such scores and interpretations from mental ability tests has seldom been explored, and this chapter considers research in the analysis of cognitive ability that might make this promise realizable.

Work in cognitive-ability testing promises to lead to better and more meaningful tests of basic cognitive skills than are now available. In so far as such skills are relevant to school and life activities generally, improvement in measuring devices may lead to more general acceptance of such measures among educators and the public. Moreover, a better understanding of the relations between abilities and human performance can facilitate efforts to improve abilities and performance. If individuals' constitutions place limits on the changes that could be effected, we need to know what those limits are. Whatever these limits may be, Carroll affirms that the possibilities for environmental manipulation of human cognitive abilities still remain wide open.

A detailed overview of research on the relationship between skills for learning and the acquisition of knowledge is presented in the chapter by Bransford and his colleagues. This research helps explain why some students learn more effectively than others and provides a foundation for efforts to assist less successful students in improving their learning abilities. As in other chapters, a fundamental theme is that comprehension, remembering, reasoning, and problem solving are influenced in important ways by the nature and organization of people's knowledge. The chapter emphasizes that in order to be useful, knowledge must be accessible in the learning and problem-solving contexts for which it is relevant. It discusses and elaborates the role of previously acquired knowledge and the types of learning activities that seem necessary in order to acquire functionally useful information. The authors give two reasons why some students may learn more effectively than others. The first is that less successful students may lack the subject-matter knowledge structures that psychologists call *schemata*, which are necessary for new learning. The second is that the knowledge may be present but insufficiently accessible. For this reason, a significant amount of research has been carried out on teaching, learning skills, and metacognitive strategies that facilitate learning.

Bransford suggests that "students need to be helped to see how thinking and learning strategies apply to each content domain (e.g., mathematics, history, physics, etc.) that they are trying to learn." He goes on to point out that the powerful strategies that students need are subject-specific and are also dependent on core concepts of the domain. Programs aimed only at general thinking skills will thus be insufficient, whereas programs that also address specific skills for specific subject matters "seem to have the potential to produce powerful educational effects."

Problem solving as a major cognitive activity in education and in daily living is the theme of the chapter by James Voss. Being able to find, refine, and solve problems is considered an important part of subject-matter competence. The solving of problems is also a significant learning activity, and much teaching and instruction is carried out by working problems that can stimulate understanding and provide practice opportunities for emerging procedural skill. Problem-solving exercises are also an important aspect of the assessment of higher levels of learning and higher levels of subject-matter knowledge.

In recent years, problem solving has been the focus of a great deal of research. Moreover, much of this research has been conducted in the context of particular academic disciplines. Voss surveys research on problem solving and emphasizes problem-solving research in particular subject matter domains. He considers the various issues involved in teaching general problem-solving skills and heuristics that are applicable and transferable to a variety of domains, and the question of what methods are most effective in teaching domain-related strategies. Increased emphasis on problem-solving activity will make it necessary for teachers and students alike to increase their familiarity with basic problem-solving concepts and for results of problem-solving theory to find their way into the classroom.

Voss emphasizes that flexibility is a key aspect of problem-solving skill, and that such flexibility comes primarily from experience. Pat methods do not, of themselves, automatically fit problems in differing contexts. Only experience in applying a rich body of knowledge to a wide variety of problem contexts can produce flexible problem-solving capability, Voss argues. Going further, however, he argues that *within* specific subject matters, it is productive to provide "appropriate problem-solving training, because such training could develop skills in argument and criticism as well as enhancing the individual's knowledge and awareness of the sociocultural world" (p. 285). Such instruction will be difficult, Voss points out, but there is at least a beginning sense of what it should be like.

ACKNOWLEDGMENTS

We are very pleased with these contributions. They are valuable today, and will remain valuable 10 years from now, when much new is known. Each chapter has helped us to see our field more clearly, and, we think, will be equally helpful to new colleagues just joining the educational profession and its scholarly research community. Rather than being the last word or the latest word on the issues temporarily before us, the chapters are a powerful first word to guide new participants into our professional and scientific world.

We are, of course, especially grateful to the authors, who took time from active research careers to write tutorials for a wider audience than their normal peer group.

Arlene Weiner is, in many respects, the third editor of this volume. In addition to technical editing, she provided many substantive insights that have made the book more accessible and more complete. She also capably handled the many tasks that authors and editors wish would disappear, for which we are also grateful.

Learning Theory

W. K. Estes
Harvard University

The principal output of the first century of research and theory on human learning and memory has been a massive accumulation of experimental and observational facts about learning in various simple, standardized tasks (most often remote from situations of practical relevance) and a number of limited generalizations, some perhaps deserving to be termed *empirical laws,* that organize and describe segments of this factual output. One can readily understand impatience with the slow pace of development of the intellectual tools we need to analyze important kinds of school learning and instruction. Nonetheless, making use of the tools now at hand can already be of value in the interpretation of research and the establishment of connections between research and practice. Further, vigorous attempts to make use of current theories outside the laboratory can contribute to their continuing refinement and elaboration (Baddeley, 1982). These thoughts have led to the orientation of this chapter toward a focus on the more general concepts and principles of learning now at hand.[1]

The aspects of learning theory to be reviewed here are dictated by potential applicability to problems of education. Thus it is sensible to start by classifying

---

[1]The overview of learning theory in this chapter is a composite of ideas drawn from earlier learning theories and from relevant aspects of more recent cognitive psychology, as organized and interpreted by the writer. To the extent feasible, it is indicated where theoretical views discussed represent a relatively broad consensus and where issues are controversial. The interpretations not attributed to any specific source are the author's responsibility and it should be understood that other investigators may disagree. For a comprehensive review of learning theories, no longer a task that can be usefully accomplished within the limits of a single chapter, the reader is referred to Bower and Hilgard (1981).

the products of education in terms of what is learned. Some principal categories are the following: (a) habits and skills, including habits of seeking and using information and skills of reading, calculating, communicating, and problem solving; (b) attitudes and values; (c) knowledge, which may be subclassified in terms of basic concepts and procedures at the first level and organized assemblages of factual knowledge at higher levels; and (d) understanding, including understanding the nature of one's self, of mankind in general, of society, and of the natural world.

A prime task of education is to supply the necessary materials and to arrange experiences for students that will lead to these kinds of learning. However, the learning is not automatic and in fact often fails. Thus, it is important to understand the learning process, what factors are important, why things often go wrong. Resources available for the task are of rather different kinds. Perhaps the most basic are the theoretical foundations of learning and instructional theory, which underlie our ability to analyze and diagnose educational problems and to guide applied research. At a more directly practical level are the knowledge and expertise about the conduct of education, drawn from practical experience and from research in educational settings.

This chapter is concerned primarily with theoretical foundations. Thus, the ideas discussed are necessarily largely abstract and removed from specific educational situations. Where possible I point out connections between abstract principles and specific problems, but for the most part these connections are developed in other chapters of this book.

The overall organization of the chapter is as follows. First, I consider the nature of the mental apparatus that accomplishes learning, characterizing its structures and processes in terms of contemporary research and theory. Next, the chapter examines the varieties of learning implicated in the formation of habits, skills, and attitudes. Third, processes basic to the acquisition of knowledge are examined.

THE INFORMATION-PROCESSING SYSTEM

In the course of any school session, a student encounters many episodes in which he or she hears or reads a message presenting some facts or concepts about the topic under study. The results of this potential learning experience may vary widely depending on circumstances. Suppose, for example, that a learning episode consisted in the presentation of a segment of film strip showing a famous person delivering some memorable speech. Typically, a student who had observed the film would recognize the episode if the same film strip were shown again, even after an interval of days or weeks. But if the student were asked to recall the episode, the result would strongly depend on a number of conditions. On an immediate test, the student would probably remember much of the episode, including even specific words, although some details would evidently not have registered at all. After a longer interval, the result might be only recall for the gist of the speech or might include scattered excerpts of the actual text depending on various aspects of the learner's approach to the task.

In general, whether information is presented via films, lectures, readings, or other kinds of experiences, the process of adding the information to the stock of knowledge and skill in the mind of the student in usable form is complex and subject to many uncertainties. The purpose of this section is to sketch in outline the modal current view as to how the memory system is organized and how it is utilized by way of the mental operations that determine whether and how information is stored and retrieved.

Organization of Memory

On one point, virtually all current investigators are agreed: Memory is not all of a piece, like such repositories as cupboards or warehouses, but comprises at a minimum several major subsystems. Some aspects of the organization of memory can be anticipated from a consideration of the ways in which it must contribute to various cognitive activities and the constraints under which it must operate.

The most basic constraint is that mental processes take time, and, in fact, are very slow in comparison to the operation of a computer. The time required for a single elementary cognitive operation, such as comparing a printed letter with its representation in memory, is of the order of 25–50 milliseconds (Sternberg, 1966), and the time needed to retrieve an item of information from memory is considerably longer (Estes, 1980). A second constraint, deriving from the first, is that, to be useful, information in memory must be organized for retrieval. A sequential record of all the experiences a child has had in school, for example, could contribute almost nothing to any constructive activity such as problem solving because it would take too long to locate needed information by searching the record. Information taken in via the senses must be sifted, classified, and entered in memory in a way that makes recovery reasonably efficient. To make this objective achievable, it appears essential that one's memory include at least the subsystems sketched in Fig. 1.1.

Primary Memory. Traditionally defined as a mental image, or representation, of perceived events that has not yet faded from awareness (James, 1890), primary memory is an essential first stage in the processing system, for intelligent filtering and selection of information is possible only if there is available a temporary record of all that has been perceived. Primary memory is necessarily transient because its contents must be continually displaced by new incoming

ACTIVATION PATHS

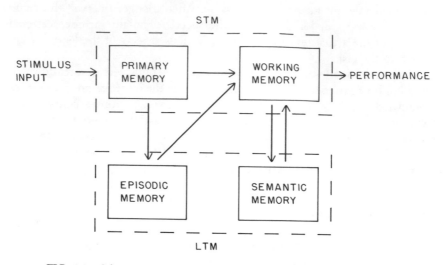

FIG. 1.1.   Schematization of the flow of information through subsystems of short-term (STM) and long-term (LTM) memory (from Estes, 1982a, Fig. 4.2, reprinted by permission of Cambridge University Press).

information, but information currently in primary memory is not necessarily wiped out all of a piece. If some aspects of a perceptual experience generate activity in emotional or motivational systems, these tend to be consolidated and preserved in secondary, or long-term, memory.

Primary memory is presumed to be passive and unselective. Hence, in any situation involving some kind of problem solving or other purposeful activity, it is essential that information in primary memory whose value or relevance is not immediately apparent be transferred to a system where it can undergo further processing, whereas primary memory is freed for new inputs.

Working Memory.   As a consequence of task requirements, or sometimes simply long-term strategies or habits, the individual sets criteria for the types of items that are selected for passage from primary memory into the limited-capacity system termed the *rehearsal buffer* (Atkinson & Shiffrin, 1968) or *working memory* (Baddeley, 1976). Here, representations of items or events, usually encoded in a more abstract form than initially perceived, can be kept in an active state by rehearsal and are subject to cognitive operations such as search and comparison. The capacity of working memory is assumed ordinarily to be only a few items (Miller, 1956), but it is expandable by appropriate practice (Chase & Ericsson, 1981). The importance of this system for education is that it serves as an entryway to long-term memory, at least for verbal material

(Atkinson & Shiffrin, 1968; Baddeley, 1976; Bower, 1975: Newell, 1973). Also, the setting or modification of selection criteria for entry of material into working memory appears to be the earliest point in information processing at which motivation influences learning.

Long-Term Memory. The long-term system is assumed to be of unlimited capacity, including all of the stored information that is retained more than a few seconds, and provides the basis for learned skills and knowledge. Several subsystems are distinguished on criteria of content and function. *Procedural memory,* not represented in Fig. 1.1, is the assemblage of stored action routines that constitute skills and habits. The storage of procedural information (effectively, stimulus–response associations, or condition–action pairs) evidently need not involve working memory, and the stored procedural information is not necessarily accessible to awareness or verbal report (Anderson, 1983; Tulving, 1983). The *episodic* system comprises memories of events in their temporal and situational contexts, whereas the *semantic* (alternatively termed *categorical* or *declarative*) system includes memory representations that are generally independent of context, for example, meanings, facts, and rules (Tulving, 1968, 1983). In a typical educational situation, the episodic system might include one's memory that one heard particular words or sentences in a lecture given on a specific occasion, whereas semantic memory would accumulate more abstract information having to do, for example, with the meanings of the words and the type of information communicated.

Presumably, most learning that occurs in educational settings has to do with semantic memory and has a cumulative character as distinguished from the memory for discrete events that characterizes episodic memory. Episodic memory appears to enter educational learning mainly as a stage or component in more complex processes, as, for example, memory for particular exemplars of categories in concept learning or memory for the outcomes of particular actions in skill learning. The organized knowledge that accumulates from such experiences need not be entirely verbal, and hence it may be preferable to designate postepisodic memory as categorical rather than semantic.

Learning that eventuates in categorical memory necessarily involves a number of stages, although these need not be temporally discrete. The stored information that forms the substrate for categorical memory must accrue from experiences in which relevant relationships among stimulus inputs or their aspects are perceived, for example, observation of use of a word in context or the relation between an exemplar and a category label. The accumulating information generally undergoes transformations as a consequence of cognitive operations such as grouping and chunking, normally occurring in the course of rehearsal, or reorganization resulting from the perception of relationships between items of information and retrieval cues that will be useful for aiding recall in test situations. Finally, accessibility of material for recall tends to decline during periods of disuse and can be maintained in an active state only as a consequence of reactivation during the interval between a learning experience and a test for recall.

Memory and Learning

All learning involves memory. However, learning is generally taken to have some cumulative aspect and some systematic relation to the individual's on-going behavior and adjustment to the environment. Memories can (although they need not) comprise merely isolated fragments of information concerning past experience. But, whereas memory may be simply memory for an event, learning is generally taken to be learning about some subject matter. In education, especially, one is concerned with learning in the sense of the acquisition of information about the world that provides the basis for intelligent behavior: knowledge of spatial relations on small and large scales, knowledge about histories of events over short- or long-time scales, factual knowledge, concepts, values, and costs associated with actions and outcomes.

Among the many different ways in which memory enters into learning, it is important to distinguish between the role of memory in the learning process and its role in representing the products of learning. This distinction relates closely to the partition of both research and theory in terms of short-term versus long-term memory. The short-term systems are essential components of the mental apparatus that accomplishes the processing of perceived items of information into forms that can be retained over the longer intervals that are of principal interest in educational research.

The concept of working memory and the processes of selective attention that operate in it offer a unified interpretation of phenomena that have traditionally been assigned to quite distinct categories. It has been well known since Thorndike's (1931) research on *belongingness* that human learners ordinarily acquire information about relationships between events or items only if they perceive these relationships as significant at the time of a potential learning experience. Thus, for example, if an individual is engaged in learning the names associated with the faces of previously unacquainted individuals and is presented in sequence with face 1–name 1, face 2–name 2, and so on, the individual will tend to learn associations that enable later recall of name 1 in the presence of face 1, and name 2 in the presence of face 2. However, no association forms to mediate recall of face 2 in the presence of name 1, even though these were experienced in just as close temporal contiguity as either of the name–face pairs. As a consequence of a normal task orientation, the learner evidently attends to the relationship between a face and the name that goes with it but not between a name and another face that simply happens to be perceived at approximately the same time. Consequently, only the former relation becomes established in working memory.

A large literature on *intentional* versus *incidental* learning has come to be interpreted in much the same way (Postman, 1976). In conformity with everyday observation, many experimental studies have shown that individuals who are instructed or otherwise motivated to learn particular materials in experimental situations exhibit much better recall than individuals who are exposed to the same material without any intention to learn. It proves also that the learner's ability to recognize the material later is essentially unrelated to the intentional–incidental distinction (Estes & DaPolito, 1967). Passive exposure to the material leads to memory traces capable of producing an experience of familiarity when the material is reencountered. However, only active attention to aspects of the situation (*retrieval cues*) relevant to later recall produces facilitation of recall over the level characteristic of incidental learning. In terms of the flow of information through the cognitive system, it appears that all of the material perceived is registered in short-term memory, but only aspects or elements relevant to a current task situation, or to the individual's current motives, are selected for maintenance by rehearsal or rehearsal-like processes in active working memory. And only information that enters working memory becomes encoded and organized in a form to enable later recall or reconstruction.

The Problem of Encoding in Memory

One point of agreement among contemporary investigators is that memory is not simply a verbatim record, but rather an encoded representation of the individual's experience. What is a code? In general, it is a representation that stands for but does not fully depict an item or event. The representation of a scene in a photograph would not be said to be encoded because it preserves all of the information in the scene (up to the resolving power of the film). In contrast, the representation of the same scene in the human memory system is said to be encoded because much of the information in the visual input is systematically discarded during processing, and the representation preserves only the values of the stimulus on certain attributes or dimensions.

Sometimes a code is sufficient to enable later reproduction of a learning experience in considerable detail, but sometimes it is sufficient only to identify which of alternative categories the experience belongs to. For example, memory for a route through a town may include specific physical features of the terrain and buildings passed during the trip, or it may take the form of a sequence of instructions regarding directions to take at various choice points. Memory for a text passage may include specific statements or may constitute only a record of the kinds of facts or ideas communicated (Anderson, 1980).

In general, there tends to be a progressive loss of information from one's initial perception of item or event to its recall at a later time. However, the loss of information is not simply a random degradation of originally recorded details. Rather, the process is selective in that information about attributes or categories relevant to later recall tends to be preserved, whereas finer or less relevant details decline in availability (Bower, 1975; Mandler & Ritchey, 1977; Norman & Rumelhart, 1970). For example, memory for speech initially includes details of the speaker's appearance, voice, and surroundings as well as fragmentary representations of particular sequences of words, but at a later time generally preserves only attributes of the message conveyed by the speech that will suffice for retrieval of the essential information tranmitted (Anderson, 1976; Kintsch, 1974).

A variety of memory codes has been identified, among them codes based on sensory dimensions, spatial and temporal location of events, semantic attributes and relations. Empirical evidence for types of encoding comes from a number of sources. One of these is the occurrence of confusion errors in recall. For example, Conrad (1964) noted that even when the mode of presentation of items such as sequences of letters or digits has been visual, subjects' errors of recall tend to be replacements of correct letters or digits with others that are like them in sound rather than with others that are visually like them. This finding is taken as evidence that the memory representation on which recall is based constitutes a recoding of the items on phonological dimensions. Whether consciously or not, people evidently prefer to rely on an auditorily based code rather than a visually based one because the former is better suited to rehearsal and more robust in the face of continuing visual inputs. Another type of evidence comes from the differential effectiveness of instructing learners to process material in ways intended to facilitate particular forms of encoding. Thus, if learners are studying lists of words that are to be recalled at a later time, recall proves to be superior if the learners are instructed to rate the words for pleasantness (thus directing their attention to semantic attributes) rather than for orthographic properties (which would direct attention to attributes unlikely to be implicated in recall).

There has been considerable debate as to whether encoding is an automatic process or one requiring voluntary attention and effort (Hasher & Zacks, 1979; Michon & Jackson, 1984). Evidently neither view is entirely correct. Encoding is basically a process of categorization and can be accomplished only if attention is directed to relevant attributes and relations. In the case of attributes that are ubiquitously involved in peoples' ordinary activities, for example, frequency and chronological order of events, attentional habits are developed that make encoding largely automatic; but under atypical circumstances, these habits may be disrupted, with the consequence that normal encoding fails to occur. In complex tasks, effective encoding of events for recall may require special skill, but once the skill develops, encoding may become automatic (as demonstrated, for example, by Chase & Ericsson, 1981, for a subject who developed an extraordinary memory span by developing the habit of encoding digit sequences in relation to familiar dates and running times). Even as difficult a categorization as distinguishing finite grammars (Reber & Allen, 1978) can be learned without apparent awareness or intent to learn, but only under conditions favorable for attention to the attributes on which encoding must occur.

Retention and Forgetting

The production of learning and the prevention of forgetting are closely intertwined aspects of education. In the literature on human learning and memory, the latter seems to have received disproportionate emphasis, perhaps because learning is of little avail unless the products are retained. The situation is a bit like harnessing power from a river. To convert water to electric power requires constructive activities, such as the designing and building of turbines. However, these activities must often be postponed while effort goes into building dikes and piling sandbags. Knowledge or skill that is forgotten is as useless as water that overflows the banks or leaks away.

Why should forgetting occur? An analysis within the information-processing framework points to several reasons.

Nonlearning. Perhaps the most important cause of apparent forgetting is failure of learning. From the vast amount of sensory information that bombards a person's senses during any waking moment, only a small part leaves any detectable trace in memory. The filter responsible for sifting out all but this small part is termed *selective attention.* During a lecture, one tries to attend to the lecturer's voice rather than to those of others murmuring in the classroom; while reading, one tries to attend to the message perceived on the printed page rather than to other events in one's surroundings. In a classical experiment on what is termed *dichotic listening* (Broadbent, 1958), the subject is instructed to attend to what is heard through one earphone and ignore what is simultaneously heard through the other. In a variety of experimental situations, it has been shown that very little, if any, of the information coming in through unattended channels is remembered (Broadbent, 1958, 1971; Fisk & Schneider, 1984; Glucksberg & Cowen, 1970; Kahneman & Treisman, 1984). There is no reason to doubt that the same is true of the analogous situations in ordinary life.

Beyond the role of attention, there are limits on the rate at which we can convert even attended information into durable memories, and consequently it is generally necessary and always beneficial to rehearse perceived items of information before going on to attend to new inputs. If only the capability of later recognition is needed, then the rehearsal can take the form of simple repetition, but if recall will be needed, more constructive activity, termed *elaborative* or *secondary* rehearsal, is essential (Woodward, Bjork, & Jongeward, 1973). The reason, in terms of current memory theory, is that appropriate retrieval cues must be stored in memory at the time of the learning experience (Tulving, 1968,

1983). The term *retrieval cue* refers to any aspect of the situation in which recall may be required or to information contained in questions that may be put to the learner in the test situation. Rehearsal that goes beyond rote repetition allows the learner to attend to relations between the rehearsed items and potential retrieval cues that are present in the learning situation or that may be generated by imaginative activity on the part of the learner. The term *activity* occurs often in discussions of the problem of retention for good reason. Effective learning is an active process.

Retrieval Failure. In his pioneering monograph on memory, Ebbinghaus (1885/1913) pointed up two somewhat paradoxical aspects of retention—that memories generally fade during periods of disuse, but that apparently long-lost memories are occasionally restored. He also outlined the state of theory at that time, one principal approach being based on the idea that memory traces gradually decay or disintegrate with time, the other that traces once stored remain in the memory system but may become inaccessible as a consequence of interference or competition from traces stored during later learning experiences. In a very influential review about a half-century later, McGeoch (1942) argued persuasively that decay theory had failed to accrue empirical support and that all forgetting might be attributable to some kind of interference, a view that dominated research on retention from that time until nearly the present.

The many experimental paradigms that have been used to study various forms of interference and the closely related interpretive concepts, such as *proactive* and *retroactive inhibition, state dependency,* and *list differentiation,* have been extensively reviewed (Postman, 1971). Given the theoretical orientation of this chapter, I bypass that large literature and proceed to analyze the problem of interference in terms of information-processing concepts.

Why should retrieval failures occur? One basic cause must be the unavailability of appropriate retrieval cues. According to the principle of *encoding specificity* (Tulving, 1968, 1983), a memory trace is generally accessible to recall only if retrieval cues present in the recall situation were encoded in the memory trace at the time of learning. A common source of retrieval failure is a disparity between the cues available at recall and those anticipated by the learner. Effective preparation for any kind of examination, for example, requires that material be studied and rehearsed in relation to the kinds of questions likely to be faced. Thus, when subjects in experiments have been instructed to prepare for recognition tests but later are unexpectedly tested also for recall, or vice versa, performance on the unexpected test has proven to be impaired (Jacoby, 1973; Tversky, 1973).

Another cause of unavailability of retrieval cues arises from the fact that they are often related to transient aspects of the learning context. By the time of the review by McGeoch (1942), experimental studies had indicated the importance of the relationship between the background setting or context at the time of learning and the context at the time of recall, and continuing research has served only to spell out many aspects of the role of context, including the mental and physiological state of the learner as well as external factors. It has been noted, further, that some random changes in context are almost inevitable over a period of time between learning and testing, and that the effects of these contextual fluctuations may be a major source of the loss of availability of memories over time that originally suggested decay theories.

In human learning, fluctuations in context exert not only direct effects on memory, by modifying the availability of retrieval cues, but also indirect effects, by modifying the way events or materials are perceived and encoded. Suppose, for example, that an individual has read a passage of printed material and then is asked whether the word "brief" occurred in the passage. If the word did occur in the passage, but in the sense of the brief presented by a lawyer at a trial, it might not be recognized on the test if the reader's current train of thought leads to interpreting the word in the sense of a short interval of time (Light & Carter-Sobell, 1970). Martin (1968) noted that in many learning situations the way particular words or symbols are encoded may fluctuate depending on the momentary context and termed this source of variability in the learning and retention process *encoding variability*. Bower (1972) brought together the concepts of temporal fluctuation and encoding variability and showed that they could account for many aspects of retention in human learning.

The way temporal fluctuation and endoding variability operate can be illustrated in terms of a simple experimental example (Estes, 1982b, pp. 135–142). Suppose that a learner has the role of a receiver in a communication network with the task of receiving and remembering messages. At some point, a message M_1 is received and the momentarily attended elements of the background context are encoded in a memory trace together with a representation of the message. If tested immediately, the subject will be sure to recall the message, but over an interval of time, availability of the contextual elements will fluctuate; the result is that at the time of a later test, some of the elements that support recall of M_1 might have become inactive and some elements that would not support recall of M_1 would have become active, so that the probability of recall would be reduced. If undisturbed by other relevant learning experiences, this process would continue until the probability of recall leveled off at an asymptote determined by the proportion of all the available elements that were active at the time of the original learning experience. Suppose, however, that shortly after the occurrence of M_1, the message M_2 were received. If tested immediately thereafter, the receiver would recall only M_2, because all active contextual elements would be encoded with that message. But over an interval of time fluctuation would occur; on a later test the sample of currently available elements would include a mixture of those associated with M_1 and M_2 and the individual would have some probability of recalling either message.

Various well-established properties of retention are readily interpreted in terms of this process. Suppose that one wanted to ensure recall of message M_1 on a delayed test. Clearly, the way to achieve this objective would be to repeat the message more than once, so that all elements that might be active at the time of the test would have an opportunity to become encoded for M_1. Further, the temporal spacing of the repetitions would be important. If they occurred very close together in time, further occurrences of M_1 would take place when the currently active message elements were already encoded for M_1 and the repetitions would be wasted. If more time were allowed between repetitions, there would be greater likelihood that elements inactive on an earlier occasion would have become active, thus allowing new learning to occur on the repetition.

Although these predictions about the course of retention and the effects of spacing of practice have been quantitatively verified only in simple experiments, it seems reasonable to suppose that the processes are quite general. But application of these general principles to more complex and less controlled situations should not be made blindly. Even in cases of complex human learning, one may expect that, other things equal, temporal distribution of practice will be beneficial for retention. However, other things may not be equal and in some instances particular factors may be at work that produce advantages for temporal massing of learning experiences. It is essential to analyze each case in terms of the contributions of general and specific factors.

Accessing memory always has somewhat the character of a search process, and like any search, this kind may sometimes fail for accidental reasons. Like telephone or intercom systems, the brain is subject to random "noise" in its operation, and consequently, theories of memory allow for the possibility that any link in an associative network varies somewhat over any interval of time in its readiness to transmit information. This property of the memory system was recognized by William James (1890), who argued that effective remembering depends on the development of a multiplicity of redundant associations to provide alternative retrieval routes, an idea now universally embodied in quantitative theories of memory.

It is important how the redundancy is achieved, however. If it arises from independent associations of many distinct retrieval cues to a given item of information, it is only beneficial. But if multiple associations emanate from a given cue, the consequent ambiguity is a hazard to retrieval. If a cue A has become associated with items B, C, and D, then the appearance of A will tend to activate memories of all three associates. The ambiguity may be resolvable by recall of the contexts in which B, C, and D were learned, but this process becomes increasingly fallible as the number of associated cues increases because it becomes progressively less likely that all of the remembered contexts will be sufficiently distinct to resolve the ambiguity. Another problem is that if a search must extend over a large number of items, memories aroused by nontarget items may send the search off in unprofitable directions, or some new input may distract the individual and cause the search to lapse before the target is located.

Ambiguity.   A related problem for recall arises when retrieval cues prove ambiguous. Many a person with quite normal memory has checked into a hotel, gone out to dinner, and on returning found that he could not remember his room number. This result is to be expected if the individual when storing the information "My room number is xxx" at check-in is attending only to aspects of the situation that are common to many hotels so that, on his return, the cue "room number" tends to evoke a number of competing memories, or if at check-in he is attending only to transient features of the situation (for example, the desk clerk) that may no longer be present when recall is needed.

It is a good general principle that recall is most efficient when a unique retrieval cue is available to provide access to the appropriate item in memory. Lack of a unique retrieval cue reduces efficiency, but need not be fatal to recall, for the consequent ambiguity can sometimes be resolved by remembering the context in which learning occurred and determining whether it matches the current context. Suppose, for example, that in some situations a pupil has been told to produce the past tense of a verb by adding "ed" and in other situations to add "en." On a later occasion, a request to produce a past tense will give rise to recall of both rules; however, the ambiguity can be resolved by remembering the circumstances under which each rule was learned and deciding which more closely matches the current situation.

The common occurrence of ambiguity and need for verification of tentative recalls makes the process of accessing long-term memory in ordinary life take on a problem-solving character. In research on how adults recall the names of high school classmates, Williams and Hollan (1981) obtained detailed "think aloud" protocols from their subjects in order to bring out details of this process. Typically, an individual would begin with some fragment of information about a classmate, which would produce recall of one or more names plus other related information about settings in which interaction with the remembered classmate had occurred. Sometimes the additional recalled information would resolve the initial ambiguity and yield confident recall of the correct name; sometimes additional cycles would be required; and sometimes all efforts would fail. Often, failure on one occasion would be followed by success on a later attempt; in these cases, it could generally be seen that the new attempt had given rise to recall of additional related information sufficient to allow the process of search and verification to proceed to a satisfactory conclusion.

Loss of Information.   The prolonged lapse in research related to decay theories of memory following the negative review by McGeoch (1942) eventually ended when the advent of methods for the analysis of short-term memory in the 1960s raised the possibility of precise tests of the possibility of spontaneous information loss. Some of the initial results appeared negative. In a study of Shiffrin (1973), for example, subjects were presented with a sequence of randomly ordered letters, then concentrated on a signal detection task designed to preclude rehearsal during a retention interval, and on a recall test at the end of the interval showed no retention loss. However, in a subsequent, related study, Reitman (1974) increased the length of the to-be-remembered letter sequence and obtained evidence of measurable forgetting over the retention interval even though there was no apparent source of competition or interference. Although more evidence is needed, it may be a general principle that the amount of irremediable information loss over a retention interval is directly related to the memory load imposed by the amount of material presented for study during a learning experience.

There are also findings indicating that even when memories for items or events are not wholly lost during a retention interval, the information retained about them may gradually lose precision. In studies of short-term recall, for example, memory for order of items may be lost even when memory for the identities of the items is retained (Conrad, 1964; Healy, 1974). An interpretation has been proposed in the form of an encoding and perturbation model (Estes, 1972a). It assumes that at the time of presentation of a list of to-be-remembered items, the relative position of each is encoded on a temporal attribute in memory. During a subsequent interval, however, noise in the operation of the memory system produces random perturbations in these encodings, so that the originally precise memory for position of an item becomes increasingly "fuzzy." It does not appear that this process can be influenced by the individual's motivation or intention to learn, but it can be slowed by repetition of the to-be-learned sequence (Cunningham, Healy, & Williams, 1984) and the difficulties it produces for effective recall can be ameliorated by measures taken to group items into small clusters that may be perceived and encoded as "chunks," or higher order units (Lee & Estes, 1977, 1981). Continuing research suggests that a similar process may operate on dimensions other than the temporal attribute (Estes, 1985).

Organization in Memory

In general, the answer to retrieval problems is organization. The difficulties that arise in lengthy memory searches can be allayed by associating clusters of items or sub-sequences of events with reference points or boundary markers. Even as simple a task as remembering the points made by a lecturer can be facilitated by clustering them into groups, set off by mental images of introductory or transitional remarks, slide presentations, or the like. Then a subsequent memory search for some particular point is facilitated because it can begin with a search over the relatively small number of boundary markers until an appropriate one is encountered, then a local search of items nearby in the memory space. These ideas have been developed more formally, with empirical support (Lee & Estes, 1981; Seamon, 1973; Shiffrin, 1970; Williams & Hollan, 1981).

Whereas memory for events or episodes is aided by attention to boundary markers (or by creation of them), memory for meanings, concepts, and factual material is typically organized in terms of categories. As apparently simple a task as recalling the states of the United States or the countries of Europe proves unexpectedly difficult if one attempts it without reference to categorical organization. In practice, however, a person has usually learned to categorize the states, say, in terms of regions (New England, Rocky Mountain states, etc.) and at recall can deal with the task in two stages: first retrieving the names of the regions, then the relatively small number of states in each. It appears that only a small number, of the order of five, items can be associated with any one element, or node (the formal counterpart of a category label) in a memory network (Mandler, 1968). Much research on categorization in semantic memory and the use of category labels as retrieval cues indicates that an effective way to circumvent this capacity limitation in human memory is to develop and use hierarchical organizations having multiple levels of categorization (for example, *animal, mammal, dog, terrier,* or *tree, evergreen, pine*). Memory for lists of words or other items is facilitated if subsets of items are associated with appropriate category labels during learning, especially if the labels are available in the test situation as cues for recall (Bower, 1970; Estes, 1976).

There is little reason to believe that hierarchical organizations arise spontaneously and inevitably, however. On the contrary, in experimental settings, their use is found to depend on instructions and other means of encouraging the use of appropriate organizational strategies (Bower, Clark, Lesgold, & Winzenz, 1969) and outside of the laboratory, the role of categorization in recall is found to depend on cultural and educational factors (Cole, Gay, Glick, & Sharp, 1971). A general principle for education is that material should be learned in relation to organizational strategies that will facilitate later recall.

GENERAL PROPERTIES OF LEARNING

Since the advent of learning theory, there have been wave-like swings of opinion from conceptions of extremely general theories, applicable across developmental and phylogenetic levels, to views of extreme specificity, presuming that principles of learning must be narrowly drawn to apply only to particular organisms in the particular situations. Hull's (1943, 1952) behavior theory perhaps represented the apex of striving for generality. Hull set the goal of behavior theory as being the formulation of a small set of axioms (referring, for example, to the effects of rewards, the way learning generalizes from one situation to another) from which specific principles might be derived for the learning of any organism under any particular set of circumstances.

This ambitious program yielded a mixture of successes and failures. The successes were importantly associated with the fact that for several decades research related to learning theory was carried out almost exclusively on a few organisms, most often laboratory rats, in a few highly simplified laboratory situations, for example, the maze or the "Skinner box." Hull's theory accounted for many results, for example the forms of learning curves, obtained in these situations, but proved difficult to extend to learning outside of the laboratory. The shortcomings of this narrow research base of learning theory were forcefully pointed out by adherents of ethology, a more naturalistic approach to animal behavior, and led in time to some rather strong reactions against the entire idea of pursuing general theories in psychology (see for example Seligman, 1970).

Debates between adherents of the extreme positions on the generality–specificity issue have been stimulating, but for purposes of directing and interpreting ongoing research on learning it seems essential to recognize the complementarity of these aspects of theory. The interpretation of nearly any instance of learning requires attention to specific characteristics of the situation and the learner. This observation is so obviously true of human learners that often instructive commonalities between human learning and lower forms of learning tend to be overlooked. General principles do not predict individual behavior, but they do provide perspective and guidance in the analysis of individual cases of learning.

It would be premature to claim laws of learning comparable to the general laws of physics. Nonetheless it seems possible to distill from the accumulation of facts and "miniature theories" some concepts and principles of considerable generality. They may not suffice to explain to anyone's satisfaction many important varieties of learning that occur in the schools or elsewhere in ordinary life, but nonetheless they seem to be worth knowing.

Redundancy.   Perhaps the most ubiquitous of these general properties, and one that might be foreseen from experience with theories of coding and information storage in nonliving systems, is that of redundancy of information storage. The idea that the result of any instance of learning is localized in some particular anatomical unit in the brain (the *engram*) has a long history in psychology, but in any simplified form it deserves to be laid to rest. A substantial segment of the career of one of the most illustrious early neuropsychologists was devoted to attempts to localize the engram, but led instead to the conclusion that the memory traces resulting from any instance of learning are widely distributed in the brain (Lashley, 1950). Little is yet known about the anatomical or biochemical form of the distributed representation, but at a conceptual level in learning theories, the prevailing view is that learning relative to any event or item of information results in changes of state of many units or elements in the memory system.

In early statistical theories of learning, these units were termed *stimulus elements,* on the presumption that the basis of learning must lie in the formation of stimulus–response associations (Estes, 1950). It has become clear, however, that the strict stimulus–response view is too narrow and that the results of learning involve information regarding many kinds of perceived or experienced relationships among events. Hence, in more recent versions of statistical learning theories it has seemed preferable to speak simply of the units of information storage or *memory elements*. An adaptive consequence of the storage of information redundantly in multiple memory units is a robustness of the system such that earlier learned information may be recalled even if only a few of the elements representing the learning are functionally available at some later time.

Sampling. Closely related to the conception of redundant storage on memory is the idea that the elements that might be involved in representation of a learning experience are not all available at once. The assumption is, rather, that for any particular instance of learning, there is a population of potentially available elements only some of which are sampled by the learner's information-processing system on any one occasion. The elements sampled correspond to the aspects of the learning situation that are actually perceived. As a consequence of variability both in the environment and in the physiological and psychological state of the learner, the particular aspects perceived vary from one encounter with a particular stimulus or situation to another, with the result that different more or less random samples of the potentially available units actually enter into the learned representation of the series of learning experiences. Some quantitative properties of the learning process that results are illustrated in Fig. 1.2, which might be taken to represent the course of the learning of a particular vocabulary item. The result of any one learning experience is an all-or-none change in the state of some particular sample of memory elements (cells in the upper portion of Fig. 1.2) that would support the correct association of a word with its definition. However, over a sequence of trials, the result is a cumulative increase in the proportion of elements in the relevant population that support this memory (cells labeled A) and hence a growth in the probability of a correct response on a test for this item. This conception provides a resolution of earlier controversies between adherents of the idea that learning is an incremental growth process versus the view that learning always occurs on an all-or-none basis on some single occasion (Bower & Hilgard, 1981). In the statistical conception, the change of state of any individual memory element is an all-or-none matter, but the way the population of elements that supports any item of learned information is categorized changes incrementally with repetitions of a given type of learning experience.

The sampling concept need only be augmented by a principle relating the state of memory to probabilities of actions in order to provide interpretations of a number of phenomena of memory in simplified situations. The principle is that, if the current state of memory includes a mixture of elements supporting the recall of different items of information or different actions, then the proba-

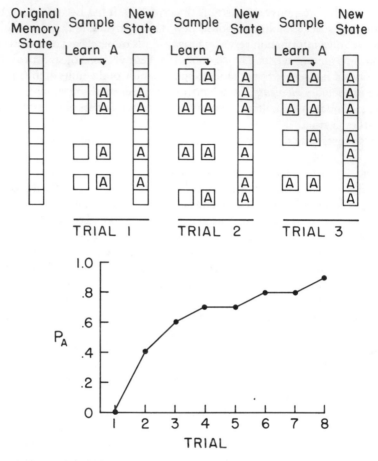

FIG. 1.2.   Learning process of stimulus sampling theory, illustrated in terms of
acquisition of the association of a word (A) and its definition. In the upper panel,
cells represent elements in the memory system, those active (sampled) on a trial
shifting from a state in which they do not to a state in which they do support
recall of word A. The lower panel shows the expected course of learning in terms
of the proportion of elements in the learned state at the beginning of each trial
(from Estes, 1982b, Fig. 2.1, reprinted by permission of Praeger Publishers).

bility of recalling any one item or action is equal to the proportion of elements
associated with it relative to the proportions associated with other items or
actions.

The way this system works in a simple transfer situation is nicely illustrated
by an experiment reported by Schoeffler (1954). In Schoeffler's study the
subject was presented with a display board on which were mounted several

rows of signal lamps and was instructed that the illumination of a combination of signal lamps signified some event (which might be interpreted, for example, as the cause of a malfunction of an item of equipment). On one trial of the experiment, the experimenter illuminated a randomly selected 50% of the lamps and indicated that these signified an event E_1, then illuminated a different randomly selected 25% of the lamps and indicated that they signified event E_2. On a subsequent memory test, a sample of lamps was illuminated in which those associated with E_1 and with E_2 were represented in a 2 : 1 ratio and the subject was asked to indicate which event would be expected to occur. On the average, event E_1 was predicted by the group of subjects with probability almost exactly .67, and similar results were obtained with other sampling combinations.

Another simple application of the same mechanism involves memory for frequencies of events. Even for events that occur too frequently for one to remember many individual instances, an individual often has relatively good memory for relative frequencies. For example, I am quite sure that there were more cloudy than sunny days in Boston during the past month, even though I can remember the weather on few individual days. The interpretation in terms of the theory is that memory elements involved in recollection of types of weather are sampled when observation of each day's weather occurs and the frequencies with which elements are sampled and associated with sun versus rain will be in the same proportion as the frequency of sunny to rainy days. Consequently, on the average, one should be expected, when asked to make such a frequency judgment, to predict the more frequent of the two kinds of events being compared with probability approximating the true relative frequency. In a number of experiments in which memory has been tested for simple events such as presentations of words on a display screen, it has been found that judgments of relative frequency are well described by the model (Whitlow & Estes, 1979). In ordinary situations, the statistically based memory for frequency often is supplemented by other kinds of information, but nonetheless the accrual of memory for frequency appears to be a rather ubiquitous and automatic process (Hasher & Chromiak, 1977). Thus, we must expect this process to provide the basis for an individual's expectations about probabilities of events—for example, probabilities with which promised rewards materialize, probabilities of success or failure on familiar tasks.

Unitization and Categorization.   Perhaps the principal limitation on the predictive value of the simple statistical model for learning relative to frequencies of events arises from the occurrence of *patterning* or *unitization*. For example, one might expect that the learning of relationships between symptoms and diseases could be interpreted quite naturally in terms of the statistical model, and the supposition proves well founded up to a point. However, substantial deviations from expectations on the basis of the model occur if the individual doing the learning perceives and attends to combinations of symptoms as patterns or higher order units, in which case it is the patterns that behave as elements in the sampling model. A learner's tendency to perceive combinations of cues as units can, of course, be influenced by instruction, but it also proves to be influenced strongly by early experience in the same type of situation. If in a particular type of problem the learner's first experience leads to perceiving symptoms or other cues as individual units, then this tendency persists, whereas if during early experience attention to patterns is rewarded, then the higher order units come to dominate performance (Estes, 1972b).

It will be apparent that the notions of redundancy and sampling lead naturally to a view of learning as basically a categorization process (in distinction to a process of continuous growth of habit strength or the equivalent, as in the theory of Hull, 1943). Prior to learning, elements of the memory system have the property only of being susceptible to activation when the individual perceives some feature or aspect of the environment. During a learning experience the activated elements are categorized into those that signify the occurrence of some item or event versus those that do not. The categorization is assumed to be permanent unless changed by new learning, so the sample of elements active on a given occasion constitutes a memory trace for the experience, with the property that when these elements are activated on some future occasion, they provide the basis for recall or recognition.

Passive and Active Aspects of Learning.   Considering the known limitations on capacity and speed of operation of the cognitive system, together with the diversity of the tasks confronting a human learner, one is prepared to find that learning is complexly organized, with current learning dependent in major respects on products of past learning. Further, one must expect that some aspects of learning will proceed automatically as incoming information is registered, whereas other aspects will require guidance by acquired learning strategies.

Hebb (1949), in his influential treatment of the neurophysiological substrate of behavior, presented a carefully documented case regarding the course of development of passive and slow versus actively directed and fast learning, both in the course of evolution of higher organisms and in the course of individual development. For animals lower on the phylogenetic scale, learning is mainly a matter of forming associations between relatively simple stimuli and responses, and the speed of forming these associations tends to be largely independent of age. In higher organisms, especially man, learning in the adult characteristically entails associations between complex patterns of stimulus information, often of a symbolic character, and complexly organized response programs. However, somewhat paradoxically, the learning of relations between complex units is generally no more difficult for the adult than the learning of simple associations, and tends to be much faster than the learning of simple associations in the infant or the very young child. The latter may be even slower than comparable learning in lower animals, whereas human adult learning is characteristically much faster. "Given a really new and unfamiliar set of sensations to be associated with motor responses, selectively, the first definite and clearcut association appears sooner in rat than in man and apparently sooner in the insect than the rat" (Hebb, 1949, p. 114).

Clearly, a major factor in these trends is the dependence of adult learning on the organization of stimulus and response units as a consequence of earlier learning. All-or-none, and apparently insightful, learning is characteristic of the mature human being but never of the infant of a higher species. But even in the adult human being, the distinction between slow and fast learning processes persists. Acquiring the ability to manipulate a complex stimulus pattern as a unit is a slow process (seen dramatically in an individual who must learn pattern vision relatively late in life following removal of a congenital cataract), whereas, once a pattern takes on unitary characteristics, learning to recognize it in a new context is very rapid. Similarly, with regard to instrumental behavior, the acquisition of single stimulus–response associations, as in eyelid conditioning, may be very slow, whereas learning to shift organized motor programs to new cues may be almost instantaneous. For brevity, I refer to the passive and relatively slow forms of learning as *perceptual* and the actively directed and relatively rapid forms as *cognitive*.

The relative rates of perceptual and cognitive learning appear to be related to differences in the way information is processed during learning, with the major distinction being whether or not working memory is involved. Perceptual learning may simply depend on the consolidation of the traces or associations set up in primary memory upon perception of a stimulus pattern, the process being largely passive and automatic. This form of learning would tend to be slow because the capacity of primary memory is limited, so newly established memory traces may be displaced by new perceptual inputs before consolidation has occurred. Thus, repeated sampling of a situation may be necessary in order for all the elements of a pattern to become associated.

In contrast, cognitive learning appears to involve information that has been selected by attentional processes for transmission into the working memory system, where memory traces of items may be maintained in an active state by rehearsal, permitting the formation of multiple associations, even following what is apparently a unitary learning experience. Cognitive learning is necessarily actively directed and selective because only a small part of the information registered in primary memory can be transmitted over what is apparently a limited-capacity serial channel to the working memory system. And it is only in the working memory system that items of information become subject to the cognitive operations that give rise to efficient retrieval schemes.

The idea that only cognitive learning utilizes working memory appears to fit in well with some observations on the apparent dissociation between perceptual and cognitive learning in cases of amnesia resulting from brain damage, where a patient may accomplish and retain learning at the perceptual level (for example acquiring familiarity with specific stimulus patterns) and manifest this learning on later tests, while at the same time being unable to remember that the learning experience ever occurred (Baddeley, 1982; Jacoby & Dallas, 1981).

It appears likely that the disappointing results of many efforts in earlier decades to obtain significant correlations between measures of learning in laboratory tasks and ability to learn in educational situations are a consequence of another such dissociation: The laboratory tasks were typically confined mainly to perceptual learning, whereas the essence of much education is cognitive learning. The effective prediction of cognitive learning ability requires that the tests used as predictors tap the information-processing mechanisms that are implicated in cognitive learning (Estes, 1982a). Some recent research on the correlational problem, evidently by taking account of this principle, is bringing out significant and substantial relationships between theoretically based measures of efficiency of elementary cognitive operations and indices of general intellectual performance (Hunt, 1978).

Graded Storage and Loss of Information.   The random sampling component of learning processes provides a way for the robustness of products of learning to increase with repeated practice, but unless modified by some organizational tendency, the variability would tend to be unadaptive. If the elements of a situation entering into learning were selected wholly at random, then it might well be that what was learned during early stages in some situation would be of no value to the learner. Similarly, if loss of information during forgetting were wholly random, then elements lost at the earliest part of a retention interval might leave no usable information.

The organizational tendency that counteracts these undesirable effects of randomness may be described as a tendency to select during learning the features of a situation relevant to task demands or motives and for representations of these features to be retained longest. Thus, for example, in a simple avoidance learning situation, some features of the environmental situation might serve only to categorize it as pleasant versus unpleasant or dangerous versus safe, whereas other, lower order, features would serve to discriminate particular aspects of the environment requiring specific selective responses.

The top-down bias in the learning process is such that the higher order features tend to be learned first and retained longest. This tendency is manifest even in simple conditioning experiments. If, for example, a tone is sounded prior to the delivery of food in a Pavlovian situation, the tone begins to evoke signs of expectation of food in the animal (increased activity level, orienting toward the food dispenser) after a very few pairings of tone and food, whereas evocation of a specific conditioned response (e.g., salivation) by the tone may develop only after a large number of trials (Estes, 1973; Hilgard & Marquis,

1940). The same tendency is seen in complex human learning situations. For example, in concept learning it is observed that once an individual has learned to categorize a collection of objects or events, information about the prototype or most typical member of a category is retained longer than the information about the classification of individual exemplars (Smith & Medin, 1981). Again, in the learning of meaningful prose material, the information required for verbatim recall of sentences that have been heard or read is lost much faster than information concerning the gist or general attributes of the information conveyed (Anderson, 1976). It is quite likely that the specific mechanisms involved in this top-down organizational tendency are different in lower and higher organisms and in lower and higher forms of learning, but the functional properties appear to be quite general.

Control Elements and Hierarchical Organization.   All of the learning theories that have achieved any substantial degree of conceptual elaboration and capability of dealing with empirical phenomena include in some form the notion of association. The concept refers to the ubiquitous tendency for perception of an object or event to evoke recall of another object or event that previously occurred more or less simultaneously with it.

In association theory prior to about 1960, there was little recognition of need for more elaborate structure than simple interitem associations. Thus, if an experimental subject were set the task of remembering a list of words following a single presentation, then, as illustrated by alternative 1 in Fig. 1.3, the resulting memory structure was conceived as one in which the first word of the list is associated with the second, the second with the third, and so on. This simple model could account for the learner's ability, on presentation with the first word of the list on a later occasion, to recall the remainder of the words. However, it would not account for the fact that in such experiments individuals typically do not recall the words in the order in which they were presented. Nor would the model be compatible with the observation that if a list is presented more than once, varying the order of the words yields little hindrance to the speed of learning. These latter observations could be accomodated, however, if the conception of association were elaborated to allow a number of items all to be associated with a common element, labeled LIST in alternative 2 of Fig. 1.3.

Further consideration of the free recall experiment suggests that alternative 2 is still too simple. As the number of words associated with a single common element increases, the speed with which they can be accessed declines and the probability that some will fail to be retrieved increases, a phenomenon termed the *fan effect* (Anderson, 1976, 1980). A way around this difficulty is provided by a multileveled structure in which only a few words are associated directly with any one common element, but several of these common elements at a given level are associated with an element at the next higher level. The resulting hierarchical or tree-like structure is portrayed as alternative 3 in Fig. 1.3. If the

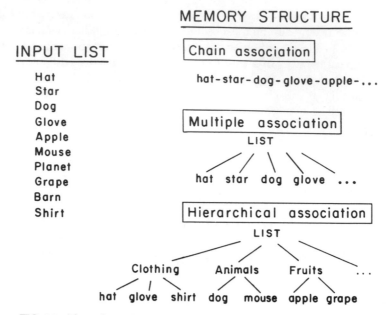

FIG. 1.3   Three alternative association models for the memory structure mediating free recall of a list of words (from Estes, 1982b, Fig. 3.14, reprinted by permission of Praeger Publishers).

common elements correspond to category labels, as in the illustration, then this model accounts also for the common tendency of individuals to cluster semantically related words during recall of a list. However, the common elements need not correspond to category labels and are simply termed *control elements* in more general models (Estes, 1972a). There is evidence that this form of organization tends to develop as learners acquire proficiency with a given subject matter (see, for example, Chi, Feltovich, & Glaser, 1981).

The memory structure comprising control elements and associations readily accommodates a number of pervasive aspects of memory. One of these is the powerful role of context. The observation (discussed previously in connection with retention) that recall, or evocation of a learned response, is optimal if the context at the time of the test is very similar to the context at the time of the original learning, suggests that when a memory representation is formed for any perceived object or event, both this representation and the representation of the context in which the learning experience occurred become associated to a common control element. The reactivation of this control element on future occasions requires the recurrence of the given item and also at least some elements of the learning context. Thus, in the parlance of networks, the control element serves as a logical AND gate. In contrast, items that are experienced at different times, like the words in the free recall list of Fig. 1.3, become connected to a common control element that functions as a logical OR gate, and the recurrence of any one of the words may reactivate the control element (and thus, in the illustration, evoke recall of the category).

The concept of a control element, or *concept node* (Anderson & Bower, 1973) in an associative network provides also a way of handling a perennial problem in cognitive psychology: How can we account for a learner's ability to accrue information about an object or event even though the exemplars or instances experienced on different occasions may vary greatly in their properties and contexts? Suppose, for example, that a child first encounters some person in a particular context, then on another occasion encounters the same person in a different context but with many changes in appearance. Why is the result not simply two distinct memory traces about two people in different contexts rather than an accumulation of information about a particular person? My proposed answer is that, on the second occasion, perception of the person activates the control element established on the first occasion, and perhaps also, to a lesser extent, control elements associated with other people resembling the given one in some respects. A decision is then made (not necessarily consciously) as to whether the activation level of one of these control elements exceeds that of the others sufficiently to meet a criterion of recognition. If so, the information added on the second occasion is referred to the same control element established on the first occasion and thus information is accumulated in memory concerning the same person. Of course false recognitions may occur, with an attendant accrual of faulty information (evidently a not uncommon event in situations that receive attention in courtrooms).

ELEMENTARY FORMS OF LEARNING

Providing favorable conditions for learning is generally agreed to be a primary function of the schools. However, the learning that goes on is much more pervasive than that programmed in the formal curriculum, including, for example, the formation of emotional dispositions, attitudes, motives, and habits. These nonintellectual forms of learning may be highly relevant both to the acquisition of knowledge and skills in the school and to the likelihood that formal education will have the desired beneficial effects on students' subsequent lives. Learning to study; learning to learn; learning to enjoy literature, art, or mathematics may be fully as important as acquiring information needed to pass examinations. Thus, the problem of understanding the variety of forms of learning that occur in school situations requires us in turn to draw on a similar variety of research traditions and the bodies of theory they have given rise to.

The organization of this survey follows so far as possible a path from the simple to the complex. Following this motif, the first main section deals with the acquisition of emotional and motivational dispositions, whose understanding draws heavily on the facts and principles of classical conditioning. However, it is found that the principles of conditioning as understood in the 1980s are quite different in important respects from those of earlier periods when the ideas of such individuals as Hull and Pavlov dominated the field. The currently most influential interpretations of conditioning draw on the concepts of information value and the distinction between short- and long-term memory systems as well as such classical concepts as excitation and inhibition. Looking first at some of the major forms of conditioning enables us to bring out in relatively simple contexts some concepts and principles that prove of wide applicability.

The distinction between selective learning and conditioning parallels in some respects the distinction between procedural and factual learning that has been emphasized in the recent work of Anderson (1976, 1983). Procedural learning, the form of learning that is directly manifest in modified performance, includes the acquisition of perceptual or motor skills and the formation of habits. Among the most ubiquitous examples in school learning are drawing, writing, and reading. The products of procedural learning necessarily embody relatively specific response programs, which are not necessarily accessible to verbal awareness and are not necessarily acquirable without actual practice. Procedural learning is typically slow and incremental and powerfully influenced by feedback from the consequences of actions—these sometimes having the character of rewards or punishments and sometimes being purely informational in nature. Principles describing how such feedback operates, and the way it depends on contingencies between behavior and other events and on temporal schedules, derive to an important extent from the operant conditioning tradition following from the early work of Skinner (1938). Principles of operant conditioning, having to do with the shaping of behavior by immediate consequences and the role of scheduling of reinforcing events, are supplemented, or complemented, in current cognitive psychology by concepts of unitization (Smith & Spoehr, 1974) and automatization (LaBerge, 1976; Schneider & Fisk, 1983; Shiffrin & Schneider, 1977).

The acquisition of factual knowledge (termed *declarative* by Anderson, 1976) includes the development of concepts and categories and the accumulation of knowledge that can be expressed in propositional form. Perhaps the most influential current approaches to factual learning are formulated in terms of the growth of associative networks, some of whose properties may be traceable back to the network models of conditioning and elementary associative learning. In contrast to procedural learning, where most research and theoretical emphasis has been focused on questions of dynamics (how learning occurs), for factual learning most attention so far has been given to questions of what is learned, how the products of learning are represented in the memory system and how knowledge is accessed in situations where it is relevant to performance.

Conditioning and Associative Learning

The term *conditioning* does not frequently appear in the current literature of cognitive and educational psychology—but neither does the term *emotion,* and the low frequencies of both may not be unrelated. A hazard is that continuing inattention to emotional, and for that matter motivational, dispositions may hinder the effective application of cognitive psychology to learning in practical situations, where emotions, motivations, and attitudes are always pertinent. Some recent work (for example Bower, 1981) shows clear evidence of influences of mood on cognitive processes in the laboratory. It seems likely, however, that understanding of the learning processes responsible for the nature and strength of emotional or motivational dispositions in specific situations is not to be found at the level of cognitive psychology, but rather at the level of basic processes of learning and conditioning.

Consideration of these basic processes will show, for example, that even though reproof and punishment may, judiciously used, have a place in the school (Walters & Grusec, 1977), one must expect that emotional reactions aroused may become conditioned to the same situational cues that the teacher is striving to associate with positive affect and attitudes. If one's purpose is to instill in students a taste for literature, art, or science, it is important that the students' early encounters with these activities be associated with positive emotions. Understanding the kinds of conditioning processes that inevitably go on in the background can help the educator arrange learning experiences for students that will favor the desired outcomes.

Although the basic learning processes may well be the same in all forms of conditioning, it is convenient to distinguish two main varieties: classical conditioning, having to do with most elementary forms of acquisition of information, and instrumental (or operant) conditioning, having to do with the modification of performance as a result of rewarding, punishing, or simply informational, consequences. Research and theory on both varieties, both historic and current, have been well summarized by Bower and Hilgard (1981). At the present time investigators of conditioning differ widely with regard to their preference for continuing to interpret conditioning in terms of classical concepts dating back to Pavlov (for example excitation, inhibition) versus an alternative terminology drawn from current work on memory and information processing. The choice does not seem critical so long as care is taken to relate the terms used to supporting observational evidence, and in the present discussion the cognitive terminology will have the advantage of better bringing out correspondences and relationships between basic learning concepts and educational motifs.

Classical Conditioning.   Conditioning, especially the classical form, seems to provide a prototype of the acquisition of elements of information, especially information concerning the signal value of a relatively neutral event (for example a light or a tone in an experimental situation) for the impending occurrence of one that is more significant to the organism (for example a shock or the presentation of food in an experimental situation). Although much of the literature on conditioning deals with the formation of relatively specific conditioned responses, for example salivation to a tone that has preceded food or an eye blink to a light that has preceded a puff of air to the cornea of the eye, we should be concerned more with situations in which learning may be described simply as the development of a tendency to anticipate a forthcoming event. A major experimental paradigm of this sort is referred to in the literature as that of the conditioned emotional response (CER). Typically, an experimental subject, for example a rat engaged in bar pressing in a Skinner box for food reward, is occasionally administered an electric shock, which typically produces a brief disturbance of the ongoing behavior. If however, on some occasion the shock is preceded by a buzzer that sounds for a few seconds, then on a later occasion the buzzer will produce clear evidence—for example immobility, quivering, cessation or at least diminution in rate of such ongoing behavior as bar pressing—that the animal now anticipates the shock (Estes & Skinner, 1941). In experiments of somewhat similar design with human subjects, an originally neutral cue that precedes a disturbing stimulus quickly acquires the capacity to evoke a changed pattern of autonomic nervous system activity, usually indexed by the galvanic skin response.[2] Typically, the learning is rapid, conditioning often being virtually complete on a single trial, and resistant to forgetting. Transfer of the effects of the conditioning from the original learning situation to new ones typically occurs in an orderly manner as a function of the degree of commonality between the old and new situations with regard either to stimulus properties or more abstract ones. In the case of an animal, the transfer would be manifest if, for example, a tone of a particular frequency were the signal stimulus in the original conditioning situation and a tone of a different frequency the test tone in a new one, probability that the test tone evokes the conditioned emotional response being a decreasing function of the difference in frequency. With human subjects, similar generalization occurs with respect to semantic properties if the signal stimulus is verbal.

Memory and Conditioning.   It seems natural enough to speak of conditioning in human beings as having to do with the establishment of memories for relationships between events, but prior to about 1970 investigators of conditioning generally found it somewhat strained or even fanciful to introduce

---

[2]The galvanic skin response (GSR) is a manifestation of an autonomic nervous system response to a sudden or traumatic stimulus.

notions of memory in relation to conditioning in animals. During the past decade or so, however, the prevailing viewpoint has changed and one sees investigators ranging from neurophysiologists, Konorski (1967) and Grossberg (1980), and investigators of animal learning (Wagner, 1979) to cognitive psychologists (Estes, 1973) finding it useful to reinterpret aspects of conditioning in terms of memory processes.

Current investigators approaching the situation from a variety of standpoints (for example Estes, 1973, 1979; Grant, 1972; Konorski, 1967; Ross & Ross, 1976; Wagner, 1978) would offer much the same conceptual account of conditioning. The information acquired by the learner concerning the relationship between a signal stimulus and a rewarding or punishing event is presumed to be mediated by memory representations of the events, representation being essentially the modern counterpart of the *memory trace* of gestalt psychology (Koffka, 1935). At the time of occurrence of the signal stimulus, a representation of it encoded in terms of its perceptual properties is established in the short-term memory system, in which it is maintained in an active state for a time by a recycling, rehearsal-like process. When the unconditioned stimulus (for example, shock or food) follows, a similar representation is formed and if the two are active jointly in the working memory system, so that the learner can attend to them together, then a representation of the conjunction of the two is formed in turn. The final stage of the process, which ensues unless the system is disturbed within a critical interval by new stimulus inputs over the same sensory channels, is the consolidation in long-term memory of a representation of the episode in terms of the attributes of the signal stimulus and unconditioned stimulus, and attributes of the context in which they occurred. On a later occasion, recurrence of the same or a similar signal stimulus in the same or a similar context tends to reactivate memory for the original experience, including the emotional or other reaction to the unconditioned stimulus. The components of the combined memory trace, for example, those associated with the signal stimulus and those associated with the context, combine multiplicatively in determining later retrieval of the memory, so even the identical signal stimulus might not evoke the memory if it occurred in a sufficiently different context.

Contiguity and Predictability.   A law or principle of contiguity has a very long history in psychology, dating back to the British Associationists and appearing, though with some reservations, in a comprehensive review of association psychology by Robinson (1932) just before the emergence of what might be termed modern learning theory. Even among the learning theorists of the 1930s, at least one (Guthrie, 1935) assumed temporal contiguity of stimulus and response to be a necessary and sufficient condition for the formation of an association. That view never became widely accepted in a strong form, however, for investigators of conditioning from Pavlov onward had recognized that at the very least conditioning in human beings can be strongly modified by verbal processes. Indeed, Cook and Harris (1937) showed that conditioned anticipation of a shock, as manifest in the "galvanic skin response," can be accomplished, or at least mimicked, by simply giving verbal information to an individual that a shock is likely to follow a signal stimulus.

Newer lines of research initiated following the advent of modern cognitive psychology have shown, further, that even in animals conditioning depends not only on contiguity of stimuli and responses but also on what might be termed the *information value* of an experienced relationship between stimulus and response events. A pioneering study with regard to this motif was reported by Kamin (1969) in an investigation of conditioning of emotional responses in rats. In the control condition of Kamin's study some originally neutral stimulus A, such as a light or the sound of a buzzer, was presented to rats shortly before the administration of an electric shock, and a CER was manifest when presentation of stimulus A subsequently caused the animals to cease an ongoing activity of operating a lever for food reward. In another condition, stimulus A was presented together with another stimulus B (for example a tone plus a light) prior to shock and on subsequent tests it was found that either A or B alone evoked the CER. Those findings were simply the standard ones in the literature of the CER. The novel aspect of Kamin's study was the introduction of a condition in which some animals were first presented with stimulus A alone followed by shock, then with A plus B together, again followed by shock, and finally with tests of A and B alone. In this case it was found that on the final tests stimulus A evoked the CER, but stimulus B did not. For the animals that had already learned that A signified impending shock, the addition of B on a later conditioning trial added nothing to the predictability of shock and, evidently as a consequence, B did not enter into learned associations as a result of the A plus B conditioning trials. A wide variety of experiments with different kinds of subjects have confirmed the general principle that a cue or stimulus is unlikely to enter into conditioning unless it adds something to the predictability of the traumatic or otherwise significant event that constitutes the unconditioned stimulus.

The principle of informativeness can have positive and negative applications. One might wish to associate positive affect with some necessary but not particularly pleasant classroom activity and attempt to produce the desired conditioning by scheduling this activity to come just before another that the students enjoy. However, temporal succession is not enough. Conditions should be arranged so that the occurrence of the first activity actually conveys information as to whether the second will be forthcoming. Contrariwise, the time of occurrence of the unpleasant activity should be clearly communicated to the students in advance, so that ordinary classroom events that precede it will not carry any additional predictive information, and therefore will not become conditioned signals for negative emotions.

What is the significance of classical conditioning for behavior? It should not be assumed that all learning that occurs has adaptive significance. However, on the whole, learning does contribute to the individual's adjustment to the environment, and understanding the nature of this relationship contributes to understanding of the learning process itself. In the case of classical conditioning, perhaps the most conspicuous adaptive aspect is the preparatory function. It is important to anticipate traumatic events in order to be able to respond quickly by flight, attack, or other appropriate action should they occur, or better yet, on occasion to take appropriate action soon enough to avert the event entirely. The anticipatory state of the organism activated by a CER serves this preparatory function by activating a family of action systems related to flight, defense, and avoidance (Bolles, 1975; Estes, 1969). Whether this partial mobilization of defensive reaction systems is adaptive in a particular case depends on the circumstances, for in some situations flight or the equivalent is inappropriate or ineffective and the emotional state simply interferes with the conduct of what would be normal behavior in the situation. In school learning situations, it would be expected that fear or other learned emotional reactions to events that might occur (such as failure on examinations or the like) would have little adaptive value but rather a disruptive or depressive effect on the kinds of constructive activity called for by school tasks.

Not all preparation has to do with traumatic events. In the rat, a signal stimulus that precedes food comes to have a broad energizing effect on families of behaviors related to food seeking and ingestion, thus facilitating trial and error activity that may lead to the learning of routes to food or the like. Although there is little direct evidence from the laboratory, one would expect much the same effects from conditioned anticipation of rewarding events by students in school environments, or, more generally, by people in a variety of everyday life situations. This positive facilitatory function of conditioned anticipatory states might be characterized as setting the stage for selective learning.

Selective Learning

Centuries of analysis of human action by philosophers, decades of research on learning by biologists and psychologists, and the everyday experience of people in varying environments all agree that much of the adaptive behavior of organisms depends on learning by experience to select actions with more favorable over actions with less favorable consequences. The reasons why selective learning often fails and the mechanisms whereby the learning is accomplished present major problems for learning theory. Progress has been made on some of these problems but others remain refractory and among these some are the source of active controversy.

A perennial source of controversy in this field has been the issue as to whether selective learning is primarily a matter of automatic strengthening of successful responses by rewards (*reinforcements*) and weakening of unsuccessful ones by punishments or whether it is, rather, a matter of acquiring information relevant to decisions. At present, the former position is perhaps most widely identified with the work of Skinner and his followers on operant conditioning and behavioral modification (Krasner, 1971; Skinner, 1938), the latter with the work of Bandura (1969, 1977) on observational learning.

The view that is exemplified in this chapter is that there is no one answer to the issue of trial and error versus observational learning. Successful performance in any situation that calls for intelligent choices or the employment of skills depends on a number of factors. In some sense, information must be acquired about the relationships between actions and outcomes. For animals, this stored information may perhaps take only the form of learned associations between stimulus, response, and outcome. For human learners, the information may take the form of verbal propositions that can arise from one's observation of one's own performance or that of other people, or it may be communicated more indirectly. Sometimes information obtained through observation or verbal communication may suffice to enable an individual to produce the desired or required performance for success on a task, but sometimes it may not. Several decades of research within the traditions both of operant conditioning and of cognitive psychology have contributed toward resolving some of these more specific issues. The following sections review some of the principal concepts and principles that have emerged.

Operant Conditioning and Behavioral Modification.   The first term in the title of this section, *operant,* refers to the specific body of principles developed by Skinner and his followers for the training of well-defined response sequences or skills under close control by schedules of rewards or punishments; the second term, *conditioning,* refers to the extension of these principles from the original research on animals to some forms of human behavior. In general, operant principles apply directly to organisms, whether human beings or lower animals, who are confined, voluntarily or not, to restricted environmental situations where the achievement of reward or avoidance of punishment depends on the occurrence of particular actions defined by an experimenter or trainer. In the original experiments of Skinner (1938), the subjects were rats confined in a small cell (a Skinner box) containing a lever that. when operated by the animal, intermittently activated a food pellet dispenser. In general, for animals in similarly limited situations, the principles developed enable the training of virtually any response sequence or skill within the animal's capability. Skinner (1953, 1968) proposed that essentially the same is true for human beings. Actual demonstrations of this extendibility have been limited so far, however, to situations that are analogous in many ways to the Skinner box—for example training simple skills or habits in institutionalized mentally defective individuals or teaching specific items of information or well-defined skills (for example adding numbers, spelling words correctly) to school children by means of "teaching machines."

Operant conditioning often has been described in terms of "shaping" the behavior of the learner and characteristically proceeds in any situation from the general to the specific. The first stage in any new situation is nearly always one of classical conditioning in which the subject learns to anticipate the occurrence of rewards or of punishing events, depending on whether the learning is to be accomplished by positive reinforcement or by avoidance, in a given locale. To illustrate a typical positive learning procedure, suppose a dog is being given to a deaf person for the purpose of providing her with surrogate ears so to speak, by letting the person know when the alarm clock or the telephone rings, or the like. The first stage in training is to bring the dog to the person's home and encourage her to play with the dog and give it tidbits, so that the animal comes to anticipate rewards in her presence. Then, with the deaf person simulating sleep and a trainer present, arrangements are made for the alarm to ring on an irregular schedule. When the alarm rings, a normal dog's first response is to become alert and move about, often toward the source. The trainer observes the dog's initial responses to the sound and categorizes them roughly into those that lead the animal in the desired direction, that is toward the deaf person, and those that do not. Then the trainer reinforces behaviors in the former category by praise or the like but does not reinforce movements toward the clock or in other undesired directions. As soon as the animal gives evidence of moving predominantly in the desired direction, the criterion for reinforcement is tightened, until after a number of episodes reward is given only if the dog actually approaches and touches the deaf person; then the deaf person takes over, and praises or rewards the animal for awaking her.

Making a reward contingent on progressively narrower classes of actions leads to the shaping of the animal's behavior from an originally diffuse pattern to the specific action desired. The next step is to make the habit durable. If a dog were rewarded for each correct response, then if on a few occasions the mistress were busy and failed to supply the reward, the animal would quickly come to expect nonreward and might discontinue its desired sentry duty. To avoid this *experimental extinction* of the newly learned response, the animal during training would be quickly shifted to a schedule of *intermittent reinforcement* in which at first occasional correct responses would receive no reward, the frequency of rewards then being progressively decreased until after a time the animal would perform the desired action reliably with only occasional reinforcement. The key principle is that the animal must have an opportunity to learn that the probability of a reward following the correct action is higher than in its absence.

Motivation and Information in the Control of Performance.   The efficacy of operant principles for the training of animals, and in some situations human beings, has been documented beyond question. However, questions may well be raised as to why reinforcers exert the effects that they do in some operant situations and also why the principles do not prove highly generalizable for the interpretation of human behavior. With regard to the first question, the evidence for the following theoretical account has been reviewed in Estes (1972c). The critical concepts are feedback from consequences of actions that facilitate or inhibit ongoing behavior and the acquisition of information that enables this feedback to be selective. The relation between motivation, or drive, and behavior can be analyzed at various levels, but for the present purposes it will suffice to observe that in general drives and motives can be classed into positive and negative categories. These categories have the properties that activation of positive motives, or, more specifically, the brain mechanisms associated with them, yields facilitation of ongoing behavior and increases activity in families of defense and flight reactions.

The basic learning process that enables drive mechanisms to become sources of selective feedback for the shaping of performance is one of acquiring information regarding relationships between changes in stimulus input from the environment and changes in activity of drive mechanisms. Consider for example a hungry animal that has found food in a particular location. The changes in stimulation accompanying approach to that location will become conditioned signals for an increase in positive feedback from drive mechanisms initially activated only during feeding. As a consequence of this learning, when the animal is later placed in the same situation and begins to explore it, changes in stimulation resulting from movements toward the previous location of food will tend to facilitate ongoing behavior, whereas decreases in such stimulation resulting from movements away will tend to inhibit ongoing behavior. This selective feedback results in the animal's approaching the location where a reward was received earlier. Nothing is known at present concerning brain mechanisms associated with human motives for achievement and the like, but their functional properties with regard to facilitation and inhibition of action seem closely analogous to those that are quite well understood for biological drives.

Given that feedback control of performance for rewarding and nonrewarding consequences of actions is so powerful, why do reward and punishment prove uncertain in their effects on ordinary human behavior? A key to the answer has been provided by the work of Nuttin (1953), who observed that human learners acquire more information about situations in which rewards and punishments occur than simply the particular correlations of these with correct and incorrect responses. Most importantly they learn to categorize situations into what Nuttin has termed *closed* versus *open* tasks. A closed task is one in which reinforcement contingencies are specific to the particular situation and are unlikely to carry over to other situations. An open task is one for which reinforcement contingencies in the training situation actually correspond with those that will exist outside and for which information to this effect is available to the learner.

Many educational and therapeutic situations are, unfortunately, of the closed character. An individual undergoing treatment for a behavior disorder may be rewarded by a therapist in the course of a treatment session for what are regarded as appropriate behaviors, but is unlikely at the same time to acquire any information leading him or her to expect similar rewards for the same behaviors outside of the treatment situation. Much the same is often true of the use of specific rewards and punishments in school situations. Reinforcement contingencies applied in education and therapy can be expected to establish habits that will lead to desired behavior outside the training situation only if the learner can be convinced that the associated actions will have similar rewarding or punishing consequences in everyday life.

COMPLEX LEARNING

Concept and Category Learning

Much of the progress toward extending learning theory to the acquisition of knowledge that has occurred in recent decades turns on the advances made by cognitive psychologists toward a theoretical characterization of the outcome of the learning process. It has come to be appreciated that the main products of educational learning are not tendencies to repeat particular successful actions or memories for particular passages of text material, but, rather, organized assemblages of concepts (Anderson, 1976; Anderson & Bower, 1973; Kintsch, 1974). The modes of organization are the province of other branches of cognitive psychology, but understanding the way concepts are learned is the task of learning theory.

Learning of Rule-Based Concepts.   According to widely accepted definitions, concept formation differs from discrimination learning primarily in the generality of what is learned. Discrimination learning prepares the individual to distinguish or identify previously experienced entities, as, for example, the members of a pair of identical twins. But concept learning prepares the learner to assign appropriately a newly encountered member of a class or category defined by the concept—for example, a newly encountered animal to the category animal or a newly encountered bird to the category bird. An important distinction within the domain of concept learning has to do with whether or not a concept is defined by some specific rule that can be discovered and utilized by the learner. Concepts encountered in formal disciplines such as mathematics or linguistics (e.g., triangle, rational number, prime number in the former; noun, verb, predicate in the latter) belong to the rule-defined category. The same appears to be true for many empirically based concepts, for example, mammal, planet, parent.

It appears that learning of rule-based concepts may proceed on either of two levels. For inexperienced learners, the process is essentially the same as discrimination learning. Initially, the learner samples more or less randomly the features or aspects of exemplars of the categories belonging to a concept and associates these with category labels. Then, as a consequence of feedback from correct or incorrect categorizations, or the equivalent information from other instruction, the learner comes to attend selectively to the features or combination of features that are actually related to category labels by the rule defining a concept. This characterization of the lower level concept learning process is the basis of what are termed *feature-frequency models* (Reed, 1973; Smith & Medin, 1981).

For more sophisticated learners, the acquisition of a concept is characteristically a more actively and rationally directed process in which some aspects of the feature frequency models, in particular the association of individual features with category labels, appear to be bypassed or subordinated to a process of hypothesis testing (Bruner, Goodnow, & Austin, 1956; Levine, 1959, 1963; Trabasso & Bower, 1968). In hypothesis models, the individual is assumed to operate from first contact with a conceptual learning situation on the premise that a solution in terms of rules is to be discovered. On first encountering an exemplar of a concept to be learned, the learner, drawing on past experience, formulates a hypothesis relating features of the exemplar to a category label, then tests this hypothesis on subsequent trials, retaining it if it leads to correct categorization and modifying it if not, until a hypothesis is shaped that leads to uniformly correct categorization. Under idealized conditions, as for example a computer simulated model dealing with a rule-defined problem, the hypothesis selection model should lead to optimally efficient concept learning. However, optimal efficiency requires that the learner maintain a completely accurate record in memory of the degree to which the conditions of each candidate hypothesis have been met by all previously experienced exemplars and that the choice of features or attributes that enter into hypotheses be uninfluenced by biases or preferences actually irrelevant to solution. In actual human learners, neither of these idealizations is completely satisfied, of course, and consequently the interpretation of concept learning must draw heavily on the psychology of memory and preference.

A substantial body of research on hypothesis selection has led to the formulation of models that account in considerable detail for the properties of performance in situations where correct classificatory behavior can be achieved by the discovery and use of simple rules (Falmagne, 1974; Millward & Wickens, 1974). However it is not clear that these models have much application to the kinds of learning that occur in school or other kinds of formal education. When, for example, pupils are learning arithmetic, mathematics, or grammar, they typically are not turned loose to deal with unfamiliar subject matter on a trial-and-error basis, discovering rules of classification if they can. Rather it is the usual practice to supply the learner with appropriate rules as a part of the instructional process and to attempt to develop skill at recognizing the circumstances under which the rules should be applied. Understanding this kind of learning is, then, for the most part a matter of understanding how propositional information is stored in memory and accessed for use under varying test conditions.

Learning of Fuzzy Categories. Much concept learning that occurs outside the laboratory has to do, not with classes strictly definable by simple rules, but rather with categorization of collections of objects or events for which no such definitions are available, hence the term *fuzzy categories.* We learn to classify plants as fruits versus vegetables, people as liberals versus conservatives, instances of mental illness as neurotic versus psychotic, but in each case without any hard and fast lines of classification that determine the class membership of all instances. Rather, correct classification turns on the degree to which members of one category, say liberals, tend to resemble each other on a number of attributes to a greater extent than they resemble members of another category, say conservatives (Rosch, 1973, 1978).

Two currently influential theoretical approaches to the learning of fuzzy categories differ considerably in the strategy adopted. In one approach, termed *prototype theory,* a special mechanism is posited, whereas in the other approach, *exemplar theory,* an effort is made to understand learning of fuzzy categories in terms of the same mechanisms and processes that have been developed to deal with other presumably simpler forms of learning.

Qualitatively, the notion of a prototype as a mental representation of a category is an old one. Sir Francis Galton (1879) suggested that we learn to recognize instances of a class of persons, such as criminals, by remembering individual instances, mentally superposing these memory traces in much the same way that one might superpose the negatives of a number of photographs of people to form a composite image, and then classifying new instances on the basis of their similarity to this composite or prototype. In more recent and more formal approaches to prototype theory (Posner & Keele, 1968; Reed, 1973) it is assumed that the information an individual stores in memory about a perceived exemplar of a category is, in effect, a list of its values on a number of relevant attributes or dimensions. The mental prototype of a category that is formed as a consequence of experience with various exemplars is simply a list of the average values of members of the category on each of the relevant dimensions. In a classification task the learner is presumed to compare an object or event presented for classification to the prototype of each relevant category, computing the average distance in a "similarity space" between the test exemplar and each of the prototypes and then classifying the examplar as belonging to the category whose prototype it is closest to. This type of model provides an account for the general properties of learning relative to fuzzy categories, in particular, for such interesting phenomena as the observation that individuals tend to classify newly encountered exemplars of a category that are close to the prototype more quickly and accurately than previously experienced exemplars that are further from the prototype. A drawback of the theory is that it assumes some rather elaborate cognitive operations on the part of the learner, for which there is little in the way of direct evidence.

In the exemplar approach (Medin & Schaffer, 1978; Smith & Medin, 1981) it is assumed that learning of categories comes down in essentials to the same process of storing memory representations of perceived stimulus patterns that enters in some degree into all forms of learning. According to the exemplar model, an individual's state of knowledge about the categories "liberal" and "conservative" takes the form, not of a mental prototype of each category, but rather of a collection of mental representations of specific individuals labeled as belonging to each category that the learner has had experience with. Classification of a new instance is assumed to be accomplished by a process in which the learner brings to mind the remembered exemplars of one category and assesses their overall similarity to the test instance, then does the same for any other candidate category, and assigns the new instance to the category to whose exemplars it is most similar on the whole. The exemplar model may well not prove to account for all aspects of human category learning, but, perhaps surprisingly, it has proven capable of generating good quantitative accounts of numerous experiments in relatively simplified situations and accounts for the phenomena that suggested prototype models without assuming as elaborate mental processes.

The different current approaches to concept learning may well prove complementary rather than competitive. It seems likely that in any new type of situation the learner initially proceeds by a more or less automatic process of storing memory representations of exemplars of categories and making new classification judgments on the basis of similarity of the new cases to remembered instances. In situations that lend themselves to quantitative characterizations of categories in the form of prototypes or rules based on defining properties, dependence on memory for specific exemplars may be superseded by a process of recognizing higher order regularities and giving priority to these as a guide to classification. There is some evidence for an overall developmental trend in children's classification learning from the more elementary to the more abstract mode (Kendler, 1983) but little is yet known about the necessary conditions for this transition either in the course of development or in the course of acquisition of skill in specific situations.

Acquisition of Knowledge

The distinction between simple forms of behavioral training and education in a broader sense turns to an important extent on the distinction between rote memorization and the acquisition of knowledge. *Rote memorization* refers to an individual's ability to recognize particular objects, to produce previously rewarded responses to specific stimuli, or to recall specific words or sentences; *the acquisition of knowledge* refers to information about a topic that can be expressed in many different ways, either verbally or in other modes. During the half century or so that learning theory has existed as an identifiable discipline, both its research base and its concepts and models have had to do mainly with simple behavioral modification or memorization. The classic learning theorists (for example Hull, 1943; Skinner, 1938) assumed that principles of learning drawn from simple situations would ultimately be extendible in a direct and more or less automatic way to more complex forms of learning. In concluding this chapter, it is appropriate to ask to what degree those expectations have been borne out.

An answer to this question that seems justifiable, not on the basis of any one study, but rather on the tenor of a great deal of current research on relatively complex forms of human learning, might be characterized as affirmative, but only within distinct limits. In order to acquire knowledge about any material, the learner must engage in activities that bring him or her into contact with the material in appropriate ways, and here the applicability of learning theory seems most clear. The formation and maintenance of habits of study, the attachment of values to products of knowledge acquisition, the employment of cognitive strategies of selective attention, rehearsal and the like, appear clearly subject to the principles that have emerged from basic learning theory. To some extent, the same may be true of some of the dynamics of knowledge acquisition, especially aspects having to do with temporal properties of study or practice, and the role of contextual factors in retrieval and retention. The limits of applicability of extant learning theory begin to be approached or exceeded when we raise questions about the nature of what is learned when one acquires knowledge and about the detailed way in which knowledge structures emerge from individual learning experiences.

Nonetheless, a succession of progressively more ambitious attempts to lay out the form that might be taken by a theory of knowledge acquisition begins to suggest some ways in which learning theory might begin to invade this more complex domain (Anderson, 1976; Anderson & Bower, 1973; Kintsch, 1974; Norman & Rumelhart, 1970).

Much activity in recent cognitive science has focused on the way knowledge and complex skills are organized in the memory system. Less attention has been given to processes of acquisition. In the most comprehensive attempt to present an "architecture" of human cognition, Anderson (1983) developed in detail a proposal for the organization of declarative memory, the repository of knowledge, and for production systems, the machinery that actually accomplishes cognitive tasks. The processes that must be responsible for the growth of declarative memory in the individual are largely bypassed, but a relatively detailed analysis is given for the acquisition of skilled performance, that is, for what Anderson terms *procedural learning.*

In Anderson's Adaptive Control of Thought (ACT) system, declarative memory takes the form of an associative network of remembered propositions or concepts. Information in declarative memory influences behavior when items are brought into short-term working memory and provides the conditions for the productions that actually control performance. A production is a condition–action pair of the general form, "If condition X is satisfied, then perform action Y." In psychological terms, a production may be viewed as a mental representation of a relation between a condition and an action, having the property that if a scan of active memory on a particular occasion finds the condition to be satisfied, then the action is carried out. The condition is typically a statement of fact in some form; the action can take the form of overt behavior or of a cognitive act such as accessing additional information from declarative memory.

The general process of procedural learning is analyzed by Anderson into stages closely corresponding to those posited by Fitts (1964) for the acquisition of motor skills. In the first stage, termed *declarative* (or *cognitive*), declarative knowledge, typically in the form of rules or prescriptions for action, is used interpretively to guide behavior. In the second stage, *knowledge compilation,* sets of productions are formed that can then run off the needed behavior without continuing references to declarative memory. In the third stage, *tuning of productions,* processes of discrimination, generalization, and strengthening by repetition increase the efficiency of the production set.

The acquisition process conceived in ACT can be illustrated in terms of the now common problem of learning to use a word-processing program. One of the first steps for the novice is to learn to manipulate the cursor, the moving symbol on the display screen that indicates where a character can be inserted or deleted. The first step in acquisition is to obtain from the reference manual or instructor a description of the rules for moving the cursor. These will typically take the form of statements such as, "To change from text to command mode, depress the escape key; to move the cursor to the left on any line, depress the keys labelled control and A." Once these propositions have been committed to memory (are represented in declarative memory), the user can begin to manipulate the cursor, typically in a fumbling fashion, by consulting his memory for the information needed to select the appropriate action at each step. With continuing experience, the action sequence needed to achieve each commonly occuring subgoal becomes "compiled" into a set of productions, which will then run off smoothly whenever the subgoal is brought into short-term memory in the course of a task. In the final stage, not necessarily distinct from the preceding one, the individual may note common elements in two or more productions and form a more general production that is more widely applicable or may note differences in the consequences of productions that had initially been treated as though equivalent. Also, commonly used productions are, in effect, moved up on a priority list so that they become more readily available.

The ingredients of these theoretical efforts to encompass the acquisition of factual and procedural knowledge appear, on the surface at least, to be defined at a qualitatively distinct level from those of more basic learning theory. However, some linkages may be discerned. For example, concepts—the most complex entities treated in basic learning theories—may serve as the most elementary units of theories of knowledge acquisition (Anderson, 1981; Anderson & Bower, 1973). Also, there are some interesting parallels between theoretical structures at the lower and higher levels. Thus, in the models flowing from the work of Anderson and Bower, concepts are interrelated in memory by means of networks having properties that resemble in many respects those of the associative networks of learning theory. Again, the *production systems* that relate memory to action in Anderson's theory are similar in form to the stimulus–response relations that link perception to action in elementary learning theories. In a *production* the response component of stimulus–response theory is replaced by an organized action program and the stimulus component by the current state of the active segment of memory. In Anderson's theory, the strength of a production (that is, its readiness for use) is related to recency and frequency of previous evocations by functions similar to those that obtain for simple stimulus–response associations. Similarly, the tuning processes that are assumed to contribute to the refinement of procedural learning in the ACT system, for example, generalization, discrimination, learning from informative feedback, are closely analogous to those assumed in general learning theory, reviewed earlier in this chapter.

There are genuine new insights in the ACT interpretation of procedural learning, but they have a basis in the cumulative results of decades of research and theory construction on both animal and human learning. Major research tasks for the immediate future will surely include efforts to work out in more detail the way in which functional properties of learning that have been incorporated in classical learning theories will be mirrored in the interpretations of more complex processes of knowledge acquistion.

SUMMARY: PROFILE OF A LEARNER

Because learning is a vast subject matter, research and the formation of theory can only advance by dealing with a particular aspect at a time. Thus a review chapter necessarily takes the form of a microcosm in which the various types of studies and types of theories extant in the field are represented. In order to understand a learner in a school or other educational situation, it is necessary to put the various topics and concepts together at least in imagination so as to provide some insight into the problems confronting the learner and the way they are resolved in actual practice. In very brief compass, it might be interesting to try to bring together from the various topics considered in this chapter a sketch of a learner as seen from the standpoint of learning theory.

Conspicuous in the basic equipment of the learner is a memory system of virtually unlimited capacity, but one whose use is limited by slow access and a pervasive tendency for declining availability of infrequently used information. Owing to these limitations, the flood of information presented to an individual by the many problem situations confronted during every waking hour would soon overwhelm the system if all of the information were automatically stored in memory. The necessary selectivity is provided primarily by an attentional system capable of setting criteria of relevance and allowing the individual's cognitive control processes to select relevant information for rehearsal and ultimate organization in the memory system, while most irrelevant information is excluded. Thus, for effective learning, a more important problem than how to memorize great amounts of information is how to develop skill at attending to what is relevant to short- and long-term task demands.

The mode of operation of the learner is characterized by concurrent activity at a number of levels. At the lowest, most automatic level of operation, much of the detail of the episodes the individual experiences is temporarily recorded in the primary memory system, which is transient, yet allows time for attention to relationships among events and selection for further processing on the basis of criteria of relevance. At the higher, more distinctively cognitive levels, the dominant working strategy of the learner is continually to seek ways of categorizing new events or items of information so that they can be dealt with as members of classes about which something is already known, rather than as novel experiences.

The process of concept learning evidently begins in a new situation with the storing in memory of representations of exemplars of categories; then new items or events are classified on the basis of their judged similarity to these remembered exemplars. Superposed on exemplar learning is a tendency to attend to features or attributes of exemplars that recur in orderly relationships to category labels and to generate hypotheses or rules that simplify the categorization of new cases.

The lower level episodic memory processes appear to operate relatively independently of motivation or current task demands, except that motivationally significant events tend to capture attention and thus to have an advantage over less significant events with regard to entry into memory organization. Motivation appears not to modify the learner's processes of memory storage directly, but rather to provide the basis for reinforcement and feedback control of attentional and cognitive strategies that direct and control the course of learning and the utilization of what is learned.

Many aspects and levels of learning theory offer some contribution to understanding the way people learn in educational settings. Perhaps most basically, education cannot go far unless the individual acquires values for the products of learning. The ways in which successful instances of learning take on value for an individual are only imperfectly understood, but there is reason to think that some of the basic processes are similar if not identical to those of classical conditioning. It is important not only to value the products of learning, but to form habits of doing the things necessary to bring learning about. The way incentives operate to influence the needed kinds of performance is understood in part by way of the theory of basic processes in trial-and-error learning and in part by recent extensions of the theory to aspects of more complex human learning.

The main reasons why learning is often difficult appear to be twofold. Firstly, learning is of little use unless the knowledge or skill acquired is retained and used in relevant situations. A substantial body of theory now offers some insight into the way retention depends on the relationships between the context in which learning occurs and the context in which the results are used or tested. Problems of retention must be solved primarily by finding ways of organizing information in memory so that it can be accessed efficiently when needed. The other principal reason for difficulty of learning lies in the fact that learning material of any complexity depends on comprehension and thus in turn on the way the learner is equipped by previous experience with the concepts basic to comprehension. The intensive research of the early 1980s has begun to provide some insight into the form in which concepts and categories come to be represented in the learner's memory system. The major problem remains of developing similar insight into the way these representations take form in the course of experience.

ACKNOWLEDGMENT

The preparation of this chapter was supported in part by NSF Grant BNS 80-26656.

REFERENCES

Anderson, J. R. (1976). *Language, memory, and thought.* Hillsdale, NJ: Lawrence Erlbaum Associates.

Anderson, J. R. (1980). *Cognitive psychology and its implications.* San Francisco, CA: Freeman.

Anderson, J. R. (1981). Concepts, propositions, and schemata: What are the cognitive units? In J. H. Flowers (Ed.), *Nebraska symposium on motivation, 1980: Cognitive processes* (Vol. 28, pp. 121–162). Lincoln, NE: University of Nebraska Press.

Anderson, J. R. (1983). *The architecture of cognition*. Cambridge, MA: Harvard University Press.

Anderson, J. R., & Bower, G. H. (1973). *Human associative memory*. Washington, DC: V. H. Winston.

Atkinson, R. C., & Shiffrin, R. M. (1968). Human memory: A proposed system and its control processes. In K. W. Spence & J. T. Spence (Eds.), *The psychology of learning and motivation: Advances in research and theory* (Vol. 2, pp. 89–195). New York: Academic Press.

Baddeley, A. D. (1976). *The psychology of memory*. New York: Basic Books.

Baddeley, A. D. (1982). Domains of recollection. *Psychological Review, 89,* 708–729.

Bandura, A. (1969). *Principles of behavior modification*. New York: Holt, Rinehart & Winston.

Bandura, A. (1977). *Social learning theory*. Englewood Cliffs, NJ: Prentice-Hall.

Bolles, R. C. (1975). Learning, motivation, and cognition. In W. K. Estes (Ed.), *Handbook of learning and cognitive processes: Vol. 1. Introduction of concepts and issues* (pp. 249–280). Hillsdale, NJ: Lawrence Erlbaum Associates.

Bower, G. H. (1970). Organizational factors in memory. *Cognitive Psychology, 1,* 18–46.

Bower, G. H. (1972). Stimulus-sampling theory of encoding variability. In A. W. Melton & E. Martin (Eds.). *Coding processes in human memory* (pp. 85–123). Washington, DC: V. H. Winston.

Bower, G. H. (1975). Cognitive psychology: An introduction. In W. K. Estes (Ed.), *Handbook of learning and cognitive processes: Vol. 1. Introduction of concepts and issues* (pp. 25–80). Hillsdale, NJ: Lawrence Erlbaum Associates.

Bower, G. H. (1981). Mood and memory. *American Psychologist, 36,* 129–148.

Bower, G. H., Clark, M. C., Lesgold, A. M., & Winzenz, D. (1969). Hierarchical retrieval schemes in recall of categorized word lists. *Journal of Verbal Learning and Verbal Behavior, 8,* 323–343.

Bower, G. H., & Hilgard, E. R. (1981). *Theories of learning* (5th ed.). Englewood Cliffs, NJ: Prentice-Hall.

Broadbent, D. E. (1958). *Perception and communication*. New York: Pergamon Press.

Broadbent, D. E. (1971). *Decision and stress*. New York: Academic Press.

Bruner, J. S., Goodnow, J. J., & Austin, G. A. (1956). *A study of thinking*. New York: Wiley.

Chase, W. G., & Ericsson, K. A. (1981). Skilled memory. In J. R. Anderson (Ed.), *Cognitive skills and their acquisition* (pp. 141–189). Hillsdale, NJ: Lawrence Erlbaum Associates.

Chi, M. T. H., Feltovich, P. J., & Glaser, R. (1981). Categorization and representation of physics problems by experts and novices. *Cognitive Science, 5,* 121–152.

Cole, M., Gay, J., Glick, J. A., & Sharp, D. W. (1971). *The cultural context of learning and thinking*. New York: Basic Books.

Conrad, R. (1964). Acoustic confusions in immediate memory. *British Journal of Psychology, 55,* 75–84.

Cook, S. W., & Harris, R. E. (1937). The verbal conditioning of the galvanic skin response. *Journal of Experimental Psychology, 21,* 202–210.

Cunningham, T. F., Healy, A. F., & Williams, D. M. (1984). Effects of repetition on short-term retention of order information. *Journal of Experimental Psychology: Learning, Memory, and Cognition, 10,* 575–597.

Ebbinghaus, H. (1913). *Memory.* (H. A. Ruger & C. E. Bussenius, trans.). New York: Teacher's College, Columbia University. (Originally published in 1885)

Estes, W. K. (1950). Toward a statistical theory of learning. *Psychological Review, 57,* 94–107.

Estes, W. K. (1969). Outline of a theory of punishment. In B. A. Campbell & R. M. Church (Eds.), *Punishment and aversive behavior* (pp. 57–82). New York: Appleton-Century-Crofts.

Estes, W. K. (1972a). An associative basis for coding and organization in memory. In A. W. Melton & E. Martin (Eds.), *Coding processes in human memory* (pp. 161–190). Washington, DC: V. H. Winston.

Estes, W. K. (1972b). Elements and patterns in diagnostic discrimination learning. *Transactions of the New York Academy of Sciences, Series II, 34,* 84–95.

Estes, W. K. (1972c). Reinforcement in human behavior. *American Scientist, 60,* 723–729.

Estes, W. K. (1973). Memory and conditioning. In F. J. McGuigan & D. B. Lumsden (Eds.), *Contemporary approaches to conditioning and learning* (pp. 265–286). Washington, DC: V. H. Winston.

Estes, W. K. (1976). Structural aspects of associative models for memory. In C. N. Cofer (Ed.), *The structure of human memory* (pp. 31–53). San Francisco, CA: Freeman.

Estes, W. K. (1979). On the descriptive and explanatory functions of theories of memory. In L. -G. Nilsson (Ed.), *Perspectives on memory research* (pp. 35–60). Hillsdale, NJ: Lawrence Erlbaum Associates.

Estes, W. K. (1980). Is human memory obsolete? *American Scientist, 68,* 62–69.

Estes, W. K. (1982a). Learning, memory, and intelligence. In R. J. Sternberg (Ed.), *Handbook of human intelligence* (pp. 170–224). New York: Cambridge University Press.

Estes, W. K. (1982b). *Models of learning, memory, and choice: Selected papers.* New York: Praeger.

Estes, W. K. (1985). Levels of association theory. *Journal of Experimental Psychology: Learning, Memory, and Cognition, 11,* 450–454.

Estes, W. K., & DaPolito, F. (1967). Independent variation in information storage and retrieval processes in paired-associate learning. *Journal of Experimental Psychology, 75,* 18–26.

Estes, W. K., & Skinner, B. F. (1941). Some quantitative properties of anxiety. *Journal of Experimental Psychology, 29,* 390–400.

Falmagne, R. J. (1974). Mathematical psychology and cognitive phenomena: Comments on preceding chapters. In D. H. Krantz, R. C. Atkinson, R. D. Luce, & P. Suppes (Eds.), *Contemporary developments in mathematical psychology: Learning, memory, and thinking* (Vol. 1., pp. 145–161). San Francisco, CA: Freeman.

Fisk, A. D., & Schneider, W. (1984). Memory as a function of attention, level of processing, and automatization. *Journal of Experimental Psychology: Learning, Memory, and Cognition, 10,* 181–197.

Fitts, P. W. (1964). Perceptual-motor skill learning. In A. W. Melton (Ed.), *Categories of human learning* (pp. 243–285). New York: Academic Press.

Galton, F. (1879). Composite portraits, made by combining those of many different persons into a single resultant figure. *Journal of the Anthropological Institute, 8,* 132–144.

Glucksberg, S., & Cowen, G. N., Jr. (1970). Memory for nonattended auditory material. *Cognitive Psychology, 1,* 149–156.

Grant, D. A. (1972). A preliminary model for processing information conveyed by verbal conditioned stimuli in classical conditioning. In A. H. Black & W. F. Prokasy (Eds.), *Classical conditioning II: Current research and theory* (pp. 28–63). New York: Appleton-Century-Crofts.

Grossberg, S. (1980). How does a brain build a cognitive code? *Psychological Review, 87,* 1–51.

Guthrie, E. R. (1935). *The psychology of learning.* New York: Harper.

Hasher, L., & Chromiak, W. (1977). The processing of frequency information: An automatic mechanism? *Journal of Verbal Learning and Verbal Behavior, 16,* 173–184.

Hasher, L., & Zacks, R. T. (1979). Automatic and effortful processes in memory. *Journal of Experimental Psychology: General, 108,* 356–388.

Healy, A. F. (1974). Separating item from order information in short-term memory. *Journal of Verbal Learning and Verbal Behavior, 13,* 644–655.

Hebb, D. O. (1949). *The organization of behavior: A neurophysiological theory.* New York: Wiley.

Hilgard, E. R., & Marquis, D. G. (1940). *Conditioning and learning.* New York: Appleton-Century-Crofts.

Hull, C. L. (1943). *Principles of behavior: An introduction to behavior theory.* New York: Appleton-Century-Crofts.

Hull, C. L. (1952). *A behavior system: An introduction to behavior theory concerning the individual organism.* New Haven, CT: Yale University Press.

Hunt, E. B. (1978). Mechanics of verbal ability. *Psychological Review, 85,* 109–130.

Jacoby, L. L. (1973). Test appropriate strategies in retention of categorized lists. *Journal of Verbal Learning and Verbal Behavior, 12,* 675–682.

Jacoby, L. L., & Dallas, M. (1981). On the relationship between autobiographical memory and perceptual learning. *Journal of Experimental Psychology: General, 110,* 306–340.

James, W. (1890). *The principles of psychology.* New York: Henry Holt.

Kahneman, D., & Treisman, A. (1984). Changing views of attention and automaticity. In R. Parasuraman & D. R. Davies (Eds.), *Varieties of attention* (pp. 29–61). New York: Academic Press.

Kamin, L. J. (1969). Predictability, surprise, attention, and conditioning. In B. A. Campbell & R. M. Church (Eds.), *Punishment and aversive behavior* (pp. 279–296). New York: Appleton-Century-Crofts.

Kendler, T. S. (1983). Labeling, overtraining, and levels of function. In T. J. Tighe & B. E. Shepp (Eds.), *Perception, cognition, and development: Interactional analyses* (pp. 129–162). Hillsdale, NJ: Lawrence Erlbaum Associates.

Kintsch, W. (1974). *The representation of meaning in memory.* Hillsdale, NJ: Lawrence Erlbaum Associates.

Koffka, K. (1935). *Principles of gestalt psychology.* New York: Harcourt Brace.

Konorski, J. (1967). *Integrative activity of the brain: An interdisciplinary approach.* Chicago, IL: University of Chicago Press.

Krasner, L. (1971). Behavior therapy. *Annual Review of Psychology, 22,* 483–532.

LaBerge, D. (1976). Perceptual learning and attention. In W. K. Estes (Ed.), *Handbook of learning and cognitive processes: Vol. 4. Attention and memory* (pp. 237–273). Hillsdale, NJ: Lawrence Erlbaum Associates.

Lashley, K. (1950). In search of the engram. In *Physiological mechanisms in animal behavior: Symposium of society of experimental biology, 4,* 454–482. New York: Cambridge University Press.

Lee, C. L., & Estes, W. K. (1977). Order and position in primary memory for letter strings. *Journal of Verbal Learning and Verbal Behavior, 16,* 395–418.

Lee, C. L., & Estes, W. K. (1981). Item and order information in short-term memory: Evidence for multi-level perturbation processes. *Journal of Experimental Psychology: Human Learning and Memory, 7,* 149–169.

Levine, M. (1959). A model of hypothesis behavior in discrimination learning set. *Psychological Review, 66,* 353–366.

Levine, M. (1963). Mediating processes in humans at the outset of discrimination learning. *Psychological Review, 70,* 254–276.

Light, L. L., & Carter-Sobell, L. (1970). Effects of changed semantic context on recognition memory. *Journal of Verbal Learning and Verbal Behavior, 9,* 1–11.

Mandler, G. (1968). Association and organization: Facts, fancies, and theories. In T. R. Dixon & D. L. Horton (Eds.), *Verbal behavior and general behavior theory* (pp. 109–119). Englewood Cliffs, NJ: Prentice-Hall.

Mandler, J. M., & Ritchey, G. H. (1977). Long-term memory for pictures. *Journal of Experimental Psychology: Human Learning and Memory, 3,* 386–396.

Martin, E. (1968). Stimulus meaningfulness and paired-associate transfer: An encoding variability hypothesis. *Psychological Review, 75,* 421–441.

McGeoch, J. A. (1942). *The psychology of human learning.* New York: Longmans, Green.

Medin, D. L., & Schaffer, M. M. (1978). Context theory of classification learning. *Psychological Review, 85,* 207–238.

Michon, J. A., & Jackson, J. L. (1984). Attentional effort and cognitive strategies in the processing of temporal information. In J. Gibbon & L. Allan (Eds.), *Timing and time perception. Annals of the New York Academy of Sciences, 423,* 298–321.

Miller, G. A. (1956). The magical number seven, plus or minus two: Some limits on our capacity for processing information. *Psychological Review, 63,* 81–97.

Millward, R. B., & Wickens, T. D. (1974). Concept-identification models. In D. H. Krantz, R. C. Atkinson, R. D. Luce, & P. Suppes (Eds.), *Contemporary developments in mathematical psychology: Learning, memory, and thinking* (Vol. 1 pp. 45–100). San Francisco: Freeman.

Newell, A. (1973). Production systems: Models of control structures. In W. G. Chase (Ed.), *Visual information processing* (pp. 463–526). New York: Academic Press.

Norman, D. A., & Rumelhart, D. E. (1970). A system for perception and memory. In D. A. Norman (Ed.), *Models of human memory* (pp. 19–64). New York: Academic Press.

Nuttin, J. R. (1953). *Tâche, Réussite, et Échec: Théorie de la Conduite Humaine.* Louvain, Belgium: Publications Universitaires de Louvain.

Posner, M. I., & Keele, S. W. (1968). On the genesis of abstract ideas. *Journal of Experimental Psychology, 77,* 353–363.

Postman, L. (1971). Transfer, interference, and forgetting. In J. W. Kling & L. A.

Riggs (Eds.), *Woodworth and Schlosberg's experimental psychology* (3rd ed., pp. 1019–1132). New York: Holt, Rinehart & Winston.

Postman, L. (1976). Methodology of human learning. In W. K. Estes (Ed.), *Handbook of learning and cognitive processes: Vol. 3. Approaches to human learning and motivation* (pp. 11–69). Hillsdale, NJ: Lawrence Erlbaum Associates.

Reber, A. S., & Allen, R. (1978). Analogic and abstraction strategies in synthetic grammar learning: A functionalist interpretation. *Cognition, 6,* 189–221.

Reed, S. K. (1973). *Psychological processes in pattern recognition.* New York: Academic Press.

Reitman, J. S. (1974). Without surreptitious rehearsal, information in short-term memory decays. *Journal of Verbal Learning and Verbal Behavior, 13,* 365–377.

Robinson, E. S. (1932). *Association theory today: An essay in systematic psychology.* New York: Appleton-Century-Crofts.

Rosch, E. R. (1973). On the internal structure of perceptual and semantic categories. In T. E. Moore (Ed.), *Cognitive development and the acquisition of language* (pp. 111–144). New York: Academic Press.

Rosch, E. R. (1978). Principles of categorization. In E. R. Rosch & B. B. Lloyd (Eds.), *Cognition and categorization* (pp. 27–48). Hillsdale, NJ: Lawrence Erlbaum Associates.

Ross, L. E., & Ross, S. M. (1976). Cognitive factors in classical conditioning. In W. K. Estes (Ed.), *Handbook of learning and cognitive processes: Vol. 3. Approaches to human learning and motivation* (pp. 103–129). Hillsdale, NJ: Lawrence Erlbaum Associates.

Schneider, W., & Fisk, A. D. (1983). Concurrent automatic and controlled visual search: Can processing occur without resource cost? *Journal of Experimental Psychology: Learning, Memory, and Cognition, 8,* 261–278.

Schoeffler, M. S. (1954). Probability of response to compounds of discriminated stimuli. *Journal of Experimental Psychology, 48,* 323–329.

Seamon, J. G. (1973). Retrieval processes for organized long-term storage. *Journal of Experimental Psychology, 97,* 170–176.

Seligman, M. E. P. (1970). On the generality of the laws of learning. *Psychological Review, 77,* 406–418.

Shiffrin, R. M. (1970). Memory search. In D. A. Norman (Ed.), *Models of human memory* (pp. 375–447). New York: Academic Press.

Shiffrin, R. M. (1973). Information persistence in short-term memory. *Journal of Experimental Psychology, 100,* 39–49.

Shiffrin, R. M., & Schneider, W. (1977). Controlled and automatic human information processing: II. Perceptual learning, automatic attending, and a general theory. *Psychological Review, 84,* 127–190.

Skinner, B. F. (1938). *The behavior of organisms: An experimental analysis.* New York: Appleton-Century-Crofts.

Skinner, B. F. (1953). *Science and human behavior.* New York: Macmillan.

Skinner, B. F. (1968). *The technology of teaching.* Englewood Cliffs, NJ: Prentice-Hall.

Smith, E. E., & Medin, D. L. (1981). *Categories and concepts.* Cambridge, MA: Harvard University Press.

Smith, E. E., & Spoehr, K. T. (1974). The perception of printed English: A theoretical perspective. In B. H. Kantowitz (Ed.), *Human information processing: Tutorials in performance and cognition* (pp. 231–275). Hillsdale, NJ: Lawrence Erlbaum Associates.

Sternberg, S. (1966). High-speed scanning in human memory. *Science, 153,* 652–654.

Thorndike, E. L. (1931). *Human learning.* New York: Appleton-Century-Crofts.

Trabasso, T., & Bower, G. H. (1968). *Attention in learning: Theory and research.* New York: Wiley.

Tulving, E. (1968). Theoretical issues in free recall. In T. R. Dixon & D. L. Horton (Eds.), *Verbal behavior and general behavior theory* (pp. 2–36). Englewood Cliffs, NJ: Prentice-Hall.

Tulving, E. (1983). *Elements of episodic memory.* New York: Oxford University.

Tversky, B. (1973). Encoding processes in recognition and recall. *Cognitive Psychology, 5,* 275–287.

Wagner, A. R. (1978). Expectancies and the priming of STM. In S. H. Hulse, H. Fowler, & W. K. Honig (Eds.), *Cognitive processes in animal behavior* (pp. 177–209). Hillsdale, NJ: Lawrence Erlbaum Associates.

Wagner, A. R. (1979). Habituation and memory. In A. Dickinson & R. A. Boakes (Eds.), *Mechanisms of learning and motivation: A memorial volume to Jerzy Konorski* (pp. 53–82). Hillsdale, NJ: Lawrence Erlbaum Associates.

Walters, G. C., & Grusec, J. E. (1977). *Punishment.* San Francisco, CA: Freeman.

Whitlow, J. W., Jr., & Estes, W. K. (1979). Judgments of relative frequency in relation to shifts of event frequencies: Evidence for a limited-capacity model. *Journal of Experimental Psychology: Human Learning and Memory, 5,* 395–408.

Williams, M. D., & Hollan, J. D. (1981). The process of retrieval from very long-term memory. *Cognitive Science, 5,* 87–119.

Woodward, A. E., Jr., Bjork, R. A., & Jongeward, R. N., Jr. (1973). Recall and recognition as a function of primary rehearsal. *Journal of Verbal Learning and Verbal Behavior, 12,* 608–617.

2

Intellectual Development

Gary M. Olson
University of Michigan

Throughout much of this century, American psychologists have viewed intelligence as what intelligence tests measure. The focus was on intelligent behavior as objectified in such tests. This view led to a predominantly psychometric approach to intellectual development. Tests of intelligence with good psychometric properties (validity, reliability) were developed, allowing investigators to measure intelligence quotients (IQs) across a broad range of ages. The primary goal was to quantify intelligence, and to differentiate children of a comparable age into different IQ strata. IQ test items were often factor analyzed in order to discover clusters of behaviors that were related (Kaufman, 1975; McNemar, 1942). From the psychometric perspective, the study of intellectual development was the study of the stability of IQ scores across ages (Honzik, Macfarlane, & Allen, 1948; McCall, Eichorn, & Hogarty, 1977; Sontag, Baker, & Nelson, 1958), of the comparability of IQ test factor structures across ages (Kaufman, 1975; McCall et al., 1977; McNemar, 1942), and of the correlations between IQ scores or factors and various forms of achievement, usually school tasks involving math or verbal abilities (Frandsen & Higginson, 1951; McNemar, 1942; Mussen, Dean, & Rosenberg, 1952).

An alternative to the psychometric approach is to focus on the underlying mental processes and structures that are responsible for intelligent behavior. Piaget is the most notable proponent of this approach in the area of intellectual development. He described what children know and what their thought processes are like at different stages of development. He used careful observations of children's behavior as the basis for his inferences about the nature of the mind. But the underlying cognitive structures were the focus of his work, not the behavior.

Recent approaches to the study of intellectual development are blends of these two approaches, giving more weight to objective, even quantified performance data than Piaget did but focusing much more on underlying mental competences than the psychometricians did. Examples of such approaches are Sternberg's (1977, 1982a, 1982b) componential view, Siegler's (Siegler & Richards, 1982) rule assessment view, and Sternberg's (1985) recent triarchic view. Each of these is a manifestation of the modern information-processing view of cognition, a view of mind strongly influenced both by the metaphor of the computer and by research in artificial intelligence, but strongly rooted in empirical observations. This is the view of intellectual development that is presented in this chapter.

This chapter presents an analysis of what intellectual development could possibly be, from the perspective of contemporary cognitive science. What is the set of possible underlying changes that would provide the basis for intellectual development? Further, what mechanisms might produce these changes? The discussion focuses on possibilities, because we still lack an empirical base sufficient for discriminating among candidate mechanisms. Actually, the most plausible view is that most of the factors or mechanisms discussed play a role at some point. Empirical data are needed to indicate which factors are influential when.

In the late 1960s, when mathematical theories of learning were quite popular, an important discussion was held on the topic of identifiability (see a recent discussion in Wickens, 1982). In essence, the issue was whether two seemingly different theories could be discriminated on the basis of a particular data set. The important result was that certain models that seem on superficial inspection to be quite different may not make discriminably different predictions with respect to a particular data set. Thus, the data set could not be used to select between the two models.

The study of intellectual development is plagued by problems of this sort, because we do not know enough about the properties of our theories to know how to discriminate among them with data. I stress two broad points in this chapter. First, we must be aware of the range of candidate factors for intellectual development. Second, many of these factors interact, complicating the task of assessing their influence. Unfortunately, theories of intellectual development tend to be imprecise, further complicating the task of differentiating among them. Although we now have a large database on what children do at different ages in different intellectual tasks, we do not have much information about theory in this area. Intensive work on theories of intellectual development, perhaps through computer simulation, could clear up some of these issues.

The goal of this chapter is to sketch a view of intellectual functioning consistent with current cognitive theory. The first section develops the conceptual framework for the discussion. A list of candidate factors that might be involved in intellectual development follows. These factors reflect a number of sources, not all of which focus on development. The next section describes a list of candidates for the mechanisms of change, a topic often neglected in discussions of intellectual development. Finally, the concluding section discusses the implications of this analysis.

CONCEPTUAL FRAMEWORK

In order to provide a framework for the discussion of mechanisms for intellectual development, I sketch a general view of how the human cognitive system is organized. This view shares strong affinities with such descriptions of the human cognitive system as those of Newell and Simon (1972), Anderson (1976,1983), and Holland, Holyoak, Nisbett, and Thagard (1986).

The cognitive system consists of a set of knowledge structures that are activated both by environmental inputs (stimuli) and by other knowledge structures (thoughts) in order to achieve goals. These knowledge structures are used and stored within a mental architecture that is characteristically human. The scope and nature of the set of knowledge structures that humans acquire is also unique. Intellectual development consists of changes in this system.

The first aspect of the cognitive system to consider is its basic architecture. Figure 2.1 shows this schematically.

Knowledge Base.   The heart of the cognitive system is the knowledge base, the store of all that is known. Anderson's (1976, 1983) ACT system proposes that the knowledge store is comprised of two distinct systems, a declarative memory

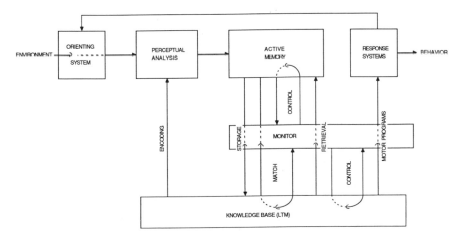

FIG. 2.1.   Overview of the cognitive system.

that consists of factual knowledge and a production memory that stores procedural knowledge. Although declarative and procedural knowledge are important subtypes of information, in general theorists have not distinguished them in the way Anderson has, opting instead for a uniform knowledge representation (Holland et al., 1986; Laird, Newell, & Rosenbloom, 1987; Rumelhart & Norman, in press). Thus, they are not sharply distinguished in the present scheme. Rather, all knowledge is assumed to be encoded in a homogeneous fashion.

One common way to describe the contents of the knowledge base is in terms of a set of production rules, called a *production system* (Anderson, 1983; Holland et al., 1986; Laird et al., 1987; Newell & Simon, 1972). Production rules consist of conditions and actions. When a condition is satisfied, the action fires. Actions may create conditions that affect the firing of subsequent productions or they may produce effects through the motor system. Table 2.1 gives several examples of production rules. Note that goals are made explicit in the conditions of the rules, and that often the actions modify the goal states.

At any given time, most of the rules in the knowledge base are inactive. As perceptual inputs and the firing of production rules modify the set of circumstances that are in force from moment to moment, different production rules are activated by having their conditions satisfied. Often more than one rule has its conditions satisfied at a time. This is known as the *competition problem.* One solution is to order the rules in some way and allow only the first rule whose conditions are satisfied to fire (Newell & Simon, 1972). Another is to place

TABLE 2.1
Examples of Production Rules from a Production System
for Subtraction
(from Neches, Langley, & Klahr, 1987)

FIND-DIFFERENCE
IF you are processing *column*
    and *number1* is in *column* and *row1,*
    and *number2* is in *column* and *row2,*
    and *row1* is above *row2*
    and *number1* is greater than or equal to *number2,*
THEN compute the difference between *number1* and *number 2*
    and write the result in *column.*

SHIFT-COLUMN
IF you are processing *column1,*
    and you are currently focused on *column1,*
    and the result in *column1* is not blank,
    and *column2* is left of *column1,*
THEN note that you are now processing *column2,*
    and note that you are focusing on *column2.*

---

strengths or levels of activation on production rules as a function of a number of variables, and select for firing that production rule that has the highest value of this variable (Anderson 1983). Yet another solution is to allow many or all production rules whose conditions are satisfied to fire, and to allow the various outcomes generated to send "messages" to a central message list that controls the next cycle of processing (Holland, 1986). In this scheme, there is a large amount of parallelism, with more than one rule active at any given moment. For present purposes, it is not essential to select a mechanism for the resolution of production competition.

Consistent with the present dominant view in cognitive psychology, there is no sharp distinction between short-term and long-term memory as separate system modules. However, at any moment in time one set of information is active and hence is more accessible than other information. This active information consists of the current perceptual input (discussed shortly) plus whatever information about goals and knowledge is currently playing a role in the firing of production rules. This active information tends to be quite volatile, easily lost through decay or interference. A distinctive characteristic of human cognition, discussed in greater detail shortly, is that only a modest amount of information can be active at any moment in time.

An important property of the information in the knowledge base is its organization. Human memory has a basically associative organization, in that the activation of information tends to activate information that is related to it. Information may be related to other information in a variety of ways. Some information is experienced together, so that temporal proximity is one basis for organizing material in memory. There is a variety of conceptual relationships among information: set relations, property lists, causal relationships, and so forth. There are also similarity relationships that play a role in the activation of information: similar sounding or appearing information is often associated. Indeed, the potential bases for the organization of information are quite large, and any given item of information is usually related to many other items in complex, tangled ways. The human knowledge base does not have a single, coherent global structure.

The organization of information plays an important role in cognition. The ease with which information can be retrieved or activated is markedly affected by its organization in memory (Bower 1970, 1972; Mandler, 1967). In turn, how easily information is accessed affects the stream of processing, both by facilitating and interfering with subsequent activities. New learning is also strongly influenced by the knowledge base. What is learned is related to what is already known, even in infancy where not much is known (Olson & Sherman, 1983).

Perceptual System. The perceptual system is the source of data about the outside world for the cognitive system. Information from each sensory modality is processed separately and in parallel, at least at the more peripheral stages. Further, each system processes input in stages, where the information is transformed and refined as it progresses toward the central system. In the central processor the information from different sensory pathways may be integrated. For example, information from vision and audition is often processed in a coordinated way, even by infants (Spelke, in press). At all ages, there is considerable parallel processing. Not only do the perceptual systems operate in parallel, but central processing can occur concurrently with perceptual processing.

The central processing system is interrupt-driven, in the sense that inputs from the perceptual processors are capable of eliciting processing that focuses on what is being sensed. Loud noises, bright lights, and motion tend to attract our attention immediately. This is biologically primitive, and continues throughout life. But as more knowledge is acquired, the relation between central processing and perceptual processing becomes more complex because of the influence of knowledge on perception (McClelland & Rumelhart, 1981; Rumelhart & McClelland, 1982). I discuss various proposals for these changes later in the chapter.

Attention. Perceptual processing is strongly affected by attention. At one level, attention is controlled by the orientation of the sensory organs. Thus, the eyes can be directed toward specific locations in the visual field or the ears can be oriented toward specific sounds to maximize the information coming into them. Items can be visually inspected by turning them round in the hand. But the sensory modalities all appear to have other forms of selectivity as well. Attention can be shifted within a single eye fixation (Jonides, 1981; Posner, 1978). From parallel or simultaneous presentation distinct visual or auditory inputs can be selected for detailed processing (Broadbent, 1958, 1971; Kahneman, 1973; Neisser, 1967). Thus, although in general much information enters the sensory systems in parallel, typically only selected aspects of it are given the most complete processing. In part these attentional processes in adults are under conscious, deliberate control. But attention is also captured involuntarily by particular kinds of salient stimuli, in the interrupt-driven fashion described in the previous paragraph.

Response System. The response system produces observable behavior. This is a complex system, and its operation and control are imperfectly understood (Gallistel, 1980; Pew, 1974; Turvey, 1977). The range of behaviors in humans is enormous: Limb movements are used to orient the body or to carry out any of a range of actions, many of them complex and highly skilled; eye and head movements are used to orient the visual and auditory system; the mouth and vocal tract are used to produce speech; and facial expressions and general body posture are used for a variety of communicative purposes. All of these behaviors produce proprioceptive stimuli that are sensed by the system, and many of them produce alterations of perceptual experiences through the other sensory modalities. For example, moving the eye changes the visual input. And, of course, many behaviors have consequences for the physical and the social world that will affect subsequent inputs to the organism.

Limits on Processing.   The cognitive system is constrained by various limits. The sensory systems are tuned to information from a particular range of possible stimulation, meaning that it is possible to know about only certain aspects of the environment.[1] However, in general, the limitations that matter most for intellectual activity are more central. The most far-reaching of these limits are various bottlenecks in processing. It is not clear whether the following bottlenecks are the same or distinct, but their effects are very similar.

One frequently described bottleneck is attentional. An incorrect but heuristically useful way to think of the attentional bottleneck is that the human cognitive system can only attend to one information stream at a time. The classic experimental demonstrations of this are in dichotic listening tasks (Broadbent, 1958, 1971) or in dual task situations (Norman & Bobrow, 1975). Also, attempting to process more than one information stream at once can lead to degraded performance on the tasks associated with each of the streams (depending on the processing loads of each task and on the payoffs for performing well in each one). Concurrent streams of information are processed incompletely, although attention can be switched to sample from one stream to another, often quite rapidly, and inferential processes can attempt to fill in missing information.

Another limitation is on the amount of internally held information that can be active. This is the traditional limit on immediate memory first described elegantly by Miller (1956). This is a limit on the amount of symbolic information that can be immediately accessible or activated at any moment. It leads to limited performance in short-term memory tasks and constrains performance in such tasks as mental arithmetic and language processing. Whether these two limits, the attentional one and the memory one, are distinct or due to common mechanisms is not settled.

Newell and Simon (1972) discussed another limit on immediate processing. They noted that although it takes on the order of hundreds of milliseconds to retrieve well-learned information, it takes considerably longer to store new information in a way that will allow it to be retrieved easily. On the basis of a survey of a wide range of verbal learning data, they estimated that it takes on the order of 5 to 10 seconds to store a chunk of information in long-term memory sufficiently well to be able to recall it. Thus, the human cognitive

---

[1]Of course, the range of information available about the world has been vastly expanded by technology (e.g., microscopes, telescopes, devices that process electromagnetic radiation that humans cannot sense).

system cannot rely on storing a lot of new information in real time as it processes environmental input. Rather, only a modest amount of the information that is attended to can be stored. This represents a further important constraint on performance in tasks where information from the environment is arriving at a rapid rate (e.g., speech).

These limits on central processing are what make human cognition so different from artificial cognition. It is not that human intelligence is limited and artificial intelligence is not. Artificial systems, although they have superior features for some characteristics (e.g., processing time, accuracy of stored information), face important limits for others (e.g., the size of the knowledge base, retrieval mechanisms). In many situations, task constraints play an enormous role in the structure of intelligent activity (Simon, 1981), in that once the task is specified there are limited degrees of freedom within which performance can vary. However, there are many situations in which the information demands in real time are high, and thus the human system cannot handle all that is going on. As we see later, there are several mechanisms by which these limits might change during development, affecting intellectual performance in a number of ways.

WHAT IS INTELLECTUAL DEVELOPMENT?

The purpose of this section is to examine the space of possible changes that could account for intellectual development, given the conceptual framework just described. As noted in the introduction, it is likely that many of these mechanisms—perhaps even all of them—have a role in intellectual development at some point during the life of the child. Furthermore, it is probable that significant features of intellectual development arise through interactions among the various factors described here. Several such significant interactions are discussed explicitly in the following sections.

Three broad classes of changes to the cognitive system are described: architectural tuning, knowledge modification, and skill modification. The first of these refers to changes in the basic hardware of the human cognitive system; the second to additions to, rearrangements of, or recodings of information in the knowledge base; and the third to changes in basic, general cognitive skills such as induction, deduction, and analogical reasoning.

Architectural Tuning

From all the evidence that has accumulated so far, it is improbable that the basic architecture of the human cognitive system changes during development (Olson, 1976; Olson & Sherman, 1983). Rather, there is evidence that aspects of the system can be tuned, in the sense that their basic operation becomes faster, less noisy, more automatic, and so on. The only exception to this generalization may be in the first few months of infancy, when certain structures that are important to cognition may change from nonfunctional to functional (e.g., the fovea; cf. Banks & Salapatek, 1983). But throughout most of infancy and later during childhood, the major architectural changes are tuning changes, not structural ones.

Sensory and Perceptual Development. The newborn infant's sensory and perceptual processes are immature when compared with those of older children or adults (e.g., Aslin, Pisoni, & Jusczyk, 1983; Banks & Salapatek, 1983). Much of this can be traced to the immaturity of the neural mechanisms at the several stages of processing that occur between the sensory organs and the brain. For example, in vision, Banks and Salapatek (1983) describe neural immaturity at the retinal, geniculate, and cortical levels, much of which has important functional significance (e.g., it limits acuity).

Sensory and perceptual processes determine the quality of the data that the organism receives from the environment. In turn, the quality of the data influences what can be learned. Major sensory defects, such as blindness or deafness, complicate cognitive development insofar as it depends on the child's interactions with the environment.

Although sensory changes primarily occur in infancy, perceptual development occurs throughout the life span (Gibson, 1969). As a result of our experience we learn to perceive the environment by learning how to select or attend to important features from the environment. There are now a number of demonstrations that show that rapid and accurate perceptual encoding is an important aspect of expertise in specific domains. Thus, the chess expert, having stored in memory thousands of meaningful board configurations, can encode a particular pattern of pieces on a board in a few seconds, as long as it reflects a meaningful arrangement (Chase & Simon, 1973). Wine tasters, chicken sorters, airplane spotters, radiologists, and skilled athletes all acquire this kind of perceptual expertise as a component of their skill (Gibson, 1969; Lesgold, 1984). The evidence is also very strong that this is an important component of cognitive development (Gibson, 1969). Much perceptual development consists of knowledge modification rather than changes in perceptual hardware.

Alertness. In order to attend to the world one must be alert. Learning is undoubtly optimal during alert states. The newborn infant has extremely limited periods of alertness. For instance, Clifton and Nelson (1976) have noted that the average period of alert awakeness in the newborn is only 5 minutes, and that 90% of such periods are shorter than 10 minutes. This severely constrains the learning, and thus will limit the rate of cognitive growth. This limitation has its major influence during early infancy, but may be important during other parts of development, such as old age.

Changes in the Central Processing Bottlenecks.   The central processing bottlenecks that were described earlier as having such major effects on human cognition are likely candidates for architectural tuning during growth and development. Although the exact source of these bottlenecks is unclear, it is most probably somewhere in the hardware of the system. It is not hard to imagine maturational changes that might affect them.

There are several ways in which developmental changes in attentional processing could affect the limited ability to attend to simultaneous inputs. The theory of Norman and Bobrow (1975) includes a limited pool of attentional resources that are available for tasks that require active decision making and monitoring. Simultaneous tasks compete for this limited pool, with performance on one or more of them being degraded when the demands of the tasks exceed the resources in the pool. There could be developmental changes in the size of the resource pool, giving younger children less ability to cope with complex, simultaneous task demands. But it is also known that the limited attentional resources can be overcome, at least to some extent, by the automatization of cognitive routines. Highly practiced tasks require much less costly monitoring or other active processing, and thus can be carried out in parallel with other tasks. As the child develops, it is likely that a number of cognitive tasks become more automatic, thus making fewer demands on this limited pool of resources. Using behavioral evidence to distinguish between changes in the pool and automaticity effects would be difficult indeed. Once again, computer simulation studies might be useful in determining how to differentiate among these possibilities.

The limited capacity of immediate memory is examined next. There are clear data that show that performance in immediate memory-span tasks changes with development. There is a regular increase in the immediate memory span with age, so regular in fact that memory span is often used as one of the subscales on intelligence tests. But what causes the increase in measured span? Olson (1973) and Simon (1974) have argued that the major source of change in digit span is the acquisition of knowledge about numbers. Miller (1956) very early demonstrated the importance of knowledge in memory span performance. It is possible to increase the functional memory span by recoding or chunking the incoming information into groups according to knowledge in long-term memory. Similarly, research shows that expert game players have better immediate recall or meaningful board configurations than novice players. Clearly, this superiority comes from the knowledge they have acquired as part of their expertise (Chase & Simon, 1973; Reitman, 1976).

A number of investigators, however, have argued that factors other than knowledge need to be taken into account. Huttenlocher and Burke (1976) studied digit-span recall in children and concluded that changes in knowledge were insufficient to explain the phenomena they observed. They argued that factors like general processing speed were more plausible than greater knowledge. Case (1978) has argued that the automatization of central processes operating within a fixed-capacity immediate-memory store accounts for the observed changes, a position similar to that of Huttenlocher and Burke (1976).

These accounts are excellent examples of the problem of identifying the various factors being discussed. If changes in immediate memory span truly signal a change in the capacity of some underlying mental structure, there is no question this would be an important feature of cognitive development. However er because such factors as the knowledge base or processing speed can have major effects on memory span performance, it is difficult to infer what is causing the change in behavior. Computer simulations that carefully examined the consequences of various architectural changes might be helpful in sorting out the possibilities.

Processing Speed and Efficiency. Cognitive processes take time. Given that the pace of external events is fixed, faster internal processing could lead to important cognitive improvements. Indeed, one of the features that artificial computational systems have that makes them superior to human processing is a much faster basic processing speed. There arc internal gains too. The faster a subprocess operates, the less likely it is to act as a bottleneck for other activities.

There is considerable evidence from reaction time studies that processing becomes faster with development (Wickens, 1974). But, as in the case of memory-span data, these changes could have several different causes. One might be an improvement in the speed of basic neural processing. This could be a consequence of the substantial neurological development that occurs in infancy and early childhood. Processing speed also improves as a result of the strengthening of associations and of the reorganization of procedures (Anderson, 1982, 1983). As subprocesses become automatized and reorganized into higher order processes, the total time it takes to complete a task tends to be reduced. Thus, both maturation and experience could contribute to faster mental processing as the child gets older.

Mental processes might also become more accurate. There are several sources of statistical uncertainty in central processing times. For one, the basic underlying nervous system structures probably operate in an aggregate and statistical fashion. For another, a host of competing influences may give rise to uncertainty for such basic processes as storage and retrieval. With neural maturation, with a knowledge base with a more differentiated organization, and with greater associative strength for many pathways, these various influences would lessen, leading to more reliable processing. This would probably also cause mental processes to run faster. All of these changes are undoubtedly more significant in the infant and young child than in the adult.

Basic System Goals.   In the adult, mental processes are probably controlled most extensively by cognitive goals, either general or specific. However, there is a substratum of basic biological goals that influences processing as well. Certainly in infancy the basic biological drives are a salient part of the baby's mental life. As the brain matures and the knowledge base expands, these may become less dominant. But at all stages of life they are very significant. Further, there are special periods of life (e.g., adolescence) when biological factors play important roles in the control of cognition, through the influence of emotions and motivation on basic system goals.

Motor Development.   Motor abilities change throughout childhood, and thus constitute potential sources for influencing cognitive development. Motor development can have at least three distinct influences on intellectual development. First, it makes possible more sophisticated exploration of the environment. Second, it allows for greater expression of intellectual activities (e.g., writing, drawing), which in turn influence environmental inputs through social interactions. Third, motor activities have been linked to early mental representations. A brief discussion of each of these follows.

Performance, in the form of locomotion, manipulation, and sensor orientation (e.g., head and eye movements), regulates the moment-by-moment perceptual inputs that provide much of the raw material for cognition. Further, skilled manipulation and precise control are components of many skills. In infancy such basic skills as grasping, orienting, sitting up, crawling, and walking can have profound effects on the infant's access to the environment and thus to information. Although the changes are not as dramatic after infancy, the child continues to develop better control over motor abilities, especially the fine motor skills involved in precise manipulation. A number of specific skills place strong demands on the motor system. For instance, typing and piano playing are examples of skills that have major motor components, but can also play a significant role in cognition. The skilled manipulation of external tools and devices can enhance or extend the usefulness of these devices for cognition.

Intelligence requires performance for its expression. Indeed, the study of infant intelligence has long been hampered by the infant's limited ability to perform, though of course this has changed with the use of innovative methods in recent decades (Harris, 1983; Olson & Sherman, 1983). The kind of intelligence expressed by an infant or child can affect the behavior of those who interact with him or her. Because social interaction contributes enormously to cognitive growth, motor development can play an important role by making various forms of interaction possible.

Major theorists such as Piaget and Bruner have implicated motor processes in the central mental activities of the infant. They have hypothesized that the contents of early cognition are closely linked to action, because the infant does not yet have symbolic representations. In particular, they have proposed that infants represent their experience in terms of their actions. For example, for Piaget the Stage IV child represents a successfully retrieved hidden object in terms of his or her action of searching for and finding it. When the object is moved to a new hiding place the child looks for it in the old location (the Stage IV Error) because the representation is in terms of action not in terms of environmental spatial coordinates. As the child grows and forms symbolic representations, motor representations become less important or dominant.

Summary: Architectural Tuning

I have presented a number of potentially significant architectural adjustments. To put these in perspective it is useful to highlight a possible change that is in all likelihood not a factor at all. There is no evidence that human intellectual processing is limited in any way by the amount of long-term storage available for retaining knowledge. This is in marked contrast to many artificial intelligence systems, in which limitations on the amount of memory readily accessible to the central processor place important limits on what can be done. There are limits that affect human long-term storage, such as the amount of time it takes to learn new information or the ease with which information can be retrieved. But capacity per se does not appear to be a factor in accounting for intellectual development.

Many of the architectural changes discussed here appear to have their major effects during the earliest stages of development. This suggests that by some age (2, 3, 4 years?) the human cognitive system may have a basically stable form, and that the major sources of intellectual development beyond this point may be due to the factors described in the next two sections. I return to this point later in the chapter.

Knowledge Modification

Knowing more is a central feature of intellectual development. Indeed, there are a number of investigators who feel that knowing more is the central feature of cognitive development (e.g., Chi, 1978; Chi & Rees, 1983). However, there are many different facets to knowing more, and in this section I review a number of them.

This section focuses on substantive, domain-specific knowledge. This knowledge can be declarative or procedural; it can also be general because it spans several domains. However, I want to contrast the knowledge discussed in this section with the more general cognitive skills described in the next section, cognitive skills such as induction, analogical reasoning, deduction, and categorization.[2]

---

[2]There are serious questions about whether domain-independent inference rules of any kind are ever acquired (Cheng & Holyoak, 1985; Cheng, Holyoak, Nisbett, & Oliver, 1986; Holland et al., 1986). But such domain-independent rules are at least candidates for cognitive development, and thus are described.

Knowledge Acquisition.   By knowledge acquisition I mean the accretion of knowledge, the adding of more things to the knowledge base. Chi (1978; Chi & Rees, 1983) has described the major effects that domain-specific knowledge have on children's performance. A child can be more expert than an adult in a specific domain (e.g., dinosaurs or chess), and thus will show more mature behavior in a range of cognitive tasks involving material from that domain.

The knowledge that is acquired in specific domains can take a number of forms. Some knowledge that can be at any of several levels of generality is purely factual or declarative. Other knowledge is procedural, representing knowledge of how to carry out various action sequences or plans within a domain. That is, one part of chess knowledge is knowing the legal moves of the individual pieces, the relative values of the pieces, and the general rules of the game. This is largely factual knowledge. But through instruction or through experience a chess player acquires knowledge of what to do in various situations. This can vary from knowledge of specific steps to follow (e.g., openings) to heuristics about what to do in certain recognizable mid- or end-game situations.

Two interrelated types of knowledge that are very important in specific domains are goals and plans or strategies to achieve these goals. As a result of learning, the child acquires numerous general and specific goals. As these goals are attempted repeatedly, the child acquires specific plans and general strategies for achieving the goals. Again, to use the chess example, the knowledge about goals is used to evaluate specific situations and knowledge about plans is used to derive moves or move sequences from these situations.

Knowledge is acquired in several ways. It can be acquired directly from experience, through induction from examples or instances. Experts in a domain like chess play many games, and from this experience learn about board patterns and move sequences. Knowledge can also be acquired by instruction. Chess experts also spend a lot of time reading about chess and discussing it with others, learning generalizations about the game from the experience of others. Knowledge can also be acquired from inference from previous knowledge. At some point, children begin to think about what it is they know, and by reasoning through a problem in a domain they can arrive at new conclusions that can then be stored and retrieved on later occasions.

In principle, knowledge can be acquired via these diverse means at any level of generality. Schank and Abelson (1977) described a hierarchy of knowledge types, from very particular domain-specific knowledge to very abstract knowledge. Those who study intelligence recognize that the ability to notice or encode relationships between domains is perhaps the most powerful part of human intelligence. Thus, the chess player who plays a variety of other board games may come to acquire general knowledge about board games or about games in general. The general cognitive skills of abstraction, generalization, and analogy formation are means by which more general types of knowledge can be acquired.

A central aspect of many theories of cognitive development is that knowledge acquisition is shaped by the present level of knowledge. Piaget called this process *assimilation,* and although the terminology has changed in contemporary theories of cognitive development, the concept is still central to most proposals. Fischer (1980), for example, has described a regular progression of knowledge through a series of levels, each of which builds upon the previous one. These levels consist of first noticing sets of specific entities, then noticing mappings from one set to another, and finally, noticing systems based on sets of mappings. This progression recurs at successive levels of development as different entities become the primitives from which sets, mappings, and systems are constructed. Thus, in Fischer's theory, in infancy, the primitive entities are sensorimotor acts, whereas in early childhood they are representational sets or systems of sensorimotor systems. As a result, the knowledge acquisition is orderly and universal, at least at a certain level of abstraction.

Why is knowledge acquired in a particular order or fashion? There are several possible accounts. One has to do with the nature of knowledge itself. Certain features of knowledge depend on other features. For example, in mathematics the concept of exponentiation builds on the concept of multiplication. Another account is that architectural features of the cognitive system constrain the order of knowledge acquisition. Certainly what can be learned in infancy is limited by sensory, perceptual, attentional, and general neurological immaturity. Finally, a variety of mechanisms for knowledge acquisition—the skills described in the next section—can constrain what can be learned. For example, incomplete or immature principles of statistical reasoning can affect the kinds of probabilistic inferences a child can add to the knowledge base.

Metacognitive awareness is one kind of knowledge on which some have placed special emphasis. Stimulated by the studies of Flavell and his colleagues (Flavell, 1979; Flavell & Wellman, 1977), a large amount of research has investigated the child's developing knowledge about how his or her cognitive system works. At root is the supposition that this in turn affects the child's cognition in a variety of ways. For example, if the child understands that immediate memory has a limited span, efforts might be made to adopt strategies to cope with the limitation. It is still an open question whether such knowledge affects cognition in a causal way (e.g., Cavanaugh & Perlmutter, 1982; Wellman, 1983), but metacognitive knowledge is an interesting candidate for a type of knowledge that is important for intellectual development.

Knowledge Reorganization. Knowledge reorganization refers to the rearrangements of the relations and superordinate categories that control our access to what we know. This is clearly one component of what it means to become expert in a domain. Studies of expert–novice differences have shown that experts organize what they know in quite different ways than do novices (Chi, Glaser, & Rees, 1983; Larkin, McDermott, Simon, & Simon, 1980; Lesgold, 1984; McKeithen, Reitman, Rueter, & Hirtle, 1981).

Piaget's stages of cognitive development refer in large part to overall knowledge reorganization. The child's progress from sensorimotor to preoperational to concrete and formal operational thought is partly due to changes in the organization of the child's knowledge. Alternatively, knowledge reorganization could refer to a change in the dominant format of knowledge. The controversy in cognitive psychology about propositional versus imaginal representations of knowledge is a controversy about knowledge format (Anderson, 1978; Kosslyn, 1980; Kosslyn & Pomerantz, 1977; Pylyshyn, 1973). Bruner's (1966) proposal that the child advances from enactive to iconic to symbolic representations is just such a proposal. He argued that the dominant format for representing knowledge changes, from a primarily sensorimotor format in infancy to a largely visual or representational code in early childhood to the abstract, symbolic code of the linguistically competent child and adult.

The idea of development as knowledge reorganization or change in format has some complications. First, at some point, reorganizing knowledge is changing format, in that a new representational scheme stores knowledge differently from the old scheme. It may be hard to distinguish operationally between changes in organization and changes in format. Second, the changes in organization are concurrent with and probably stimulated by the acquisition of new knowledge. It should be possible to distinguish acquisition and reorganization, but care will need to be taken. A number of criteria for differentiating among different representations of knowledge are discussed in Mandler (1983) and in Rumelhart and Norman (in press).

A special type of knowledge-reorganization process is the automatization of procedural knowledge. Through practice, processes that formerly took considerable time and cognitive effort can come to be performed quickly and effortlessly. Anderson (1982, 1983) has called this process knowledge compilation, and in the context of his ACT production system has described the details of how such a process would work. Such automatization is an important part of how experts and novices differ (Chi et al., 1983; Larkin et al., 1980).

Summary: Knowledge Modification

Knowledge modification is probably the least controversial potential source of intellectual development. No theorist would deny that knowing more is a central characteristic of such development. But what does knowing more mean? Perhaps the most controversial recent claim on this matter is that the differences seen in intellectual development are essentially expert–novice differences (Chi, 1978; Chi & Rees, 1983). Proper evaluation of this claim requires examining the broad range of possible contributors to intellectual development in order to differentiate the role of knowledge modification from either architectural changes or skill modification.

Skill Modification

Intelligent activity draws on a number of cognitive skills, most of which are probably domain specific. However, there are many general cognitive skills that potentially could be used in many different domains. Some of these are basic system skills (e.g., recognition) that surely exist, perhaps even from the outset, and whose contribution to intellectual development are enormous. These basic skills may themselves undergo change as part of development, further enhancing the power of the cognitive system. Others of these skills may or may not exist in a domain-independent way: The issue is still open and controversial in a number of important areas (Holland et al., 1986).

There are three broad classes of cognitive skills. In the first class are the basic operations of memory, including association, recognition, and recall. The second class consists of skills that derive general knowledge from experience, and includes such skills as induction and categorization. The third class consists of skills that interrelate or recombine existing knowledge to form new knowledge, and includes deduction, statistical reasoning, and analogical reasoning. Of course, these different classes of skills are highly interrelated in practice.

Basic Memory Processes

Association. One of the most basic properties of the mind is that experiences, whether from the environment or internally generated, can become associated in memory with later memory retrieval dependent on these associative connections. The centrality of associations for human memory is undisputed. What has become clear from research on memory is that the traditional view, of association by contiguity under the control of environmental reward and punishment, is far too simple to be correct (Anderson & Bower, 1973). In particular, human memory does not consist of all the same kinds of connections between mental entities. Instead, the relationships stored in memory tend to be of special types, which could be labeled as *is-similar-to, is-followed-by,* and *is-caused-by.* Whether these relationships are learned or are innate is still an open question, although there is sufficient research with infants to suggest that many of these relationships are present quite early (Harris, 1983; Olson & Sherman, 1983).

Recognition. Recognition involves the matching of encodings of environmental inputs with information stored in memory. Like association, it is a primitive process in that it is present as early as it can be measured, and in contrast to other basic skills does not seem to change appreciably during development (Olson, 1976; Olson & Sherman, 1983). Because recognition is a direct function of knowledge, changes in the knowledge base will drastically affect recognition performance. But the basic skill itself may change little.

Recall. In contrast to association or recognition, recall abilities change remarkably during development. Piaget (1952, 1954, 1962; Piaget & Inhelder, 1973) has argued that recall does not emerge until the end of infancy. This is probably too conservative a view, because there is evidence of recall-like phenomena throughout much of infancy (Ashmead & Perlmutter, 1980; Huttenlocher, 1974; Mandler, 1983; Olson & Sherman, 1983). But recall abilities develop remarkably throughout early childhood (Kail, 1984; Kail & Hagen, 1977; Ornstein, 1978), in large part because the ability to retrieve information from memory on the basis of a partial cue is heavily dependent on strategies that seem to have to be learned (Kobasigawa, 1977). Because memory is so central to most cognitive activity, the development of the ability to recall information is a basic feature of intellectual development.

Generalization from Experience

A distinctive property of intelligent activity is the recognition and exploitation of generalizations and abstractions from experience. From the lowest level perceptual classifications to the most abstract conceptual constructs, it is the ability to categorize experience on the basis of similarities and differences that gives intelligence its obvious adaptive advantage. A series of closely related cognitive skills is involved.

Induction. Broadly speaking, induction is reasoning from the particular to the general. The classic examples of induction have to do with observing a certain number of instances of a phenomenon and reaching a general conclusion. Will the sun rise tomorrow? Will this ball fall when I drop it? None of these events has a logical certainty associated with it, but on the basis of past experience each is highly probable. Thus, induction is a form of statistical reasoning, of drawing conclusions about the relative likelihood of various events or activities. It specifically refers to drawing of general conclusions about events or objects on the basis of empirical observations of particulars.

Recently, there has been much interest in the study of inductive mechanisms in both humans and machines (e.g., Anderson, 1983; Holland, 1975; Holland et al., 1986; Michalski, Carbonell, & Mitchell, 1983, 1986; Mitchell, Carbonell, & Michalski, 1986). This work has shown that induction is not merely blind generalization. Induction is strongly influenced by existing knowledge. The kind of conclusion reached about a series of observations depends on the learner's assumptions about the nature of the phenomenon being observed. For example, the likelihood of concluding that a particular species of bird has the color of the one instance we have observed is greater than the likelihood of concluding that all members of a particular ethnic group of people are fat from having observed one fat person. This is because of our knowledge about the variability of these properties in the kinds of populations we are examining (Nisbett, Krantz, Jepson, & Kunda, 1983). In short, one's knowledge of the domain in question determine both the kind of generalization made and the strength of the generalization in relation to a specified amount of data.

Inductive reasoning is closely tied up with our concepts of causality, chance, variability, and central tendency, as well as with particular knowledge about the domain. Changes in inductive reasoning skills are a plausible source of developmental change, although undoubtedly it will be difficult to differentiate changes in general inductive skills from the acquisition of specific domain knowledge.

Categorization. Categorization abilities represent a special form of inductive reasoning. Categorization refers to the formation of classes or categories of experience on the basis of some shared properties or similarities. Further, it refers to such grouping under conditions where it is also known that the individual members of the category are different. In other words, the members of the category are similar in some ways but differ in others.

Research on the nature of natural categories (cf. Rosch & Lloyd, 1978; Smith & Medin, 1981) has stimulated much interest in exactly how categorical information is represented. Because categorical knowledge is inherently statistical, there is interest in how both central tendencies of categories and the variability of instances is represented (Fried & Holyoak, 1984). Further, as is now well-known, natural categories tend to have fuzzy boundaries and membership in them is graded (Rosch, 1978).

There is a large body of research on the development of categorization. Recent research has shown that infants display categorization skills during the first year (Olson & Strauss, 1984). But much research on young children has shown that there are important developmental trends in how the child arrives at and represents categorical information (Carey, in press; Markman & Callanan, 1984). As with the more general case of induction, changes in categorization skills may contribute to intellectual development. But again, distinguishing between changes in a general skill and changes in specific knowledge will require careful analysis.

Recombination of Knowledge

Another important source of knowledge is new knowledge obtained from old knowledge. This source cannot be sharply distinguished from the preceding source in all cases, because arriving at new general knowledge about experience often depends on the use of prior knowledge, and the recombinations of knowledge described here often depend on environmental inputs of various sorts. But the primary focus of the skills described in this section is the deriving of new knowledge, either particular or general, from knowledge that already exists.

Deduction. Deduction refers to the reaching of logically necessary conclusions from premises on the basis of general principles of inference. Although deductive principles need not be explicitly taught to be used, at least in our society, certain simple forms of deduction often are part of the schooling of children. The categorical syllogism often constitutes the student's first introduction to deductive reasoning, and not surprisingly, psychologists have studied syllogistic reasoning in some detail (Johnson-Laird, 1983, 1985; Revlin & Mayer, 1978). However, deductive principles are much more general than this, as evidenced by a variety of formal schemes developed by logicians.

Aristotle described deductive rules as the laws of thought, and throughout much of intellectual history scholars have treated logic as though it characterized an asymptotic state of human reasoning. A number of developmental psychologists have studied the acquisition of logical thought, assuming that developmental progress was being made toward the asymptote that logic described (e.g., Inhelder & Piaget, 1958; Osherson, 1974a, 1974b, 1975, 1976).

This is not an implausible view. Deductive reasoning is clearly a powerful basis for deriving or verifying new knowledge, a point long appreciated by both philosophers and logicians and one that a number of artificial intelligence programs have attempted to exploit. However, a growing body of evidence has suggested that humans may never achieve something approaching a general, domain-independent deductive reasoning system (see Cheng et al., 1986; Holland et al., 1986). In this view, humans acquire a number of pragmatic reasoning schemas associated with particular domains, allowing them to reason with satisfactory accuracy within specific domains but not allowing them the power of general deductive methods (Cheng et al., 1986).

Deductive reasoning abilities, as defined by performance on tasks such as syllogisms, vary developmentally, and thus, whatever the best way to characterize the asymptotic nature of these abilities, the skills involved represent an important facet of intellectual development.

Principles of Statistical Reasoning. Inductive reasoning, or the reaching of general conclusions from the observation of instances, is one important type of statistical reasoning (see discussion in the preceding section). But statistical reasoning also covers many cases in which conclusions about uncertain events are reached by reasoning from other probabilistic knowledge. For instance, assessments of relative likelihoods of events given certain preconditions are quite common in everyday life. Humans have many flaws as intuitive statisticians (Kahneman, Slovic, & Tversky, 1982: Nisbett & Ross, 1980), although even young children are capable of making accurate statements about probability (Piaget & Inhelder, 1975). Given the importance of this kind of reasoning, and the discrepancy between human abilities and those of the normative disciplines (probability theory, statistics), statistical reasoning abilities are a good candidate for an important influence on intellectual development.

Plausible Reasoning.   Much human reasoning is based on plausibility rather than logical certainty. For instance, in answering questions, the respondent often does not know the answer but can make a plausible guess. Collins (1978; Collins & Michalski, in press; Collins, Warnock, Aiello, & Miller, 1975) has studied this process in some detail. He examined how people arrived at and defended answers to questions such as "Is the Nile longer than the Mekong River?" or "Can a goose quack?" The generation of plausible answers to such questions uses a number of principles of plausible reasoning that have been recently formalized by Collins and Michalski (in press). Such principles are clearly very important for reaching informed guesses about novel situations from knowledge already available in long-term memory. We know almost nothing about how such abilities might develop, but they constitute an important domain to investigate, because reasoning on the basis of plausibility covers so many real-world situations.

Analogical Reasoning.   Reasoning by analogy often is taken as one of the hallmarks of human intelligence, and indeed most psychometric conceptions of intelligence honor this view by including tests of analogical reasoning as part of what it is that the intelligence tests measure. There is little doubt that analogical reasoning plays an important role in learning and problem solving (Holyoak, 1984), although theorists disagree on the extent of its importance. Research on analogical reasoning in artificial intelligence and cognitive psychology has flourished recently (e.g., Carbonell, 1983, 1986; Forbus & Gentner, 1986; Gentner, 1983; Holyoak, 1984; Sternberg, 1977; Winston, 1980), reflecting the belief of cognitive science researchers in the importance of this form of reasoning.

A growing literature on analogical reasoning in children is beginning to make clear the extent to which the component abilities of such reasoning develop (Pellegrino, 1985; Sternberg, 1977, 1982a). Because analogical reasoning necessarily involves issues of knowledge representation, recognition. memory retrieval, and such reasoning processes as comparison and evaluation, deciphering exactly what is happening as analogical reasoning performance changes with development will be tricky. Good cognitive science models should help.

Summary: Skill Modification

The list of cognitive skills just reviewed is not exhaustive. However, it suggests the range of skills whose development could play a substantial role in intellectual development. As we have seen again and again in our brief review, distinguishing clearly between the development of a particular skill and the development of some other feature of the cognitive system (e.g., the knowledge base) is extremely tricky, and will require careful theoretical and empirical analysis. Further, as mentioned before, it is an open question as to how general any of these skills are. The child may acquire skills within specific domains that do not extend very well to other domains. It will take theoretical as well as empirical research to sort out these matters.

MECHANISMS OF CHANGE

The main goal of this chapter has been to focus on the question of what could change during intellectual development. But before summing up, it is worth speculating on what produces these changes. What mechanisms lead to the differences that are so clearly observed between children of different ages? As many reviewers of the topic of intellectual development have pointed out, scholars have had much more success at describing what intellectual life is like at various stages of development than in describing how it got to be that way. As in the previous section, my goal here is to describe a list of candidates without necessarily implicating specific ones as being correct. Once again, the most probable situation is that a number of these mechanisms are important contributors to intellectual development.

Organismic Factors

Organismic factors refer to factors within the organism that could lead to developmental change. One set consists of a broad range of biological factors, whereas another involves spontaneous cognitive changes. Organismic factors contrast with environmental ones, described in later sections.

Biological Change

Certainly, biological changes play a considerable role in the early stages of intellectual development. The human brain is immature at birth, and it is clear that a number of perceptual and cognitive functions are constrained by this during the early months of life (e.g., Banks & Salapatek, 1983; Olson & Sherman, 1983). Further, postnatal brain development may be correlated with major cognitive functions such as language (Lenneberg, 1967), making plausible the hypothesis that the functions have a substantial biological basis. Similarly, during adolescence there are major biological changes, this time of a primarily hormonal character, that could have an important impact on intellectual functioning.

There are several classes of biological change that might affect intellectual development.

Neural Changes. The number of neurons is more or less fixed at birth, but there are a number of other changes that occur postnatally. It is now clear that there are enormous morphological changes having to do with the number of *connections* among neurons that occur postnatally, although one must be cautious about associating these morphological changes with cognitive functioning (Goldman-Rakic, Isseroff, Schwartz, & Bugbee, 1983; Lund, 1978; Parmelee & Sigman, 1983). There are also substantial postnatal changes in the conduction speed of neural information (Gamstorp, 1963). Partly this is due to the changes in connectivity just discussed, and partly it is due to the formation of myelin sheaths that speed the conduction of neural signals (Yakovlev & Lecours, 1967). As was noted earlier, changes in central processing speed could play a significant role in general intellectual development.

Although these general changes in neural functioning can be documented, the link between the changes and details of intellectual functioning cannot be drawn. Thus, although changes in the nervous system are a candidate for a general mechanism for intellectual development, little more can be said than that during certain periods there are correlations between changes in neural functioning and changes in cognitive abilities. Perhaps the new work on connectionist models will eventually provide insight into what effect, if any, underlying neural changes might have on cognition (McClelland & Rumelhart, 1986; Rumelhart & McClelland, 1986).

Hormonal Changes. There is growing appreciation of the influence of hormonal activity on behavior. Perhaps the single most important domain in which hormonal influences have been implicated is that of gender differences. Prenatally, hormones play a major role in gender differentiation (Money & Earhardt, 1972), and it has been speculated that this may in turn lead to certain differences in cognition (Broverman, Klaiber, Kobayashi, & Vogel, 1968; Petersen, 1979). Similarly, the hormonal storm that is adolescence may produce further changes (Petersen & Taylor, 1980).

Skeletal and Neuromuscular Changes. Changes in the body and in the coordination and effectiveness of motor systems are potentially of great significance for cognition. Certainly the development of manipulation and locomotion in the infant have major impacts on cognitive growth. Further, as the child gets larger, its perspective on the world changes. In *The Phantom Tollbooth,* (Juster, 1964) Milo encounters a small boy who seems to be suspended in the air.

"Well," said the boy, "in my family everyone is born in the air, with his head at exactly the height it's going to be when he's an adult, and then we all grow up toward the ground. When we're fully grown up or, as you can see, grown down, our feet finally touch. . . . You certainly must be very old to have reached the ground already."

"Oh no," said Milo seriously. "In my family we all start on the ground and grow up, and we never know how far until we actually get there."

"What a silly system." The boy laughed. "Then your head keeps changing its height and you always see things in a different way? Why, when you're fifteen things won't look at all the way they did when you were ten, and at twenty everything will change again." (pp. 104–105)

Spontaneous Cognitive Changes

Psychology has long looked to either nature or nurture for explanations of psychological growth. Either it is wired in, or it is acquired through interaction with the environment. Because of this, relatively little attention has been given to more or less spontaneous reorganizations of knowledge. To be sure, certain theorists have talked about such changes. But there is little theory specifying the mechanisms whereby such changes might occur.

Holland's (1975, 1986) theory of adaptive systems is an example of a formal computational theory in which spontaneous changes play a central role. Drawing upon a biological metaphor, he proposed that the elementary units of cognition (which he calls classifiers) spontaneously recombine to generate new candidate internal representations that may be useful for classifying environmental or behavioral regularities. This mechanism generates new representations that may or may not fit the environment. Further, the recombinations are not based on random selections from classifiers. Instead, changes occur by recombinations of classifiers that have good records based on their past ability to predict the next state or to bring the system needed rewards. But the mechanism is spontaneous in that it generates novel patterns that are not based on direct immediate experience.

Holland's system is suggestive of a number of mechanisms that could be proposed whereby cognitive elements are mixed and combined according to various rules, all in isolation from current experience. Such spontaneous, novel combinations could be a major source of adaptive advances in intellectual functioning.

Environmental Factors

All theories of intellectual development have assumed that there are major inputs from the environment. What are the exact mechanisms by which the environment comes to influence intellectual functioning? Theories have varied widely on how explicitly they have defined the possible mechanisms and at what level the mechanisms operate. For instance, stimulus–response theories have been very explicit about local, atomistic mechanisms, although traditionally they have had difficulties in accounting for structures at a more general level. In contrast, Piaget has described the kinds of structures that exist at a very general level, but has been silent about the mechanisms whereby cognition advances from one stage to the next.

The environment consists of two broad sets of influences on the child, the inanimate world and the social world. It goes without saying that there are important interactions between the two. Brief descriptions of the major factors in these two realms are described next.

The Inanimate Environment

The child's interactions with the inanimate world constitute a major influence on intellectual development. This is in part because understanding the inanimate world constitutes a major portion of the knowledge that is acquired. It is no accident that Piaget devoted so much attention in his theory to the child's developing understanding of the physical world.

The child is not a passive recipient of information about the world. From the earliest moments, the child actively explores the world. Initially, the infant's limited manipulatory and locomotor skills confine this exploration to eager looking. But as reaching, grasping, crawling, standing, and walking enter the infant's repertoire of motor skills, the exploration of the inanimate world takes on an increasingly sophisticated character. It is important to stress that the infant is biologically predisposed to explore the world. It takes no coaxing on the part of parents to get the child to examine objects or to attend to activities and events.

What features of the child's interactions with the nonsocial world play an important role in intellectual development? On the one hand, it is important for the child to extract regularities from the world in order to form categories and concepts. Research on infant categorization abilities shows that such regularities can be extracted quite early (Olson & Sherman, 1983; Olson & Strauss, 1984). However, it is also important that the child notice discrepancies between his or her knowledge and objects or events in the world. Once again, the infant appears to be biologically predisposed to attend to inputs that are discrepant in just this way (Kagan, Kearsley, & Zelazo, 1978). Infants look longer at novel events and objects, and this enhances their ability to move beyond their current level of understanding.

In summary, during infancy the child is predisposed to notice aspects of the inanimate environment that play a major role in intellectual development. These interactions require, of course, an environment that has both some minimal level of complexity to it as well as noticeable regularity.

From the very beginning persons are attractive to the infant (Olson, 1981; Sherrod, 1981). As the child develops, social stimulation comes to have, if anything, an increasingly important role in the child's intellectual development.

Social Interaction.   Social interactions, especially with the primary caregiver, are important to the infant's social and emotional development. But these interactions are also a significant part of intellectual development (Clarke-Stewart, 1973; Flavell & Ross, 1981). Such interactions provide several things. First, they offer controlled exposure to the elements of the social and nonsocial world, helping to regulate the child's learning experiences. The child's attention can be controlled through social interaction, providing a richer source of learning experiences than would arise spontaneously. Clearly, this is one of the things that is missing in the deprived environments that produce poor developmental outcomes. Second, because children as well as adults modulate their input to reflect the child's state of development (Shatz & Gelman, 1973), the social world is a source of environmental input that is tailored to the child's current abilities. Most theories stress the importance of optimal levels input for the child (Case, 1985). Third, the social world is an especially rich source of contingent stimulation. Detailed studies of mother–infant interactions have shown how responsive mothers are to the specific behaviors of the child (e.g., Schaffer, 1977, 1984; Stern, 1985). These contingencies could improve the learning of important knowledge and skills, such as causality. Finally, social interaction provides the arena for two special forms of environmental input that are particularly important for intellectual development, namely, play and imitation.

Play.   Play is an especially important form of social interaction. The routines of play provide the child with major opportunities to learn about the regularities of both the social and nonsocial world. Play very early on provides a mechanism for the construction of symbolic representations (Garvey, 1977, 1984; Piaget, 1962), and thus may be a crucial bridge to the acquisition of language. Play may also provide the child an opportunity for exploration and experimentation, vehicles for the generation and evaluation of hypotheses.

Imitation.   Imitation is another especially important form of social interaction. Observing what others do is an extremely important source of learning, and there is ample evidence that it plays an important role during childhood (Guillaume, 1971; Piaget, 1962). Imitation can be instructed intentionally, as when parents try to get the child to "do as I do." Or it can occur simply as a result of the child observing what is going on around him or her. Either way,

76

from infancy on (Meltzoff & Moore, 1983) it is a central mechanism for the child's learning about the world (Bandura, 1971).

IMPLICATIONS AND CONCLUSIONS

My goal in this chapter has been to survey candidates for what might constitute intellectual development, given a cognitive science perspective on the organization of mental activities. There are numerous theories of intellectual development, each stressing different factors (see Case, 1985; Siegler & Richards, 1982; Sternberg & Powell, 1983 for excellent reviews of the various major theories). Pinning down exactly what factors are involved at what point would require a much larger enterprise than can be undertaken in this chapter. Indeed, it is not clear the data base exists yet to sort out the details. But thinking through the space of possibilities is a prerequisite to this larger enterprise.

We have examined several major categories of changes. One has to do with changes in the basic characteristics of the cognitive system itself. Because it seems unlikely that the basic organization of the system changes, it is more accurate to characterize these changes as ones of architectural tuning. A second category is change in the knowledge base. To develop intellectually is to know more or to know better, in the sense of having one's knowledge organized or represented in a more effective fashion. Finally, intellectual development may in part consist of the development of any of a number of basic, general skills, such as induction or deduction.

Intellectual development consists of a number of different but coordinated changes that occur during the child's life. Although there is continuity in the basic architecture of the mind, there are a number of profound internal changes that lead to the kind of changes in intellectual performance that signal development.

During infancy, there are many biological changes that shape mental activity. The immaturity of the brain and of the sensory and motor pathways in and out of it severely constrain the newborn. During the first 2 years these constraints are sharply lessened as postnatal neurological development proceeds. These changing constraints are one major factor in shaping early intellectual development.

Another major factor during early development is the enlarging knowledge base. The infant knows nothing about the world, although many of the factors that control attention and learning appear well suited for learning useful, adaptive things about the world. But much early intellectual behavior is affected by the limited knowledge of the infant.

During toddlerhood, biological factors play a decreasingly important role in intellectual development, and environmental factors, especially social interactions, play, and imitation, become central. The development of language is the single most influential shaping factor in intellectual development, and this dominates the preschool years. With the help of language, basic cognitive skills that shape information acquisition and organization evolve. Memory skills, problem-solving skills, and a wide range of reasoning skills undergo major development.

The mind of the child at the time school begins has stabilized as a biological entity although there are important upheavals to come during adolescence. A large knowledge base has been established, and many basic cognitive skills have emerged. The school years represent a period of intense and disciplined environmental input, once again with major effects on intellectual development. As we have seen, there is great diversity in the possible changes in the knowledge base that can occur. Sentiment as to the relative weights of specific knowledge and general skills in schooling seems to swing, but most cognitive science researchers feel that many of the specific factors we discussed in these two areas have important roles.[3]

ACKNOWLEDGMENT

Preparation of this chapter was supported in part by a Research Career Development Award (HD 00169) and by a Research Grant (HD 10486) from the National Institute of Child Health and Human Development. Keith Holyoak, Judy Olson, and Henry Wellman provided helpful comments on earlier drafts of this chapter.

REFERENCES

Anderson, J. R. (1976). *Language, memory, and thought.* Hillsdale, NJ: Lawrence Erlbaum Associates.

Anderson, J. R. (1978). Arguments concerning representations for mental imagery. *Psychological Review, 85,* 249–277.

Anderson, J. R. (1982). Acquisition of cognitive skill. *Psychological Review, 89,* 369–406.

Anderson, J. R. (1983). *The architecture of cognition.* Cambridge, MA: Harvard University Press.

Anderson, J. R., & Bower, G. H. (1973). *Human associative memory.* Washington, DC: V. H. Winston.

Ashmead, D. H., & Perlmutter, M. (1980). Infant memory in everyday life. In M. Perlmutter (Ed.), *New directions for child development: Children's memory* (Vol. 10, pp. 1–16). San Francisco: Jossey-Bass.

---

[3]For the interested reader, there are a number of recent volumes that reflect the attempt to apply ideas and concepts from cognitive science to schooling and intellectual development (e.g., Berger, Pezdek, & Banks, 1987: Chipman, Segal, & Glaser, 1985; Dillon & Sternberg, 1986; Glaser 1978, 1982; Nickerson, Perkins, & Smith, 1985; Segal, Chipman, & Glaser, 1985).

Aslin, R. N., Pisoni, D. B., & Jusczyk, P. W. (1983). Auditory development and speech perception in infancy. In M. M. Haith & J. J. Campos (Eds.), *Handbook of child psychology* (Vol. 2): *Infancy and developmental psychobiology* (pp. 573–687). New York: Wiley.

Bandura, A. (1971). *Psychological modeling: Conflicting theories.* Chicago: Aldine-Atherton.

Banks, M. S., & Salapatek, P. (1983). Infant visual perception. In M. M. Haith & J. J. Campos (Eds.), *Handbook of child psychology* (Vol. 2): *Infancy and developmental psychobiology* (pp. 435–571). New York: Wiley.

Berger, D. E., Pezdek, K., & Banks, W. P. (1987). (Eds.). *Applications of cognitive psychology: Problem solving, education, and computing.* Hillsdale, NJ: Lawrence Erlbaum Associates.

Bower, G. H. (1970). Organizational factors in memory. *Cognitive Psychology, 1,* 18–46.

Bower, G. H. (1972). A selective review of organizational factors in memory. In E. Tulving & W. Donaldson (Eds.), *Organization of memory* (pp. 93–137). New York: Academic Press.

Broadbent, D. E. (1958). *Perception and communciation.* New York: Pergamon Press.

Broadbent, D. E. (1971). *Decision and stress.* New York: Academic Press.

Broverman, D. M., Klaiber, E. L., Kobayashi, Y., & Vogel, W. (1968). Roles of activation and inhibition in sex differences in cognitive abilities. *Psychological Review, 75,* 23–50.

Bruner, J. S. (1966). On cognitive growth. In J. S. Bruner, R. R. Olver, & P. M. Greenfield (Eds.), *Studies in cognitive growth* (pp. 1–67). New York: Wiley.

Carbonell, J. G. (1983). Learning by analogy: Formulating and generalizing plans from past experience. In R. S. Michalski, J. G. Carbonell, & T. M. Mitchell (Eds.), *Machine learning: An artificial intelligence approach* (Vol. 1, pp. 137–161). Palo Alto, CA: Tioga.

Carbonell, J. G. (1986). Derivational analogy: A theory of reconstructive problem solving and expertise acquisition. In R. S. Michalski, J. G. Carbonell, & T. M. Mitchell (Eds.), *Machine learning: An artificial intelligence approach* (Vol. 2, pp. 371–392). Los Altos, CA: Morgan Kaufmann.

Carey, S. (in press). *Conceptual change in childhood.* Cambridge, MA: MIT Press.

Case, R. (1978). Intellectual development from birth to adulthood: A neo-Piagetian interpretation. In R. S. Siegler (Ed.), *Children's thinking: What develops?* (pp. 37–71). Hillsdale, NJ: Lawrence Erlbaum Associates.

Case, R. (1985). *Intellectual development: Birth to adulthood.* New York: Academic Press.

Cavanaugh, J. C., & Perlmutter, M. (1982). Metamemory: A critical examination. *Child Development, 53,* 11–28.

Chase, W. G., & Simon, H. A. (1973). Perception in chess. *Cognitive Psychology, 4,* 55–81.

Cheng, P. W., & Holyoak, K. J. (1985). Pragmatic reasoning schemas. *Cognitive Psychology, 17,* 391–416.

Cheng, P. W., Holyoak, K. J., Nisbett, R. E., & Oliver, L. M. (1986). Pragmatic versus syntactic approaches to training deductive reasoning. *Cognitive Psychology, 18,* 293–328.

Chi, M. T. H. (1978). Knowledge structures and memory development. In R. S. Siegler (Ed.), *Children's thinking: What develops?* (pp. 73–96). Hillsdale, NJ: Lawrence Erlbaum Associates.

Chi, M. T. H., Glaser, R., & Rees, E. (1983). Expertise in problem solving. In R. Sternberg (Ed.), *Advances in the psychology of human intelligence* (Vol. 1, pp. 7–75). Hillsdale, NJ: Lawrence Erlbaum Associates.

Chi, M. T. H., & Rees, E. T. (1983). A learning framework for development. In M. T. H. Chi (Ed.), *Trends in memory development research* (pp. 71–107). Basel: S. Karger.

Chipman, S. F., Segal, J. W., & Glaser, R. (Eds.). (1985). *Thinking and learning skills, Vol. 1. Research and open questions.* Hillsdale, NJ: Lawrence Erlbaum Associates.

Clarke-Stewart, K. A. (1973). Interactions between mothers and their young children: Characteristics and consequences. *Monographs of the Society for Research in Child Development, 38,* (Whole No. 153).

Clifton, R. K., & Nelson, M. N. (1976). Developmental study of habituation in infants: The importance of paradigm, response system, and state. In T. J. Tighe & R. N. Leaton (Eds.), *Habituation: Perspectives from child development, animal behavior, and neurophysiology* (pp. 159–205). Hillsdale, NJ: Lawrence Erlbaum Associates.

Collins, A. (1978). Fragments of a theory of human plausible reasoning. In D. L. Waltz (Ed.), *Theoretical issues in natural language processing—2.* Urbana, IL: University of Illinois.

Collins, A., & Michalski, R. S. (in press). The logic of plausible reasoning. A care theory. *Cognitive Science.*

Collins, A., Warnock, E. H., Aiello, N., & Miller, M. L. (1975). Reasoning from incomplete knowledge. In D. Bobrow & A. Collins (Eds.), *Representation and understanding: Studies in cognitive science* (pp. 383–415). New York: Academic Press.

Dillon, R. F., & Sternberg, R. J. (Eds.). (1986). *Cognition and instruction.* Hillsdale, NJ: Lawrence Erlbaum Associates.

Fischer, K. W. (1980). A theory of cognitive development: The control and construction of hierarchies of skills. *Psychological Review, 87,* 477–531.

Flavell, J. H. (1979). Metacognition and cognitive monitoring: A new area of cognitive-developmental inquiry. *American Psychologist, 34,* 906–911.

Flavell, J. H., & Ross, L. (1981). (Eds.) *Social cognitive development: Frontiers and possible futures.* New York: Cambridge University Press.

Flavell, J. H., & Wellman, H. M. (1977). Metamemory. In R. V. Kail, Jr. & J. W. Hagen (Eds.), *Perspectives on the development of memory and cognition* (pp. 3–33). Hillsdale, NJ: Lawrence Erlbaum Associates.

Forbus, K. D., & Gentner, D. (1986). Learning physical domains: Toward a theoretical framework. In R. S. Michalski, J. G. Carbonell, & T. M. Mitchell (Eds.), *Machine learning: An artificial intelligence approach* (Vol. 2, pp. 311–348). Los Altos, CA: Morgan Kaufmann.

Frandsen, A. N., & Higginson, J. B. (1951). The Stanford-Binet and the Wechsler Intelligence Scale for Children. *Journal of Consulting Psychology, 15,* 236–238.

Fried, L. S., & Holyoak, K. J. (1984). Induction of category distributions: A framework for classification learning. *Journal of Experimental Psychology: Learning, Memory, and Cognition, 10,* 234–257.

Gallistel, C. R. (1980). *The organization of action: A new synthesis.* Hillsdale, NJ: Lawrence Erlbaum Associates.

Gamstorp, J. (1963). Normal conduction velocity in ulnar, median and peroneal nerves in infancy, childhood and adolescence. *Acta Paediatrika, Stockholm Supplement, 146,* 68–76.

Garvey, C. (1977). *Play.* Cambridge, MA: Harvard University Press.

Garvey, C. (1984). *Children's talk.* Cambridge, MA: Harvard University Press.

Gentner, D. (1983). Structure-mapping: A theoretical framework for analogy. *Cognitive Science, 7,* 95–119.

Gibson, E. J. (1969). *Principles of perceptual learning and development.* New York: Appleton-Century-Crofts.

Glaser, R. (Ed.). (1978). *Advances in instructional psychology* (Vol. 1). Hillsdale, NJ: Lawrence Erlbaum Associates.

Glaser, R. (Ed.). (1982). *Advances in instructional psychology* (Vol. 2). Hillsdale, NJ: Lawrence Erlbaum Associates.

Goldman-Rakic, P. S., Isseroff, A., Schwartz, M. L., & Bugbee, N. M. (1983). The neurobiology of cognitive development. In M. M. Haith & J. T. Campos (Eds.), *Handbook of child psychology* (Vol. 2): *Infancy and developmental psychobiology* (pp. 281–344). New York: Wiley.

Guillaume, P. (1971). *Imitation in children.* Chicago: University of Chicago Press.

Harris, P. L. (1983). Infant cognition. In M. M. Haith & J. J. Campos (Eds.), *Handbook of child psychology* (Vol. 2): *Infancy and developmental psychobiology* (pp. 689–782). New York: Wiley.

Holland, J. H. (1975). *Adaptation in natural and artificial systems.* Ann Arbor, MI: University of Michigan Press.

Holland, J. H. (1986). Escaping brittleness: The possibilities of general purpose learning algorithms applied to parallel rule-based systems. In R. S. Michalski, J. G. Carbonell, & T. M. Mitchell (Eds.), *Machine learning: An artificial intelligence approach* (Vol 2, pp. 593–623). Los Altos, CA: Morgan Kaufmann.

Holland, J. H., Holyoak, K. J., Nisbett, R. E., & Thagard, P. R. (1986). *Induction: Processes of inference, learning, and discovery.* Cambridge, MA: MIT Press.

Holyoak, K. J. (1984). Analogical thinking and human intelligence. In R. J. Sternberg (Ed.), *Advances in the psychology of human intelligence* (Vol. 2, pp. 199–230). Hillsdale, NJ: Lawrence Erlbaum Associates.

Honzik, M. P., Macfarlane, J., & Allen, L. (1948). The stability of mental test performance between 2 and 18 years. *Journal of Experimental Education, 4,* 309–324.

Huttenlocher, J. (1974). The origins of language comprehension. In R. L. Solso (Ed.), *Theories in cognitive psychology: The Loyola symposium* (pp. 331–368). Hillsdale, NJ: Lawrence Erlbaum Associates.

Huttenlocher, J., & Burke, D. (1976). Why does memory span increase with age? *Cognitive Psychology, 8,* 1–31.

Inhelder, B., & Piaget, J. (1958). *The growth of logical thinking from childhood to adolescence.* New York: Basic Books.

Johnson-Laird, P. N. (1983). *Mental models.* Cambridge, MA: Harvard University Press.

Johnson-Laird, P. N. (1985). Deductive reasoning ability. In R. J. Sternberg (Ed.), *Human abilities: An information processing approach* (pp. 173–194). New York: Freeman.

Jonides, J. J. (1981). Voluntary versus automatic control over the mind's eye's movement. In J. B. Long & A. D. Baddeley (Eds.), *Attention and performance IX* (pp. 187–203). Hillsdale, NJ: Lawrence Erlbaum Associates.

Juster, N. (1964). *The phantom tollbooth*. New York: Random House.

Kagan, J., Kearsley, R. B., & Zelazo, P. R. (1978). *Infancy: Its place in human development*. Cambridge, MA: Harvard University Press.

Kahneman, D. (1973). *Attention and effort*. Englewood Cliffs, NJ: Prentice-Hall.

Kahneman, D., Slovic, P., & Tversky, A. (Eds.). (1982). *Judgment under uncertainty: Heuristics and biases*. New York: Cambridge University Press.

Kail, R. V. (1984). *The development of memory in children* (2nd ed.). San Francisco: Freeman.

Kail, R. V., Jr., & Hagen, J. W. (Eds.). (1977). *Perspectives on the development of memory and cognition*. Hillsdale, NJ: Lawrence Erlbaum Associates.

Kaufman, A. S. (1975). Factor analysis of the WISC-R at eleven age levels between 6½ and 16½ years. *Journal of Consulting and Clinical Psychology, 43,* 135–147.

Kobasigawa, A. (1977). Retrieval strategies in the development of memory. In R. V. Kail & J. W. Hagen (Eds.), *Perspectives on the development of memory and cognition* (pp. 177–201). Hillsdale, NJ: Lawrence Erlbaum Associates.

Kosslyn, S. M. (1980). *Image and mind*. Cambridge, MA: Harvard University Press.

Kosslyn, S. M., & Pomerantz, J. R. (1977). Imagery, propositions, and the form of internal representations. *Cognitive Psychology, 9,* 52–76.

Laird, J. E., Newell, A., & Rosenbloom, P. S. (1987). Soar: An architecture for general intelligence. *Artificial Intelligence, 33,* 1–64.

Larkin, J., McDermott, J., Simon, D. P., & Simon, H. A. (1980). Expert and novice performance in solving physics problems. *Science, 208,* 1335–1342.

Lenneberg, E. H. (1967). *Biological foundations of language*. New York: Wiley.

Lesgold, A. M. (1984). Acquiring expertise. In J. R. Anderson & S. M. Kosslyn (Eds.), *Tutorials in learning and memory: Essays in honor of Gordon Bower* (pp. 31–60). San Francisco: Freeman.

Lund, R. D. (1978). *Development and plasticity of the brain: An introduction*. New York: Oxford University Press.

Mandler, G. (1967). Organization and memory. In K. W. Spence & J. T. Spence (Eds.), *The psychology of learning and motivation* (Vol. 1 pp. 327–372). New York: Academic Press.

Mandler, J. M. (1983). Representation. In J. H. Flavell & E. M. Markman (Eds.), *Handbook of child psychology* (Vol. 3): *Cognitive development* (pp. 420–494). New York: Wiley.

Markman, E. M., & Callanan, M. A. (1984). An analysis of hierarchial classification. In R. J. Sternberg (Ed.), *Advances in the psychology of human intelligence* (Vol. 2, pp. 325–365). Hillsdale, NJ: Lawrence Erlbaum Associates.

McCall, R. B., Eichorn, D. J., & Hogarty, P. S. (1977). Transitions in early mental development. *Monographs of the Society for Research in Child Development, 42* (Serial No. 171).

McClelland, J. L., & Rumelhart, D. E. (1981). An interactive activation model of context effects in letter perception, Part 1: An account of basic findings. *Psychological Review, 88,* 375–407.

McClelland, J. L., & Rumelhart, D. E. (1986). *Parallel distributed processing: Explora-*

tions in the microstructure of cognition. Vol. 2. Psychological and biological models. Cambridge, MA: MIT Press.

McKeithen, K. B., Reitman, J. S., Rueter, H. H., & Hirtle, S. C. (1981). Knowledge organization and skill differences in computer programmers. Cognitive Psychology, 13, 307–325.

McNemar, Q. (1942). The revision of the Stanford-Binet Scale. Boston: Houghton-Mifflin.

Meltzoff, A. N., & Moore, M. K. (1983). The origins of imitation in infancy: Paradigm, phenomena, and theories. In L. P. Lipsitt (Ed.), Advances in infancy research (Vol. 2, pp. 265–301). Norwood, NJ: Ablex.

Michalski, R. S., Carbonell, J. G., & Mitchell, T. M. (Eds.) (1983). Machine learning: An artificial intelligence approach (Vol. 1). Palo Alto, CA: Tioga.

Michalski, R. S., Carbonell, J. G., & Mitchell, T. M. (Eds.) (1986). Machine learning: An artificial intelligence approach. (Vol. 2). Los Altos, CA: Morgan Kaufmann.

Miller, G. A. (1956). The magical number seven, plus or minus two: Some limits on our capacity for processing information. Psychological Review, 63, 81–97.

Mitchell, T. M., Carbonell, J. G., & Michalski, R. S. (Eds.). (1986). Machine learning: A guide to current research. Boston: Kluwer.

Money, J., & Earhardt, A. A. (1972). Man & woman. Boy & girl. Baltimore, MD: The Johns Hopkins University Press.

Mussen, P., Dean, S., & Rosenberg, M. (1952). Some further evidence on the validity of the WISC. Journal of Consulting Psychology, 16, 410–412.

Neches, R., Langley, P., & Klahr, D. (1987). Learning, development, and production systems. In D. Klahr, P. Langley, & R. Neches (Eds.), Production system models of learning and development. (pp. 1–53). Cambridge, MA: MIT Press.

Neisser, U. (1967). Cognitive psychology. New York: Appleton-Century-Crofts.

Newell, A., & Simon, H. A. (1972). Human problem solving. Englewood Cliffs, NJ: Prentice-Hall.

Nickerson, R. S., Perkins, D. N., & Smith, E. E. (Eds.). (1985). The teaching of thinking skills. Hillsdale, NJ: Lawrence Erlbaum Associates.

Nisbett, R. E., Krantz, D. H., Jepson, D., & Kunda, Z. (1983). The use of statistical heuristics in everyday life. Psychological Review, 90, 339–363.

Nisbett, R. E., & Ross, L. (1980). Human inference: Strategies and shortcomings of social judgment. Englewood Cliffs, NJ: Prentice-Hall.

Norman, D. A., & Bobrow, D. G. (1975). On data-limited and resource-limited processes. Cognitive Psychology, 7, 44–64.

Olson, G. M. (1973). Developmental changes in memory and the acquisition of language. In T. E. Moore (Ed.), Cognitive development and the acquisition of language (pp. 145–157). New York: Academic Press.

Olson, G. M. (1976). An information processing analysis of visual memory and habituation in infants. In T. J. Tighe & R. N. Leaton (Eds.), Habituation: Perspectives from child development, animal behavior, and neurophysiology (pp. 239–277). Hillsdale, NJ: Lawrence Erlbaum Associates.

Olson, G. M. (1981). The recognition of specific persons. In M. E. Lamb & L. R. Sherrod (Eds.), Infant social cognition: Empirical and theoretical considerations (pp. 37–59). Hillsdale, NJ: Lawrence Erlbaum Associates.

Olson, G. M., & Sherman, T. (1983). Attention, learning, and memory in infants. In

M. M. Haith & J. T. Campos (Eds.), *Handbook of child psychology* (Vol. 2): *Infancy and developmental psychobiology* (pp. 1001–1080). New York: Wiley.

Olson, G. M., & Strauss, M. S. (1984). The development of infant memory. In M. Moscovitch (Ed.), *Infant memory* (pp. 29–48). New York: Plenum.

Ornstein, P. A. (Ed.). (1978). *Memory development in children.* Hillsdale, NJ: Lawrence Erlbaum Associates.

Osherson, D. N. (1974a). *Logical abilities in children: Organization of length and class concepts, empirical consequences of a Piagetian formalism* (Vol. 1). Hillsdale, NJ: Lawrence Erlbaum Associates.

Osherson, D. N. (1974b). *Logical abilities in children: Logical inference, underlying operations* (Vol. 2). Hillsdale, NJ: Lawrence Erlbaum Associates.

Osherson, D. N. (1975). *Logical abilities in children: Reasoning in adolescence: Deductive inference* (Vol. 3). Hillsdale, NJ: Lawrence Erlbaum Associates.

Osherson, D. N. (1976). *Logical abilities in children: Reasoning and concepts.* (Vol. 4). Hillsdale, NJ: Lawrence Erlbaum Associates.

Parmelee, A. H., Jr., & Sigman, M. D. (1983). Perinatal brain development and behavior. In M. M. Haith & J. T. Campos (Eds.), *Handbook of child psychology* (Vol. 2): *Infancy and developmental psychobiology* (pp. 95–155). New York: Wiley.

Pellegrino, J. W. (1985). Inductive reasoning ability. In R. J. Sternberg (Ed.), *Human abilities: An information-processing approach* (pp. 195–225). New York: Freeman.

Petersen, A. C. (1979). Hormones and cognitive functioning in normal development. In M. A. Wittig & A. C. Petersen (Eds.), *Sex-related differences in cognitive functioning* (pp. 189–214). New York: Academic Press.

Petersen, A. C., & Taylor, B. (1980). The biological approach to adolescence: Biological change and psychological adaptation. In J. Adelson (Ed.), *Handbook of adolescent psychology* (pp. 117–155). New York: Wiley.

Pew, R. W. (1974). Human perceptual-motor performance. In B. H. Kantowitz (Ed.), *Human information processing: Tutorials in performance and cognition* (pp. 1–39). Hillsdale, NJ: Lawrence Erlbaum Associates.

Piaget, J. (1952). *The origins of intelligence in children.* New York: Norton.

Piaget, J. (1954). *The construction of reality in the child.* New York: Basic Books.

Piaget, J. (1962). *Play, dreams and imitation in childhood.* New York: Norton.

Piaget, J., & Inhelder, B. (1973). *Memory and intelligence.* New York: Basic Books.

Piaget, J., & Inhelder, B. (1975). *The origin of the idea of chance in children.* New York: Norton.

Posner, M. I. (1978). *Chronometric explorations of mind.* Hillsdale, NJ: Lawrence Erlbaum Associates.

Pylyshyn, Z. (1973). What the mind's eye tells the mind's brain: A critique of mental imagery. *Psychological Bulletin, 80,* 1–24.

Reitman, J. S. (1976). Skilled perception in Go: Deducing memory structures from inter-response times. *Cognitive Psychology, 8,* 336–356.

Revlin, R., & Mayer, R. E. (Eds.). (1978). *Human reasoning.* New York: Wiley.

Rosch, E. (1978). Principles of categorization. In E. Rosch & B. B. Lloyd (Eds.), *Cognition and categorization* (pp. 27–48). Hillsdale, NJ: Lawrence Erlbaum Associates.

Rosch, E., & Lloyd, B. B. (Eds.). (1978). *Cognition and categorization.* Hillsdale, NJ: Lawrence Erlbaum Associates.

Rumelhart, D. E., & McClelland, J. L. (1982). An interactive activation model of context effects in letter perception, Part 2: The contextual enhancement effect and some tests and extensions of the model. *Psychological Review, 89,* 60–94.

Rumelhart, D. E., & McClelland, J. L. (1986). *Parallel distributed processing: Explorations in the microstructure of cognition. Vol. 1. Foundations.* Cambridge, MA: MIT Press.

Rumelhart, D. E., & Norman, D. A. (in press). Representation in memory. In R. C. Atkinson, R. J. Herrnstein, G. Lindsey, & R. D. Luce (Eds.), *Handbook of experimental psychology.* New York: Wiley.

Schaffer, H. R. (Ed.). (1977). *Studies in mother-infant interaction.* New York: Academic Press.

Schaffer, H. R. (1984). *The child's entry into a social world.* New York: Academic Press.

Schank, R., & Abelson, R. (1977). *Scripts, plans, goals and understanding.* Hillsdale, NJ: Lawrence Erlbaum Associates.

Segal, J. W., Chipman, S. F., & Glaser, R. (Eds.). (1985) *Thinking and learning skills. Vol. 1. Relating instruction to research.* Hillsdale. NJ: Lawrence Erlbaum Associates.

Shatz, M., & Gelman, R. (1973). The development of communication skills: Modifications in the speech of young children as a function of the listener. *Monographs of the Society for Research in Child Development, 38* (Whole No. 152).

Sherrod, L. R. (1981). Issues of cognitive-perceptual development: The special case of social stimuli. In M. E. Lamb & L. R. Sherrod (Eds.), *Infant social cognition: Empirical and theoretical considerations* (pp. 11–36). Hillsdale, NJ: Lawrence Erlbaum Associates.

Siegler, R. S., & Richards, D. D. (1982). The development of intelligence. In R. J. Sternberg (Ed.), *Handbook of human intelligence* (pp. 897–971). New York: Cambridge University Press.

Simon, H. A. (1974). How big is a chunk? *Science, 183,* 482–488.

Simon, H. A. (1981). *The sciences of the artificial* (2nd. ed.). Cambridge, MA: MIT Press.

Smith, E. E., & Medin, D. L. (1981). *Categories and concepts.* Cambridge, MA: Harvard University Press.

Sontag, C. W., Baker, C. T., & Nelson, V. L. (1985). Mental growth and personality development: A longitudinal study. *Monographs of the Society for Research in Child Development, 23,* (Serial No. 68).

Sophian, C. (1980). Habituation is not enough: Novelty preferences, search, and memory in infancy. *Merrill-Palmer Quarterly, 26,* 239–257.

Spelke, E. (in press). The development of intermodal perception. In L. Cohen & P. Salapatek (Eds.), *Handbook of infant perception* (Vol. 3). New York: Academic Press.

Stern, D. N. (1985). *The interpersonal world of the infant: A view from psychoanalysis and developmental psychology.* New York: Basic Books.

Sternberg, R. J. (1977). *Intelligence, information processing, and analogical reasoning: The componential analysis of human abilities.* Hillsdale, NJ: Lawrence Erlbaum Associates.

Sternberg, R. J. (1982a). A componential approach to intellectual development. In R. J.

Sternberg (Ed.), *Advances in the psychology of human intelligence* (Vol. 1, pp. 413–463). Hillsdale, NJ: Lawrence Erlbaum Associates.

Sternberg, R. J. (1982b). Reasoning, problem solving, and intelligence. In R. J. Sternberg (Ed.), *Handbook of human intelligence* (pp. 225–307). New York: Cambridge University Press.

Sternberg, R. J. (1985). *Beyond IQ: A triarchic theory of human intelligence.* New York: Cambridge University Press.

Sternberg, R. J., & Powell, J. S. (1983). The development of intelligence. In J. H. Flavell & E. M. Markman (Eds.), *Handbook of child psychology* (Vol. 3): *Cognitive development* (pp. 341–419). New York: Wiley.

Turvey, M. T. (1977). Preliminaries to a theory of action with reference to vision. In R. Shaw & J. Bransford (Eds.), *Perceiving, action, and knowing.* Hillsdale, NJ: Lawrence Erlbaum Associates.

Wellman, H. M. (1983). Metamemory revisited. In M.T.H. Chi (Ed.), *Trends in memory development research* (pp. 31–51). Basel: S. Karger.

Wickens, C. D. (1974). Temporal limits of human information processing: A developmental study. *Psychological Bulletin, 81,* 739–755.

Wickens, T. D. (1982). *Models for behavior: Stochastic processes in psychology.* San Francisco: Freeman.

Winston, P. H. (1980). Learning and reasoning by analogy. *Communications of the ACM, 23,* 689–703.

Yakovlev, P. I., & Lecours, A. R. (1967). The myelogenetic cycles of regional maturation of the brain. In A. Minkowski (Ed.), *Regional development of the brain in early life* (pp. 3–70). Philadelphia: F. A. Davis.

Motivation

Carol S. Dweck
University of Illinois

Most of the chapters in this volume deal with the processes involved in effective learning and performance of cognitive tasks. This one does as well. However, instead of analyzing the specific skills required to succeed at a cognitive task, this chapter analyzes the motivational processes that affect success at that task. That is, it examines the factors, aside from skill itself, that affect the pursuit, attainment, and display of cognitive skills. These are cognitive factors (beliefs, inferences) and affective factors that influence children's choice and initiation of tasks, as well as the intensity and persistence with which they pursue them.

Much of the research reviewed consists of experimental laboratory work that closely examines the workings of these factors—that focuses on specific motivational variables (measured or manipulated) and their relation to specific aspects of task choice, task pursuit, and task performance. As the motivational variables that appear to facilitate or impede learning are identified, research on conditions that foster them are reviewed. Throughout, I consider research that speaks to the applicability of these findings to educational settings and that explores the implications of the findings for children's long-term academic achievement.

Motivational Myths

The components of adaptive motivational patterns have been poorly understood. Many common-sense analyses have been limited and have not provided a basis for effective practices. Indeed, all of the following common-sense beliefs have been called into question or seriously qualified by recent research:

1. the adaptive patterns of young children (challenge seeking, love of learning, etc.) would automatically continue unabated if not sabotaged by the coercive, evaluative practices of adults.

2. large amounts of praise and success will establish, maintain or reinstate adaptive patterns.

3. "brighter" children have more adaptive patterns—are more likely to choose personally challenging tasks or to persist in the face of difficulty.

As the chapter proceeds through a systematic analysis of motivational factors, it will become clear that young children's adaptive patterns may not automatically remain intact through developmental change and may not automatically transfer to tasks involving long-term achievement goals; that well-intended "reinforcement" practices may not increase the probability that a child will seek intellectual tasks, approach them with confidence, or persist when tasks pose difficulties; that children considered brightest may not be less susceptible to debilitating patterns, although the presence and impact of these patterns may be less apparent to educators during the grade school years. As we will see, motivation on cognitive tasks consists of a complex interplay of factors, and motivational patterns that impede learning are by no means the province of less "bright," poorly treated students.

Thus, although we have far to go before motivational effects on cognitive performance are fully understood, research has begun to shed light on the nature and workings of important motivational factors, and hence to suggest conditions that may foster desirable patterns. Before we turn to this research, let us first define more clearly what is meant by *motivation* and by *adaptive* or *facilitating motivational patterns*.

Definition of Motivation and Facilitating Patterns

The study of motivation deals with the causes of goal-oriented strivings (Atkinson, 1964; Beck, 1983; Dollard & Miller, 1950; Hull, 1943; Veroff, 1969). Achievement motivation involves striving toward a particular class of goals—those involving competence. As I discuss later, one may further identify two subclasses of achievement goals: (a) *learning goals,* in which individuals strive to increase their competence, to understand or master something new; and (b) *performance goals,* in which individuals strive either to document, or gain favorable judgments of, their competence or to avoid negative judgments of their competence (Dweck & Elliott, 1983; Nicholls, 1981; Nicholls & Dweck, 1979).[1]

It is proposed that desirable/adaptive/facilitating motivational patterns are basically those that promote the establishment, maintenance, and attainment of personally challenging and personally valued achievement goals. Maladaptive patterns, then, would be associated with a failure to establish reasonable, valued goals, to maintain effective striving toward those goals, or ultimately to attain valued goals that are potentially within one's reach.

Learning goals and performance goals may both be associated with vigorous achievement activity. It is still suggested, however, that they tend to be differentially associated with adaptive and maladaptive patterns—that learning goals predict the pursuit and mastery of challenging tasks more reliably than do performance goals.

Major Motivational Variables

Facilitating and maladaptive motivational patterns can be conceptualized in terms of three major variables: (a) *goal value:* the salience and attractiveness of achievement goals; (b) *goal expectancy:* the subjective probability of goal attainment; and (c) *means value:* the attractiveness or aversiveness of the activities necessary for goal attainment. These variables and their component processes play critical roles in determining whether achievement activities are undertaken and whether effective achievement striving is maintained (see, e.g., V.C. Crandall, 1967, 1969; V.J. Crandall, 1963; Dweck & Elliott, 1983; McClelland, Atkinson, Clark, & Lowell, 1953; Weiner, 1972).

These factors will vary by individual and by situation. That is, there will be important differences among people in their tendency to value achievement goals (or to value particular achievement goals), in their tendency to form and maintain high expectancies of success, and in their tendency to enjoy achievement tasks and settings. There are also strong situational influences on goal value, goal expectancy, and means value. In many situations there will be cues that highlight certain goals (e.g., evaluative cues), that affect subjective probabilities of success (e.g., task-difficulty cues), and that speak to the attractions of the activities at hand (e.g., interest value of the material).

Individual differences in how one tends to approach and respond to situations (one's motivational "sets") will combine with situational cues to determine values and expectancies. Sometimes, when situational cues are clear (i.e., not subject to alternative interpretations), diverse individuals may tend to look

---

[1]The word "performance" is used in several ways, not only in connection with performance goals. I use it also when I refer to the child's task activity (performance of a task) and to the product of that activity (level of performance). The meaning should be clear from the context.

similar (e.g., see Dweck, Davidson, Nelson, & Enna, 1978). That is, there will be situations that appear to bring out facilitating (or debilitating) patterns for the moment in most individuals, for example, situations that create high (or low) goal value, high (or low) expectancy, and high (or low) interest. However, when we speak of an individual's "having" adaptive patterns, we mean that these patterns are displayed readily and widely, that his or her sets will override or reinterpret a variety of situational cues that might, say, lower others' expectancies and values or cause others to abandon effective striving.

Individual differences, then, are not seen as the *presence* or *absence* of adaptive and maladaptive patterns. Rather, individual differences are conceived in terms of the *probability* that such patterns will be elicited across situations.[2] Indeed, later I argue that effective intervention consists not simply of creating an environment in which children's maladaptive tendencies do not come into play, but in promoting more adaptive tendencies that will generalize to less utopian settings.

It might be also noted here that although I speak of individuals having particular facilitating or debilitating patterns, I do not speak of individuals having high or low achievement motivation. This is because the latter implies that achievement motivation is a unitary characteristic that is present in particular amounts, and because it fails to take account of the different achievement goals toward which individuals may strive. Instead, facilitating and debilitating patterns can have many bases, can take many forms, and can occur with respect to different goals.

The Nature of Motivational Variables

Hypothetical Constructs.   It is important to remember that motivational variables are constructs that psychologists have formulated to help explain behavior. They are hypothesized mediating variables intended to describe something within the individual that will clarify the relationship between antecedent conditions and consequent behavior. They are postulated mediators of people's responses to events.

To say that motivational factors are hypothetical constructs is not pejorative. Constructs appear to be necessary. Perhaps it would be preferable to understand goal-oriented behavior in achievement situations without recourse to invisible processes, but this does not appear likely. Descriptions of external stimuli and overt behavior no longer seem to hold the promise of providing a

---

[2]This inherent probabilistic character of individual differences may be what has led some people to question the existence of intraindividual consistency or to deem certain individual differences (e.g., sex differences) *unreliable*. Yet, individual differences conceived in this way are not expected to occur in every situation or on every measure. The question then becomes under what circumstances they are likely to occur and with what consequences.

satisfying explanation of motivated behavior. Nor does a simple description of the reinforcement history tell us what is directing the individual's behavior in the present. It appears that we need also to talk about such things as how individuals interpret situational cues or performance outcomes, and how these judgments/inferences/beliefs affect subsequent behavior. Indeed, as we will see, including such constructs in our analyses has allowed us to understand why apparently similar events can have widely discrepant effects on behavior and why apparently dissimilar events can have highly similar effects. It has allowed us to begin to see why positive outcomes sometimes seem to decrease the probability of a given behavior or why seemingly negative outcomes can increase its probability.

Thus, the question becomes not whether constructs are desirable, but which constructs are useful. As we will see, the constructs that have proven most fruitful in exploring achievement motivation are those that are most specific, most clearly defined, most precisely measurable and manipulable. They are ones that provide a link between antecedent events and consequent behavior that can be clearly articulated and tested. Although broad constructs like self-concept have had wide appeal, they have not been as useful in illuminating motivational processes. (See Damon & Hart, 1982, for a cogent discussion of why the global variable "self-esteem" has failed to fulfill its promise as a predictive or explanatory construct.) The more specific constructs may well be components of what people have meant by self-concept, but an emphasis on specific constructs appears to promise a clearer picture of motivational effects on cognitive performance.

Affect Versus Cognition. A question that often arises is whether motivation is affect or cognition. It is both. Clearly, both cognition and affect can influence goal-directed behavior in achievement situations (Beck, 1983; Covington, 1983a; Parsons, 1983; Weiner & Graham, 1984). Another frequent question concerns which is primary, affect or cognition. It appears that the answer is "either." Most of the processes I consider can be seen as having primary cognitions (not necessarily conscious) that generate affect—underlying beliefs or inferences that result in emotional states such as fear, excitement, dejection, pride. To say that in many cases affect may not be primary is by no means to say it is unimportant. Such consequent affective states may have enormous impact on subsequent behavior. In fact, it may sometimes be the affect rather than the underlying cognition that directly spurs approach to or avoidance of a task or that results in deteriorated or improved performance (Weiner & Graham, in press). Of course, there are also cases in which the affect appears to be primary and no underlying cognitions can be identified. Some activity preferences (what one enjoys, finds interesting) may fall into this category (see, e.g., Zajonc, 1980).

In short, motivational processes are best seen as an interplay of cognitive and affective factors that influence the initiation and maintenance of goal-directed striving.

Present Approach

Overview of Framework.   Figure 3.1 represents, in a general and simplified fashion, the motivational processes that come into play in an achievement situation. It is important to note that although many of these processes have important cognitive components and bear systematic relationships to behavior, I do not propose that these processes are typically conscious, logical, explicit or deliberate on the part of the child. Rather, like most psychological processes, they are likely to be unconscious and often to involve biased judgments. For example, when we say a child formulates an expectancy or makes an attribution for an outcome, we do not mean that the child has deliberately gone through a logical inference process and has emerged with an explicit answer, although this may sometimes occur. It is the task of the researcher to make these processes explicit, to measure them precisely, and to clarify their relationships to antecedent conditions and consequent behavior.

As depicted in Fig. 3.1, we may conceive of the child as entering a potential achievement situation with a repertoire of cognitive skills and with a host of motivational sets. Motivational sets include (a) *beliefs* (e.g., favored views about the nature of competence, about the level of one's competence, about what variables influence outcomes, etc.); (b) *inference rules* (e.g., preferred modes of computing task difficulty, deciding the causes of outcomes); (c) *salient representations* (e.g., tendencies to focus on aversive or pleasurable

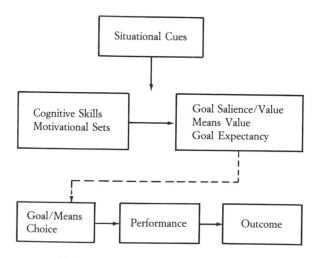

FIG. 3.1.   Proposed motivational processes.

means or on desirable or undesirable outcomes); and (d) *values and interests* (personal hierarchy of what is important and enjoyable).

Situational cues (e.g., about the nature of the task, the evaluator, potential rewards) are then interpreted in light of these sets to yield some salient, valued goals, some expectancy of reaching those goals, and some idea of how pleasant or aversive the route to those goals will be. A course of action—which, if any, achievement goals to pursue and how—is then chosen. If a task is undertaken, then as it is performed and outcomes occur, this information feeds back into the system, potentially altering the goal value, goal expectancy, or means value. Broadly speaking, as long as values and expectancies remain high, strivings will persist.

Relationship to Past Theories. Past approaches have differed in the extent to which they have focused on specific mediators of achievement behavior versus general energizers of achievement behavior (see Dweck & Elliott, 1983 for a detailed review of different theoretical models). For example, the evaluation anxiety approach (Mandler & Sarason, 1952; Sarason, Davidson, Lighthall, Waite, & Ruebush, 1960; Sarason & Mandler, 1952; Wine, 1971, 1982), the social learning approach (Battle, 1965, 1966; V.C. Crandall, 1967, 1969; V.J. Crandall, 1963; V.J. Crandall, Katkovsky, & Preston, 1960, 1962), and the attributional approach (Weiner, 1972, 1982; Weiner; Frieze, Kukla, Reed, Rest, & Rosenbaum, 1971; Weiner & Kukla, 1970; for the related learned helplessness approach, see Dweck & Goetz, 1978) have all sought to measure more-or-less specific motivational variables, to test hypotheses about the relationships of these variables to specific aspects of achievement behavior, and to test mechanisms through which the focal variables affect behavior. In contrast the need-for-achievement tradition (Atkinson, 1957, 1964; Atkinson & Feather, 1966; Heckhausen, 1967; McClelland et al., 1953) has tended to focus on global, generalized motives that are seen as energizing and directing virtually all aspects of achievement behavior. The need-for-achievement approach has thus involved the use of global measures (such as the Thematic Apperception Test—Murray, 1938) to provide an index of the underlying motives and to predict future behavior.

Although our approach perhaps has more in common with past approaches that emphasize specific mediators, we find much of value in the need-for-achievement tradition as well. First, the question of what *instigates* achievement striving is a critical one and has not always received sufficient attention in other theories. Second, the theory gives a prominent role in the direction of behavior to affect (positive and negative anticipatory goal responses such as anticipatory pride or shame), a role that the more cognitive theories tended sometimes to ignore.

Yet the findings from these different approaches need not be seen as incompatible. Indeed, when one looks more closely at the global motive measure (i.e., "unpacks" it), one finds that the individual categories of responses look quite similar to the more specific mediators that are being studied by others. That is, the global motive measure in some ways appears to be the grand sum of the cognitive and affective processes that are found by others (e.g., Diener & Dweck, 1978) to unfold over time in achievement situations. It may be this property of the measure that has made it useful for purposes of prediction, but it may be this same property that has made it less useful for understanding the moment-to-moment specifics of motivational processes, and hence the more precise patterns of individual differences or situational influences (although see Atkinson & Birch, 1970, 1974). Therefore, although I draw on the many valuable findings of this tradition, and although I speak of particular generalized sets, beliefs, or predispositions, I do not tend to speak in terms of motives. Perhaps an analogy to another domain serves to clarify this issue further.

The postulation of needs and motives as explanations of human behavior was part of a broader theoretical tradition that emphasized drives (biologically based and acquired) as energizers and directors of behavior (e.g., Hull, 1943, 1952; Miller, 1951). Yet even when we examine the most clearly biologically based drives, such as hunger, it becomes apparent that global motives or drives do not illuminate with sufficient precision the diverse patterns and mechanisms of eating behavior. As an individual matures, food consumption can come to serve a variety of goals, and can come under the control of the individual's beliefs. For instance, aside from quelling hunger, eating can serve such goals as regulating weight, promoting health, having novel gustatory experiences, or showing oneself to have cultivated tastes. Moreover, the selection and pursuit of goals will be directed by the beliefs individuals have about themselves, about the means to goal attainment, about the reasons for past success or failures, and so on. Although one must always be careful not to lose the big picture by proliferating details, we believe that complex motivational systems are best understood by distinguishing different goals and attending to component processes within goals.

Thus the present approach, building on past approaches, represents an attempt to (a) define and develop the distinction between two classes of goals in achievement situations (i.e., learning goals vs. performance goals); (b) delineate a sequence of processes involving specific mediators, each linked to behavior in testable ways; and (c) suggest the ways in which generalized sets can direct the sequence of motivational processes.

This focus on more specific mediators has several advantages. What is most important is that it has allowed researchers to begin to understand with greater clarity and coherence:

1. individual difference patterns other than simple approach or avoidance behavior

2. situational influences—how various classes of situational cues systematically affect achievement behavior

3. developmental change—how specific achievement patterns emerge given environmental influences and the general context of cognitive change

4. instructional practice and ameliorative interventions—how specific practices influence particular mediators to promote or alter motivational patterns.

With an emphasis on specific mediators, researchers have begun to construct a picture of motivational processes that is sufficiently detailed to dispel intuitively appealing motivational myths.

Overview of Chapter

In the next several sections I examine the major classes of motivational factors, focusing chiefly on goal value and goal expectancy. Within each, I delineate patterns that appear to foster the initiation and maintenance of effective striving, as well as patterns that appear to interfere with the adoption and attainment of achievement goals. I also examine determinants of these patterns and consider implications for practice.

Specifically, the Goal Value section examines available research on the different achievement goals, and suggests how an emphasis on "learning" goals versus "performance" goals promotes choice of personally challenging tasks, more widespread persistence in the face of obstacles, and higher quality efforts, particularly for children who are most vulnerable to debilitation in achievement situations. Indeed, this section suggests that the different types of goals impart an entirely different character to achievement situations, shifting not only the purpose of the activity, but also affecting such things as the standards for judging success, the meaning of outcomes, and the level of intrinsic interest in the task (means value). What orients children toward the different goals? I review research indicating that viewing and valuing intelligence as a stable trait predisposes children to adopt performance goals, whereas viewing intelligence as a dynamic quality that grows through effort appears to orient children toward learning goals. I conclude the section by examining the implications of the different views of intelligence and the different achievement goals for teacher expectancy effects.

The section on Goal Expectancy examines the nature and basis of expectancies associated with challenge seeking and effective striving. As one might expect, it is expectancies that are high, stable, and resilient that tend to be related to challenge seeking and effective striving. However, surprisingly often, it is not the children with the highest competence who have clearly the highest, most stable or resilient confidence. To illuminate this puzzling discrepancy between children's actual competence and their expectancy of success, I turn to the process of expectancy formation. By examining research on how children engage in task analysis, on the standards they adopt to gauge success and failure, and on the ways in which they process their achievement outcomes, I suggest mechanisms through which inappropriate and maladaptive expectancies can be formed.

This section further examines the different bases and character of expectancies within the two types of achievement goals, suggesting that performance goals lead to expectancies that are more vulnerable or brittle and that two of the major maladaptive expectancy patterns—evaluation anxiety and learned helplessness—occur within the performance-goal framework. Although much well-meant educational practice retains the performance-goal framework and attempts to create confidence with respect to performance goals by providing success, research evidence suggests that a more fruitful alternative is to (a) aim interventions directly at the specific mediators involved in the maladaptive pattern, rather than hoping that children will draw the intended inference from success experiences; and (b) create an emphasis on learning goals and personally challenging tasks. I also point out that virtually all motivational interventions have occurred with unsuccessful students (i.e., those with skill deficits as well as maladaptive motivational tendencies). Yet, as noted, the research findings indicate that many very able students are not confident, challenge seeking, or persistent, and may thus profit from similar interventions.

The Developmental Issues section examines the profound changes in achievement motivation that take place in the early school years. It is during these years that maladaptive patterns appear to fall into place, with many children exhibiting increasing pessimism, anxiety, or apathy. I pose the question of why the self-initiating, self-maintaining, and self-reinforcing achievement motivation system of younger children is not more widely maintained over these years, and propose two major factors to help account for this: the changing nature of the tasks and the changing definition of ability. I suggest that these changes may lead children toward performance goals, thus creating conditions in which maladaptive patterns develop. What is the role of the school in this undesirable state of affairs? As I consider the evidence, it appears not so much that schools squelch the natural enthusiasm and confidence of children, as that they fail to teach the *new* sets of skills or foster the *new* motivational frameworks that are necessary for the growth of adaptive patterns on intellectual tasks in the school setting.

Finally, the Conclusion section brings together the major points of the previous sections and develop the implications for long-term achievement. For example, it explores ways in which the motivational patterns delineated here can help account for differential attraction to and differential achievement in different subject areas (e.g., sex differences in math vs. verbal achievement). In particular, this section analyzes the characteristics of math versus verbal subject areas as they are acquired over the school years, and suggests that each set of characteristics provides a match with a different motivational pattern, such that many children who seek and persist in one subject area may avoid or abandon striving in the other. This chapter ends by developing further the idea that what is desirable in a mature motivational system is the ability to generate personally valued long-term goals, and to act in ways that maximize the probability of attaining them.

GOAL VALUE

Achievement Goals

The study of achievement motivation, as noted earlier, is the analysis of the determinants of goal-oriented striving, where the goals relate to competence. These goals fall into two categories: learning goals and performance goals. When one has a learning goal, one aims at *increasing* one's competence, at understanding, mastering, figuring out something new. Performance goals, in contrast, center around concerns about *validating* one's competence. When one has performance goals one aims at (a) obtaining favorable judgments of one's ability, and/or (b) avoiding unfavorable judgments of one's ability (Dweck & Elliott, 1983; Elliott & Dweck, 1981; Nicholls & Dweck, 1979).

An *achievement situation* is defined by the adoption of an achievement goal on the part of the individual. It is not defined by the availability of such goals within a situation. That is, an adult may construct a situation that highlights learning or performance goals, but it is not an achievement situation for the child, if he or she does not explicitly or implicitly adopt an achievement goal. Similarly, whether an achievement situation is chiefly a learning or performance situation depends on the child's goal rather than on the nature of the task. If a child is given a new set of material to tackle but does so with the goal of obtaining a competence judgment (e.g., by rapidity of learning or mastery), then we would call it predominantly a performance situation. If a child approached a test or contest with the goal of getting tips on how to improve his skills, then we would say that this was predominantly a learning situation. We assume that virtually everyone values learning and prefers positive to negative judgments. However, children will differ in the degree to which they value and adopt achievement goals, and which ones they value and adopt.

It is important to note that the various achievement goals may be held (and attained) simultaneously. In a given situation one may seek to learn, to obtain favorable competence judgments, and to avoid unfavorable judgments. However, in other situations these goals may come into conflict, and the child may feel that he or she has to choose between learning and performance goals (becoming smarter vs. looking smart) or between the two performance goals (attempting to look smart vs. avoiding looking incompetent). Achievement goals may also combine or conflict with nonachievement goals and it seems reasonable to expect that the more one's achievement goals are compatible with one's other goals (such as being popular, having fun, or acquiring material rewards), then the more likely they are to be pursued. It is also reasonable to expect that the more attractive, interesting, or enjoyable the means to a goal are (i.e., the higher the means value), the more likely the goal is to be pursued (see Dweck & Elliott, 1983).

In summary, an achievement situation is defined by the adoption of one or more achievement goals. The adoption of a given achievement goal will depend on its salience to the individual and on its value relative to other competing achievement and nonachievement goals. The next section considers some of the factors that contribute to the relative salience of learning versus performance goals and examines the many consequences of adopting one type of achievement goal over the other.

Learning and Performance Goals Contrasted

Although both learning and performance goals can promote active, effective striving on challenging tasks, the research evidence is beginning to suggest that performance goals may create a context that is less conducive to this. As we see, viewing a given situation as an occasion for an ability judgment (as opposed to an opportunity for learning) can transform the achievement process in a great many ways, altering for example the type of standard likely to be used, the variables on which expectancies are based, one's perceived and actual control over desired outcomes, the perception and impact of failure, the enjoyment of high-effort tasks, and one's attitude toward educators and peers.

Although few studies as yet have explicitly induced and compared (or measured and compared) learning versus performance goals (see M. Bandura & Dweck, 1981; Elliott & Dweck, 1981), many have manipulated the salience and value of performance goals, and hence the relative value of the two types of goals. This has been done, for example, by instituting a competitive versus individual reward structure (e.g., Ames, Ames, & Felker, 1977), by varying the alleged diagnosticity of the task vis-à-vis important abilities (e.g., Nicholls, 1975), by introducing an audience or evaluator versus allowing the individual to perform privately or focussing his or her attention on the task (e.g., Brockner & Hulton, 1978; Carver & Scheier, 1978; E. Diener & Srull, 1979), by presenting the task with "test" instructions versus "game" or neutral instructions (e.g., Entin & Raynor, 1973; Lekarczyk & Hill, 1969; McCoy, 1965; I.G. Sarason, 1972).

Taken together, the results suggest that highlighting performance goals relative to learning goals can have the effects discussed following on motivational factors and on consequent achievement behavior.

Standards.   Standards are the level of performance or learning that a child feels he or she must attain in order to be successful. Performance goals appear to foster the adoption of normative standards of success, as opposed to personal or autonomous standards, which can be more flexible and progressive, that is, heightened with task experience (see, e.g., Ames & Ames, 1981; Carver & Scheier, 1981; E. Diener & Srull, 1979; Nicholls, 1981, 1983). Normative standards typically entail an evaluation of a final product or level of performance relative to others. They thus create a win–lose situation in which the effects of past successes, considerable personal progress, or an excellent product, can be obliterated by a comparative judgment (Ames & Ames, 1981). In contrast, personal standards, particularly those based on one's progress, mark gains in learning that are permanent, and allow one to maintain the effects of past successes, even in the face of a present failure (Ames & Ames, 1981). Moreover, with personal standards, however stringent, the supply of success can equal the demand (see, e.g., Covington & Beery, 1976).

Expectancies.   If, when one seeks a favorable ability judgment, expectancies of success are likely to be based on estimates of one's ability relative to others, then one may need to estimate this *before* choosing or embarking on a task (lest one obtain a negative judgment of ability). Thus the estimate must be high in order to initiate performance on a challenging task (M. Bandura & Dweck, 1981; Elliott & Dweck, 1981). And the expectancy needs to *remain* high to sustain involvement. Yet there is evidence to suggest that a performance set (e.g., Anderson & Jennings, 1980: portraying task performance as indicative of "ability" vs. "strategies") eliminates the expectation of improvement over trials when an initial failure has occurred.

When one has learning goals, however, one's expectancies may weigh effort more heavily, that is, how much time and work must be expended to reach the learning goal, given the task and given one's present skill level. In addition, one can try out a task in order to gain more information about one's likely rate of progress. Thus, with a learning goal, one need not perceive before the fact that one's existing task-related skills are greater than others', or even that one's rate of progress will be greater, in order to embark on a challenging task. Indeed, in studies by Elliott and Dweck (1981), in which learning and performance goals were experimentally manipulated, and M. Bandura and Dweck (1981), in which learning and performance goals were assessed, children with learning goals chose challenging tasks regardless of whether they thought they had high or low ability relative to other children. In contrast, children with performance goals avoided challenge if they had doubts about their normative ability.

Perceived Control.   Given the different nature of the two goals, a learning goal can be expected to enhance a child's sense of control over outcomes, a variable that has often been linked to effective achievement behavior (A. Bandura,

1977, 1980; Harter & Connell, 1981; Weisz & Stipek, 1982). Perceived control, although related to expectancy, refers not only to the likelihood of an outcome, but also to its contingency—its relationship to one's own behavior.

Within a performance goal, several factors intervene between one's input and a desired outcome, and the individual may have little control over these factors. For example, when striving to succeed according to a normative standard, one has virtually no control over the performance of one's reference group. Or when striving for a competence judgment from a given evaluator, one may have little to say about the criteria the evaluator uses in judging your product.

Within a learning goal, however, one more often has control over the factors related to goal attainment. That is, if one's goal involves progress or personal mastery, then the effort-outcome relationship is more direct. There is usually not a separate outcome that occurs later and that depends on others. Moreover, I suggest that within a learning framework instructors or peers are more likely to be perceived as resources for goal attainment rather than potential obstacles.

Task Choice.   Performance goals compared to learning goals appear to promote defensive strategies designed to protect against negative judgments of ability. Thus, when oriented toward performance goals, individuals with low expectancies are sometimes found to choose excessively easy tasks on which success is insured or excessively difficult ones on which failure does not signify low ability (and one can earn respect for a valiant attempt; see deCharms & Carpenter, 1968; Moulton, 1965; Raynor & Smith, 1966). Even individuals with high expectancies of success may sacrifice a potentially fruitful learning opportunity that involves risk of errors for an opportunity to look smart (Elliott & Dweck, 1981).

An orientation away from performance goals appears to foster tackling of more appropriately challenging tasks, regardless of the individual's perceived level of ability (Meyers, Folkes, & Weiner, 1976; Nicholls, 1983). Similarly, an explicit orientation toward learning goals encourages a choice of learning tasks over performance opportunities, even when the learning task involves likely displays of ignorance (Elliott & Dweck, 1981).

Task Pursuit.   In addition to affecting task choice, the defensive protection against negative judgments that may accompany performance goals can manifest itself in aspects of task pursuit as well. For example, when one is required to perform on a challenging task, one may attempt to reduce its diagnosticity of one's ability by minimizing effort or by introducing other factors that can serve as excuses for poor performance. Berglas and Jones (1978) have termed this strategy *self-handicapping,* that is, the employment of devices that reduce the likelihood of success but that serve as protection against a failure that signifies low ability. Others have also noted the face-saving potential of low effort investment in the face of threatened failure (Covington & Omelich, 1979a, 1979b; Frankl & Snyder, 1978; Nicholls, 1976).

Finally, performance goals and learning goals are differentially associated with debilitation in the face of obstacles. The more a child focuses on learning or progress, the greater the likelihood of maintaining effective strategies (or improving one's strategies) under failure (Bandura & Schunk, 1981; Elliott & Dweck, 1981; cf. also Anderson & Jennings, 1980; C.I. Diener & Dweck, 1978).

In short, an appropriately challenging task on which one exerts high effort (and on which external impediments are not apparent) can yield a particularly telling competence judgment. Thus, with performance goals, low or shaky expectancies of success may lead one to shun the very tasks that foster learning and mastery experiences, or to pursue them in ineffective ways.

Outcome Attribution and Satisfaction. Once again, within a learning framework the focus is likely to be on effort versus ability. Ames, Ames, and Felker (1977), for example, found that with an autonomous reward structure, success and failure outcomes were seen as reflecting effort, and children's pride in their performance (in both the success and the failure conditions) was related to the degree of effort they perceived themselves to have exerted. However, within the competitive reward structure, outcomes were seen more as reflecting on their ability and on their luck. Pride in performance was related to the degree of ability and luck they believed themselves to have. Thus, competitive failure yielded little basis for personal pride or satisfaction.

Consonant with these results are those of Elliott and Dweck (1981), who found that, in the face of obstacles, children with learning goals did not tend to attribute outcomes to lack of ability, to show performance disruption, or to exhibit negative affect, even if they perceived themselves as having low ability relative to others.

M. Bandura and Dweck (1981) also found the differential emphasis on effort with learning and performance goals. Children with learning goals were significantly more likely than children with performance goals to say they would feel smarter after a high effort mastery experience than after a low effort mastery experience (see also Nicholls, 1983). In addition, when asked to indicate their affective reactions to low-effort mastery, children with learning goals were more likely than children with performance goals to choose "bored" or "disappointed" versus "proud" or "relieved."

Finally, within a performance framework, one's own outcome satisfaction may be in conflict with those of one's peers. Ames, Ames, and Felker (1977) found children's own satisfaction and their perception of others' satisfaction with performance to be negatively correlated under the competitive reward structure ($-.70$), but not in the autonomous reward structure ($.06$), even though their relative outcomes were identical in the two conditions. In addition, in rating how deserving of rewards (stars) both persons were given their level of performance, children were more magnanimous toward the poorer performer (whether it was self or other) in the noncompetitive condition than they were in the competitive one. Indeed, in the noncompetitive condition, they even awarded the losing other slightly more stars than they awarded themselves.

Task Interest.   The evidence suggests that the characteristics of learning situations are ones that are more likely to foster and maintain interest in the task. First, it appears from the foregoing discussion that challenging tasks and ones that pose obstacles are less likely to create negative affect (and more likely to create positive affect) for children with learning versus performance goals (M. Bandura & Dweck, 1981; Elliott & Dweck, 1981). The findings just discussed also suggest that high effort is itself more likely to be experienced as pleasurable in a learning situation than in a performance situation. In the former, high effort appears to engender pride in one's work (Ames et al., 1977; M. Bandura & Dweck, 1981), and it more or less directly produces progress; in the latter, high effort can be associated with the shame of displaying low ability (Ames et al., 1977; Covington & Omelich, 1979a, 1979b; Nicholls, 1976).

Finally, it was suggested above that learning goals may foster a greater sense of personal control. The intrinsic motivation literature suggests that greater perceived control often is associated with greater task interest and enjoyment: situational factors that imply that others control outcomes or constrain behavior seem to precipitate a decline in intrinsic motivation (Deci, 1975; Deci & Ryan, 1980; Lepper, 1980; Lepper & Greene, 1978; Maehr & Stallings, 1972; Ryan, Mims, & Koestner, in press; Salili, Maehr, Sorensen, & Fyans, 1976).

Cognitive Sets and Achievement Goals

We have mentioned numerous situational factors that may orient children toward learning or performance goals, but there are also beliefs or cognitive sets that children have that can differentially orient them toward these goals. An example of this is the child's conception of intelligence—his or her theories about the nature of smartness. In my own work, I have found that different children favor different theories of intelligence—smartness as a dynamic growing quality or smartness as a fixed trait, a static entity—and the theory they favor predicts the achievement goal they select. M. Bandura and Dweck (1981) found that children who endorsed the "incremental" theory (e.g., "Smartness is something you can increase as much as you want to") were significantly more likely to adopt learning goals on an experimental task than children who endorsed the "entity" theory (e.g., "You can learn new things, but how smart you are stays pretty much the same"). That is, children who thought smartness was increasable chose tasks that would increase their competence, whereas children who thought smartness was a stable entity were more likely to choose tasks that would secure a positive judgment of their existing competence or avoid a negative judgment.

These findings were replicated on a large junior high school—incremental theorists were significantly more likely than entity theorists to report a preference for classroom tasks that were learning oriented ("Hard, new, and different so I could try to learn from them") versus performance oriented ("Fun and easy to do, so I wouldn't have to worry about mistakes," "Like things I'm good at so I could feel smart," or "Real hard so mistakes wouldn't mean I'm not smart").

As a further test of the relationship between children's theories of intelligence and their goal choice, Dweck, Tenney, and Dinces (1982) sought to determine whether experimentally manipulating children's theories of intelligence would affect their goal choices in predicted ways. In this study, children were differentially focused on one theory or the other by means of reading passages that embodied either an incremental or an entity theory of intelligence (these passages were as similar as possible in all other respects and were presented as one of several passages that dealt with a variety of topics in psychology). As part of another task, children were then asked to choose the kind of problems they would prefer to work on when the experimenter returned at a later date. As might be expected from the previous studies, children who were given the incremental theory passage were significantly more likely to choose the problems that reflected the learning goals than children given the entity theory passage. Thus children's ideas about intelligence (whether naturally occurring or experimentally induced) appear to be related to whether they view tasks as learning opportunities or competence judgments.

As discussed in the section on development, although younger children tend to have a more incremental view of intelligence, in the middle grade-school years children become increasingly aware of normative definitions of ability and trait views of intelligence (Harari & Covington, 1981; Nicholls, 1978; Ruble, 1983; Stipek, 1981, 1984). They then have available to them alternative conceptions of ability, and therefore have a choice of which to focus on and which to use as a guide for their achievement behavior. As Dweck and Elliott (1983) pointed out, perhaps the most "mature" view represents an integration of the two theories, that is, a recognition of present differences in relative ability but an emphasis on individual growth in ability.

It is interesting to note (along with Covington, 1983b, and Gould, 1981) that Alfred Binet, the inventor of the IQ test, was clearly an incremental theorist. He believed that not only specific skills, but basic capacity, were enhanced through his training procedures: "It is in this practical sense, the only one accessible to us, that we say that the intelligence of these children has been increased. We have increased what constitutes the intelligence of a pupil: the capacity to learn and to assimilate instruction" (Binet, 1909/1973, p. 104).

We have been highlighting some of the benefits of an incremental theory and learning goals; however, as with virtually everything, extremes can be maladaptive. For example, it could be maladaptive if this orientation were accompanied by an inability to come to terms with personal limitations or limits on attainment, or if individuals with this orientation felt smart and worthwhile *only* when they were working and striving (see Janoff-Bulman & Brickman (1981) for a cogent discussion of maladaptive overpersistence). Also self-defeating might be an excessive disregard for the judgments of others or the performance requirements of one's setting, resulting in a failure to function within the larger educational or professional environment. Clearly, one's personal learning goals must be coordinated with the demands of one's environment (e.g., passing tests, publishing research results, etc.). In ideal cases, the two are not at odds.

Of course, these perils are by no means necessary concomitants of learning goals. They simply serve to illustrate that any adaptive orientation carried too far may no longer be adaptive, and to suggest that what is adaptive must always depend on the environment in which one is functioning.

Summary and Implications

In summary, an incremental theory of intelligence and learning goals appear to promote a different stance toward achievement situations than do an entity theory and performance goals. With the former, a child can be seen as approaching potential achievement situations asking: What can I learn? How can I figure this out? With the latter, children may sooner ask: Can I do it? Will I look smart? Will I reveal my ignorance? (see Dweck & Elliott, 1983; Langer & Dweck, 1973; Nicholls, 1979b). As the research evidence shows, both can foster challenge seeking and persistence. However, the former appears to do so regardless of a child's level of confidence, whereas with the latter appears to do so chiefly when there is a high and sustained level of confidence. This relationship is summarized in Table 3.1.

When we add to this the fact that confidence seems more difficult to maintain within a performance framework, we are led to the position that challenge seeking and persistence are better facilitated by attempts to foster a learning orientation than by attempts to instil confidence within a performance framework.

Nonetheless, much current educational practice aims at creating high-confidence performers, and attempts to do so by programming frequent success and praise (see Brown, Palincsar, & Purcell, 1984, for a discussion of this issue). How did this arise? I suggest that misreadings of two popular phenomena may have merged to produce this approach. First was the growing belief in "positive reinforcement" (interpreted as frequent praise for small units of

TABLE 3.1
Achievement Goals and Achievement Behavior

Goal Orientation	Confidence in Present Ability	Task Difficulty Choice	Persistence
Performance	Lo ——→ Avoid challenge		Lo
	Hi ——→ Seek challenge		Hi
Learning	Lo ⟍ Hi ⟋	Seek challenge (that fosters learning)	Hi

behavior) as the way to promote desirable behavior. Yet a deeper understanding of the principles of reinforcement would not lead one to expect that frequent praise for short, easy tasks would create a desire for long, challenging ones or promote persistence in the face of failure. On the contrary, continuous reinforcement schedules are associated with poor resistance to extinction, and errorless learning, as evidenced by Terrace's (1969) renowned pigeons, has been found to produce bizarre emotional responses following nonreinforcement.

Second was a growing awareness of teacher expectancy effects. A widely known study (Rosenthal & Jacobson, 1968) showed that teachers' impressions about students' ability (e.g., manipulated via test information) actually affected students' performance, such that the students' performance fell more in line with the teachers' expectancies. The research on this "self-fulfilling prophecy" raised serious concerns that teachers were hampering the intellectual achievement of children they labeled as having low ability. On the basis of the following assumptions, one remedy was thought to lie in making low-ability children feel like high-ability children by means of a high success rate. The first assumption was that high-IQ children are thriving (have adaptive motivational patterns) and that low-IQ children are not (have motivational patterns that interfere with learning). The second assumption, building on the first, was that the adaptive patterns of high-IQ children stem from their classroom successes, which reaffirm their high ability and instil confidence, and that the maladaptive patterns of the low-IQ child stem from failures, which reaffirm their low ability and undermine confidence. The implication, then, was to make every child feel like a high-IQ child by camouflaging existing differences among children and by programming frequent success experiences.

In view of the implications that were drawn from teacher expectancy effects, it is interesting to note that the original researchers (see, e.g., Rosenthal, 1971, 1974; Rosenthal & Jacobson, 1968) appeared to frame their work within (and provide teachers with) an incremental theory of intelligence.[3] Specifically, in the Rosenthal and Jacobson (1968) study, teachers were told that the "test for intellectual blooming" indicated that the target children would show remarkable gains in intellectual competence during the school year. Moreover, the original researchers, when hypothesizing about possible mechanisms through which gains were produced, thought in terms of teachers having stimulated intellectual growth through challenge, and, in reviewing work on negative expectancy effects, lamented that "lows" seem to be given too little work, and work that is too easy, to spur cognitive gains (Rosenthal, 1971). (Cf. Brown et al., 1984, who argue cogently that it is not ill treatment, but a failure to teach the necessary high-level skills, that accounts for much of the achievement deficit of low reading groups.) Thus, these researchers were oriented toward producing intellectual growth in children rather than simply giving them an illusion of smartness.

The next section examines the kinds of expectancies in children that are associated with challenge seeking and persistence, and the conditions that foster them. We see, first, that high-achieving children are by no means models of desirable motivational patterns. Second, the research is clear in indicating that continued success on personally easy tasks (and sometimes even on difficult tasks within a performance framework) is ineffective in producing stable confidence, challenge seeking, and persistence. Rather, procedures that specifically address motivational mediators and that provide experiences with challenging tasks (often involving some failure) within a learning framework seem to bring about more adaptive patterns (Andrews & Debus, 1978; A. Bandura & Schunk, 1981; Brown et al., 1984; Chapin & Dyck, 1976; Covington, 1983b; Dweck, 1975; Fowler & Petersen, 1981; Relich, 1983; Schunk, 1982).

GOAL EXPECTANCIES

One might suppose that children who had the highest IQ scores, achievement test scores, and grades would be the ones who had by far the highest expectancies for future test scores and grades, as well as for performance on novel, experimental tasks. Surprisingly often, this is not the case. In fact, one of the things that makes the study of expectancies particularly intriguing is that measures of children's actual competence do not strongly predict their confidence of future attainment. For example, for grade-school children, correlations between competence measures and expectancies on experimental tasks tend to

---

[3]See Dweck and Bempechat (1983) for a discussion of how teachers' theories of intelligence might influence the theories and goals children adopt (cf. Ames, 1983; Babad & Inbar, 1981; Babad, Inbar, & Rosenthal, 1982; Cooper & Good, 1983; Heckhausen & Krug, 1982; Weinstein, 1983).

run .30's and below (M. Bandura & Dweck, 1981; Crandall, 1969; Stipek & Hoffman, 1980a; see also Phillips, 1984).

One might also suppose that high-achieving children would be much less likely than low achievers, when encountering an obstacle, to attribute their difficulty to a lack of ability, and to show deteriorated performance. But this supposition, too, is often contradicted by the evidence (e.g., Licht & Dweck, 1984a, 1984b; Stipek & Hoffman, 1980; see also C.I. Diener & Dweck, 1978, 1980).

This section begins by asking: Who has confidence? That is, how are expectancies of future attainment related to past attainment? It then asks why high achievers as a group do not always have appreciably higher confidence. How can we understand why a substantial subgroup of high achievers has low expectancies, attributes failures to a lack of ability, and shows performance decrements under failure? And why, if expectancies are important determinants of achievement behavior, are these children nonetheless high achievers in grade school? And what about low achievers with high confidence? On what might their confidence be based? When would their expectancies be a spur to achievement, and when would they interfere with effective goal pursuit? Thus, this section examines the process of expectancy formation, turning to a consideration of the bases of reasonable, high and stable expectancies—ones that appear to promote choice of, and persistence on, appropriately challenging tasks.

Competence Versus Confidence: Relationship of Past Attainment to Future Expectancies

As just noted, there does not seem to be as close or consistent a link as one would expect between children's ability to perform well at a task (as indicated by task-specific measures, by past performance on related tasks, or by general measures of achievement) and their expectancy that they will perform well at the task.

In the study by M. Bandura and Dweck (1981) cited earlier, children were divided into high- and low-confidence groups based on whether or not they expected to reach their standard on the experimental task. The standard consisted of how many problems out of the 10 they needed to get right to feel satisfied, and this was compared to how many they actually expected to get right. For the low-confidence group, the mean standard was 6.83 and the mean expected number correct was 4.58. For the high-confidence group, the mean standard was 4.76 and the mean expected number correct was 6.40. In addition, on another measure (not used for classification) low-confidence children expected significantly more children to outperform them than did the high-confidence children. What is most interesting in the present context is that the low-confidence children tended to have somewhat *higher* achievement test scores (mean of 82.5 percentile for low-confidence vs. 76.1 for high-confidence—although clearly, a high achieving group on the whole). Is it that the low-confidence children did not know they were "smart"? No, they did not appear to be unaware of their relative standing. Specifically, when estimating their rank in their class, the low-confidence children rated themselves as somewhat nearer to the top than the high-confidence children. In short, although the low-confidence children did not have poor opinions of their past attainment or abilities, they faced the upcoming task with low expectancies of absolute and relative performance. (See Phillips, 1984, for an extensive study of high-achieving students who *do* have unduly low perceptions of their ability.)

A tendency toward lower expectancies among higher achievers has been especially noted in girls. For example, findings reported by V.C. Crandall (1969) suggest that bright girls are particularly likely to underestimate future performance (given what past performance would warrant). Stipek and Hoffman (1980a), in a study of first- and third-grade children, show a *negative* correlation for the third-grade girls between teachers' ratings of achievement and students' expectancies of success on the experimental tasks—the brighter a girl was considered to be, the fewer problems she expected to solve correctly ($\bar{x}$ bright = 2.6, average = 7.8, low = 8.2 out of 10). Although much research suggests that children's (including girls') perceptions of their relative standing in class becomes fairly accurate by the second and third grades (Frey & Ruble, 1983; Nicholls, 1978, 1979a; Stipek, 1984; Weinstein, 1983), the above findings suggest that this knowledge may not always be used (or perceived as relevant) in predicting future performance. Consonant with this view are the findings of Parsons, Meece, Adler, and Kaczala (1982) from their study of students enrolled in high school math courses. Although males and females did not differ in their perceptions of their current math ability or in their performance expectancy for their current math course, females reported significantly lower expectancies than did males for *future* math courses.

In a related vein, the tendency to blame intellectual failures on a lack of ability, or to show impaired performance under failure, does not appear to be closely related to measures of ability or task proficiency. For example, in the series of studies by C.I. Diener and Dweck (1978, 1980), measures of task proficiency prior to failure (ease of learning, sophistication of strategy used) did not predict children's attributions or response to subsequent failure. Once again, these tendencies are not necessarily related to perceived attainment or ability, Nicholls (1979a) obtained teachers' and students' rating of students' attainment in reading (Grades 2–8). Although girls' ratings of their attainment were higher than boys' (and teachers concurred in this assessment), girls were still more inclined than boys to attribute failure to low ability. Moreover, in a study by Licht and Dweck (1984a) that examined the impact of initial confusion on subsequent learning, high-achieving girls (who also rated themselves as bright) showed greater debilitation than low-achieving girls. Whereas in the *no-confusion* condition, the brighter the girl (by her own self-rating) the more likely she was to master the new material ($r = .47$), in the confusion condition the brighter the girl, the *less* likely she was to reach the mastery criterion ($r = .38, p_{diff} < .02$). (For boys in this study the correlation between self-rated ability and task performance increased from the no-confusion to the confusion condition: $r = .15$ and $.34$, respectively.)

In short, being a high achiever and knowing one is a high achiever does not appear to translate directly into high confidence in one's abilities when faced with difficulties, or even into the maintenance of one's ability to perform or learn under these conditions. Although, of course, learning disabilities or retardation may also give rise to such patterns (Butkowsky & Willows, 1980; Weisz, 1979), it is clear that low confidence or fragile confidence is not the sole province of the low-achieving, "failure-prone" child.

If there is a sizable proportion of high achievers with low or shaky confidence or performance disruption under failure (see Phillips, 1984), and if these variables are important to achievement, then why are these children still high achievers? Achievement may lag as a result of performance debilitation or task avoidance. That is, both the presence of failure or the opportunity to avoid challenging subject areas may lead to cumulative skill deficits in children with maladaptive patterns. For good students, grade school may not provide either of these. It may not present either tasks that are difficult enough to create failure and debilitation or the choice of not pursuing a given subject area. For these reasons, maladaptive patterns may not yet typically come into play. Licht and Dweck (1984a) have shown, however, in an experiment conducted in classrooms, that when confusion does accompany the initial attempt to learn new material, mastery of the material is seriously impaired for these children.

It may be only in subsequent school years that these maladaptive tendencies will have their impact on achievement, when these children may elect to avoid challenging courses of study, drop out of courses that pose a threat of failure, or show debilitation of performance under real difficulty. Thus, our studies may create conditions that good students will encounter fully only in later years, but that reveal underlying patterns already in place in the grade-school years.

The Formation and Maintenance of Expectancies

Why is it that high achievers (and perhaps girls in particular) do not have consistently and appreciably higher expectancies than lower achieving children? Why might some low achievers have overly high expectancies? If actual competence and past successes do not directly and by themselves drive confidence judgment, what else must be considered? We turn now to the process of expectancy formation to illuminate factors that may lead to appropriate, high, stable and resilient expectancies versus unduly low or fragile ones or unduly high, unrealistic ones.

Dweck and Elliott (1983) present a detailed, step-by-step analysis of expectancy formation. In the present discussion, we focus on three major parts of the process: (a) the way children analyze tasks, (b) the standards children adopt for judging success, and (c) the way children process outcomes.

As we see, the establishment and maintenance of appropriately high expectancies are fostered by a tendency to (a) *think strategy* (i.e., to engage in task analysis that focuses on strategy formulation, particularly on challenging tasks, under evaluative pressure and when obstacles arise); (b) *think progress* (i.e., to adopt challenging standards that are based on personal progress vs. inflated norms); and (c) *focus on past and future success,* and on effort and strategy as causes of and cures for failure.

For each of the three component processes—task analysis, standard setting, outcome processing—I first suggest some ways in which learning goals can foster higher and more sustained confidence by focusing children on strategy and progress. I then turn to two groups of children who show maladaptive patterns involving unduly low expectancies—high anxiety and learned helplessness, associated with low confidence under evaluative pressure and plunging confidence in the face of failure. I suggest ways in which children with these syndromes focus on factors and engage in practices that undermine confidence of success, despite more than adequate skills for attaining success.

Task Analysis

A great deal of research points to the conclusion that a key ingredient for generating high and stable expectancies, as well as for optimizing performance, is a tendency to "think strategy" when approaching a task, and to keep thinking strategy when difficulties arise (Anderson & Jennings, 1980; Covington, 1983a; C.I. Diener & Dweck, 1978; Dusek, Kermis, & Mergler, 1975; Meichenbaum, 1977; Wine, 1982). Indeed, the most effective programs for training cognitive skills that generalize across tasks are ones that focus on teaching children to formulate systematic problem-solving strategies (see Brown, Bransford, Ferrara, & Campione, 1983). In the motivational domain, a slightly different question arises. Here we ask: When do children fail to use the skills they have, and who are the children who are most vulnerable to this disruption? As we see, among children who clearly have mastered these "metacognitive skills" are many who fail to use them precisely when they are most needed—when tasks are challenging and the stakes are high.

Previous sections have noted the way in which performance versus learning goals can transform achievement processes. With respect to task analysis, I suggested that children with performance goals may concentrate much of their task analysis on gauging the difficulty of the task and calculating their chances of gaining favorable ability judgments. With a learning goal, children may go more directly to generating possible strategies for mastering the task. I propose here that the former tendency—focusing on task difficulty and ability versus strategy planning and implementation—may characterize children with maladaptive evaluation anxiety or learned helplessness. First, the timing and occurrence of task analysis for different children is examined. Then the nature of their analytic activity is discussed.

Children who have high evaluation anxiety or who exhibit learned helplessness in the face of failure appear to be particularly likely to cease generating problem-solving strategies when these strategies are most called for.[4] Highly anxious children often show adequate strategizing under nonevaluative conditions, but as soon as evaluative pressure is heightened (e.g., via task instructions, task description), their attention turns from task strategies, and they begin to focus more on such things as personal inadequacies, performance deficiencies, irrelevant aspects of the task, or cues from the evaluator (Doris & S.B. Sarason, 1955; Ganzer, 1968; Hill, 1972; Meichenbaum & Butler, 1978; Nottelman & Hill, 1977; I.G. Sarason, 1975; I.G. Sarason & Stoops, 1978; S.B. Sarason et al., 1960; Wine, 1971, 1982). It certainly can be argued that loss of confidence may precede the cessation of strategizing, but it can also be argued that recovery of confidence is thereby made improbable. Moreover, Meichenbaum and Butler (1978) have shown that when highly anxious students are taught to use their anxiety as a cue to be task relevant, debilitation markedly decreases.

In contrast to highly anxious children, helpless children do not tend to evidence performance disruptions under evaluative conditions until some sort of failure is experienced, whereupon strategizing ceases and deterioration may be quite rapid and quite pronounced (e.g., C.I. Diener & Dweck, 1978, 1980; Weiner, 1972, 1974, 1982). Kuhl (1981) has noted interfering "state-oriented" (vs. action-oriented) cognitions among helpless college students, and C.I. Diener and Dweck (1978, 1980) have monitored the progressive abandonment of active strategizing among helpless children following the onset of failure, along with the attendant increase in task-irrelevant statements. Their mastery-oriented counterparts, who showed no evidence of greater proficiency prior to failure, in most cases maintained, and in many cases increased, the sophistication of their problem-solving strategies under failure. This was accompanied by

---

[4]Both evaluation anxiety and learned helplessness are often assessed via questionnaires—for example, the Test Anxiety Scale for Children (Sarason et al., 1960) that assesses children's preoccupation with and somatic reactions to evaluative situations or, for helplessness, the Intellectual Achievement Responsibility Scale (Crandall, Katkovsky, & Crandall, 1965) that assesses children's attributions for their intellectual–academic successes and failures.

an increase in solution-oriented self-instructions and self-monitoring. Thus, although helpless and mastery-oriented children do not appear to differ in strategic skills, they appear to differ greatly in when they use them.

An important aspect of task analysis relates to how one partitions one's analytic efforts. A recent study by Cunnion (1984) suggested that girls compared to boys may key more on task complexity and less (or later) on generating efficient task strategies. Cunnion compared girls' and boys' solution strategies (as verbalized during problem solving) on the Raven's Progressive Matrices Test, a nonverbal intelligence test. Each problem on the test consists of a three-by-three matrix of patterns with the lower right pattern missing. The child must choose from an array the pattern that correctly completes the matrix. Whereas girls in this study tended to enumerate the various stimulus dimensions and track them over the different dimensions of the matrix before aiming for a final solution, boys tended to key on a subset of dimensions and aim at a more efficient solution. (In fact, there was a tendency for fewer boys to notice that an inserted "catch" problem had two solutions, depending on the dimension attended to.) Thus, girls' more analytic strategy may sometimes buy them greater accuracy or deeper solutions; however it is possible that such attention to task details or complexities may sometimes lead them to overestimate the task difficulty, and hence underestimate their likely performance (see also Foersterling, 1980; Licht & Dweck, 1984b; Parsons, 1983). Boys' earlier attention to solution strategies may engender or maintain higher expectancies.

There is much research to suggest that unsuccessful students (e.g., poor readers) may have insufficient appreciation of task difficulty cues, and for this reason may sometimes have inappropriately high expectancies. Specifically, work by Baker and Brown (in press); Bransford et al. (1982); Stein, Bransford, Franks, Owings, Vye, & McGraw (1982); suggested that more successful students are more attuned to task difficulty cues, are more likely to appreciate the subtleties and complexities of an intellectual task. They are also more likely to recognize when their initial ideas were in error and why. Thus, higher achieving students may analyze tasks in ways that permit them to appreciate, and prepare for, task difficulty. However, it is suggested that perhaps overanalysis of complex tasks prior to strategy formulation can unduly lower confidence.

Another critical aspect of task analysis relates to the comparison of perceived difficulty to one's own ability. In contemplating difficult tasks in the future, what aspect of his or her ability does a child invoke to gain a sense of probable outcome: a body of present, specific skills and knowledge or a repertoire of more general problem-solving strategies and learning skills? Even within an entity theory, which depicts intelligence as fixed, children may differ in what they do to get a reading on their intelligence, in what they take to be evidence of high ability.

The fact that there are many children who rate their past attainment and normative ability as superior but do not expect to display superior performance in the future suggests that perhaps they are matching the perceived requirements of future, more difficult tasks against their *present* knowledge, without allowing for intervening learning or on-task strategizing. That is, they may be asking whether they could perform now, as opposed to learn or figure out at the appropriate time. In this way, such children may view their "ability" as having been sufficient for past tests, but not for future more stringent ones.

This possibility clearly requires further investigation, but if correct, may help us understand why the expectancies of vulnerable children are found to be particularly low with respect to future, novel tasks (Lenney, 1977). Indeed, to the extent that future courses in mathematics (vs. verbal areas) tend to involve skills or conceptual frameworks clearly different from (and presumably more difficult than) the ones one has already mastered, this tendency might be particularly pronounced in mathematical areas (see Dweck & Licht, 1981; Licht & Dweck, 1984a, 1984b; see also the Conclusion section). Later, I propose that this analysis may help to clarify why such children stand ready to attribute failure to low ability when their ability should have been more than amply validated by past performance.

To summarize, given that a child has the problem-solving skills to succeed on a task, the research suggests that high confidence and optimal performance may be fostered by thinking strategy, thinking it soon, and thinking it even more when obstacles arise.

Standards

Standards have been defined as the level of performance or learning that a child feels he or she must attain in order to feel successful. It has been suggested that the most salutary standards appear to be those that focus on one's own progress and that represent a personal challenge, (i.e., that require, but are attainable through, high effort). It has been noted that learning goals tend to promote the adoption of such standards but that performance goals may focus children on normative standards that have a win–lose nature and that place success beyond the reach of many.

Although normative standards might reasonably appear to favor children who are doing well, some evidence suggests the possibility that certain children inflate how well others are likely to do. For example, C.I. Diener and Dweck (1980) asked children, after eight successfully solved problems, to indicate on a 1 to 10 scale how well they thought they had done up to that point, and then how well they thought most kids their age would do. Helpless children had thus far performed at least as well as mastery-oriented ones—helpless children were using the most advanced problem-solving strategy 50% of the time compared to 41% for mastery-oriented children. Although helpless and mastery-oriented children evaluated their own performance similarly (6.39 and 7.00, on a 10-point scale), their estimated level of other children's performance was significantly different (7.25 and 5.89). That is, helpless children imagined a more proficient comparison group than did their mastery-oriented peers.

In a related vein, Dweck, Goetz, and Strauss (1980) asked children to predict their grades for each subject on their upcoming report card, as well as to indicate how well they thought they would do in each subject compared to other children in their class. Girls had received significantly higher grades than boys on the preceding report card and were to receive significantly higher grades on the report cards which they were predicting. Although girls accurately predicted higher grades for themselves than boys did for themselves, girls still predicted they would do less well compared to others than did boys. Girls, it appears, may have imagined a higher achieving peer group than boys did. This appears consonant with Lenney's (1977) conclusion that sex differences in expectancy are particularly likely to occur when social comparison norms are introduced, with females showing a decrease and males an increase over their expectancies in more autonomous conditions.

In summary, when using normative standards of success, certain children may perceive themselves to be falling short, when in reality they are not.

We have suggested that challenging tasks and high standards within an autonomous framework bring out the best in children—strategy formulation, high effort, high satisfaction. We have noted, too, that when children adopt high-value performance goals but with low confidence, they may choose excessively easy or difficult tasks in order to avoid negative judgments of their ability. These courses of action, if habitual, may further undermine their confidence in their abilities. Unfortunately, some educators appear to have seized on the idea of lenient standards and easy successes as a means of instilling confidence in children. Yet, this very regime has been shown to create the perception of low ability (Meyer et al., 1979; cf. Meyer, 1982). I will return to this issue following an examination of how children process achievement outcomes.

Processing Outcomes

The research indicates that appropriately high and stable expectancies are associated with a tendency to highlight one's successes as indicative of future outcomes, and to key on effort and strategy as causes and cures for failure (Anderson & Jennings, 1980; Covington, 1983b; Diener & Dweck, 1978, 1980; Dweck, 1975; Schunk, 1982). Learning goals, as we have seen, focus children on effort as a chief cause of outcomes, and even in the face of failure allow children to retain positive judgments of their ability and high expectancies of future success. Performance goals, however, place more emphasis on ability and luck. They thus may foster a debilitating pattern for children who tend to use ability as the explanation for their negative outcomes, but luck as the reason for successes (rather than vice versa). We turn now to a consideration of such tendencies.

Attributions.   A wealth of research findings over the past decade has linked low expectancies and fragile expectancies (as well as performance deterioration in the face of obstacles) to the tendency to attribute failure to a lack of ability (vs. effort, strategy or luck; Butkowsky & Willows, 1980; Covington & Omelich, 1981; Relich, 1983; Stipek & Hoffman, 1980b; Weiner, 1972, 1974, 1983). Indeed this tendency, which is found more frequently among females than among males (Dweck & Reppucci, 1973; Frey & Ruble, 1983; Licht, 1984; Licht & Shapiro, 1982; Nicholls, 1975; Parsons, 1983; Parsons et al., 1982; Relich, 1983) serves as a defining characteristic of learned helplessness (Butkowsky & Willows, 1980; Diener & Dweck, 1978; Dweck, 1975; Dweck & Reppucci, 1973; Relich, 1983; Rholes, Blackwell, Jordan, & Walters, 1980) and appears to be part and parcel of high evaluation anxiety (Doris & Sarason, 1955; Ganzer, 1968).

Experimental work in which attributions have been manipulated provides evidence that they are a cause of children's responses to outcomes. Attributions have been manipulated both more directly (e.g., by means of instructional sets or explicit feedback; e.g., Anderson & Jennings, 1980; Andrews & Debus, 1978; Dweck, 1975; Schunk, 1982) and less directly (e.g., by means of feedback contingencies or outcome sequences: Dweck et al., 1978; Weiner et al., 1971; see also Weiner, 1972, 1974, 1982, 1983). They have been manipulated both in short-term experimental sessions (e.g., Anderson & Jennings, 1980; Dweck et al., 1978) and in longer term training studies (Andrews & Debus, 1978; Dweck, 1975; Fowler & Peterson, 1981; Relich, 1983; Rhodes, 1977; Schunk, 1982). Results from these studies lend support to the view that attributions mediate the expectancy and performance changes that result from success and failure.

As suggested, one of the most consistent findings in this literature is that attributions of failure to a lack of ability predict declining expectancies, decreased persistence, and impaired performance in the face of difficulty. Some children making these attributions become incapable of solving the same problems they solved only shortly before. In contrast, attributions of failure to insufficient effort, faulty strategy, or bad luck predict maintenance of high expectancies, high persistence, and good performance under failure. Indeed these attributions often predict heightened effort and improved performance during failure (e.g., use of more sophisticated strategies) and following failure (e.g., increased speed and accuracy compared to prefailure performance; see Dweck & Goetz, 1978).

It is interesting to note that children who display this more mastery-oriented response may often not even make attributions when obstacles arise (Diener & Dweck, 1978). Instead of dwelling on their difficulty and the imagined reasons for it, these children may often go directly to formulating strategies designed to remedy the difficulties and bring about success. Interestingly, these strategies are both cognitive and motivational; they consist of solution hypotheses, as well as self-instructions designed to foster confidence (e.g., "I did it before, I can do it again."), to spur effort ("The harder it gets, the harder I need to try."), and to aid concentration ("I should slow down and try to figure this out."). Thus, not only are there differences in the attributions made by vulnerable children and their less vulnerable counterparts, there are also differences in their tendencies to make attributions, that is, to focus on the causes of failure versus the cures for it.

Outcome Salience.   For children with vulnerable expectancies, negative outcomes appear to be particularly salient, and ambiguous situations appear to be more readily perceived as failures. For example, Meunier and Rule (1967) found that their high-anxious subjects responded to no-feedback trials as though they were failure trials (reporting extremely low confidence), whereas low-anxious subjects treated these like success trials. Crandall (1969) and Lenney (1977) in reviewing research on sex differences in expectancy suggested that when there are mixed outcomes or contradictory messages about ability, females may tend more to focus on the negative, and males on the positive (see also Nicholls, 1975; Relich, 1983).

In their research on learned helplessness, Diener and Dweck (1980) found strikingly different recall of successes and failures by helpless and mastery-oriented children, despite equivalent performance. Specifically, after successfully solving the first eight problems, helpless children recalled solving only 5.46 problems on the average, whereas mastery-oriented children more accurately recalled solving 7.57 problems. After four subsequent failure problems, helpless children recalled failing to solve 6.14 problems, whereas mastery-oriented children more accurately reported only 3.71 unsolved problems. Thus, although they had twice as many success outcomes as failure outcomes, helpless children actually recalled having had slightly more failures than successes (cf. Alloy & Abramson, 1979; Lewinsohn, Mischel, Chaplain & Barton, 1980 for data on differential recall of positive and negative events by depressed and nondepressed individuals).

In short, helpless versus mastery children, high versus low-anxious children, and girls versus boys are often found to evidence lower and/or more fragile expectancies of success on achievement tasks. This vulnerability may be linked to a tendency for negative outcomes to appear more salient to these groups, for failure to be more readily perceived in ambiguous situations, and for failure more than success to be seen as indicative of ability and predictive of future outcomes.

But why would individuals with acknowledged ability and a reasonable history of success so readily perceive failure and lose faith in their ability? Although the answer is far from clear, I offer one possibility, building on an earlier proposal.

Diagnosing One's Intelligence.   As suggested throughout, some children are oriented toward an entity theory of intelligence and performance goals. But, further, as just suggested, even within an entity view children may differ in how they diagnose their intelligence, in what constitutes evidence of high or low ability. Thus, for some of these children, high ability or being smart may be judged by the adequacy of existing skills and knowledge for immediate solution of difficult tasks. Ability, in this view, rather than equipping you to strategize or learn effectively, would eliminate the necessity for appreciable strategizing or further learning prior to mastery. That is, high ability, rather than being something that makes effort effective, is something that should make effort unnecessary; rather than being something that enables you to conquer difficult tasks, is something that, if present, should make tasks easy, concepts clear, and answers obvious. Difficulties, confusion, or failure, then, by indicating the inadequacy of existing knowledge for the task at hand, may thus signal to these children that their underlying ability is inadequate, that they are not smart enough. Indeed evidence can be found in Nicholls (1978) of pronounced sex difference in reasoning about ability and its relationship to effort, one that is consistent with the view we are proposing.

Why doesn't prior success, even when considerable, provide more confidence of overcoming obstacles? First, as previously noted, past success may speak only to the adequacy of existing skills for past (easier) tasks. Second, I suggest the paradoxical notion that for some of these children, the very experiences that would be expected to build confidence—previous mastery of difficult tasks—may sometimes undermine it. That is, mastery of difficult tasks by means of high effort and intensive strategizing, may for these children directly call into question their ability—for, were it not for such high effort (and perhaps the "luck" of hitting on the right strategy), their skills would clearly have been inadequate. And indeed there is a fair amount of evidence to suggest that vulnerable children (e.g., girls) more often than their confident counterparts (e.g., boys) attribute their successes to high effort or luck rather than to high ability (Bar Tal & Darom, 1979; Licht, 1984; Licht & Shapiro, 1982; Nicholls, 1975, 1978; Parsons, et al., 1982;). Thus, within this framework, mastery experiences may not build faith in future mastery, but instead may even at times instill doubts about future mastery.

This analysis may shed light on why, for example, after solving eight consecutive challenging problems, helpless children in the Diener and Dweck (1980) study believed that their chances of solving subsequent problems of the same type were only about 50%. Such children may perceive themselves to be functioning on the edge of their abilities, and difficult tasks, whether mastered or not, may serve to emphasize the precariousness of their position.

In short, this hypothesis—that vulnerable children key on the sufficiency of present knowledge as an index of intelligence—provides one way of tying together a set of disparate and puzzling phenomena, and perhaps of gaining insight into a motivational system that provides so few paths from competence to confidence.

Summary and Implications

The many ways in which children, even the most competent ones, can undermine their confidence have been noted. This is accomplished chiefly by focusing on the wrong things: on task difficulty rather than strategy, on inflated norms rather than personal progress, on failures rather than on successes as predictive of the future.

Because some children worry about failure, expect failure, perceive failure, or become mired in failures, it has often been thought that supplying a large storehouse of success might alter their focus. Yet it is becoming clear that simply programming successes does little to build the high, stable, and resilient expectancies that accompany challenge seeking and persistence (Dweck, 1975; Relich, 1983). Rather, the procedures that yield desired changes appear to be ones that incorporate challenge, and even failure, within a learning-oriented context, and that address the underlying processes—task analysis (Brown et al., 1984; Covington, 1983b; Meichenbaum & Asarnow, 1982), standard setting (A. Bandura & Schunk, 1981), and the processing of outcomes (Andrews & Debus, 1978; Dweck, 1975; Fowler & Petersen, 1981; Relich, 1983; Rhodes, 1977; Schunk, 1982). These procedures yield not just learning of specific content, but the mastery of more generalized cognitive and motivational strategies.

The task analysis and standard-setting studies have, quite reasonably, been conducted with children who are unsuccessful students, those who lag behind their age mates in reading and math and who show evidence of deficiencies in "metacognitive" skills. Yet the present analysis suggests that some kind of intervention may be in order for bright children who technically have the skills (the "how-to" analyze), but not the "what," "how much," and "when." Such children may need to be instructed in when to seek efficient strategies versus analyzing task complexity or when and how much to assess mastery strategies versus consulting existing "knowledge." For example, in contemplating a future math course (e.g., calculus), it appears fruitful to emphasize mastery experiences and strategies, and simply to check that one has specific skill prerequisites. It seems less fruitful to ask whether one's present, specific knowledge is sufficient to solve calculus problems now. As another example, in the Cunnion (1984) study described previously, there was overall no sex difference in performance, but there often is found to be a sex difference when the same test is administered with a time limit. It is possible that girls' tendency to conduct an exhaustive search puts them at a particular disadvantage under these conditions, and that an ability to switch gears into an "efficient strategy mode" would be beneficial. The key, of course, is to attain the flexibility to match one's strategy to the situation.

Motivational training in processing outcomes (e.g., instructing children to attribute failure to effort and strategy versus ability) has also been conducted primarily with less successful students (who display both a lag in skill level and a maladaptive response to difficulty). Again, the foregoing research suggests that some of the brightest students, who in grade school as yet show little or no obvious impairment in the school environment, may be prime candidates for such motivational interventions. Among these are children (e.g., bright girls) who have had early, consistent, and abundant success, yet despite this (or perhaps even because of this) do not relish the presence or the prospect of challenge.

In summary, although much research remains to be done, the evidence thus far indicates that generating a learning framework, providing experience with mastering difficulty or coping with failure within that framework, and giving explicit attention to cognitive–motivational mediators can create the conditions for building both abilities and confidence in those abilities.

DEVELOPMENTAL ISSUES:
THE EARLY SCHOOL YEARS

It has long been noted that young children arrive at school with great confidence and exuberance, but that over the next few years many become increasingly pessimistic, anxious, or apathetic. This regrettable change has typically been blamed solely on faulty educational practice, with the assumption that except for these practices the youthful optimism would inevitably continue to flourish. This section examines the precise changes in achievement beliefs that take place over the early school years, and asks how best to understand them. We suggest that the many cognitive changes (e.g., in the understanding of causal factors or in the positing of psychological traits) and the change to new kinds of tasks (intellectual ones) are not superficial changes, and in themselves make it unlikely that former patterns will automatically transfer and persist.

Achievement Patterns: Before and After

The last few sections have examined maladaptive achievement patterns involving goal value, goal expectancies, and means value. The literature suggests that consistent maladaptive patterns of beliefs and behavior are not frequently detected in young children, but that by second and third grade some of the beliefs associated with maladaptive patterns have become more common, and that by fourth and fifth grade, maladaptive behavior (such as task avoidance, and performance impairment) accompanies those beliefs (Miller, 1982; Rholes et al., 1980; Stipek, 1984; Weisz, 1979).

The young (preschool) child appears to have everything one would wish in an achievement motivational system. It is self-initiating, in that there is a plethora of high-value learning goals that children seem naturally to pursue with confidence. It is self-maintaining, in that the means seem inherently involving or pleasurable and expectancies appear hardy and resilient in the face of obstacles. And, it is self-reinforcing, in that progress and mastery provide direct rewards.

When children arrive at school, this system seems still to be operating. Kindergarteners and first graders almost uniformly have high perceptions of their ability, with most of them reporting that they rank at the top of their class (Marshall, Weinstein, Middlestadt, & Brattesani, 1980; Nicholls, 1978, 1979a; Stipek, 1981, 1984). They have extremely high expectancies of success that they tend to maintain in the face of repeated failures (e.g., Parsons & Ruble, 1977; Stipek & Hoffman, 1980a). They take credit for their successes, even "chance" successes (Miscione, Marvin, O'Brien, & Greenberg, 1978; Weisz, 1980, 1981), but clearly do not tend to focus on failures, to see them as indicative of low ability, or to show debilitation under failure (Rholes et al., 1980; Ruble, Parsons, & Ross, 1976). Younger children are also more likely than older ones to name intrinsic factors (learning goals or interest in the work) as reasons for their school work, as opposed to extrinsic factors, such as grades (see Stipek, 1984). Finally, they tend to use personal standards (such as mastery or task completion), as opposed to normative ones for judging success (Frey & Ruble, 1983; Heckhausen, 1981; Ruble, Boggiano, Feldman, & Loebl, 1980; Stipek, 1984).

The optimistic, self-enhancing biases of first graders occur despite the fact that they are not unaware of counterevidence. For example, they are already aware of the classroom ability hierarchy. Although they do not yet assume their place in that hierarchy, they are quite capable of rank ordering other class members fairly accurately (Stipek, 1981). Similarly, although they do not yet lower their expectancies readily in the face of repeated failures, they are quite capable of taking this information into account, and, in fact, do revise expectancies downward when they are judging another child's performance or when their own failure outcomes are made more salient (Stipek, Roberts, & Sanborn, 1982; Stipek & Hoffman, 1980a).

By the second and third grades, children's self-ratings and self-rankings come more into line with their report card grades and teachers' ratings, their expectancies become more conservative, their confidence declines under failure, and failure begins to have an impact on their rating of their task ability (e.g., Nicholls, 1978, 1979a; Rholes et al., 1980; Stipek, 1981, in press). Much of this can be interpreted as evidence of children's becoming increasingly "realistic," or perceptive about task difficulty and outcome cues. Therefore, many of these changing beliefs are not in themselves alarming, particularly when they do not predict maladaptive behavior. By the fourth and fifth grades, however, children's achievement behavior has become systematically related to children's beliefs, whether these beliefs are accurate or not. For example, attributions of failure to a lack of ability are now associated with lowered persistence and impaired performance (Rholes et al., 1980). Maladaptive patterns appear now to be in place.

Thus, over the course of the first 5 school years, the self-initiating, self-maintaining, and self-reinforcing system seems for many children to be running out of steam. Although many characteristics of the early system appear desirable (and possible) for older children pursuing cognitive tasks, these characteristics do not appear to be as widely maintained as one might wish. Why not? In the discussion that follows, two major factors are considered: the changing nature of the tasks and the changing definition of ability. I propose that these changes help shift the emphasis away from learning goals and toward performance goals, thus creating the conditions for maladaptive patterns to take hold.

The Changing Nature of Tasks

I suggest that the shift from physical or concrete tasks in the preschool years to increasingly complex and abstract cognitive tasks over the grade-school years in itself makes it difficult for learning goals to be maintained. Indeed, we propose that a new set of skills must be learned in order for children to sustain learning goals over these and subsequent years.

When one considers the tasks that preschool children typically pursue and master, prominent among these are physical tasks (e.g., skipping, catching a ball) and cognitive tasks with clear concrete or physical components (e.g., puzzles). For such tasks, even for young children, reasonable goals and means can be self-chosen, independently pursued, and self-judged. This is largely due to the fact that these tasks provide a clearly envisionable end-state to strive for, a visible process, clear signs of progress, and clear indications that one has arrived at the end-state. Moreover, the goals and means seem to have inherent value for children. But what about solving long math problems or comprehending reading passages?

As school tasks become more intellectual and abstract, things become less clear. What is important to know? Why? How do you learn, solve, or understand it? How do you know when you have or haven't? How do you know why you have or haven't? Will you? When? The new "metacognitive" requisites of such tasks—generating effective means and monitoring progress—have received considerable attention (see Brown et al., 1983). However, the new motivational demands—identifying high value goals and maintaining confidence and interest—have received less systematic investigation. All we can say with assurance is that many children who succeed in meeting the new cognitive demands do not succeed in meeting the new motivational ones.

As if it were not difficult enough to maintain learning goals and high confidence under these circumstances, these same years mark the emergence of an entity theory of ability and normative standards for judging ability. Thus not only do children now need the judgment of others to assess their work, that judgment may take on a new meaning.

Changing Theories of Ability

Over the first few school years, there emerges a new set of beliefs about the content of ability, the malleability of ability, the means of judging ability, and along with these beliefs, a desire to document this ability. First, there appears to be a change over the first few school years in what is meant by smartness. Early definitions invoke effort, conduct, and work habits as part of the concept, whereas later ones specifically exclude these factors (Blumenfeld, Pintrich, Wessels, & Meece, 1981; Frey & Ruble, 1983; Nicholls, 1978; Stipek, 1981; Stipek & Tannatt, 1984; Weinstein, 1983). Early school work does, in fact, involve an unclear mixture of these factors, and praise on these tasks tends to be a rather diffuse mélange of social reinforcement and performance feedback (Brophy, 1981). Many school tasks in later years tend to be more clearly a matter of cognitive skill, and the feedback children receive becomes more clearly tied to the correctness of their answers.

Second, children's early theories tend to portray ability as a mutable quality that can be increased by working hard and studying—that is, their theories tend to be more incremental in nature (Harari & Covington, 1981; Stipek, 1981, in press). In the first few grade-school years, children appear to learn the entity theory as well. They can now begin to conceive of ability as a more stable trait that is revealed (rather than modified) by effort (Harari & Covington, 1981; Nicholls, 1978; Stipek, 1981, in press; see also Dweck & Elliott, 1983). They can now ask "Am I smart?" Concomitant with this dawning hypothesis about ability is a great upsurge in children's quest for social comparison information about performance (Frey & Ruble, 1983; Ruble, 1983; Stipek, 1984; Stipek & Tannatt, 1984; Veroff, 1969). Although kindergarten children tend to make numerous peer comparisons, it is only at the end of first grade or in second grade that these comparisons come to focus specifically on relative progress or performance.

It does not seem to be simply a case of the schools forcing this view of ability on impressionable children, for it is at about this same time that a general interest in psychological traits emerges (see Damon & Hart, 1982; Dweck & Elliott, 1983). Moreover, these changes appear to occur even in schools in which ability comparisons are not made salient (see Frey & Ruble, 1983). What seems most likely is that school provides a setting in which children can formulate and test new hypotheses about intellectual ability at a time when they are cognitively equipped to do so. As implied earlier, it is not particularly alarming that children notice individual differences in progress or performance, for these differences exist. What is important is what children ultimately make of these differences. In this view, then, the issue is not whether children ever entertain an entity theory but whether they integrate it with an incremental theory and maintain an emphasis on personal progress. The danger arises when the entity theory remains predominant and leads children and their educators into practices that do not promote learning.

Summary and Implications

In this section I described the marked changes in achievement patterns that occur over the first few years of school. I then suggested that the changing nature of the tasks and changing conceptions of ability render difficult the maintenance of learning goals and thereby set the stage for the emergence and stabilization of maladaptive patterns. Although these changes toward maladaptive patterns may not always be the "fault" of the school, it certainly becomes the task of the school to facilitate the development of adaptive ones. The section that follows explores some of the possible long-term consequences of the maladaptive patterns examined here. It concludes by outlining the characteristics of an adaptive motivational system in the mature individual.

CONCLUSION

Long-term Effects of Motivational Patterns

Math Versus Verbal Achievement.   Discrepancies between males and females in mathematical achievement have long been a source of puzzlement to researchers. Although in the grade-school years girls equal boys in mathematical achievement (and surpass them in verbal achievement), in the junior high and high school years, boys pull ahead and remain ahead in math achievement (Donlon, Ekstrom, & Lockheed, 1976; Ekstrom, Donlon, & Lockheed, 1976; Fennema & Sherman, 1977; Hilton & Berglund, 1974; Maccoby & Jacklin, 1974). A wide assortment of explanations has been advanced, ranging from claims about the nature of the genetic equipment (Benbow & Stanley, 1980) to arguments about the impact of sex-role stereotypes (Sherman & Fennema, 1977). Without ruling out other explanations, we add a motivational explanation based on the research findings reviewed above. Specifically, the fact that the two sexes often display different motivational patterns, and the fact that the academic subject areas in question differ in major ways aside from the skill they require, suggest that perhaps motivational patterns contribute to these achievement discrepancies.

This suggestion is made even more plausible when one considers that (a) sex differences in math achievement are greatest among the brightest students (Astin, 1974; Fox, 1976) and (b) sex differences in motivational patterns and associated behavior appear to be greatest among the brightest students: Bright girls compared to bright boys (and compared to less bright girls) seem to display shakier expectancies, more frequent failure attributions to lack of ability, lower preference for novel, challenging tasks, and more frequent debilitation in the face of failure or confusion (Licht, 1984; Licht & Dweck, 1984a; Stipek & Hoffman, 1980). Moreover, some characteristics of math versus verbal areas are precisely ones that would work against individuals with this pattern, but would favor individuals with the more confident, challenge-seeking pattern (see Dweck & Licht, 1981; Licht & Dweck, 1984b, for a more detailed discussion of these characteristics).

First, as suggested earlier, new units and new courses in math, particularly after the grade-school years, tend to involve new skills, new concepts, or even entirely new conceptual frameworks (e.g., algebra, geometry, calculus). These new skills and concepts are not only different from, but are often more difficult than, ones the child has mastered in the past. In the verbal areas, however, once the basic skills of reading and writing are mastered, one does not as typically encounter leaps to qualitatively different tasks, tasks requiring mastery of completely unfamiliar verbal skills. Increments in difficulty appear to be more gradual and, by college, most English courses require essentially the same skills. (Even the learning of foreign languages does not typically involve learning an entirely new conceptual framework). This is not to say that one's ideas and one's means of expression do not become increasingly sophisticated, but rather that there tend not to be abrupt changes in tasks and task requirements.

This general difference between math and verbal areas may have several important psychological consequences. For one thing, as children ponder future math courses the greater novelty and difficulty of the future courses compared to present ones (i.e., the greater discrepancy between what one knows and what one needs to know do do well in the future) would be expected to precipitate declines in confidence for bright girls but not for bright boys. Indeed, as previously noted, Parsons et al. (1982) found significant sex differences in expectancies for future math courses even when females and males were equivalent in their perceptions of their present math ability and in their expectancies for their present math courses.

Another consequence of this proposed difference between math courses and highly verbal courses is that children are more likely to experience failure or confusion at the beginning of a new unit or course. This might be expected to produce debilitation (or escape attempts, such as course dropping) in bright girls, but perseverance in bright boys. And, indeed, direct support for this prediction of differential debilitation comes from the Licht and Dweck (1984a) study just described, in which confusion (or no confusion) attended the introduction of new subject matter. Moreover, an extensive study of sex differences in achievement cognitions and responses to failure recently completed by Licht (1984) yields further evidence. On the basis of their grades, Licht divided her subjects into A, B, C, and D students and, among other measures, administered the Diener and Dweck discrimination learning task. A significant sex difference was found among the A students (and only among the A students) in their response to failure, with the A girls showing the greatest debilitation of the eight groups and with the A boys being the only group to show facilitation. In addition, in line with our previous point, Licht found a strong sex difference in task preferences between A girls and A boys: The A girls much preferred tasks they knew they were good at, whereas A boys preferred ones they would have to work hard to master.

Another characteristic of math that may make it less compatible with girls' motivational pattern is the clarity and all-or-nothing quality of the outcome—one commits oneself to a specific answer that is objectively scored and deemed right or wrong. Thus, perhaps more than in verbal areas, outcomes will be seen as reflecting on ability and children who are so inclined will tend to attribute their failures to a lack of ability. Indeed, sex differences in attributions (with girls more than boys attributing failure to ability, and boys more than girls attributing success to ability) appear to be found more often for mathematical than for verbal areas (Licht, 1984).

In summary, math appears to differ from verbal areas in ways that would make it more compatible with the motivational pattern of bright boys and less compatible with that of bright girls. Thus, given two children with equal math aptitude and math achievement in the grade school years, but with these differing motivational patterns, we would predict precisely the sex differences in course taking and long-term achievement that are found to occur.

With increasing age, children will make increasingly consequential decisions, and maladaptive patterns may begin to impair their achievement and constrict their future choices. Maladaptive patterns such as those displayed by bright girls may even fail to foster intellectual growth in general. In a 38-year longitudinal study of IQ change (measured at mean ages of 4.1, 13.8, 29.7, 41.6), Kangas and Bradway (1971) found that for males the higher the preadult level the more they gained in later years, whereas for females the higher the preadult level the less they gained in later years. In fact, of the six groups in the study (males and females with high, medium, and low preadult IQs), all showed surprisingly large gains over the years (between 15 and 30 points) except the high IQ females, who showed little gain (about 5 points). Although there are many possible interpretations of these results, the general picture suggests that bright females, compared to bright males, are not thriving. Our analysis suggests that appropriate motivational interventions may help prevent some of the achievement discrepancies between the sexes.

The Self-Regulating Motivational System

I have suggested throughout that by pursuing a series of short-term performance goals, individuals may fail to pursue a course of action that leads them to where they would wish to arrive. As previously suggested, as choices take on increasing importance for the future, the ability to place the current situation in a long-term context becomes critical. I also suggest that as situations become less structured (e.g., following high school or college), self-regulation vis-à-vis long-term goals becomes increasingly critical.

While one is in school, relatively well-defined tasks present themselves automatically, along with fairly specific standards, deadlines, rewards, and punishments. After school, for many, there is less structure given by the environment, and individuals often are called on to provide their own goals, means, spurs to action or persistence, and rewards for progress. That is, the individual becomes increasingly responsible for defining and acting in accordance with his or her long-term best interest. In a sense, mature individuals must be able to step out of the immediate situation and ask: What are my long-term goals? What courses of action are consonant or dissonant with them? What do I know about (my) motivational processes that is pertinent? How can I structure my situations, restructure my cognitions, or alter my attentional focus to maximize desirable behavior?

Thus, skills that served children well in the more structured school environment may no longer be sufficient following school, and long-term attainment may be better predicted by the presence of these higher order motivational processes. To the extent that we understand the workings of motivational processes we will be in a better position to promote the acquisition of adaptive patterns and to facilitate long-term attainment.

ACKNOWLEDGMENTS

The author is grateful for the invaluable assistance of Janine Bempechat, the many contributions of Ellen Leggett, and the tireless technical assistance of Ruth Bronk and Terry Kovich. The author also acknowledges the support of grant BNS 79-14252 from the National Science Foundation and Grant HD 18238 from the National Institute of Mental Health.

REFERENCES

Alloy, L. B., & Abramson, L. Y. (1979). Judgment of contingency in depressed and nondepressed students: Sadder but wiser? *Journal of Experimental Psychology: General, 108,* 441–485.

Ames, R. (1983). Teachers' attributions for their own teaching. In J. M. Levine & M. C. Wang (Eds.), *Teacher and student perceptions: Implications for learning.* Hillsdale, NJ: Lawrence Erlbaum Associates.

Ames, C., & Ames, R. (1981). Competitive versus individualistic goal structures: The salience of past performance information for causal attributions and affect. *Journal of Educational Psychology, 73,* 411–418.

Ames, C., Ames, R., & Felker, D. W. (1977). Effects of competitive reward structure and valence of outcome on children's achievement attributions. *Journal of Educational Psychology, 69,* 1–8.

Anderson, C. A., & Jennings, D. L. (1980). When experiences of failure promote expectations of success: The impact of attributing failure to ineffective strategies. *Journal of Personality, 48,* 393–407.

Andrews, G. R., & Debus, R. L. (1978). Persistence and the causal perceptions of failure: Modifying cognitive attributions. *Journal of Educational Psychology, 70,* 154–166.

Astin, H. (1974). Sex differences in scientific and mathematical precocity. In J. C. Stanley, D. P. Keating, & L. H. Fox (Eds.), *Mathematical talent: Discovery, description and development.* Baltimore, MD.: The Johns Hopkins University Press.

Atkinson, J. W. (1957). Motivational determinants of risk-taking behavior. *Psychological Review, 64,* 359–372.

Atkinson, J. W. (1964). *An introduction to motivation.* Princeton, NJ: Van Nostrand.

Atkinson, J. W., & Birch, D. (1970). *The dynamics of action.* New York: Wiley.

Atkinson, J. W., & Birch, D. (1974). The dynamics of achievement-oriented activity. In J. W. Atkinson & J. O. Raynor (Eds.), *Motivation and achievement.* Washington, DC: Winston.

Atkinson, J. W., & Feather, N. T. (Eds.). (1966). *A theory of achievement motivation.* New York: Wiley.

Babad, E. Y., & Inbar, J. (1981). Performance and personality correlates of teachers' susceptibility to biasing information. *Journal of Personality and Social Psychology, 40,* 553–561.

Babad, E. Y., Inbar, J., & Rosenthal, R. (1982). Teachers' judgment of students' potential as a function of teachers' susceptibility to biasing information. *Journal of Personality and Social Psychology, 42,* 541–547.

Baker, L., & Brown, A. L. (in press). Metacognition and the reading process. In P. D. Pearson (Ed.), *A handbook of reading research.* New York: Longman.

Bandura, A. (1977). Self-efficacy: Toward a unifying theory of behavioral change. *Psychological Review, 84,* 191–215.

Bandura, A. (1980). The self and mechanisms of agency. In J. Suls (Ed.), *Social psychological perspectives on the self.* Hillsdale, NJ: Lawrence Erlbaum Associates.

Bandura, A., & Schunk, D. H. (1981). Cultivating competence, self-efficacy, and intrinsic interest through proximal self-motivation. *Journal of Personality and Social Psychology, 41,* 586–598.

Bandura, M., & Dweck, C. S. (1981). *Children's theories of intelligence as predictors of achievement goals.* Unpublished manuscript, Harvard University, Cambridge, MA.

Bar Tal, D., & Darom, D. (1979). Pupils' attributions for success and failure. *Child Development, 50,* 264–267.

Battle, E. S. (1965). Motivational determinants of academic task persistence. *Journal of Personality and Social Psychology, 2,* 209–218.

Battle, E. S. (1966). Motivational determinants of academic competence. *Journal of Personality and Social Psychology, 4,* 634–642.

Beck, R. C. (1983). *Motivation: Theories and principles.* Englewood Cliffs, NJ: Prentice-Hall.

Benbow, C. P., & Stanley, J. C. (1980). Sex differences in mathematics ability: Fact or artifact. *Science, 10,* 1262–4.

Berglas, S., & Jones, E. E. (1978). Drug choice as a self-handicapping strategy in response to noncontingent success. *Journal of Personality and Social Psychology, 36,* 405–417.

Binet, A. (1973). *Les idees modernes sur les enfants.* Paris: Flamarion. (Original work published 1909)

Blumenfeld, P. C., Pintrich, P. R., Wessels, K., & Meece, J. (1981, March). *Age and sex differences in the impact of classroom experiences on self-perception.* Paper presented at the annual meeting of the Society for Research in Child Development, Boston.

Bransford, J. D., Stein, B. S., Vye, N. J., Franks, J. J., Auble, P. M., Mezynski, K. J., & Perfetto, C. A. (1982). Differences in approaches to learning: An overview. *Journal of Experimental Psychology: General 3,* 390–398.

Brockner, J., & Hulton, A. J. B. (1978). How to reverse the vicious cycle of low self-esteem: The importance of attentional focus. *Journal of Experimental Psychology, 14,* 564–578.

Brophy, J. (1981). Teacher praise: A functional analysis. *Review of Educational Research, 51,* 5–32.

Brown, A. L., Bransford, J. D., Ferrara, R. A., & Campione, J. C. (1983). Learning, remembering, and understanding. In P. Mussen (Gen. Ed.), J. H. Flavell & E. M. Markman (Vol. Ed.), *The handbook of child psychology* (Vol. 1). New York: Wiley.

Brown, A. L., Palincsar, A. S., & Purcell, L. (1984). Poor readers: Teach don't label. In U. Neisser (Ed.), *The academic performance of minority children: A new perspective.* Hillsdale, NJ: Lawrence Erlbaum Associates.

Butkowsky, I. S., & Willows, D. M. (1980). Cognitive-motivational characteristics of children varying in reading ability: Evidence for learned helplessness in poor readers. *Journal of Educational Psychology, 72,* 408–422.

Carver, C. S., & Scheier, M. F. (1978). Self-focusing effects of dispositional self-consciousness, mirror presence, and audience presence. *Journal of Personality and Social Psychology, 36,* 324–332.

Carver, C. S., & Schier, M. F. (1981). Attention and self-regulation: A control-theory approach to human behavior. New York: Springer-Verlag.

Chapin, M., & Dyck, D. G. (1976). Persistence in children's reading behavior as a function of a length and attribution retraining. *Journal of Abnormal Psychology, 85,* 511–515.

Cooper, H. M., & Good, T. L. (1983). *Pygmalion grows up: Studies in the expectation communication process.* New York: Longman.

Covington, M. V. (1983a). Motivated cognitions. In S. G. Paris, G. M. Olson, & H. W. Stevenson (Eds.), *Learning and motivation in the classroom.* Hillsdale, NJ: Lawrence Erlbaum Associates.

Covington, M. V. (1983b). Strategic thinking and the fear of failure. In S. Chipman, J. Segal, R. Glaser (Eds.), *Thinking and learning skills: Current research and open questions* (Vol. 2). Hillsdale, NJ: Lawrence Erlbaum Associates.

Covington, M. V., & Beery, R. (1976). *Self-worth and school learning.* New York: Holt, Rinehart & Winston.

Covington, M. V., & Omelich, C. L. (1979a). Effort: The double-edged sword in school achievement. *Journal of Educational Psychology, 71,* 169–182.

Covington, M. V., & Omelich, C. L. (1979b). It's best to be able and virtuous too: Student and teacher evaluative responses to successful effort. *Journal of Educational Psychology, 71,* 688–700.

Covington, M. V., & Omelich, C. L. (1981). As failures mount: Affective and cognitive consequences of ability demotion in the classroom. *Journal of Educational Psychology, 73*(6), 796–808.

Crandall, V. C. (1967). Achievement behavior in the young child. In W. W. Hartup (Ed.), *The young child: Reviews of research.* Washington, DC: National Association for the Education of Young Children.

Crandall, V. C. (1969). Sex differences in expectancy of intellectual and academic reinforcement. In C. P. Smith (Ed.), *Achievement-related motives in children.* New York: Russell Sage.

Crandall, V. C., Katkovsky, W., & Crandall, V. J. (1965). Children's beliefs in their own control of reinforcements in intellectual-academic situations. *Child Development, 36,* 91–109.

Crandall, V. J. (1963). Achievement. In H. Stevenson (Ed.), *Child psychology: Sixty second yearbook of the National Society for the Study of Education.* Chicago: University of Chicago Press.

Crandall, V. J., Katkovsky, W., & Preston, A. (1960). A conceptual formulation for some research on children's achievement development. *Child Development, 31,* 787–797.

Crandall, V. J., Katkovsky, W., & Preston, A. (1962). Motivational and ability determinants of young children's intellectual achievement behaviors. *Child Development, 33,* 643–661.

Cunnion, M. (1984). *Sex differences in problem-solving strategies.* Unpublished doctoral dissertation, Harvard University, Cambridge, MA.

Damon, W., & Hard, D. (1982). The development of self-understanding from infancy through adolescence. *Child Development, 53,* 841–864.

deCharms, R., & Carpenter, V. (1968). Measuring motivation in culturally disadvantaged school children. In H. J. Klausmeier & G. T. O'Hearn (Eds.), *Research and development toward the improvement of education.* Madison: Dembar Education Services.

Deci, E. L. (1975). *Intrinsic motivation.* New York: Plenum.

Deci, E. L., & Ryan, R. M. (1980). The empirical exploration of intrinsic motivational processes. In L. Berkowitz (Ed.), *Advances in experimental social psychology* (Vol. 13). New York: Academic Press.

Diener, C. I., & Dweck, C. S. (1978). An analysis of learned helplessness: Continuous changes in performance, strategy, and achievement cognitions following failure. *Journal of Personality and Social Psychology, 36,* 451–462.

Diener, C. I., & Dweck, C. S. (1980). An analysis of learned helplessness: II. The processing of success. *Journal of Personality and Social Psychology, 39,* 940–952.

Diener, E., & Srull, T. K. (1979). Self-awareness, psychological perspective, and self-reinforcement in relation to personal and social standards. *Journal of Personality and Social Psychology, 37,* 413–423.

Dollard, J., & Miller, N. E. (1950). Personality and psychotherapy. New York: McGraw-Hill.

Donlon, T., Ekstrom, R., & Lockheed, M. (1976, September). *Comparing the sexes on achievement items of varying content.* Paper presented at the meeting of the American Psychological Association, Washington, DC.

Doris, J., & Sarason, S. B. (1955). Test anxiety and blame assignment in a failure situation. *Journal of Abnormal Psychology, 30,* 335–338.

Dusek, J. B., Kermis, M. D., & Mergler, N. L. (1975). Information processing in low- and high-test anxious children as a function of grade level and verbal labelling. *Developmental Psychology, 11,* 651–652.

Dweck, D. S. (1975). The role of expectations and attributions in the alleviation of learned helplessness. *Journal of Personality and Social Psychology, 31,* 674–685.

Dweck, C. S., & Bempechat, J. (1983). Children's theories of intelligence: Impact on learning. In S. G. Paris, G. M. Olson, & H. W. Stevenson (Eds.), *Learning and motivation in the classroom.* Hillsdale, NJ: Lawrence Erlbaum Associates.

Dweck, C. S., Davidson, W., Nelson, S., & Enna, B. (1978). Sex differences in learned helplessness: II. The contingencies of evaluative feedback in the classroom and III. An experimental analysis. *Developmental Psychology, 14,* 268–276.

Dweck, C. S., & Elliott, E. S. (1983). Achievement motivation. In P. Mussen (Gen. Ed.), E. M. Hetherington (Vol. Ed.), *Handbook of child psychology* (Vol. 4). New York: Wiley.

Dweck, C. S., & Goetz, T. E. (1978). Attributions and learned helplessness. In J. H. Harvey, W. Ickes, & R. F. Kidd (Eds.), *New directions in attribution research* (Vol. 2). Hillsdale, NJ: Lawrence Erlbaum Associates.

Dweck, C. S., Goetz, T. E., & Strauss, N. L. (1980). Sex differences in learned helplessness: IV. An experimental and naturalistic study of failure generalization and its mediators. *Journal of Personality and Social Psychology, 38,* 441–452.

Dweck, C. S., & Licht, B. G. (1981). Learned helplessness and intellectual achievement. In J. Garber & M. E. P. Seligman (Eds.), *Human helplessness: Theory and applications.* New York: Academic Press.

Dweck, C. S., & Reppucci, N. D. (1973). Learned helplessness and reinforcement responsibility in children. *Journal of Personality and Social Psychology, 25,* 109–116.

Dweck, C. S., Tenney, Y., & Dinces, N. (1982). [Implicit theories of intelligence as determinants of achievement goal choice] Unpublished data, Harvard University.

Ekstrom, R., Donlon, T., & Lockheed, M. (1976, April). *The effect of sex-biased content in achievement test performance.* Paper presented at the meeting of the American Educational Research Association, San Francisco, CA.

Elliott, E. S., & Dweck, C. S. (1981). *Children's achievement goals as determinants of learned helplessness and mastery-oriented achievement patterns: An experimental analysis.* Unpublished manuscript, Harvard University, Cambridge, MA.

Entin, E. E., & Raynor, J. O. (1973). Effects of contingent future orientation and achievement motivation on performance in two kinds of tasks. *Journal of Experimental Research in Personality, 6,* 314–320.

Fennema, E., & Sherman, J. (1977). Sex-related differences in mathematics achievement, spatial visualization, and affective factors. *American Educational Research Journal, 14,* 51–71.

Foersterling, F. (1980). Sex differences in risk-taking: Effects of subjective and objective probability of success. *Personality and Social Psychology Bulletin, 6,* 149–152.

Fowler, J. W., & Peterson, P. L. (1981). Increasing reading persistence and altering attributional style of learned helpless children. *Journal of Educational Psychology, 73,* 251–260.

Fox, L. (1976). Sex differences in mathematical precocity: Bridging the gap. In D. P. Keating (Ed.), *Intellectual talent: Research and development.* Baltimore, MD: The Johns Hopkins University Press.

Frankl, A., & Snyder, M. L. (1978). Poor performance following unsolvable problems: Learned helplessness or egotism? *Journal of Personality and Social Psychology, 36,* 1415–1423.

Frey, K. S., & Ruble, D. N. (1983). *What children say to each other when the teacher's not around: Self-evaluation and social comparison in the classroom.* Unpublished manuscript, Princeton University, Princeton, NJ.

Ganzer, V. J. (1968). Effects of audience presence and test anxiety on learning and retention in a serial learning situation. *Journal of Personality and Social Psychology,8,* 194–199.

Gould, S. J. (1981). *The mismeasure of man.* New York: Norton.

Harari, O., & Covington, M. V. (1981). Reactions to achievement behavior from a teacher and student perspective: A developmental analysis. *American Educational Research Journal, 18,* 15–28.

Harter, S., & Connell, J. P. (1981, August). *A structural model of children's self percep-tions of competence, control, and motivational orientation in the cognitive domain.* Paper presented at the meeting of the International Society for the Study of Behav-ioral Development, Toronto.

Heckhausen, H. (1967). *The anatomy of achievement motivation.* New York: Academ-ic Press.

Heckhausen, H. (1981). The development of achievement motivation. In W. W. Har-tup (Ed.), *Review of child development research* (Vol. 6). Chicago: University of Chicago Press.

Heckhausen, H., & Krug, S. (1982). Motive modification. In A. Steward (Ed.), *Moti-vation and society: Essays in honor of David C. McClelland.* San Francisco: Jossey-Bass.

Hill, K. T. (1972). Anxiety in the evaluative context. In W. W. Hartup (Ed.), *The young child* (Vol. 2). Washington, DC: National Association for the Education of Young Children.

Hilton, T., & Berglund, G. (1974). Sex differences in mathematics achievement—A longitudinal study. *Journal of Education Research, 67,* 231–7.

Hull, C. L. (1943). *Principles of behavior.* New York: Appleton-Century-Crofts.

Hull, C. L. (1952).*A behavior system.* New Haven, CT: Yale University Press.

Janoff-Bulman, R., & Brickman, P. (1981). Expectations and what people learn from failure. In N. T. Feather (Ed.), *Expectancy, incentive, and action.* Hillsdale, NJ: Lawrence Erlbaum Associates.

Kangas, J., & Bradway, K. (1971). Intelligence at middle age: A thirty-eight year fol-low-up. *Developmental Psychology, 5,* 333–37.

Kuhl, J. (1981). Motivational and functional helplessness: The moderating effect of state versus action orientation. *Journal of Personality and Social Psychology, 40,* 155–170.

Langer, E. J., & Dweck, C. S. (1973). *Personal politics.* Englewood Cliffs, NJ: Prentice-Hall.

Lekarczyk, D. T., & Hill, K. T. (1969). Self-esteem, test anxiety, stress, and verbal learning. *Developmental Psychology, 1,* 147–154.

Lenney, E. (1977). Women's self confidence in achievement settings. *Psychological Bulletin, 84,* 1–13.

Lepper, M. R. (1980). Intrinsic and extrinsic motivation in children: Detrimental effects of superfluous social controls. In W. A. Collins (Ed.), *Minnesota symposium on child psychology* (Vol. 14). Hillsdale, NJ: Lawrence Erlbaum Associates.

Lepper, M. R., & Greene, D. (Eds.). (1978). *The hidden costs of reward: New perspectives on the psychology of human motivation.* Hillsdale, NJ: Lawrence Erlbaum Associates.

Lewinsohn, P. M., Mischel, W., Chaplain, W., & Barton, R. (1980). Social competence and depression: The role of illusory self-perceptions? *Journal of Abnormal Psychology, 89,* 203–212.

Licht, B. G. (1984). Unpublished data, Florida State University.

Licht, B. G., & Dweck, C. S. (1984a). Determinants of academic achievement: The interaction of children's achievement orientations with skill area. *Developmental Psychology, 20,* 628–636.

Licht, B. G., & Dweck, C. S. (1984b). Sex differences in achievement orientations: Consequences for academic choices and attainments. In M. Marland (Ed.), *Sex differentiation and schooling.* London: Heinemann.

Licht, B. G., & Shapiro, S. H. (1982, September). *Sex differences in attributions among high achievers.* Paper presented at the meeting of the American Psychological Association, Washington, DC.

Maccoby, E. E., & Jacklin, C. N. (1974). *The psychology of sex differences.* Stanford, CA: Stanford University Press.

Maehr, M. L., & Stallings, W. M. (1972). Freedom from external evaluations. *Child Development, 43,* 177–185.

Mandler, G., & Sarason, S. B. (1952). A study of anxiety and learning. *Journal of Abnormal and Social Psychology, 47,* 166–173.

Marshall, H. H., Weinstein, R. S., Middlestadt, & Brattesani, K. A. (1980, April). *"Everyone's smart in our class": Relationship between classroom characteristics and perceived differential teacher treatment.* Paper presented at the American Educational Research Association, Boston.

McClelland, D. C., Atkinson, J. W., Clark, R. A., & Lowell, E. L. (1953). *The achievement motive.* New York: Appleton-Century-Crofts.

McCoy, N. (1965). Effects of text anxiety on children's performance as a function of instructions and type of task. *Journal of Personality and Social Psychology, 2,* 634–641.

Meichenbaum, D. (1977). *Cognitive-behavior modification: An integrative approach.* New York: Plenum Press.

Meichenbaum, D., & Asarnow, J. (1982). Cognitive-behavior modification and metacognitive development: Implication for the classroom. In P. C. Kendall & S. D. Hollon (Eds.), *Cognitive-behavioral interventions: Theory, research, and procedures.* New York: Academic Press.

Meichenbaum, D., & Butler, L. (1978). Toward a conceptual model for the treatment of test anxiety. Implications for research and treatment. In I. G. Sarason (Ed.), *Test anxiety: Theory research, and applications.* Hillsdale, NJ: Lawrence Erlbaum Associates.

Meunier, C., & Rule, B. G. (1967). Anxiety, confidence and conformity. *Journal of Personality, 35,* 498–504.

Meyer, W. U. (1982). Indirect communications about perceived ability estimates. *Journal of Educational Psychology, 74,* 888–897.

Meyer, W., Bachmann, M., Brevimann, U., Hempelmann, M., Plöger, F., Spiller, H. (1979). The informational value of evaluative behavior: Influences of praise and blame on perceptions of ability. *Journal of Educational Psychology, 71,* 259–268.

Meyers, W. W., Folkes, V., & Weiner, B. (1976). The perceived informational value and affective consequences of choice behavior and intermediate difficulty task selection. *Journal of Research in Personality, 10,* 410–423.

Miller, A. (1982). *Self-recognitory schemes and achievement behavior: A developmental study.* Unpublished doctoral dissertation, Purdue University, West Lafayette, IN.

Miller, N. E. (1951). Learnable drives and rewards. In S. S. Stevens (Ed.), *Handbook of experimental psychology.* New York: Wiley.

Miscione, J. L., Marvin, R. S., O'Brien, R. G., & Greenberg, M. T. (1978). A developmental study of preschool children's understanding of the words "know" and "guess." *Child Development, 49,* 1107–1113.

Moulton, R. W. (1965). Effects of success and failure on level of aspiration as related to achievement motives. *Journal of Personality and Social Psychology, 1,* 399–406.

Murray, H. A. (1938).*Explorations in personality.* New York: Oxford University Press.

Nicholls, J. G. (1975). Causal attributions and other achievement related cognitions. Effects of task outcome, attainment value, and sex. *Journal of Personality and Social Psychology, 31,* 379–389.

Nicholls, J. G. (1976). Effort is virtuous but it's better to have ability. Evaluative responses to perceptions of effort and ability. *Journal of Research in Personality, 10,* 306–315.

Nicholls, J. G. (1978). The development of the concepts of effort and ability, perception of academic attainment, and the understanding that difficult tasks require more ability. *Child Development, 49,* 800–814.

Nicholls, J. G. (1979a). Development of perception of own attainment and causal attributions for success and failure in reading. *Journal of Educational Psychology, 71,* 94–99.

Nicholls, J. G. (1979b). Quality and equality in intellectual development. *American Psychologist, 34,* 1071–1084.

Nicholls, J. G. (1981). *Striving to demonstrate and develop ability: A theory of achievement motivation.* Unpublished manuscript, Purdue University, West Lafayette, IN.

Nicholls, J. G. (1983). Conceptions of ability and achievement motivation: A theory and its implications for education. In S. G. Paris, G. M. Olson, & H. W. Stevenson (Eds.), *Learning and motivation in the classroom.* Hillsdale, NJ: Lawrence Erlbaum Associates.

Nicholls, J. G., & Dweck, C. S. (1979). *A definition of achievement motivation.* Unpublished manuscript, University of Illinois, Champaign, IL.

Nottelman, E. D., & Hill, K. T. (1977). Test anxiety and off-task behavior in evaluative situations. *Child Development, 48,* 225–231.

Parsons, J. E. (1983). Expectancies, values, and academic behaviors. In J. T. Spence (Ed.), *Achievement and achievement motivation.* San Francisco: Freeman.

Parsons, J. E., Meece, J. L., Adler, T. F., Kaczala, C. M. (1982). Sex differences in attributions and learned helplessness. *Sex Roles, 8,* 421–432.

Parsons, J. E., & Ruble, D. N. (1977). The development of achievement-related expectancies. *Child Development, 48,* 1075–1079.

Phillips, D. (1984). The illusion of incompetence among high-achieving children. *Child Development, 55,* 2000–2016.

Raynor, J. O., & Smith, C. P. (1966). Achievement related motives and risk-taking in games of skill and chance. *Journal of Personality, 34,* 176–198.

Relich, J. D. (1983). Attribution and its relation to other affective variables in predicting and inducing arithmetic achievement. Unpublished doctoral dissertation, University of Sydney, Sydney, Australia.

Rhodes, W. A. (1977). *Generalization of attribution retraining.* Unpublished doctoral dissertation, University of Illinois, Champaign IL.

Rholes, W. S., Blackwell, J., Jordan, C., & Walters, C. (1980). A developmental study of learned helplessness. *Developmental Psychology, 16,* 616–624.

Rosenthal, R. (1971). Teacher expectations and their effects upon children. In G. S. Lesser (Ed.), *Psychology and educational practice.* Glenview, IL: Scott, Foresman.

Rosenthal, R. (1974). *On the social psychology of the self-fulfilling prophecy: Further evidence for Pygmalion effects and their mediating mechanisms.* New York: MSS Modular Publications.

Rosenthal, R., & Jacobson, L. (1968). *Pygmalion in the classroom.* New York: Holt, Rinehart & Winston.

Ruble, D. N. (1983). The development of social comparison processes and their role in achievement-related self-socialization. In E. T. Higgins, D. N. Ruble & W. W. Hartup (Eds.), *Social cognition and social development: A sociocultural perspective.* New York: Cambridge University Press.

Ruble, D. N., Boggiano, A. K., Feldman, N. S., & Loebl, J. H. (1980). A developmental analysis of the role of social comparison in self-evaluation. *Developmental Psychology, 16,* 105–115.

Ruble, D. N., Parsons, J. E., & Ross, J. (1976). Self-evaluative responses of children in achievement settings. *Child Development, 47,* 990–997.

Ryan, R. M., Mims, V., & Koestner, R. (in press). The relationship of reward contingency and interpersonal context to intrinsic motivation: A review and test using cognitive evaluation theory. *Journal of Personality and Social Psychology.*

Salili, F., Maehr, M., Sorensen, R., & Fyans, L. (1976). A further consideration of the effects of evaluation on motivation. *American Educational Research Journal, 13,* 85–102.

Sarason, I. G. (1972). Experimental approaches to test anxiety: Attention and the uses of information. In C. D. Spielberger (Ed.), *Anxiety and behavior: Current trends.* New York: Academic Press.

Sarason, I. G. (1975). Anxiety and self-preoccupation. In I. G. Sarason & C. D. Spielberger (Ed.), *Stress and anxiety* (Vol. 2). Washington, DC: Hemisphere.

Sarason, I. G., & Stoops, R. (1978). Test anxiety and the passage of time. *Journal of Consulting and Clinical Psychology, 46,* 102–109.

Sarason, S. B., Davidson, K., Lighthall, F., Waite, F., & Ruebush, B. (1960). *Anxiety in elementary school children.* New York: Wiley.

Sarason, S. B., & Mandler, G. (1952). Some correlates of test anxiety. *Journal of Abnormal and Social Psychology, 47,* 561–565.

Schunk, D. H. (1982). Effects of effort attributional feedback on children's perceived self-efficacy and achievement. *Journal of Educational Psychology, 74,* 548–556.

Sherman, J., & Fennema, F. (1977). The study of mathematics by high school girls and boys: Related variables? *American Educational Research Journal, 14,* 159–68.

Stein, B. S., Bransford, J. D., Franks, J. J., Owings, R. A., Vye, N. J., & McGraw, W. (1982). Differences in the precision of self-generated elaborations. *Journal of Experimental Psychology: General, 3,* 399–405.

Stipek, D. J. (1981). Children's perceptions of their own and their classmates' ability. *Journal of Educational Psychology, 73,* 404–410.

Stipek, D. J. (1984). *Developmental aspects of achievement motivation in children.* In R. Ames & C. Ames (Eds.), *Research on motivation in education* (Vol. 1): *Student motivation.* New York: Academic Press.

Stipek, D. J., & Hoffman, J. M. (1980a). Children's achievement related expectancies as a function of academic performance histories and sex. *Journal of Educational Psychology, 72,* 861–865.

Stipek, D. J., & Hoffman, J. (1980b). Development of children's performance-related judgments. *Child Development, 51,* 912–914.

Stipek, D. J., Roberts, T., & Sanborn, M. (1982). *The effect of reward and perspective on children's performance expectations for themselves and another child.* Unpublished manuscript, University of California at Los Angeles, Los Angeles, CA.

Stipek, D. J., & Tannatt, L. M. (1984). Children's judgment of their own and their peers' academic competence. *Journal of Educational Psychology, 76,* 75–84.

Terrace, H. S. (1969). Extinction of a discriminative operant following discrimination learning with and without errors. *Journal of the Experimental Analysis of Behavior, 12,* 571–582.

Veroff, J. (1969). Social comparison and the development of achievement motivation. In C. P. Smith (Ed.), *Achievement-related motives in children.* New York: Russell Sage.

Weiner, B. (1972). *Theories of motivation: From mechanism to cognition.* Chicago: Markham.

Weiner, B. (Ed.). (1974). *Achievement motivation and attribution theory.* Morristown, NJ: General Learning Corp.

Weiner, B. (1982). An attribution theory of motivation and emotion. In H. Krohne & L. Laux (Eds.), *Achievement, stress, and anxiety.* Washington, DC: Hemisphere.

Weiner, B. (1983). *Principles for a theory of student motivation and their practice within an attributional framework.* In R. Ames & C. Ames (Eds.), *Student motivation* (Vol. 1). New York: Academic Press.

Weiner, B., Frieze, I. H., Kukla, A., Reed, L., Rest, S., & Rosenbaum, R. M. (1971). *Perceiving the causes of success and failure.* Morristown, NJ: General Learning Press.

Weiner, B., & Graham, S. (1984). *An attributional approach to emotional development.* In C. Izard, J. Kagen, & R. Zajonc, (Eds.), *Emotion, cognition and behavior.* Cambridge, MA: Harvard University Press.

Weiner, B., & Kukla, A. (1970). An attributional analysis of achievement behavior. *Journal of Personality and Social Psychology, 15,* 1–20.

Weinstein, R. S. (1983). *Student mediation of classroom expectancy effects.* In J. B. Dusek (Ed.), *Teacher expectancies.* Hillsdale, NJ: Lawrence Erlbaum Associates.

Weisz, J. R. (1979). Perceived control and learned helplessness among mentally retarded and non-retarded children. *Developmental Psychology, 15,* 311–319.

Weisz, J. R. (1980). Developmental change in perceived control: Recognizing noncontingency in the laboratory and perceiving it in the world. *Developmental Psychology, 16* (5), 385–390.

Weisz, J. R. (1981, August). *Achievement behavior, contingency judgments, and the perception of control.* Paper presented at the Meetings of the International Society for the Study of Behavioral Development, Toronto.

Weisz, J. R., & Stipek, D. J. (1982). Competence, contingency, and the development of perceived control. *Human Development, 25,* 250–281.

Wine, J. D. (1971). Test anxiety and direction of attention. *Psychological Bulletin, 76,* 92–104.

Wine, J. D. (1982). Evaluation anxiety: A cognitive-attentional construct. In H. W. Krohne & L. Laux (Eds.), *Achievement, stress, and anxiety.* Washington, DC: Hemisphere.

Zajonc, R. B. (1980). Feeling and thinking: Preferences need no inferences. *American Psychologist, 35,* 151–175.

Intellectual Abilities and Aptitudes

John B. Carroll
*University of North
Carolina at Chapel Hill*

This is not a standard textbook chapter on intelligence. It does not discuss such matters as criticisms of intelligence tests; the question of test bias; social class, race, and sex differences; and other, somewhat peripheral issues, such as the representation of abilities in the brain. Treatments of these and other topics may be found in textbooks and handbooks such as those by Anastasi (1982b), Brody and Brody (1976), Butcher (1968), Jensen (1980, 1981), Pyle (1979), Sternberg (1982b), Vernon (1961, 1979), and Willerman (1979).

Instead, this chapter gives major emphasis to the multifactorial interpretation of intelligence, the identification and definition of abilities, and ways of relating abilities to the knowledge bases, cognitive operations, and cognitive strategies involved in the performance of intellectual tasks. It presents points of view and information, as needed, on the nature of abilities, the nature/nurture issue, the importance of the dimensional analysis of abilities, the development of abilities, and the abilities measured by widely used tests. It offers a model, the Ability/Difficulty Interaction (A/DI) Model, for defining abilities and relating them to experimental studies and analyses of intellectual performances that have been conducted in cognitive psychology. It cannot provide complete coverage of either the multifactorial analysis of abilities or the analysis of cognitive processes, but it suggests and illustrates ways in which relationships between these two fields can be fruitfully studied. It is based on the premises that intellectual abilities and their psychological bases can be scientifically studied and that solid progress can be made toward a generally acceptable and well-founded theory of individual differences in abilities (Carroll & Horn, 1981).

New Views of Intellectual Abilities and Aptitudes

During the first 5 or 6 decades of the intelligence testing movement, the view accepted by many workers in the field was that intelligence is a single entity in the individual that is more or less fixed, rooted in the constitution of the individual and largely determined by genetic factors. Although it was granted that environmental influences were also manifested in intelligence test scores, such environmental influences often were considered simply as "noise" that interfered with obtaining completely accurate estimates of the individual's "true" genetic intelligence.

Over the past 2 decades, however, a view that is almost the exact opposite of this has been promoted. It is held by a number of distinguished authorities that intelligence is not a fixed entity characteristic of the individual. Rather, a score on an intelligence test (however expressed) is regarded as being simply "a measure of what the individual has learned to do and what he or she knows at the time [of testing]" (Anastasi, 1981, p. 6). It is seen as a measure of the extent to which the individual has acquired generalized cognitive skills that are widely applicable in solving problems, learning new ideas and facts, and dealing with life's problems. If genetic influences are in any degree responsible for the score that an individual is able to attain on a so-called intelligence test, such influences are seen as arising from complex interactions of genes with environmental factors. In any case, environmental factors, such as experience and learning, are regarded as important determiners of score levels.

Further, it is urged by many authorities that the most useful way of studying intelligence and intellectual abilities is to examine the detailed processes involved in the tasks set on ability tests. As Glaser (1972) said, "A fruitful approach is the conceptualization of individual difference variables in terms of the process constructs of contemporary theories of learning, development, and human performance" (p. 9). An early attempt to do just this was made by Carroll (1976) in his admittedly armchair analysis of a number of intellectual abilities in terms of the memory components used in the tasks, the cognitive operations and strategies used by individuals in performing the tasks, and the types of responses required. Carroll emphasized that all performances required in intellectual ability tests could be regarded as cognitive *tasks,* and that in consequence it should be possible to study ability test performances by methods more prevalent in laboratories of experimental psychology than in laboratories of psychometrics. Such possibilities had already been explored in investigations by Hunt and colleagues (Hunt, 1974, 1976; Hunt, Frost, & Lunneborg, 1973; Hunt, Lunneborg, & Lewis, 1975), initiating a line of research that has increasingly flourished (e.g., Bisanz, Danner, & Resnick, 1979; Chiang & Atkinson, 1976; Cohen & Sandberg, 1980; Egan, 1981; Keating & Bobbitt, 1978; Spiegel & Bryant, 1978; Sternberg, 1977).

As a result of many social forces, psychologists have begun to take very seriously the possibility of improving and enhancing intellectual abilities through special programs of training, coaching, education, and other types of intervention. Detterman and Sternberg (1982) published a volume in which some of these possibilities were surveyed. An assumption underlying this direction of inquiry is that whatever genetic factors may be involved in determining intellectual abilities, environmental factors make substantial contributions to their variance, and that these environmental factors can be manipulated, partly through analysis of cognitive task requirements and partly through devising treatments that will enable individuals better to meet such requirements.

This is not to say that older views of intelligence and aptitudes have been completely abandoned. The notion that there exists a strong "general" or "g" factor of intelligence, as originally proclaimed by Spearman (1927), has been staunchly defended by such writers as Jensen (1980, 1981) and Eysenck (1979; see also Eysenck vs. Kamin, 1981). Both Jensen and Eysenck see the genetic component of intelligence variance as being very large, perhaps as large as 80% of the total variance corrected for attenuation. Nevertheless, these writers are careful to point out that general intelligence is not a *thing,* but an abstraction revealed in performances of people on tests and other tasks, and in the substantial correlations of those performances over a wide variety of tasks. They emphasize the cognitive analysis of these tasks—their complexity and other characteristics—in attempting to define general intelligence (see, for example, Jensen, 1981, pp. 59–62).

Some Points of View Adopted Here

Tests are not the only means to gain information on people's intellectual abilities, aptitudes, and abilities; they are only the most widely used methods. But tests must be regarded as simply indicators of performance at a given point of time under given conditions. If these limitations are taken into account, it is believed that the analysis of test performances can be revealing and informative.

As Anastasi (1980) observed, terms like *intelligence, ability, aptitude,* and even *achievement* have acquired certain unfortunate surplus meanings over the years—surplus meanings in which notions of genetic determination, trait constancy, and test bias play some role. Authors and publishers of intelligence tests have tended to substitute more neutral terms in naming their tests. Nevertheless, some of the *core* meanings of these terms are valuable and should be retained.

On intelligence: The old saying, originated by Boring (1923), that intelligence is what the intelligence tests test, can be taken seriously by pursuing it to examine the tests carefully and analytically in terms of the cognitive skills, knowledges, and processes the presence or absence of which they test. Through methods that are considerably elaborated upon here, it becomes evident that *intelligence* is a term that refers to some composite of many abilities, some of which are of a quite general and widely applicable character, others of which have to do with much more narrowly constrained domains of performance. The term *intelligence* need have no special implication regarding the degree to which a particular level of performance is determined either by genetic or environmental factors.

On ability: This is probably the most neutral term of the lot. It may be taken to refer merely to present capability to perform some class of tasks (assuming the individual is at least awake, attentive, motivated, etc.), with no implication as to how such a capability has arisen. At the same time, its use usually implies that the capability is a more than ephemeral characteristic of the individual— that it has developed or been acquired over days, weeks, months, or years, and that it will still be present on further occasions in the foreseeable future. This is because, as pointed out by Carr and Kingsbury (1938), ability is a predictive concept that refers to the possibility of repeating an act or performance at a later time. They add that ability "is an attributive definition of the reactive nature of the individual in virtue of his possession of those constitutional conditions upon which the occurrence of the act [or performance] is contingent and which render possible its future performance" (p. 355).

On aptitude: An aptitude, we may assume, is an ability (however acquired) that is in some way, or to some substantial extent, prerequisite for further development or learning, in such a way that a measure of aptitude can be helpful in predicting the amount of that further development or learning. Just as the term *ability* carries no necessary surplus meaning concerning the source of an ability, the term *aptitude* need carry no such surplus meaning either. On this basis, almost any ability may represent an aptitude for some kind of development or learning.

On achievement: Clearly, an achievement is a learned capability to perform something, but its attainment in some way depends on the intellectual capacity or aptitude present in the learner. Repeatedly we find, in research on the precursors of achievement, that degrees of achievement, given equal amounts of time and opportunity to learn, are associated with, or correlated with, measures of intellectual abilities and aptitudes taken prior to learning experiences. Elucidating the nature and source of these associations and correlations requires detailed analysis of the requirements of the learning task as well as of the particular aptitudes that are involved in the associations.

In my view, it is possible to draw a clear distinction between aptitude and achievement, if the time relationships between measures of the two constructs, and certain other conditions, are carefully observed (Carroll, 1974a, 1974b). The "jangle fallacy" proposed by Kelley (1927), whereby aptitude and achievement were asserted to be simply different terms for the same thing, arises only if these relationships and conditions are ignored. Correlations between aptitude and achievement measures taken concurrently cannot be used as evidence either for or against an aptitude/achievement distinction. But when ability A, measured at a time *a* which is prior to an individual's starting a learning task, predicts rate of learning or eventual performance on that task as indexed by measure B taken at time *b* (subsequent to learning), with no substantial change in measure A taken at time *b*, ability A can be called an aptitude for the learning task.

A Point of View on the Nature–Nurture Problem

From nuances in the previous discussion, it is obvious that one of the most sensitive issues in the field of testing is the nature–nurture problem, that is, the extent to which abilities are determined by individuals' genetic constitutions and maturational potentialities. The issue is very resistant to resolution, not only because of the complexity of possible genetic and environmental mechanisms but also because of difficulties in obtaining and interpreting data that can give unassailable answers. Authorities differ enormously in their views on the issue (Anastasi, 1982a; Eysenck vs. Kamin, 1981; Jensen, 1972, 1981; Vernon, 1979), ranging from those who, like Kamin, believe that evidence for any degree of intelligence heritability is so slim that one cannot reject the hypothesis that it is zero, to those who, like Eysenck and Jensen, believe that the evidence supports the claim that it is as much as 80%. The widely cited peccadillos (or worse) of Burt (see Hearnshaw, 1980) in handling data pertinent to the issue have certainly done much harm in warping attitudes of both scientists and the public on this matter. I do not claim expertise in the relevant phases of behavioral genetics and must resign myself to relying on the arguments and opinions of those who seem most competent to judge the issue. DeFries and Plomin (1978, p. 501), for example, stated that "a prudent person has no alternative but to reject the hypothesis of zero heritability" of tested cognitive ability, and Tyler (1978) averred that "there is no longer any argument about the statement that heredity plays some part in the development of abilities and personality traits" (p. 40). In a review of Eysenck and Kamin's (1981) debate, I (Carroll, 1982b) mentioned my feeling that

> the question of the relative weight of heredity and environment in the determination of abilities [is] of little moment. Because one can do little about heredity, I could not care whether the heritability of any ability was .2, .5, or even .8, as long as there was a chance (as seemed reasonable) that environment, education, and other nongenetic factors had some role and that such factors could be to some extent controlled or manipulated in social or educational programs. I would be more interested in the *limits* to which abilities can change or be improved, and it seemed that the appropriate stance to take was that these limits were wide open until they were proved to be otherwise. (p. 242)

I have found it profitable to examine the question of what the limits to the environmental enhancement of abilities would be, given different values for the amount to which heredity and environment affect abilities. For simplicity, assume that we can distinguish the effect of "pure heredity" from all other effects, including those of genetic–environmental covariance, and that the effects of heredity and environment (including learning, etc.) are expressed in terms of the respective proportions of variance for which they account in an ability. Assume further that the ability or trait in question is measured with perfect reliability.

It is convenient to assume that the effect of the environment is normally distributed over a population, and that it can be expressed in sigma units. Individuals with extreme degrees of environmental deprivation, let us suppose, have an "environmental advantage" of -3, while individuals who have already profited from great environmental advantage might be at, let us say, $+3$ on this scale. In a population, the average amount of environmental advantage would be expressed as 0 on our scale. Let us suppose, now, that the effect of some environmental intervention (e.g., a training or coaching course designed to enhance the ability in question, or an environmental enrichment program like Headstart) can also be measured on this same scale. That is, the effect of a particular intervention might be, say, to increase an individual's advantage by one sigma unit; another intervention might have a larger effect, say 3 sigma units.

Let us observe the probable effect of a given amount of change in environmental advantage on a measure of an ability or trait, given different values of the proportions of variance contributed by "pure" heredity as opposed to all other factors. For convenience, this measure is in what may be called "IQ units," that is, measures scaled so that the standard deviation of the ability is 17 (for this is the approximate standard deviation of many IQ measures). (It can also be assumed that the mean IQ in the population is 100, but this mean does not figure in our calculations.) The results are shown in Table 4.1.

If the variance of a trait or ability is determined only by pure genetic factors (G), no amount of change in environmental advantage can produce any change in the trait, so we see a row of zeros in the first row of the table, for a proportion of genetic variance equal to unity. On the other hand, if the variance of a trait or ability is determined only by nongenetic factors (in which case the variance from G is .00 and the variance from E, that is, nongenetic factors, is 1.00), the amount of change in the trait that can be produced by a given amount of change in environmental advantage is the maximum possible for that amount of change, that is, 17 points for each sigma unit of change in environmental advantage. These values are shown in the last row of the table.

What is of interest is to examine the possible gains that could be produced by increases in "environmental advantage" when the proportion of genetic

TABLE 4.1

Theoretical Expected Gains, in IQ Units, from Given Increases in
Environmental Advantage, in Sigma Units, as a Function of the Proportions of
Genetic (G) and Non-Genetic (E) Variance in a Trait, Assuming Perfect
Reliability of the Trait Measurement

Variance Proportions		Increase in Environmental Advantage						
G	E	0	1	2	3	4	5	6
1.00	.00	0	0	0	0	0	0	0
.95	.05	0	4	8	11	15	19	23
.90	.10	0	5	11	16	22	27	32
.85	.15	0	7	13	20	26	33	40
.80	.20	0	8	15	23	30	38	46
.75	.25	0	9	17	26	34	43	51
.70	.30	0	9	19	28	37	47	56
.65	.35	0	10	20	30	40	50	60
.60	.40	0	11	22	32	43	54	65
.55	.45	0	11	23	34	46	57	68
.50	.50	0	12	24	36	48	60	72
.45	.55	0	13	25	38	50	63	76
.40	.60	0	13	26	40	53	66	79
.35	.65	0	14	27	41	55	69	82
.30	.70	0	14	28	43	57	71	85
.25	.75	0	15	29	44	59	74	88
.20	.80	0	15	30	46	61	76	91
.15	.85	0	16	31	47	63	78	94
.10	.90	0	16	32	48	65	81	97
.05	.95	0	17	33	50	66	83	99
.00	1.00	0	17	34	51	68	85	102

variance is rather high, say as high as 80%, as claimed by some authorities.
From the table we can see that for this value of genetic variance there can be a
change of almost 8 IQ points for each sigma unit of change in environmental
advantage. An intervention program that produces 3 sigma units of change in
environmental advantage would be expected to produce an increase of 23 IQ
points—a substantial, perhaps even surprising amount—in the trait or ability
in question.

With lesser amounts of genetic variance, say 60%, ability changes produced
by increases in environmental advantage are even greater, but not really *much*
greater. For example, 3 sigma units of increase in environmental advantage
would be expected to produce an increase of 32 IQ units in the ability, that is,
about 40% greater than the 23 units produced if genetic variance is 80%. The
point is that as long as genetic variance is less than 100%, substantial increases

in ability could be expected to be produced by increases in environmental advantage, even if genetic variance is as high as 80%. This is because the amount of ability change increases as the *square root* of the proportion of nongenetic variance.

The amounts of increase shown in the table, even for rather high values of genetic variance, are not out of line with average ability increases of, say, 10 to 20 IQ points reported for "successful" programs of environmental intervention (see, for example, programs cited by Caruso, Taylor, & Detterman, 1982). One can gain much reassurance from the observation that even if genetic variance is as high as 60% to 80%, there is considerable play for the operation of environmental interventions. From this standpoint, the negative reactions that many people have to claims of high heritability values for intellectual abilities are hardly justified. Nobody knows, and perhaps nobody will ever know, the "true" values of the heritability of intellectual traits in any population. But values in the range 60% to 80% do not seem unlikely, and they are not inconsistent with the notion that environmental interventions, especially for individuals with substantial amounts of environmental disadvantage, can produce substantial increases in measured abilities.

CONCEPTUAL, DIMENSIONAL, AND DEVELOPMENTAL ANALYSES OF INTELLECTUAL PERFORMANCES

Explicating Definitions of Abilities

What is an ability? What is a *cognitive* ability? What is "intelligence"? What is "IQ"? The literature of individual differences and psychological testing contains voluminous discussion intended to answer such questions. Here I hope to circumvent the philosophical tangles and cul-de-sacs entailed in these discussions; instead, I wish to direct attention to the possibility of arriving at *scientifically* justifiable definitions. I entertain the hypothesis that one can define abilities in terms of special and precisely described relations between characteristics of individuals and the characteristics of tasks that require or involve these abilities.

It is useful, however, first to examine some aspects of previous endeavors to define *intelligence* and intellectual or cognitive abilities. I would prefer not to refer to *intelligence* in the singular, because the evidence suggests that there is not a single unitary kind of intelligence. But intelligence is so often referred to in the literature as a singular entity that some use of this term is almost unavoidable. If there are different kinds of intelligences, as seems likely, they have yet to be definitively established by an appropriate series of scientific investigations.

In the past, psychologists have fashioned and refined their concepts of ability and intelligence from the forms that these concepts take in common experience and in the mind of public. Sternberg, Conway, Ketron, and Bernstein (1981) have shown that the "implicit" conceptions of intelligence held by experts in psychological testing are rather similar to those held by the public, as indexed by responses to questionnaires concerning behaviors characteristic of "intelligence" or subvarieties, "academic intelligence" and "everyday intelligence," that were inquired about by these authors. Their results, they suggested, support Neisser's (1979) proposal that intelligence is to be understood in terms of "prototypes," that is, that persons are regarded as being "intelligent," "academically intelligent," or whatnot, to the extent that they are perceived to have the characteristics of imagined ideals of "an intelligent person," "an academically intelligent person," and so on. There seem to be several different prototypical concepts of intelligence, depending on what constellation of features is present in the prototype. Among such features are "practical problem-solving ability," "verbal ability," and "social competence." Even concepts of motivation and cognitive style enter into some prototypes: Intelligent persons are conceived of as being energetic, deliberate, and efficient; they manifest "dedication and motivation in chosen pursuits." Persons with high degrees of social competence are seen as "accepting others for what they are," and people with good problem-solving ability are conceived of as tending to "listen to all sides of an argument" and "keep an open mind." These latter behaviors look more like cognitive styles than manifestations of abilities.

There are undoubtedly many other domains of human behavior in which prototypes of high ability exist in laypersons' minds. We often speak of special talents in music, art, mechanical ingenuity, scientific research, creative writing, public speaking, mathematics, or memory, without being able, necessarily, to specify the exact behaviors that would be characteristic of persons with any one of these talents. For example, there are so many ways in which people can be successful public speakers—so many different behaviors exhibited by successful public speakers—that "the successful public speaker" can only be regarded as a popularly held prototype. (There may not be much difference, actually, between a prototype and a stereotype.)

As Sternberg et al. (1981) pointed out, *explicit* theories (of intelligence) are "constructions of psychologists or other scientists that are based or at least tested on data collected from people performing tasks presumed to measure intelligent functioning" (p. 37). A similar observation could be made about an explicit theory of *any* ability. Our concern here is with how explicit theories of ability can be developed and verified.

In the case of "intelligence," the history of psychologists' attempts to measure this prototype has often been recounted (see, for example, Carroll, 1982a). Initially, it was thought that measures of sensory discrimination and simple reflex and reaction processes would provide valid measures, but after these appeared not to reflect intelligent behavior sufficiently well, psychologists turned to the development of tasks demanding more complex mental operations and skills. Binet and Simon (1905) are generally credited with pioneering the way toward a more adequate means of measuring intelligence, by developing a great variety of intellectual tasks, scaled along a mental age continuum. Since Binet's time, such tasks have been devised in great profusion to measure various hypothesized aspects of intelligence and other cognitive abilities. These tasks have been "validated" as measures of intellectual abilities chiefly by noting their correlations with other tasks (or composite measures derived from such tasks), with age progression, with success in school, and with various other criteria. But such validation procedures have often been criticized for circularity (e.g., Block & Dworkin, 1976).

It is worth noting that the behaviors listed by Sternberg et al.'s (1981) respondents as characteristic of intelligent persons are in the majority of instances oriented around classes of tasks. For example, to say that a person has "practical problem-solving ability" as evidenced by the person's being able to "reason logically and well," "identify connections among ideas," and "see all aspects of a problem" implies that the person does well with *tasks* that involve reasoning, identifying connections between ideas, and seeing all aspects of a problem. To say that a person has good verbal ability as shown by the person's "speaking clearly and articulately" implies that the person does well in a task situation in which clear and articulate speaking is important to effective task accomplishment.

These considerations lead one to focus on the relations between abilities and tasks. We may define a *task* as any setting or situation that requires a person to undertake some action or actions in order to achieve a specifiable objective, final result, or terminal state of affairs. Tasks can come in all sizes and shapes. The individual "items" of typical intelligence and ability tests are tasks that are small in size—although they may, of course, differ in difficulty and demand characteristics. Tasks of greater extent may occur in certain performance tests—like the requirement to lead a platoon of men in building a crude bridge, a task used in OSS assessment procedures (Office of Strategic Services, Assessment Staff, 1948). Even the simplest task, however, may entail a rather complex set of requirements and processes. Sanders (1980), for example, suggested six processing stages in a choice reaction-time task. Sternberg (1977) recognized at least five stages in the solution of an analogical reasoning problem. Obviously, the more complex the task, the more component stages or aspects one might expect the task to contain.

We can raise—but hardly settle at this point—the issue of how detailed we have to be in analyzing tasks into processing stages or other elements. Sanders' (1980) paper is part of a growing literature in cognitive psychology on the question of how processing stages in cognitive tasks can be identified and differentiated (see also Salthouse, 1981). One might imagine that tasks could be divided almost infinitely into processing stages, but in practice it is probable that some unit of analysis of a "right" or appropriate size would be acceptable. One possibility would be the "components" postulated by Sternberg's (1977, 1980b) "componential analysis."

Tasks involve not only a variety of information-processing stages, but also, almost always, some kind of *content* consisting of the stimuli that they may include, or that may be encountered in their performance. Implicit in many tasks, also, are the particular task instructions that must be adopted and understood in order that the task may be effectively accomplished. Tasks set in ability tests nearly always are preceded by instructions as to what the examinee is expected to do, and one part of the task, therefore, is the requirement that examinees understand these instructions. (For many tasks of everyday life, performers may set or adopt their own instructions, unless such instructions come from external sources.)

In view of the possible combinations of instructions, contents, and processing stages, there is an almost infinte variety of possible tasks. Those who construct or devise ability tests have capitalized on these possibilities in creating the multitude of tasks that can be found in tests of "intelligence" and other cognitive abilities. Each aspect of a task can be varied. Instructions can be made simple or complex (and *statements* of instructions, which are to be distinguished from the instructions themselves, may be made either clear or opaque); the stimuli involved in the tasks can be selected to be familiar or unfamiliar, simple or complex, easy or difficult to perceive, and so on; the required processing stages can be made few or many.

Research in ability testing has proceeded in the spirit of experimentation by introducing variations in task elements in order to note their consequences for test reliability, test validity, test intercorrelations, and other test properties. In this sense, ability testing research may be said to be a branch of experimental psychology, contrary to an opinion that a historian of psychology once offered (Boring, 1957, p. 570).

Variations in certain properties of tests have been studied extensively in the psychometric theory of mental tests (e.g., Lord & Novick, 1968) but almost exclusively in terms of variations in "item difficulties," that is, the proportions of representative samples of examinees that are found to pass, or arrive at the keyed correct answers to, the items of a test. In the theory of mental tests, almost no attention is given to what makes items or test tasks "easy" or "difficult" for examinees. It is recognized that task difficulty can be dependent on the psychophysical properties of stimuli, the familiarity or unfamiliarity of stimulus content, the complexity of task requirements, and other task attributes, but there exists no widely accepted, well-developed systematic and general theory in respect to these matters. An early contribution to such a theory was made by Guilford (1937); more recent discussions are those of Berger (1982) and Campbell (1961).

A Model of Ability and Task Difficulty:
The Ability/Difficulty Interaction (A/DI) Model

Regardless of what makes tasks easy or difficult, it is useful to formulate a model of the relationship between ability and task difficulty. Here, I offer a general model, based largely on psychophysical theory, that I believe can be applied to the analysis of any intellectual ability. It can be presented most clearly with the consideration of a "simple" case, the analysis of pitch discrimination ability. Later, extrapolation to intellectual abilities is attempted.

Intimately connected with psychophysical theory is the notion that ability to detect stimuli, or notice their differences, is dependent on levels of stimulus attributes, or on differences in those levels. Psychophysical theory concerns the relations between stimulus attributes and the probability that such attributes will be detected or noticed. Relationships of this sort have been worked out for a variety of attributes of physical stimuli (Engen, 1971). Individuals differ in their ability to detect such attributes, and such abilities may be characterized by reference to psychophysical scales. For example, the ability to detect differences in the pitch of tones can be characterized by specifying quantitatively the amount of pitch difference at which an individual has, say, a 50% probability of detecting the difference. This is then defined as the limen or threshold of pitch discrimination for the individual.

Given the possibility of determining and arranging individuals' limens along a psychophysical scale, it becomes possible to characterize individual differences very explicitly in terms of such a scale. The ability in question becomes defined precisely in terms of stimulus attributes and the relation of these attributes to differences in ability.

Further, it becomes possible, in such cases, to define a *person characteristic function* that specifies, *for a given individual,* the relation between the individual's probability of stimulus attribute detection and the physical scale itself. The theory of the person characteristic function (although he did not call it that) was worked out by Mosier (1940, 1941), and was further developed by Carroll (1983a) in an analysis of the properties of a well-known test of pitch discrimination ability—a subtest of the Seashore Measures of Musical Talent (Seashore, 1919; Seashore, Lewis, & Saetveit, 1939). In this instance, the ability measured by the test can be defined directly in terms of task characteristics. There could hardly be debate about what kind of ability is being measured, once certain psychometric problems are clearly understood and resolved, as Carroll attempted to do, countering a suggestion that had been made by Guilford (1941) that the test measures three distinct abilities. (Guilford's suggestion turns out to have been based on a statistical artifact.)

Let us look more carefully at the person characteristic function. This function might take any of a number of forms, except that the function would most reasonably be limited to a monotonic form, because the probability of correctly

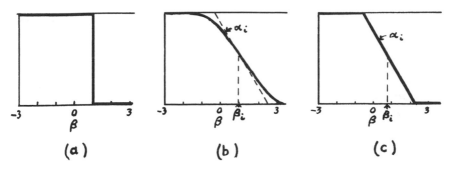

FIG. 4.1.   Three possible forms of the person characteristic function.

performing tasks could be expected always to decrease with the difficulty of the tasks. Three possible forms are illustrated in Fig. 4.1.

The quantity β is a parameter that specifies the difficulty of a task. Figure 4.1a represents what may be called the Walker–Guttman function (Walker, 1931; Guttman, 1941) that implies that a particular individual, i, will "pass" any task with a difficulty less than or equal to β_i (the critical or liminal value for that individual), but "fail" any task with a difficulty greater than β_i. The Walker–Guttman function is an ideal that is rarely if ever attained in practice.

Figure 4.1b represents the familiar normal ogive function or a logistic approximation to it. This function has two parameters for any individual i, the position parameter β_i and a slope parameter α_i. The position parameter is defined as the value of β at which the individual has a true probability of success of .5. The slope parameter has to do with the spread of task difficulties over which the individual's probabilities of success are reasonably close to .5, or more precisely, it has to do with the dispersion of the person characteristic function over the task difficulty continuum.

Figure 4.1c represents the function assumed by the so-called *quantal hypothesis* of psychophysics proposed by von Békésy (1930; see Engen, 1971, pp. 33–34.) Although the underlying theory of the neural quantum may be only rarely applicable in the theory of ability tests, this function appears to be useful either on its own merits or as a simplification of the more complex normal ogive and logistic functions. Carroll (1983a) found generally better fits to pitch discrimination data when using the quantal model than when using the logistic function. Like the normal ogive or logistic function, this function has both a position parameter and a slope parameter. An interesting property of the function is that it postulates ranges of the difficulty continuum where the true probability of success is 1 and other ranges where the true probability of success is 0. Thus, the function may better satisfy one's intuitive feeling that for many ability continua, some individuals should have no problem whatsoever with easy tasks, and some individuals would have no possibility whatsoever of performing difficult tasks.

Exactly what model of the person characteristic function applies best in any particular case is a matter for empirical determination. The important point in the present discussion is that the person characteristic function is directly useful in defining an ability, in the sense that variations in ability are indexed by reference to the position parameter β of this function, which in turn is referenced to specifiable variations in a task characteristic.

In the simple case of pitch discrimination ability, we can *define* the ability by saying that individuals differ with respect to the position of their threshold parameters along the dimension in which the tasks in the pitch discrimination test vary, namely, the amount of difference in pitch between two tones that are presented. This situation is represented in Fig. 4.2.

Although the question is not of immediate concern to problems of defining ability traits, it is interesting to speculate about the status of the slope parameter α of the person characteristic function. There is a clear possibility that this represents a property of the *task variation or difficulty dimension,* not a property of individual differences. The limited amount of evidence thus far available suggests that the parameter can be, for any given task variation dimension, either constant over individuals, or functionally related to the task difficulty parameter β. The observation that slopes are very unlikely to be infinite (as they would be in the Walker–Guttman function shown in Fig. 4.1a) implies that there are theoretical limits to the reliability of a test with a given number of items. I cannot take space to develop this point more fully, as it is not sufficiently pertinent to the present discussion.

Although the reader may rather readily see the thrust of this discussion as it pertains to the "simple" case of pitch discrimination ability, it may not be easy to perceive how it applies to the total range of cognitive abilities, including

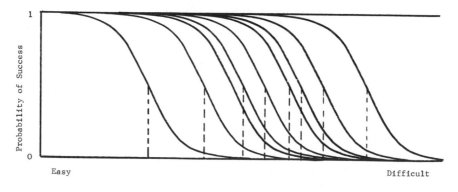

FIG. 4.2 Person characteristic curves on a trait, for a small sample of individuals.

abilities ordinarily covered under the term *intelligence.* On the way to clarifying that point, it is necessary to turn our attention to the dimensional analysis of abilities.

The Dimensional Analysis of Abilities

As has already been observed, tasks can differ in many dimensions—not only in stimulus characteristics, but also in complexity, number of processing stages, and the like. If we knew nothing about cognitive abilities, we might suppose that there is a separate ability corresponding to any dimension in which cognitive tasks might vary. This is unlikely, of course, but it might constitute a kind of initial hypothesis about the range of possible kinds of abilities.

In principle, one might take any pair of tasks that could be scored on a pass–fail basis and attempt to determine whether they measure, or depend on, the same ability. This would be done by administering the tasks to a typical sample of subjects and seeing whether there is agreement in the pass–fail scores between the two tasks. In an ideal case, suppose that exactly the same proportions of examinees pass the two tasks, and that all who pass one task also pass the other. One would be tempted to infer, then, that the two tasks measure the same ability, because such findings would indicate that all who pass the two tasks have β_i parameters equal to or greater than a certain quantity β on the same difficulty continuum; the parameter β would characterize the difficulty level of both tasks on this continuum.

An ideal case of this sort is improbable in practice, for various reasons. For one thing, even if the two tasks do in fact measure precisely the same ability, the slope parameter α is likely to be such that there would not be perfect agreement of the "pass" scores between the two tasks. Second, it is unlikely that the two tasks would have precisely the same β parameter (i.e., be of the same difficulty). Third, it is unlikely that any two tasks would depend on precisely the same ability or combination of abilities. Nevertheless, this ideal case can be regarded as a model for interpreting the results of the many efforts that psychologists have made to determine the dimensions of abilities. Stated in a slightly different way, this ideal case can be regarded as a model for justifying the "correlational" method that has been widely employed in this field. The way in which it can be used to justify the correlational method will take us on a further excursion in psychometric theory.

If psychologists attempted to determine the dimensions of abilities solely by looking at agreements between pass and fail scores on pairs of tasks assembled from some collection of such tasks, a number of difficulties would be encountered. One difficulty stems from the fact that there are problems in assessing the agreement between pass and fail scores on pairs of tasks and inferring the extent to which two tasks measure the same ability or combination of abilities.

As has been shown a number of times (Carroll, 1945, 1961; Ferguson, 1941), the Pearsonian product-moment correlation is an inadequate indicator of whether two tasks measure the same ability when the tasks are of different difficulties (i.e., have different proportions of passing scores). The tetrachoric correlation has been proposed as a coefficient that avoids this difficulty, and with care it can be used, but it has several limitations: It is less statistically reliable than the Pearsonian coefficient, it depends on a possibly undesirable assumption of normality in the underlying distribution of ability, and it is subject to bias due to an interaction between task difficulty and the possibility of passing a task by chance guessing (Carroll, 1945). Despite considerable work by psychometricians in attempting to resolve the statistical problems involved, there have been relatively few attempts to determine the dimensions of ability by studying agreements between passing scores on pairs of cognitive tasks. (Examples of such studies, however, are factor analyses of Stanford–Binet intelligence items by Jones, 1949, 1954; Stormer, 1967; and Wright, 1939, using tetrachoric correlations and generally showing that the Stanford–Binet measures a number of different abilities.)

Very early on in the history of mental testing, psychologists learned to construct psychological tests as *collections* of tasks, or *items,* as they came to be called. Generally, the items of a test exhibited, or were selected on the basis of, considerable similarity in their task characteristics. For example, a "vocabulary test" would be constructed by developing a series of multiple choice items using key words of different degrees of familiarity and incidence frequency in word counts. A "mechanical ability" test would be constructed from series of tasks that appeared to be similar in that they involved certain kinds of manipulation of physical objects. As psychometric theory developed, test constructors learned to select items for tests in terms of indices of "item validity," that is, correlations of item scores with total test scores. From the perspective adopted here, such indices may be interpreted as indices of the extent to which an item is similar to other items in a test with respect to either the abilities measured or the task characteristics, or both. Recent developments in test theory have made it possible to test whether a set of items or tasks that differ in difficulty fits a model such that all the items are homogeneous in whatever they measure (Gustafsson, 1977).

Many psychological tests have been designed in such a way that they contain items of different degrees of difficulty, despite recommendations from some authorities that to maximize reliability, the items of a test should be of approximately equal difficulty (near 50% passing after correction for any chance guessing effects). Actually, designing tests containing items of different difficulties is reasonable in that the items tend to define a difficulty continuum, and the total test score (e.g., number of items correct) tends to indicate where an individual with a given total score falls on this difficulty continuum. This is also true even if the items are of approximately equal difficulty, because the α parameters of difficulty continua are such as to cause the total scores to spread individuals along the difficulty continuum. In any case, the use of multiple items in a test avoids the difficulties previously mentioned in connection with determining correlations between single items. It enables the use of more straightforward linear correlation statistics (although it should be noted that even these statistics entail certain widely ignored problems; see Carroll, 1961).

If, in addition, the items are sufficiently similar in what they measure (as indicated by satisfactory item validities), the difficulty continuum measured by a test can be regarded as reflecting a single ability (or combination of abilities). It would follow, then, that the ability measured by the test is (at least approximately) defined in terms of the difficulty continuum established by the items, and eventually in terms of the gradations in task characteristics that are represented by items of different difficulties.

Further, it would follow that if scores on two tests are found to have a high intercorrelation, they are measuring the same ability to the extent that the difficulty continua defined by the tests are similar. The ability (or combination of abilities) that is measured in common by the two tests could be further defined by examining the way in which the tasks contained in the items vary with their difficulties.

In contrast, if the scores of two tests are found to have a correlation of zero or near zero, it is unlikely that they measure the same abilities, because their difficulty continua are dissimilar. The scores on the two tests place individuals at uncorrelated positions on the respective difficulty continua, and it is likely that these continua would be found to be quite dissimilar with respect to variations in task characteristics of their items.

The line of reasoning just pursued provides an initial but powerful justification for the "correlational method" that has been extensively used in the study of the dimensions of human abilities. It is incomplete and limited chiefly in the sense that the correlational method has not ordinarily been exploited to the extent of examining (except perhaps in a vague and subjective way) item/task characteristics in relation to difficulty continua. Also, users of the correlational method in the dimensional study of abilities have not always adequately attended to the homogeneity of the tasks contained in given tests. To use the A/DI model proposed here, it is necessary that the tasks arranged on a difficulty scale be as homogeneous as possible in all respects except those that account for variation in difficulty. One technique that is useful in identifying abilities and in establishing homogeneous difficulty scales is factor analysis.

Factor Analysis and the Dimensional Analysis of Abilities

Although it is not the only statistical method applicable to the problem (other multivariate methods are useful also), the technique known as *factor analysis* has been the one most widely employed in the dimensional analysis of abilities.

In this context, factor analysis as an enterprise seeks to determine the least redundant set of dimensions by which to describe the abilities of individuals as they are revealed in the performance of tasks such as those included in ability tests. It would be inappropriate here to go into the details of factor-analytic methods and procedures; elsewhere I have attempted to provide useful guides (Carroll, 1983b, 1985). I wish only to look at factor analysis from the perspective that is developed here.

As an extension and exploitation of the correlational method, factor analysis attempts to identify latent dimensions or "factors" on which individuals can in theory be measured, in such a way that scores on these factors, when appropriately weighted by coefficients (factor "loadings" or the like) can predict or account for these individuals' scores on manifest variables. This is what is implied in the fundamental equation of factor analysis:

$$y_{ji} = w_{j1}x_{1i} + w_{j2}x_{2i} + \ldots w_{jm}x_{mi} + w_{ju}x_{ui}$$

That is, the standardized score, y_{ji}, of individual i on variable j is regarded as the sum of the individual's scores, $x_{1i}, x_{2i}, \ldots, x_{mi}$ on common factors 1, 2, . . . , m, plus the individual's score, x_{ui} on a factor unique to test j (composed of specific and error components), each weighted by a coefficient w associated with the particular factor and variable. One object of factor analysis is to use the least number of factors in this equation, over the set of variables studied in any particular investigation. Another object is to make as many of the coefficients in the equation for any given variable as close to zero as possible, that is, to describe any particular variable in the simplest way possible. This is usually accomplished by appropriate "rotations" of the factors according to "simple structure" criteria, which may yield either uncorrelated or correlated factors depending on the nature of the data. In some procedures of factor analysis, for example, in Schmid and Leiman's (1957) hierarchical description of variables, the number of factors may be increased somewhat in order that they may be orthogonal (i.e., uncorrelated). In this case, some factors are more "general" than others, and indeed there are sometimes several levels of generality.

Factors are interpreted by examining the characteristics of variables on which they have high factor weights and contrasting them with characteristics of variables on which they have low or near zero ("vanishing") loadings. Although this is not usually explicit, such interpretations actually refer to the characteristics of the *tasks* that give rise to the variables. A set of variables that all have high loadings on a given factor are usually found to contain tasks that are similar in one or more respects—in type of content, in type of cognitive processing required, in type of response required, and so on. These task characteristics are usually quite different from those observed in the tasks associated with other factors found in a set of variables. If, for example, one factor loads highly on tasks that require a knowledge of relatively unfamiliar vocabulary, and another factor loads highly on tasks that involve mental manipulation of visual spatial forms, it is obvious that these sets of tasks have quite different characteristics.

Further, insofar as the variables contain difficulty continua (as they normally do in ability testing), the identification of a factor implies that the variables with high loadings on it have similar difficulty continua, that is, that the tasks arrayed along those continua tend to be gradated along similar dimensions.

Factor analysis must be regarded not only as a statistical technique but also as a wide-ranging scientific enterprise. The factorial analysis of a particular set of variables measured on a particular sample of individuals cannot normally be expected to yield final and conclusive results. Only series of factorial investigations, with explorations of different hypotheses about the number and nature of ability factors, can be expected to yield such results. Hypotheses about factors are to be tested by varying the task characteristics of test variables and noting the consequences of such variations for the obtained factorial structures. In this sense, factor analysis should be conceived of as a branch of experimental psychology.

Factor-analytic investigations of typical mental ability tests, conducted over most of the present century, have given rise to various theories of intelligence. These theories can be arrayed along a continuum ranging from the theory that intelligence is best identified with a strong "general" factor that arises from positive correlations among all mental ability tests, to a theory that intelligence is to be interpreted as the sum of many separate and independent abilities. The theory that intelligence is a general factor is most closely associated with Spearman (1904, 1927); current advocates of such a theory, albeit with certain modifications and reservations, are Eysenck (1979), Humphreys (1979), Jensen (1980, 1981), and McNemar (1964). The theory that intelligence (if it exists at all) is the sum or integration of many independent abilities is represented in Guilford's (1967) "structure-of-intellect" theory. Neither of these types of theory, in my opinion, is adequate or precise enough to account for all the data now available about dimensions of mental or cognitive abilities. My preference is for some type of hierarchical theory such as those put forth by Vernon (1961, 1979), Cattell (1971), and Horn (1978a, 1978b). Such a theory is consistent with the higher order analyses of correlated (oblique) factors described by Thurstone (1947) and Cattell (1978) if one is also permitted to orthogonalize correlated factors by the techniques developed by Schmid and Leiman (1957).

Presently available evidence (some of which has been summarized, for example, by Carroll, 1983b; Ekstrom, 1979; and Horn, 1978a, 1978b) indicates that one can postulate the existence of some 30 to 50 factors, of different degrees of generality, in cognitive ability. The findings made thus far are not sufficiently clear and comprehensive to enable one to make any definitive specification of what factors exist or how many there are. Discrepancies among the findings of different investigations occur because of differences in selection of the variables analyzed, samples of subjects tested, and factor-analytic methodologies employed. Some of these discrepancies can be resolved by reanalyses of existing data; others could be resolved only through new empirical research.

Many of the factors at the so-called primary level are well established and appear over and over again in factor-analytic investigations of cognitive ability tests and performances. Among these are factors named Induction, Logical Reasoning, General Reasoning, Verbal Comprehension, Number Facility, Spatial Orientation, Visualization, Speed of Closure, Flexibility of Closure, Perceptual Speed, Associative Memory, Memory Span, Associational Fluency, Expressional Fluency, Ideational Fluency, and Word Fluency. These names, it should be noted, are given only for convenience; the more exact identification and interpretation of each factor could be given only through an extended description. Many other primary factors are only tentatively established, for example, factors pertaining to the auditory modality (Horn & Stankov, 1982; Stankov & Horn, 1980), and future research may be expected to disclose still more. It is quite possible that identification and interpretation of many of the "well-established" factors may have to be revised in the light of reanalyses of published data and further empirical research. For example, Lohman (1979) has proposed a new way of aligning various factors in the spatial ability domain.

At the second-order level, some six or seven factors may be regarded as reasonably well established. A list of such factors might include, for example, the six second-order ("second stratum") factors identified by Hakstian and Cattell (1978) in a study of 20 primary abilities: Fluid Intelligence, Crystallized Intelligence, Visualization Capacity, General Perceptual Speed, General Memory Capacity, and General Retrieval Capacity. Hakstian and Cattell also found at the third-order level three factors that they named Original Fluid Intelligence, Capacity to Concentrate, and School Culture, but this set of factors must be regarded as only very tentative pending further research.

Carroll (1980a, 1983b) has listed factors that appear in correlational studies of tasks used in experimental cognitive psychology, such as the stimulus-matching task introduced by Posner (1978; Posner & Mitchell, 1967), the short-term memory scanning task studied by S. Sternberg (1969, 1975), the traditional choice-reaction task, and a series of reading tasks studied by Frederiksen (1982) and Jackson and McClelland (1979). Some of these are the following, with only tentative identifications: Visual Duration Threshold, Slope of Choice Reaction Time (with respect to the logarithm of the number of choices), Accuracy of Complex Information Processing, Speed of Mental Comparisons, Slope of Visual and Memory Search Processes (with respect to stimulus set size), Encoding Multi-letter Arrays, Phonemic Translation, and Depth of Processing in Word Recognition. The relationships of these factors to the better established primary and second-order factors mentioned previously are at present very unclear. E. Hunt (1978), Jensen (1982), and P. A. Vernon (1983) are among investigators finding significant (albeit usually low) correlations of these factors with more traditional measures of cognitive ability. Extensive investigations will be needed to clarify these relationships.

Despite statistical problems that have already been mentioned, factor analysis can be applied at the item level to establish homogeneous ability/difficulty scales.

Developmental Analyses of Abilities

A proper theory of ability cannot be developed unless the abilities identified by factor analysis or other means can be observed at different ages and have some degree of stability over the life span. In particular, the A/DI model proposed here cannot be applied satisfactorily unless a task difficulty continuum has some relevance to the development or change of an ability.

The ability factors mentioned in the preceding section have been disclosed in investigations using subjects at age levels ranging from childhood to old age, but chiefly in studies using adolescents and young adults (e.g., college students and young military personnel). The better established factors have been identified in some form at every age except infancy and early childhood. Nevertheless, closer examination of the findings is needed to suggest answers to a number of questions:

1. How does an ability develop and change over the life span? If levels of an ability can be expressed quantitatively, what changes in these levels are noted over the course of an individual's life span?

2. Can an ability change in nature, qualitatively, over the course of an individual's life span?

3. Are the same abilities identifiable at different ages? Is there, as originally proposed by Garrett (1938, 1946), progressive differentiation of abilities over the period of growth to adulthood? Do distinctions between abilities tend to diminish or disappear in later adulthood or old age?

4. Do particular measures of ability change in factorial composition with age? When individuals of different levels of development perform a given task, do they "use" the same abilities, or different abilities?

Satisfactory answers to most of these questions would obviously have to come from longitudinal studies in which the same individuals are followed and tested over long periods of time, but because longitudinal studies are difficult to conduct and present many methodological problems of their own (Bayley, 1970, p. 1173), much of the available evidence is based on cross-sectional studies in which different groups of subjects in different age ranges are tested. (See a comprehensive review by Siegler & Richards, 1982.)

The Course of Development of an Ability

The basic data we have to work with are the responses of individuals of different ages to tasks that vary in their characteristics. From the perspective adopted here, a satisfactory ideal model is one in which individuals of different ages would be arrayed along a task difficulty continuum according to their person characteristic functions. The identification of a situation for which this is true would constitute evidence that a single ability (or a uniform constellation or combination of abilities) affects task performance. If we then observe the performances of a single individual over time, we would note any changes that might occur in that individual's position parameter on the task difficulty continuum. If the change is significant and in a positive direction, we would infer that growth in the ability had occurred—through maturation, learning, or some other effect. If the change is in a negative direction, we would infer some kind of decline in the ability—caused perhaps by a physiological debility, or through forgetting.

I am aware of few instances in which such a view of ability changes has been employed by investigators. It could be employed with certain scales on standard intelligence tests (e.g., the vocabulary scale of the Stanford–Binet, or the "criterion referenced" scales of the British Ability Scales; Elliott, Murray, & Pearson, 1978–1982, that have been established on the basis of a Rasch, 1980, model). Normally, growth or decline of abilities has been observed on the basis of gross test scores or derived indices such as the mental age (e.g., Hindley, 1981); in such cases some skepticism can be expressed as to whether the growth or decline has been observed in a single ability or in some undefined combination of abilities.

With this reservation, it can be stated that the almost universal observation is that during childhood and adolescence, abilities increase in absolute terms (although some may reach an asymptote around the beginning of adolescence), and that during adulthood and the later years of life, some abilities may continue to increase whereas other abilities may decline in at least some individuals. Pertinent information on average changes in some important abilities may be gained from an examination of the scaled scores of the Wechsler intelligence scales (Wechsler, 1974, 1981) and from data summarized by Bayley (1970). As far as I am aware, there exist no satisfactory compilations of growth and decline data for factored abilities. Thurstone (1955) presented preliminary data on the differential growth of certain mental abilities; further information might be gleaned from the numerous reports of individual studies in the literature.

Writers in the field of ability testing often have concerned themselves with what often is called the *stability* or *constancy* of abilities. This issue has to do with whether individuals tend to maintain the same *relative* position, with advancing age, with respect to normative groups. That is, even though an individual may advance in ability in absolute terms, does the individual's relative position on the ability stay the same, advance more rapidly, or fall behind, with respect to the abilities of others in the individual's age cohort? During the early history of intelligence testing, there was much interest in whether the IQ is constant. Because the IQ (whether computed from the ratio of mental age, (MA) to chronological age, (CA) or as a "deviation IQ") is a relative measure, it is obvious that it cannot be constant if mental growth curves do not form a family of perfectly parallel trajectories. Nevertheless, it has often been possible to identify cases in which the IQ is approximately constant over a range of ages. It is likely, however, that the constancy would diminish if relative positions of different components or factors of IQ-measured intelligence were considered. In general, concern with the constancy of the IQ has dissipated with the realization that the course of development of an ability can be anything but uniform. Growth on particular abilities can occur in fits and starts, as it were— with rapid growth over certain periods and minimal growth over others. A consequence of this is that correlations between relative positions tend to decrease with the amount of time difference between testings. Anderson (1939) attempted to account for such correlations through the use of his "overlap hypothesis," that assumes that mental growth over a given period is uncorrelated with status at the beginning of the period. At this writing, the overlap hypothesis is generally discredited because its basic assumption is not borne out by data (Pinneau, 1961), and in any case change scores tend to be quite unreliable (Thorndike, 1966). On the whole, although there are indeed sometimes substantial changes in relative positions of individuals, there is an impressive amount of constancy in mental ability growth data (Bayley, 1970).

Qualitative Changes in Abilities

Although there has been some speculation to the effect that there may be qualitative changes in abilities over the life span, as far as I am aware there is no good research basis for making such an assertion. To be sure, if we define an ability in terms of a task difficulty scale, there will be "qualitative" differences in the tasks as we scan from the easy tasks to the more difficult tasks, and such differences contribute to the specification of the difficulty scale. But the basic ability as defined by those tasks remains the same. The temptation to conceive qualitative differences in ability occurs in connection with certain notions of global ability, such as "writing ability," which corresponds to a global prototype of a "good writer" who possesses many different skills. "Writing ability" is a composite of a number of different abilities, which might include verbal ability, knowledge of writing conventions (spelling, punctuation, etc.), ideational fluency, expressional fluency, and planning ability, let us say, in addition to knowledge of a particular subject area about which one might write. The apparent qualitative differences in global writing ability at different periods of development actually arise from the fact that different kinds of ability are important at different periods.

Developmental Differentiation of Abilities

It is generally agreed that it is difficult to find differentiated ability factors in infancy (say, below 2 years of age), and what abilities can be identified during infancy—mostly in the sensorimotor realm—rarely show significant correlations with abilities measured at later ages. Bayley (1970) stated that no general factor ability can be identified in the first 3 years. She remarked that the apparent lack of stability of factors during this period cannot be attributed to lack of reliability of measures, however. In her studies, conducted with the Berkeley Growth Study sample studied longitudinally from infancy to 36 years of age, the only impressive correlations between abilities measured in infancy and in later years concern the acquisition and use of language. With newer techniques of observing infant abilities, however, there are some indications that other abilities, such as recognition memory measured at 4 to 7 *months* of age, can be significantly predictive of verbal intelligence scores at 4 to 7 *years* of age (Fagan & McGrath, 1981; Lewis & Brooks-Gunn, 1981). McCall (1981) drew a conclusion of "cautious optimism" from such studies.

Reinert's (1970) comprehensive and technologically sophisticated review of research on the hypothesis that abilities become more differentiated with increasing age levels is useful, despite having been completed some years ago. Reinert pointed out that there can be different bases for differentiation hypotheses. Either in cross-sectional or longitudinal studies, data points can be grouped by chronological age, by ability levels (usually, by IQ), or even by levels of a personality variable. Grouping subjects by ability levels, for example, could show whether abilities are more differentiable for subjects of higher IQ than for those of lower IQ. After reviewing more than 60 studies designed to investigate one or another aspect of differentiation hypotheses, Reinert concluded that although there is "sufficient evidence to indicate the existence of age-related changes in the factorial pattern of intelligence, the data are too contradictory to permit a clear-cut description of the nature of these changes" (p. 467). The difficulty in drawing conclusions stems from major differences in the factor-analytic methodologies employed by different investigators. It appears that the reanalyses of data recommended by Reinert have still yet to be done. A more recent longitudinal study by Atkin et al. (1977) provides some support for the age differentiation of factor structures over Grades 5 through 11. In a cross-sectional comparison, Undheim (1978), however, found little support for age differentiation of broad ability factors over the age range 10 to 13.

To date, studies of age- or ability-differentiation hypotheses have used only factor-analytic approaches, conclusions being drawn from the number of factors identified at different ages or ability levels. The problem of determining the proper number of factors for explaining a set of data is one of the most notoriously difficult problems in factor analysis, not always resolvable by the most sophisticated methods of confirmatory factor analysis because the issue is one of comparative levels of statistical significance that are dependent on sample size as well as number of factors. (If, for example, with a sample of 200 cases, five factors yield residuals with a chi-square significance level of $p = .12$, whereas six factors yield $p = .40$, how many factors should be accepted? Conservatively, five, but one could argue for six. If the sample size is increased to 1,000 and the probability values decrease to .015 and .09 respectively, how many factors are to be accepted? Certainly not just five, and probably more than six.)

If abilities do in fact become differentiated with increasing age or ability levels, what would this mean? It seems implausible that at a given age level, a factor would appear out of nowhere, when it had not appeared at an earlier age (assuming the set of variables investigated is held constant). Close examination of studies reviewed by Reinert shows that with successive age levels, factors tend to "split." That is, if factor A appears at a given age, factors B and C appear at a later age, both B and C showing considerable similarity to factor A. (In Buss & Royce's, 1975, terms, the factors "diverge.") According to the theory just proposed, a factor corresponds to a scale of task difficulty. The occurrence of factor differentiation might therefore reflect a bifurcation of a difficulty scale. Our factor A might correspond to the lower level of a difficulty scale that at some point bifurcates to form two scales that show up as factors B and C. Bifurcation of a difficulty scale might reflect a situation where easy tasks demand only one ability, whereas more complex tasks require more than one ability—either in the sense that a given task could be performed with *either* of two abilities, or in the sense that a given task requires critical levels on two abilities. For example, simple numeration tasks might require only one general ability, whereas more complex numerical tasks might require not only this general ability but also a knowledge of the properties of the decimal number system. I am not aware of any attempts to explicate a finding of factor differentiation in terms of notions suggested here, or something like them. What is needed is the development of models that might help to explain factor differentiation effects if indeed such effects can be demonstrated.

Ability Changes in Adulthood and Later Years

Recent reviews of various findings and issues in the development and possible decline of abilities in adulthood and later years are to be found in compilations by Birren and Schaie (1977), Knox (1977), Poon (1980), and Salthouse (1982). Reviews by Botwinick (1977) and by Willis and Baltes (1980), included in these works, are especially pertinent; these authors complain that most research on intelligence changes in this age period is based on measures designed for much younger individuals—children and young adults—and oriented chiefly toward academically related aspects of intelligence. There is some merit in this complaint, but it is still true that most tasks set on ability tests are not inappropriate for older adults; they involve mental operations and skills that are relevant throughout life. Considering that the school curriculum is designed to prepare the student for later life, the fact that intelligence tests are concerned with school-related abilities cannot be used to condemn them as being inappropriate for measuring abilities in later life. My conjecture would be that the difficulty scales implicit in ability tests used in research on changes in the adult years are simply slight upward extensions of those inherent in data from children and young adults.

Studies based largely on cross-sectional data have for a number of years been suggesting that considerable declines in intellectual abilities take place in the adult years, particularly in abilities subsumed under fluid intelligence. Research with longitudinal data, however, suggests that at least some of these apparent declines are due to cohort effects. The average measured ability of the population appears to have been increasing over the past half century, with increased education, better lifestyles, and so on. Thus, in cross-sectional studies, younger subjects (born and raised at later times) tend to have higher scores than older subjects. The conclusion from studies in which attempts are made to control cohort effects (e.g., Schaie & Labouvie-Vief, 1974) appears to be that for many individuals there is little if any decline in most abilities up through age 60 or so. Nevertheless, there are methodological problems in controlling for cohort effects. Horn's (1980) suggestion that there is substantial decline in "fluid intelligence" abilities over the "vital years of adulthood" (age 20–60) deserves serious attention, particularly because it is based on voluminous data and a well-articulated hierarchical theory of mental functions.

Nearly all investigators agree that aging is accompanied by a slowing of many behavioral processes, including cognitive processes, and that this slowing probably has a central, neurophysiological basis beyond the mere effect of slowed peripheral sensory and motor response processes (Birren, Woods, & Williams, 1980).

"Dedifferentiation" or convergence of abilities—the opposite of the differentiation process suggested for earlier ages—has been proposed. Cunningham (1980) found little evidence for this, because similar factor structures are observed at different ages during adulthood, both in cross-sectional and longitudinal studies. Some factors tend to become more highly correlated with increasing age, but Cunningham regarded this as attributable to increasing interdependence of skills represented by different factors. The effect could be explained in other ways, however (cohort effects?), and only more detailed and intensive research with the actual task performances of adults could aid in resolving the issue.

Theory of Ability Change

It has been assumed here that an ability corresponds to a scale of task difficulty. Ordinarily, such a scale of difficulty would be established on the basis of cross-sectional data (e.g., the responses of a representative sample of like-aged individuals to a series of tasks that are similar in all respects except those that differentiate them in difficulty). Individual differences in probability of successful performance, as a function of task difficulty, would place individuals at different points on such a scale. An interesting and important question is whether such a scale would also constitute a *developmental* scale. That is, can age-related changes in abilities over time be properly registered on such a scale, and if so, can they be shown to be lawfully related to variables that would explain those changes? It seems that such a question has never been thoroughly investigated and definitively answered (if, indeed, it has ever been posed in this way!). Here I assume that it could eventually be answered in the affirmative, at least for many types of ability scales. This seems likely because individual differences noted in cross-sectional data are usually interpretable as attributable to differences in levels of development (however such levels may have been attained). Methodological issues in establishing developmental scales and interpreting age-related changes on such scales are extensively discussed by Wohlwill (1973), although only incidentally in relation to intellectual ability scales.

Variables associated with both maturation (as biologically given) and general and specific learning experiences, always in interaction with one another, have traditionally been posited as accounting for increases of abilities registered in absolute terms on developmental scales. A comprehensive review of the classical evidence on this point is provided by J.M. Hunt (1961), who, without denying the role of biological and genetic factors, urged a careful look at the important role of learning and experience. Hunt's book is one of the earliest to emphasize the possible role of current information-processing theories in interpreting and guiding interventions to increase abilities. This theme is taken up and expanded in many more recent discussions, such as those by Buss (1973a, 1973b), Keating (1979), and Sternberg (1982a; see also Detterman & Sternberg, 1982). In commenting on one intervention study, J.M. Hunt (1981) suggested that intervention must be carefully designed to match individuals' "epigenetic stages" of mental development.

A similar trend is noticeable in discussions of possible declines of ability in the elderly and ways of preventing or minimizing such declines (Poon, 1980; Willis, Blieszner, & Baltes, 1981). It is hypothesized that declines are neither inevitable nor predetermined by neurobiological factors—rather, that they can be to some extent controlled through interventions that focus on information-processing operations and strategies that can be adopted or learned by elderly people.

163

These developments imply that ability measurements and scales, if they are to be used effectively in research and practice, must be designed and calibrated to reflect the development of information-processing operations and strategies. It is doubtful that conventional ability measurements go very far in fulfilling this requirement, but they can possibly be adapted to meet it to some extent. Whether it will be necessary to develop new types of instruments is a matter for investigation.

Treatments of Dimensional and Developmental Aspects of Abilities in Individual and Group Tests

We refer to a series of well-known and widely used tests or test batteries for assessing individuals' intellectual abilities and aptitudes. Details about these instruments and the very extensive research connected with them may be found in such books or chapters as those by Anastasi (1982b), Boehm and Sandberg (1982), Kaplan and Saccuzzo (1982), Kaufman (1979, 1982), Lutey and Copeland (1982), Matarazzo (1972), and Sattler (1982), and much useful information, including experts' reviews of tests, is obtainable from Buros's (1953, 1959, 1965, 1972, 1978) series of *Mental Measurements Yearbooks* and from his compilation (1975) of reviews of intelligence tests. Here, we can make only a few pertinent remarks about these tests.

Factorial Composition

In nearly every case, the factorial composition of a test or test battery is at present not completely clear, whether because of inadequate design of the instrument or because of research efforts that are incomplete or methodologically suspect. The archetype of an individual test, the Stanford–Binet Intelligence Scale, measures a potpourri of imperfectly correlated abilities, as has been shown in a number of studies (Jones, 1949, 1954; Ramsey & Vane, 1970; Stormer, 1967; Wright, 1939). The MA or IQ derived from it emphasizes verbal, fluency, and reasoning abilities; memory, spatial, and many other important aptitudes are only slightly represented in it. A "general intelligence" factor is represented in the IQ only to the extent (about half its variance) that some of these abilities tend to be correlated. The factorial composition of the several Wechsler scales (the WPSSI, WISC, and WAIS) is fairly well established. Two robust but substantially correlated factors have emerged in nearly every study: a verbal comprehension or language factor, and a "perceptual organization" factor that is some composite of abilities in the spatial domain. A third factor has been variously interpreted as "freedom from distractability" and "freedom from disruptive anxiety," but it could also be interpreted as an ability to deal with certain types of symbols. The "full-scale IQ" derived from a Wechsler series can be thought of as a composite of a general intelligence factor, a verbal ability factor, and a spatial ability factor. Correlations between Stanford–Binet and Wechsler IQs are high, but only as high as their common factorial compositions permit.

Factorial compositions of various other commonly used ability scales are problematical. The Raven Progressive Matrices test, in its several versions (Raven, 1938–1965), has often been thought to be a good measure of g, but some factorial studies (e.g., Adkins & Lyerly, 1952) indicate that it also taps abilities in the spatial and perceptual speed domains. The Peabody Picture Vocabulary Test obviously puts heavy emphasis on verbal abilities, as does the Illinois Test of Psycholinguistic Abilities.

Not well known in the United States, the British Ability Scales (Elliott et al., 1978–1982) provide a refreshing exception to the previous statements. This series of 23 individually administered scales for children in the 2- to 17-year-old range includes measures of factors of Reasoning, Spatial Imagery, Perceptual Matching, Short-Term Memory, Verbal Ability, and Verbal Fluency in such a way that the factorial composition of each scale is fairly clear, with separate evaluations of accuracy and speed where necessary. Although derivation of global IQs is provided for, the emphasis is on the separate scales (which are, as mentioned here, "criterion-referenced").

So much for individually administered tests. Factorial compositions of traditional group-administered tests of intelligence are if anything less clear than for individually administered tests. Many of these tests, such as the California Test of Mental Maturity (Sullivan, Clark, & Tiegs, 1963), the Kuhlmann–Anderson Intelligence Test (Kuhlmann & Anderson, 1963), and the Henmon–Nelson Intelligence test (J. L. French, 1973), have a distinctly academic flavor in that they employ a pencil-and-paper format and often involve reading and writing. The almost universal use of time limits entails an inevitable intrusion of speed factors (of different sorts, and to different extents) into test scores. Thus, total scores on these tests reflect some combination of a general intelligence factor, a verbal ability or "crystallized intelligence" factor, and speed.

A number of multifactor test batteries are available but seem not to be widely used except in research. The first of these was Thurstone and Thurstone's (1946, revised in 1962) SRA Primary Mental Abilities battery (PMA), available in five levels for Grades K–12 (or above) and offering tests of factors identified as Verbal Meaning, Perceptual Speed, Number Facility, Spatial Relations, and Reasoning. A more recent test series of this kind is Hakstian and Cattell's (1976) Comprehensive Ability Battery (CAB), designed for high school students and offering tests on more than 20 primary mental abilities. Because the PMA and the CAB are direct outcomes of factor-analytic studies, the factor compositions of the subtests are about as clear as they can be made, except for the intrusion of speed factors in some tests because of the use of time limits. Generally, factor scores tend to be correlated, and Hakstian and Cattell (1978) have published a higher order analysis of these correlations. Educational

Testing Service (ETS; Ekstrom, French, & Harman, 1976) has sponsored the availability of "reference tests" for 23 intellectual ability factors, but these are designed only as marker tests for factor-analytic research. Although of considerable value for this purpose, they are not well enough standardized and refined for use in counseling or other operational purposes, and their factorial composition is not always as clear as might be desired due to the lack of control of speed and other aspects. These tests, however, might well form the basis for a much needed revised and improved series that could be used not only in factor-analytic research but also in educational practice.

The Nature of Test Scores

Most of the tests just mentioned yield test scores that are intended to place the examinee either on some sort of age scale, such as "mental age," or on a "point" scale that indicates the position of the examinee relative to some normative group—such as those of comparable chronological age or grade level. That is, they are always in some sense "norm-referenced." Even a mental age score, although interpretable in absolute terms, is a norm-referenced measure because it permits assessing whether an individual is ahead or behind his or her chronological age group in mental development. The IQ (whether computed from the ratio of MA to CA or on the basis of a deviation score) is simply a more refined indicator of relative status.

The need for norm-referenced scores is understandable in operational contexts, and in many cases such scores may constitute the only type of meaningful score that could be formed. ("Raw" scores such as "number correct" have obvious limitations.) But norm-referenced scores by themselves fail to give useful information concerning the actual level of ability, in concrete terms, demonstrated by an examinee. Such scores do not indicate, in particular, the threshold level of difficulty that the examinee can achieve; in other words, such scores do not directly communicate the position of the testee on a meaningful difficulty scale.

Recent advances in the theory of testing (Hambleton, 1982) have given impetus to the development of "criterion-referenced" scores that are intended to indicate the meaning of test scores in terms of actual behaviors and responses. This development has been particularly pronounced in connection with educational achievement tests, where test performances are to be evaluated relative to the achievement of specific educational objectives. The technique of criterion-referencing can, however, be applied in the case of ability testing. It is exemplified in the scoring of the aforementioned British Ability Scales (Elliott et al., 1978–1982), which yield (along with norm-referenced scores) "Rasch-based" scores that are independent of norms and that can be interpreted in terms of levels of difficulty achieved by testees.

The criterion referencing of ability test scores need not rely on the Rasch model. What is required is any way of referencing scores to the level of difficulty of tasks that the testee can pass with a probability of 50% (after correction for any chance success effects), and a way of describing that level of difficulty in some objective, or preferably absolute, manner. For example, criterion-based scores on a vocabulary test would indicate what kinds of words are at the borderlines of the individual's vocabulary mastery; they might indicate something about the size of the individual's vocabulary. Criterion-based scores on a reasoning ability test would indicate what kinds of reasoning problems the individual can easily master, and what kinds the individual has pronounced difficulty with. With further investigation, such scores might indicate what mental operations the individual can easily perform, and what mental operations the individual is unlikely to perform at his or her stage of mental development.

The possibility of developing criterion-based scores and interpretations for mental ability tests has seldom been explored, but seems to have great promise. The remainder of this chapter considers research in the analysis of cognitive ability tasks that might make this promise more fully realizable. The A/DI model proposed here is directly related to the construction of criterion-referenced scales, because a task difficulty continuum should facilitate the specification of performances and behaviors at different points on this scale. It may also facilitate the development of equal-interval scales of performance that would be useful in studies of growth and change of abilities.

THE A/DI MODEL AS A BASIS FOR DEFINING ABILITIES AND RELATING THEM TO COGNITIVE REQUIREMENTS OF TASKS

Theory and Methodology

Defining an Ability

According to the A/DI model, an *ability* is a person characteristic that interacts with a series of tasks graded in "difficulty" (as specially defined) such that there is a point (a threshold level) on the difficulty scale where the person has a theoretical probability of 50% of performing a task "correctly" or acceptably with respect to some criterion, and such that as easier tasks are attempted, the theoretical probabilities of success increase from 50%, eventually to 100%, and as more difficult tasks are attempted, the probabilities decrease from 50%, eventually to 0%. It is assumed that the tasks are similar in all respects except those that differentiate them in difficulty, and that it can be established psychometrically that they all measure a homogeneous ability, for example by demonstrating fit to a "Rasch model" that assumes measurement of a single ability or constellation of abilities (Gustafsson, 1977). Individual variation in ability is manifested in the fact that individuals' threshold levels are at different points on the task difficulty scale. For each individual, therefore, the threshold level constitutes a parameter indicating degree of ability.

This model can be applied to the analysis of abilities such as those measured by typical intelligence and aptitude tests, particularly when the abilities have been well identified and established by factor-analytic or other psychometric procedures. Further, the model can be used in interpreting abilities in terms of the types of knowledge bases and cognitive processes that are associated with these abilities.

The manner in which an ability can be defined by this model can readily be conceived in a simple case like the testing of pitch discrimination ability, where it is possible to imagine a series of tasks that are highly similar in all their characteristics except one, namely the difference in pitch of two presented tones, the task being to detect the difference in pitch (for example by reporting which tone is higher in pitch).

Difficulties may be foreseen, however, in applying the model to tasks that are more complex in the sense that they may vary in numerous characteristics. Although tasks may be graded in difficulty according to the proportions of individuals in a sample or population performing them correctly or acceptably, these difficulty levels are a complex function of the various characteristics of the tasks, which may interact with different abilities. It may therefore be difficult to define any one ability by observing variations in task characteristics.

To introduce possible solutions to such complications, we need to discuss, in addition to several other problems, (a) notions of task difficulty, and (b) the characterization of knowledge bases, cognitive processes, and other psychological phenomena in the performance of tasks.

Task Variation and Task Difficulty

Let us rule out, at the outset, any consideration of the *subjective* or *judged* difficulty of a task, because there is rarely need for subjective judgments of task difficulty and they are often of questionable reliability and validity. The *empirical* difficulty of a task is usually determined as the proportion of test individuals, in some supposedly representative sample, who are able to perform the task "correctly" or according to some preconceived standard of acceptability. The scaling of such proportions will obviously depend on the nature of the sample; to investigate relations between such proportions in different samples, or to relate them to more intrinsic measures of difficulty such as those discussed here, it is often helpful to subject them to some form of transformation, for example, to normal deviate values or to values required by the Rasch (1980) model of test scores.

Campbell (1961) introduced a distinction between *intrinsic* and *extrinsic* determinants of task difficulty. In general, she regarded intrinsic determinants as those inherent in the content, structure, and layout of a task, and thus determinable from analysis of the task without any consideration of subjects' responses. Extrinsic determinants of task difficulty were those associated with variations in subjects' backgrounds, experiences, motivation, and attentiveness, and with the particular conditions under which a task might be presented to subjects, for example, the nature of the instructions or any cues that might be given deliberately or inadvertently. There seem to be some logical confusions in Campbell's discussion; for example, she regarded novelty as an "intrinsic" determinant and unfamiliarity of content as an extrinsic determinant. Nevertheless, the distinction between intrinsic and extrinsic determinants is useful. For our present purposes, let us consider an *intrinsic* determinant of task difficulty any characteristic of tasks in which variation can occur over tasks and that can be specified by some objective or operational means without reference to subject characteristics. Preferably, task characteristics should be scalable or statable in quantitative terms. For example, verbal content could be scalable in terms of word frequency, sentence length, or other types of indices. The complexity of reasoning tasks could be scaled in terms of the number of elements to be processed and the number and types of processes by which these elements are to be operated on by a human subject. The ideal case would be one in which empirical difficulty data are highly predictable from a model that involves task characteristics as its parameters. The model itself would specify the scale of intrinsic task difficulty. Successive investigations employing improved and usually more detailed models would eventuate in more nearly perfect predictions. Here, I cite a number of such models from the literature.

Cognitive Requirements of Tasks

The phrase *cognitive requirements of tasks* is here used to refer to any and all aspects of (a) stimulus content insofar as it evokes cognitive responses, (b) experiential or knowledge bases that individuals may be required to call on in task performance, (c) the cognitive operations and "strategies" that may be involved in such performances, and (d) the types of overt response that tasks may require subjects to make in order to demonstrate performance capability.

At least some type of experiential or knowledge base is probably called on in connection with any type of stimulus content, but some types of content emphasize such bases more than other types. For example, verbal content may involve materials in a particular language, varying in familiarity and complexity. In contrast, certain types of nonverbal content may place few demands on a knowledge base, instead putting demands on basic perceptual, learning, and memory processes.

Whatever demands a task may place on experiential and knowledge bases as opposed to perceptual, learning, and memory processes, various cognitive processes may be involved in performance of the task. There is as yet no agreed upon list or classification of such cognitive processes, although investigations using the A/DI model might lead toward more adequate specifications than are now available, for example in the lists offered by Carroll (1976, 1980a, 1981), Snow (1981), and Sternberg (1980b).

At least some of the cognitive processes elicited by a task can be obligatory and intrinsic to the task, whereas others may be optional and somehow dependent on subject characteristics, or on the particular conditions under which a task is presented. Processes of the latter type may be referred to as cognitive *strategies*. If tasks are so structured as to enable them to be performed with different cognitive strategies, this may make for complications in using the A/DI model unless, as is conceived possible, the strategies employed by different individuals can be shown to depend on levels of different abilities.

The types of responses required by tasks are usually intrinsic and obligatory, and can be interpreted in terms of intrinsic cognitive processes employed in producing those responses.

Relating Task Difficulty Scales and Task Cognitive Requirements

We now come to the fundamental assumption of the A/DI model, namely, that *the cognitive requirements of a task are related to, and detectable by analysis of, variations in task characteristics observable over a task difficulty continuum that has been established by psychometric techniques as constituting a homogeneous ability continuum.* Such an assumption—or perhaps it can be called a theorem—seems justified a priori because as task difficulty increases, tasks call for more of certain cognitive requirements—a greater knowledge base, more cognitive capacity to handle quantity and complexity of information, or some combination of these. In any event, the A/DI model is either confirmable or falsifiable in particular cases.

Just how relations between task difficulty and cognitive requirements can be shown to be related is a matter for study. Undoubtedly different types of cases will present themselves, and each must be dealt with in the optimal way possible. Some illustrations are introduced here, with suggestions concerning procedures of analysis and interpretation. Several further issues must be discussed, however, before these illustrations can be presented.

The Problem of Factorially Complex Difficulty Scales

At least two somewhat different cases must be considered:

Scales Involving a Primary and a Higher Order Factor.   As has been suggested previously in a brief and very sketchy survey of factor-analytic results, many ability tests are factorially complex in the sense that they load on both a "primary" factor like Verbal Knowledge (V) and a more "general" or "group" factor such as "crystallized intelligence" (*Gc*)—and perhaps also on a still higher order factor such as *g*. This can be true even though a statistical test may show that the set of items (tasks) of which they are composed is homogeneous in the ability or abilities they test. A test of the homogeneity of a series of items can show only that they are homogeneous in testing a single *constellation* of abilities. That constellation can sometimes be truly unitary, with no possibility of further breakdown or analysis into further separate abilities. Items testing pitch discrimination ability may be unitary in this sense. Such "unitary" abilities are rare in the cognitive ability domain, however. The more usual case is that of a primary factor that also shows substantial weighting on factors at one or more higher levels, and such cases offer a challenge to the use of the A/DI model.

A possible solution for this case is to attempt to observe variations in two or more task characteristics, one associated with the "primary" factor and the other associated with the higher order factor. We might expect to find that these task variations are correlated over the difficulty scale: As one characteristic changes, so also does the other, perhaps in the nature of things. But the variation in the task characteristic that is associated with a primary factor might be observable only in the particular series of tasks under study, whereas variations in task characteristics associated with a higher order factor are also observable in other kinds of tasks—tasks associated with other primary factors. The assumption is that particular kinds of task characteristics are associated with particular latent traits that may be either of a "primary" or a "higher order" nature. One would expect, also, that a task characteristic that is associated with a "primary" factor would be observed to vary in the same way in all tests that show significant loadings on that primary factor. Similarly, a test characteristic associated with a higher order factor would be observed to vary in the same way on all tests that show significant loadings on that higher order factor. (Presumably, also, correspondences could be established between task difficulty scales of different tests of a particular factor on the basis of whatever metric is established for that task characteristic.)

Another possibility needs to be considered, namely that task difficulty characteristics associated with primary factors may be assignable to experiential or knowledge bases, whereas those associated with higher order factors are assignable to variations in cognitive requirements that tap the capacities involved in the acquisition of those knowledge bases given environmental opportunities to do so. Hunt and Lansman (1982) have suggested that attentional capacity (as linked to *g*) "may be a factor in acquiring vocabulary but may not be a factor when taking a vocabulary test" (p. 247). Vocabulary knowledge, as measured by a score on a vocabulary test, or other verbal test, would simply be an index of the extent to which vocabulary had been acquired, as a function of attentional capacity and environmental opportunities to acquire a verbal knowledge base. (See also the discussion on p. 183, of a study by Marshalek, 1981.)

Scales Involving any Two or More Primary Factors. Factor analytic results inevitably reflect phenomena observed in groups, but not necessarily in individual members of a group. For example, suppose that a particular scale is found to have significant loadings on two factors—call them A and B. One possible interpretation of such a finding is that some individuals "use" ability A in performing the tasks of this scale, whereas other individuals "use" ability B. (By "using an ability," we mean simply that an individual's ability parameter is sufficiently high to permit successful performance with respect to whatever task parameter is relevant, regardless of the individual's parameter on some other ability, which might be quite low.) But another possibility is that the tasks require *both* abilities A and B roughly in the proportions indicated by the respective factor loadings. Factor analysis, by itself, has no direct way of indicating which of these possibilities obtains in a specific case. It is as yet unclear whether use of the A/DI model could distinguish these two possibilities, but at least the first of these possibilities was apparently illustrated in two studies (MacLeod, Hunt, & Mathews, 1978; Mathews, Hunt, & MacLeod, 1980) of performance on Clark and Chase's (1972) sentence verification task, by investigating fits of models of task difficulty for individuals having different ability patterns.

The Problem of Speeded Tasks

An implicit assumption in the previous discussion is that the dependent variable is accuracy: task difficulty is indexed by the proportion of individuals who perform a task "accurately." In many cognitive tasks, however, a dependent variable of interest may be the speed of performance, measured either in time per unit of performance (e.g., time to make a response, or RT) or performance per unit of time. In such cases speed of performance can be a function of task difficulty—easier tasks being performed faster, and it is often possible to establish models of task characteristics that predict speed. For example, Sternberg (1977) established models of analogical reasoning task difficulty that predicted "solution times" with apparently high accuracy. If it is desired to convert such models to make specifications in terms of more conventional indices such as proportions of individuals meeting a certain criterion, this could be done by viewing tasks as having "pseudodeadlines," in which case difficulty would be indexed by the proportion of individuals performing a task within some specified time. This type of treatment could if necessary be given to "component scores" that presumably specify times for stages of task performance. Note that in Sternberg's componential analysis the components are taken directly to represent the cognitive processes (encoding, inference, mapping, etc.) involved in task performance.

A similar problem arises in connection with certain "fluency" factors, where individuals are asked to make as many different responses as possible within a given time. The dependent variable can be studied either directly or as the proportion of individuals rendering a certain number of responses within a given time. Task difficulty still inheres in the nature of the stimuli and any constraints that are imposed on acceptable responses.

The methodology developed by White (1982) may be of use in modeling performances on speeded tasks. Speed, accuracy, and persistence in attempting a solution constitute separate parameters. Although speed and accuracy parameters may be correlated positively or negatively in a particular sample performing a particular task, they are logically distinct and must be so treated in any model of performance. Investigators must be alert to the possibility of speed-accuracy trade-offs.

Application of the A/DI Model to Selected Domains

Here I give illustrations of the feasibility of defining abilities, in three selected domains (reasoning, spatial ability, and verbal ability), in terms of continua of task characteristics. Unfortunately, the literature is largely silent about the detailed characteristics of individual tasks or items. Eysenck (1981, p. 83) has correctly said that the "fundamental unit of analysis [in defining an ability] should be the item," but partly because of space limitations and partly for purposes of protecting test security, few published articles give sufficient details about individual items to permit thorough analysis from the literature. Even test manuals rarely give information on characteristics (difficulties, etc.) of individual items. In fact, a thorough analysis could be made only from data on individual item responses. This section includes suggestions on how researchers could make such analyses from their own data.

The Domain of Reasoning Ability

Various kinds of reasoning abilities have always been regarded as closely related to intelligence, often highly loaded on a g or general intelligence factor. From the days of Spearman (1923, 1927) psychologists have been concerned with the nature of the cognitive processes involved in reasoning tests and the way in which such tests operate to measure intelligence. Spearman enunciated hypotheses about the nature of intelligence as exhibited in intelligence tests— hypotheses that are remarkably similar to those proposed (e.g., by Sternberg, 1977) in recent years, during which psychologists have paid detailed attention to these processes by studying them in experimental as well as psychometric contexts.

In factor-analytic studies (J. W. French, 1951; Thurstone, 1938) there have been fairly clear indications that several "primary" reasoning factors can be identified. Certainly an Induction factor is found in tests where the subject's task is to discover a rule or principle governing presented stimulus material, and a Deduction or Logical Reasoning factor is found in tests where the task is to produce or evaluate conclusions that logically follow from given premises. The ETS factor reference kit (Ekstrom et al., 1976) also postulates a General Reasoning factor associated mainly with quantitative reasoning problems, but this factor appears to be complex and not easily distinguished from the other reasoning factors. There is as yet little detailed psychological investigation of the tasks involved in this factor, in contrast to the Induction and Deduction factors. Our consideration here is therefore mainly limited to the Induction and Deduction factors, which appear to be factorially distinct even though substantially correlated.

It is usually considered that factors in the reasoning domain are covered, at a second-order of analysis, by a factor labeled *Gf*, "fluid intelligence" (Horn, 1978a, 1978b). It should be an interesting exercise to see whether the A/DI model can be applied so as to define both the primary factors and the second-order factor, but the literature does not permit us to pursue such an exercise at this time.

Inductive Ability Tasks

Among the tests having high loadings on this factor (and depending on test content, sometimes loadings on other factors) are various types of series completion, analogy, and figural matrix tests. In every case, the subject's task is to examine the stimulus material and infer one or more rules that need to be applied to produce or choose a correct solution to the item. It is not normally necessary for the subject to state the rule explicitly; a correct solution, however (apart from any chance guessing effects), presumably entails at least an implicit awareness of the appropriate rule. I find relevant studies of six item types, which are discussed here.

The Letter Series Completion Test.   A sample item is: jkqrklrslmst__?__ . Simon and Kotovsky (1963) developed a notation to describe the patterns of alphabetic letter sequences that must be discovered by subjects to solve such a problem. Holzman, Glaser, and Pellegrino (1976) reported finding a rank order correlation of .802 between the number of characters required to notate the patterns for 15 items and the number of errors made in these items by Simon and Kotovsky's group of high school students. Correlations of .789 and .773 were reported by these authors for a group of children in Grades 1 to 6. These findings suggest that a further analysis of relations between task characteristics of letter series problems and item difficulty could yield a reliable and objective method of determining a criterion-referenced score on this type of task, that is, a score that specifies what types of problems an examinee is likely to be able to solve or not to solve. In a further paper, Kotovsky and

Simon (1973) postulated four basic subroutines for correct solution: (a) the detection of interletter relations, (b) the discovery of periodicity, (c) the completion of a pattern description, and (d) extrapolation. Some of these subroutines entail the use of a particular knowledge base (the alphabetic order of letters); others involve fundamental cognitive operations such as temporary storage in memory, comparison, and so on. Possibly a multivariate analysis of item characteristics in relation to individual performances could isolate the relative importance of these routines and their relevance for a particular individual. (See, for example, the technique employed by Whitely & Schneider, 1981, discussed later. See also an improved rationale for the scaling of letter-series tasks; Butterfield, Nielsen, Tangen, & Richardson, 1985.)

Geometric Analogy Tasks. At least three investigations of this type of task yield findings that suggest how its scores could be made criterion-referenced by detailed study of task characteristics. R. J. Sternberg (1977, pp. 255–286) included a geometric analogy experiment in the series of investigations of his componential theory of intelligence. Task difficulty was evaluated by rated figure complexity and number of elements to be encoded. Sternberg was able to predict solution times under various task conditions ($r = .90$) from a model that incorporated task difficulty in an encoding parameter, but the correlation is in part due to variations in task conditions. Sternberg's data indicate that task difficulty is relevant, but he did not investigate this matter in a way detailed enough for my present purposes. Mulholland, Pellegrino, and Glaser (1980) examined geometric analogy task performance in 28 adults and found that reaction times for correct solution of true analogies were highly predictable from the number of elements in the stimulus materials, the number of "transformations" involved, and their product. Errors were also highly predictable from task characteristics (see the original article for details). Whitely and Schneider (1981) used a linear logistic model (Fischer, 1973) to analyze item difficulty (error) data from 211 undergraduates who were administered geometric analogy items from the Cognitive Abilities Test (Thorndike, Hagen, & Lorge, 1954–1974), testing Mulholland et al.'s model and then two more elaborated models. For Mulholland et al.'s model, number of elements was a significant variable but number of transformations was not. (Note the difference in subject populations, also that Whitely and Schneider did not investigate using the product of the two variables.) A second model also used number of elements, but transformations were separately classed as either distortions or displacements. In this model, in which item difficulties were predicted with $r = .68$, number of elements was not significantly related to item difficulty, but increased displacements made items harder, whereas increased number of distortions slightly decreased item difficulty, in agreement with previous findings cited by Whitely and Schneider. With further subdivisions of displacements and distortions, a third model produced slightly better predictions ($r = .73$). It is possible, of course, that further analyses of task characteristics could yield even better predictions. According to Whitely and Schneider, with the use of Gustafsson's (1977) procedure all the items were found to be homogeneous in the sense of testing a common ability or abilities.

In two of these studies, there was external validation of models through correlations of model data with scores on conventional reasoning tests. In Sternberg's (1977) experiment, although "interval" and "component" scores alone (based solely on models of solution times—see original text for definitions and details) did not have significant correlations with external variables, they did when combined with error rates. For example, highly significant multiple correlations of .80 ($N = 24$) were obtained for certain interval scores and error rates in predicting scores on the Cattell Culture-Fair test and the Lorge–Thorndike analogies test. This would suggest that the tests were more sensitive to level of ability than to speed of solution. One would expect error rates to be more relevant for level of ability than for speed. Mulholland et al. (1980) obtained $r = .69$ between error rates on their experimental items and scores on the Cognitive Abilities Test (CAT) geometric analogy subtest given with no time limits. Whitely and Schneider did not obtain data on any external variable because their analyses dealt with items taken directly from the CAT subtest, each item given by overhead projector with a fixed presentation time of 25 seconds (the average time available under standard test instructions); accuracy was the only dependent variable of interest. Thus, their results should be reasonably generalizable to geometric analogies tests given under normal conditions.

"People Piece" Analogies.   This type of analogies task, particularly well suited to his purposes, was used by Sternberg (1977, pp. 173–221) and its data were analyzed extensively. The stimuli were cartoon-like line drawings of people that were made to vary systematically in binary dimensions of height (tall, short), girth (fat, thin), color (red, blue), and sex. The items varied in the numbers of attribute values changed from the A to B and from the A to C terms of the analogy, and in the number of values by which the D term differed from the correct answer; because of item construction constraints, there could be only 75 types of items. The numbers of attribute values that were changed constituted task characteristics that were entered in equations of a model of analogical reasoning, with the result that estimates of the parameters ("components") of the model were dependent on them. Solution times were clearly dependent on the number of feature changes (see Sternberg's Fig. 7.3 and 7.4), and apparently error rates were as well, although error rates were generally low. Sternberg found a correlation of .96 between observed solution times and those predicted by the best of his models. Some of this correlation is undoubtedly due to cueing conditions, but it appears that task characteristics played a

large role in determining the dependent variables. A number of highly significant correlations (up to $-.80$) were found between solution times and external
variables, namely, scores on Word Grouping, Letter Series, and Cattell reasoning, and a reasoning factor score based on these and other tests, particularly
when the data were from later sessions when subjects had more nearly approached asymptotic performance. From Sternberg's data, it should be possible to characterize a given solution score in terms of combinations of task
characteristics associated with it. Determination of task characteristics associated with a liminal performance (a 50% chance of solution within a given time)
would also be feasible in principle.

Verbal Analogies.   There have been a number of investigations of verbal analogies of the conventional type found on various intelligence and scholastic
aptitude tests. It must be noted, however, that verbal analogies items frequently
contain a vocabulary load that is logically independent of any processes in
performing an analogy task per se. Carroll (1980b) showed that vocabulary
load is the almost exclusive source of task difficulty in verbal analogy items
found on the Scholastic Aptitude Test (SAT) sponsored by the College Board.
That is, few examinees fail these items because they do not know how to
perform analogical reasoning (they can pass items if the vocabulary load is
within their reach); they fail them mainly because they do not have adequate
knowledge of the word meanings involved.

In Sternberg's (1977, pp. 222–254) verbal analogy experiment, conducted
with 16 Stanford University undergraduates selected for a range of abilities,
items were not used if they were too difficult or "seemed to rely primarily on
vocabulary or general information" (p. 223). Task difficulty was controlled by
selecting analogy terms according to ratings of associative relatedness that were
also used in the mathematical modeling. The correlation between solution
times and those predicted by the best model was .93 but it is not clear to what
extent this was accounted for by the selection of terms in the analogy tasks;
some was undoubtedly due to cueing conditions. Nevertheless, for given cueing
conditions, there were a number of significant correlations of solution times
with external variables, including both scores on a reasoning test and scores on
a vocabulary test. The correlations with the vocabulary test do not necessarily
mean that Sternberg failed to control vocabulary load adequately; vocabulary
scores could be in part an indicant of reasoning ability. In any event, the
findings suggest that it would be possible to specify a scale of task difficulty in
terms of task characteristics as specified by the semantic distance ratings used
in constructing the items. Probably this possibility could be enhanced by using
a wider range of ability than Sternberg used, but on the other hand the model
would have to be adjusted to take account of the familiarity of terms, through
use of word frequency or related indices (Rubin, 1980).

Numerical Analogies.   An example of a numerical analogy item, as studied by Holzman, Pellegrino, and Glaser (1982), is the problem 20 : 16 : : 11 : 7 : : 6 : __?__ . Items were regarded as varying on two dimensions: number of operations or "transformations" and ambiguity. Items were classified as ambiguous whenever the first pair of numbers permitted a multiplication or division inference but the rule for the problem was addition or subtraction (e.g., 11 : 22 : : 7 : 18 : : 28 : __?__) or when two types of operations were combined. In multiple regression analyses, these variables predicted proportions of correct solutions with multiple correlations of .851, .884, and .851, respectively, for groups of average-IQ children, high-IQ children, and adults. Holzman et al. (1982) remark:

> The magnitudes of the [regression] coefficients vary across the three groups. Although number of operations had substantial effects on performance in all three groups, its relative importance seemed to decline at the higher age and IQ levels. This reflects the increasing importance of the ambiguity variable for the high-IQ and adult subjects. (p. 366)

The authors made further analyses in which the magnitudes of numbers and the types of numerical operations were also shown to be associated with item difficulty. I would conjecture that with more detailed techniques, further analyses could be made of these data to predict item difficulty (after a normal ogive transformation) more accurately than was shown in this article, possibly in a unified model that would take account of subject as well as task characteristics. Scores on reasoning with numerical analogies could thus be made criterion referenced in the sense that given scores would be associated with characteristic patterns of tasks.

Progressive Matrices.   Such matrices are found in the Cattell Culture-Fair Test and are the single item type utilized in three series of tests by Raven (1938–1965). An item consists of a 3 X 3 matrix, one cell of which is not given; figural materials are systematically varied over rows and columns and the subject's task is to choose, among presented alternatives, what figural shape should appear in the blank cell if the rules implicit in the matrix are to apply. The subject must therefore discover what rules govern the "progression" of materials over rows and columns. This type of test is often regarded as a good measure of *g*, or at least of an induction factor. Adkins and Lyerly (1952) found subsets of Standard Progressive Matrices tests loaded on a factor they interpreted as "hypothesis verification," although one set also loaded on a perceptual speed factor.

Nährer (1980) studied 10 specially constructed progressive matrix items, using Fischer's (1973) linear logistic model. Certain parameters (variation, superimposition, pattern, spatial arrangement, horizontality, and verticality, each with possible values of 0, 1, or 2) by which the complexity of the solutions was assessed, were shown to give moderate prediction (cross-validating data from a previous study) of empirical item difficulty parameters: I compute $r = .38$ from his data. Possibly the constrained nature of Nährer's sample of items precluded any better predictions, but his technology might well be employed in studies of a wider range of items.

It appears that Raven's Coloured Progressive Matrices test (primarily for younger children and retardates) may be factorially complex, with three or possibly four distinguishable and interpretable factors (Carlson & Jensen, 1980; Corman & Budoff, 1974). Any attempt to establish task difficulty scales as a function of item characteristics therefore would have to be concerned with the analysis of sets of items with high and univocal loadings on separate factors. I am unaware of any attempt to do this.

A further complicating consideration is that, as E.B. Hunt (1974) suggested, progressive matrices items can be performed either by analytic or holistic strategies.

In these studies of inductive reasoning, it is evident that the major way in which the tasks vary is the complexity of the rule or rules that are involved in solution. The modeling of item difficulty is accomplished by assigning weights to different characteristics of stimulus materials. Although no direct evidence can be found in the literature (because data are not reported by individuals, or even by groups of individuals of different ability levels), it appears that an individual's level of inductive ability is related to the level of rule complexity that the individual can readily perceive and apply. The task characteristics that control task difficulty are presumably related to the cognitive processes involved in rule eduction, such as those suggested by Sternberg (1977).

Deductive Ability Tasks

Tasks loading on this factor require the subject to form or choose a conclusion that logically follows from given premises. Among types most often employed in ability tests and given most study in cognitive psychology are the linear syllogism (e.g., A is longer than B; B is longer than C; which is shortest?), the categorical syllogism (e.g., All A are B; some C's are A. True or false: Some C's are B), and the conditional syllogism (e.g., if A, then B; A is true; is B true?). Sternberg (1982c, pp. 254ff.) provides a guide to the rather extensive literature on these tasks, focusing on the linear syllogism, for which there are several models that claim to represent the cognitive processes involved in performance. All models involve task characteristics in predicting solution time and errors, but differ in their interpretation of how subjects deal with these elements. Sternberg's (1980a) "mixed" linguistic-spatial model appears to be superior in its fit to data. In an experiment testing the model, 32 types of 3-term series problems were varied in five binary dimensions: (a) the markedness of the adjective in the first premise, (b) the markedness of the adjective in the second premise, (c) the markedness of the question adjective, (d) affirmative versus negative premises, (e) correct answer in first versus second premise. These dimensions are incorporated in a model that predicted, in experimental data, a composite of latency and error data with a squared canonical correlation of .849. These findings suggest that with further analysis it should be possible to specify scales of task difficulty for both speed and level of accuracy aspects of performance on this task. Space does not permit giving details on how Sternberg relates his parameters to cognitive processes; the reader is referred to his article.

In concluding this section on various types of reasoning and problem solving abilities, an observation that seems to emerge from our considerations may be noted, namely, that abilities have to do not so much with the overall structure or design of tasks as with how subjects handle aspects of the tasks as they vary on the difficulty scale. Different cognitive processes and knowledge bases are required or mobilized as tasks become more difficult. Verbal analogies that call for knowledge of words of low familiarity are a clear illustration of the importance of the knowledge base. An example where a particular cognitive process is called for by more difficult items is that cited by Pellegrino and Glaser (1980, p. 149), where more difficult items increase memory load requirements.

The Domain of Visuospatial Abilities

The domain of visuospatial factors is complex. Lohman (1979, p. 132) suggests that these factors can be sorted into those that involve mainly simple speed processes and those that involve complex processes properly measured by power (level of mastery) tests:

Speed factors:	Process
Cs (Speed of closure)	Identify
K (Left-right orientation)	Orient (left & right)
M (Spatial memory)	Remember
Ps (Perceptual speed)	Match
SR (Spatial relations)	Transform
Complex process factors	
SO (Spatial orientation)	Orient
Vz (Spatial visualization)	Visualize

It is interesting to note that in Lohman's view the factors show a direct correspondence with processes; processes are regarded as increasing in complexity as one reads down the list just given. (Processes can also become complex *within* factors; for example, factor Cs permits variation in the complexity or difficulty of visual materials to be identified, for example by degrading of the stimulus.) Of these factors, it appears that detailed experimental studies have concentrated on only three, namely Spatial Relations, Spatial Orientation, and Spatial Visualization. Pellegrino and Kail (1982) review this work, some of which is also considered by Cooper and Regan (1982), although it appears that the latter authors do not observe distinctions between the separate factors, concerning themselves with a global view of "spatial aptitude." Space does not permit a comprehensive discussion of available results, and I do not cover Egan's interesting work on Spatial Orientation; I can only offer tentative conclusions and suggestions from the perspective of the theoretical model of task difficulty proposed here.

Spatial Relations Tasks

According to Lohman, a spatial relations factor is found only in certain tests like Cards, Flags, and Figures (Thurstone, 1938) that involve presentation of spatial forms in different rotated positions and the requirement to check matches between stimuli. He remarks: "Although mental rotation is the common element, the factor probably does not represent speed of mental rotation. Rather, it represents the ability to solve such problems quickly, by whatever means" (p. 127). He seems to imply that different mental processes can be used to solve items. I adopt the view, however, that the *critical* element is speed of mental rotation whenever no other process is readily possible (compare views expressed by Cooper & Regan, 1982).

Pellegrino and Kail (1982) reported a number of detailed studies of stimulus matching by mental rotation, using stimuli that were either familiar alphanumeric symbols or figures taken from the Space test of the Primary Mental Abilities (PMA) battery (Thurstone & Thurstone, 1946). The latter are unfamiliar figures composed of irregularly convoluted lines. In addition to error rates, four parameters derived from subject response times when angular disparity between stimulus pairs was varied produced a multiple R of .57 with PMA Space test scores; this result suggested that "the particular speed differences that account for aptitude differences involve a basic mental rotation process and the speed of encoding, comparing, and rotating unfamiliar stimuli" (p. 323). However, further analysis suggested that there was also a component associated with switching a representation from identity to its mirror image. Using this component in the modeling of response speeds produced much better predictions, particularly when the possibility of subjects' using different solution strategies was allowed for. From the studies reported by Pellegrino and Kail, it seems clear that individual differences in spatial relations tasks are fundamentally related to a mental rotation process, even though certain tasks introduce complications when they use unfamiliar stimuli or involve mirror images. I conjecture that the purest task difficulty scale for spatial relations tasks would be one in which (a) only "same" judgments are involved in the tasks that are scaled; (b) the unfamiliarity of the stimuli is minimized by appropriate selection of stimuli, or perhaps by raising familiarity through practice; (c) task variation would be only in angular disparity; and (d) the dependent variable is speed of response, or probability of correct response within a deadline. For a reasonable experimental setting, the tasks might nevertheless have to be interspersed among tasks in which "different" judgments and less familiar stimuli would be involved. This conjecture, of course, would have to be tested in fresh experimental studies.

Spatial Visualization Tasks

Lohman (1979) stated that spatial visualization "is represented by a wide variety of tests such as Paper Folding, Form Board, WAIS Block Design, Hidden Figures, Copying, etc." (p. 127). These are usually administered under unspeeded conditions, and the dependent variable is more likely to be accuracy rather than speed. Task difficulty appears to be controlled mainly by the complexity or unfamiliarity of the stimulus materials. The cognitive process involved appears to be the encoding of the stimulus, that is, forming a mental representation of the stimulus or some transformation of it that is sufficiently stable to permit further mental operations with it.

Support for the notion that the critical element in Spatial Visualization is the encoding of the stimulus is found in various experimental results reported or discussed by Pellegrino and Kail. For example, they note that different slopes for reaction time as a function of angular disparity are found for familiar alphanumeric symbols as opposed to unfamiliar PMA stimuli. They also note the radically different slopes found for two-dimensional alphanumeric stimuli versus the complex three-dimensional block figures studied by Metzler and Shepard (1974). Apart from the effects of angular disparity, the critical differences in the regression lines are associated with stimulus complexity or unfamiliarity. It appears that there has been no study in which complexity or familiarity of stimuli has been systematically varied and related to speed and accuracy data. I would conjecture that a "pure" spatial visualization task difficulty scale would be one in which the critical variation in tasks would center in stimulus complexity (as it might be indexed by number of elements, asymmetry, or other variables) and/or unfamiliarity (as indexed by amount of prior exposure, practice, use of conventional vs. "strange" forms, etc.).

The Domain of Verbal Abilities

Various types of tests are found to load on a factor traditionally labeled V: tests of vocabulary, reading comprehension, composition (writing) ability, listening comprehension, interpretation of proverbs, many (but not all) tests of verbal analogies, and so on. Consistently, tests of vocabulary, and indeed any tests that put a demand on knowledge of the meanings of words in the examinee's native or best acquired language, have highest loadings on this factor. Nevertheless, there are indications that the factor extends to other types of language knowledge and skill, such as comprehension of complex ideas presented in prose with low vocabulary load but complex syntax.

It would be easy, although possibly misleading, to construct a task difficulty scale for vocabulary knowledge as measured by typical multiple-choice vocabulary tests. Word frequency as indexed by word counts such as those of Thorndike and Lorge (1944), Kucera and Francis (1967), or Carroll, Davies, and Richman (1971) would be one variable correlating fairly highly with empirical item difficulty. Other variables, such as concreteness versus abstractness (Spreen & Schulz, 1966) and age of acquisition (Carroll & White, 1973) would probably increase the correlation significantly. These variables, however, would indicate little about cognitive processes, for tests of vocabulary are primarily measures of a knowledge base. It is somewhat paradoxical that vocabulary tests nevertheless show high correlations with a general factor, and especially with the crystallized intelligence factor described by Horn and Cattell (1966). It would be a mistake, however, to suppose that this is because a higher order factor of intelligence is required in the choice of answers in a multiple-choice test. The cognitive processes in selecting correct answers, given that the relevant word meanings are known, must surely be of a fairly elementary character.

Marshalek (1981) addressed himself to making a process analysis of vocabulary knowledge, using a sample of 74 high school seniors representing a bivariate distribution of verbal and spatial ability. Three types of vocabulary tests were used: a multiple-choice test requiring only "vague knowledge" of word meanings (i.e., selecting from clearly distinctive meanings), a multiple-choice test requiring "accurate recognition" of word meanings (i.e., selecting from closely related meanings, only one being truly correct), and a test requiring free-response definitions of words presented. Vocabulary words were systematically varied along dimensions of word frequency and concreteness versus abstractness.

Word frequency and abstractness were related to item difficulty only when precise meanings and definitions were required, a result that was interpreted as showing that words and their meanings can exist in states of knowledge that vary in completeness and precision.

Reference tests given to the sample included tests of reasoning, reading comprehension, and spatial ability. Reasoning scores were related to vocabulary measures in several interesting ways: (a) subjects with low reasoning ability had pronounced difficulty in the formulation of good word definitions; (b) reasoning ability was related to vocabulary knowledge primarily over the bottom half of the vocabulary distribution, whereas in the top half it made little difference; and (c) reasoning ability correlations with vocabulary increased as the degree of precision of knowledge required increased. Correlations with reading comprehension tests were higher for vocabulary tests with words of high and medium word-count frequency than for tests with relatively rare words. Subjects with high spatial ability seemed to have had an advantage in acquiring the meanings of concrete words, but not those of abstract words.

The variables Marshalek used provided little direct information about cognitive processes. The total pattern of results, however, led him to conclude that the cognitive processes involved in vocabulary knowledge occur primarily during the *acquisition* phase rather than at the time of taking a vocabulary test. Tests of knowledge of the exact meanings of high and medium frequency words are more practical indicators of vocabulary than tests of knowledge of low frequency words because, as he put it, "high frequency words are words to which everyone is exposed; failing to comprehend them must result mainly from failure to extract meanings during the acquisition or definition stages rather than from lack of exposure" (p. 62). Such failures are presumably due to low general intelligence or reasoning ability. Marshalek's results suggest also that acquisition of the meanings of low frequency words tends to occur mainly among people who are above a certain level of reasoning ability and who have long and consistent exposure to such words through reading and similar forms of experience.

Verbal ability is not indexed only by vocabulary knowledge. It is also indexed by comprehension of verbal materials presenting relatively complex ideas— even with a low vocabulary load. An example of an attempt to measure reading comprehension according to levels of "readability" or reading difficulty is found in the Degrees of Reading Power tests developed by the New York State Board of Education (see Kibby, 1981). The reading passages on these tests constitute, in effect, a scale of task difficulty, and their positions on the scale can be modeled by parameters conventionally used in readability formulas that reflect not only word frequency but also syntactical complexity.

On the other hand, there has been some difficulty in attempting to show that verbal ability correlates with performance on a well-known "sentence verification" task developed by Clark and Chase (1972) and extensively studied by cognitive psychologists. For example, from a study using 84 college students, Lansman (1981) reported difficulties in fitting either Clark and Chase's or Carpenter and Just's (1975) model of sentence verification. (These models involve parameters pertaining to the use of falsification, negation, and linguistically marked adjectives.) Further, parameters derived from these models had generally nonsignificant correlations with fluid intelligence scores. Possibly these findings are due to the relatively restricted range of verbal ability in the sample, but it is also likely that the task is simply too easy even for individuals with only a moderate degree of verbal ability. A sentence verification task that would involve more advanced linguistic phenomena, such as the use of conditional clauses and embedded constituents, might show greater relation with traditional tests of verbal ability.

CONCLUDING DISCUSSION

This chapter, particularly the third section, has not been easy to write. The primary goal has been to present a perspective on the nature of cognitive abilities, the multifactorial character of the domain, and the ways abilities are related to learned knowledge and skill and to cognitive processes. A second goal has been to make suggestions on a research methodology for further investigations of these matters. On the one hand, it has been difficult to select important ideas and findings from the vast literature that already exists on these topics, but on the other hand it has been difficult to find truly useful and relevant materials to illustrate the proposed research methodologies. The study of cognitive abilities from the perspectives I propose is still in its infancy, and investigators have not yet covered much ground. But even in presenting illustrative material, space limitations have precluded a full discussion of the technically sophisticated theory and detail that is present in the sources.

Readers will undoubtedly wonder: in all this material, where does one find the cognitive processes we seek? Are they contained in the "factors" of ability? Are they implied in scales of task difficulty? Are they contained in the models that predict placement of tasks on these scales? And where are the "cognitive strategies" that many think are obvious determinants of performance? Finally, where does all this lead, in terms of possible practical applications?

The answers to these queries are varied. Cognitive processes *are* sometimes contained in factors, but often embedded so deeply in them, so to speak, that they may not be immediately apparent. They may constitute the "essence" of an ability factor. Examples are the cognitive processes implicit in the Spatial Visualization factor—the formation of a spatial representation—and in the Spatial Relations factor—the mental rotation of a spatial representation. But even in these cases the inference that a cognitive process is the essence of the factor comes only through analysis of what is *critical* in controlling task difficulty, leading to conjectures about how the factor might be measured in a more purified form than is manifested by tests or variables that have not been cleaned of extraneous sources of variance. The tests commonly used in measuring Spatial Visualization and Spatial Relations are only a starting point.

Cognitive processes can also be implied in scales of task difficulty. In the examples just given, they are implied in the fact that task difficulty is controlled by variations in task characteristics that call for different amounts or efficiencies of ongoing cognitive processes, such as spatial form encoding or mental rotation of such forms. In the case of Spatial Rotation, it is probable that only a *single* parameter controls task difficulty, that is, angular disparity between mental representations, from which it may be inferred that the corresponding cognitive process is unitary. In the case of Spatial Visualization, it is possible that a number of stimulus parameters might have to be used to predict task difficulty—number of elements, their size and orientation, amount of competing context, and so on. This would suggest that a number of separate perceptual processes might occur during the encoding of a stimulus. Although it might be satisfactory to summarize such processes by regarding them as constituting a single process, the parameters themselves might correspond to separate constituent processes or components. If such components can be isolated by experimental or theoretical models, and if these components appear to be different sources of ability variance, the separate parameters that control task difficulty might be said to correspond to separate cognitive processes. Such a state of affairs may obtain in the case of parameters controlling the difficulty of inductive reasoning tasks. See, for example, Carroll's (1980c) reanalysis of certain data published by Sternberg (1977) on analogical reasoning tasks.

When task difficulty is controlled by parameters that refer to past experiences of subjects (amount of learning, amount of exposure to stimuli, etc.), the task difficulty continuum has to do with the properties of a knowledge base. The relevant cognitive processes are not those occurring during task performance but those that occurred in the acquisition of the knowledge base. An example of this was seen in our discussion of the Verbal Knowledge factor. Other examples would be seen in a consideration of various factors in the memory domain, except that some of the components would not pertain to the knowledge base but to processes during task performance. For example, memory span performance is controlled partly by the knowledge base properties of the stimuli (digits, words, etc.) and partly by cognitive processes occurring during task performance (e.g., encoding of stimulus order).

Accounting for variations in subject cognitive strategies in terms of the A/DI model presents a problem. The notion that subjects use different cognitive strategies would correspond to the notion that a different model of task difficulty, with different variables and parameters, would apply for any given cognitive strategy. To date, the clearest example of how this might be true has been provided by the work of MacLeod et al. (1978; see also Mathews et al., 1980), who show that different models of sentence verification task performance apply for groups differing in patterns of verbal and spatial ability. Another example may be seen in studies of visual stimulus matching performance described by Cooper (1982), except that in this case it appears that strategy can be controlled to some extent by instructions, and the instructions become, in effect, part of the definition of the task.

For the analysis of cognitive strategy effects it may be suggested that one initially assume a "pure" A/DI model that operates in the same way for all subjects, subsequently investigating variations from this model that would be a function either of subjects' ability patterns or task variations produced by variations in instructions.

Toward what end does all this work lead? First of all, I think it leads toward better understanding of the phenomena we are addressing. This is, after all, a primary goal in research. The investigations of recent years have helped us to understand better the nature of human abilities and their bases in skill, knowledge, and cognition. I expect that much further progress can and will be made—whether or not it is precisely along lines suggested here.

An intermediate end to be served by work in cognitive ability testing would be the devising of better and more meaningful tests of basic cognitive skills than are now available. In so far as such skills are relevant to school and life activities generally—and it is hard to deny that they are of major weight—any improvement in measuring devices would possibly lead to more general acceptance of such measures among educators and the public.

Ultimately, however, a better understanding of relations between abilities and human performance cannot but be beneficial to efforts to change abilities and performances in desired ways. Once we achieve a better understanding of what cognitive skills and knowledge bases are involved in various desirable human endeavors, we can begin to operate on those cognitive skills and knowledge bases to effect changes. Certainly knowledge bases can be enlarged through instruction and learning, and many cognitive skills could probably be enhanced through training and practice. If individuals' constitutions place limits on the changes that could be effected, we need to know what those limits are. In closing, I reiterate a theme introduced near the beginning of this chapter, namely, that the possibilities for environmental manipulation of human cognitive abilities still remain wide open.

REFERENCES

Adkins, D., & Lyerly, S. (1952). *Factor analysis of reasoning tests.* Chapel Hill, NC: University of North Carolina Press.

Anastasi, A. (1980). Abilities and the measurement of achievement. In W. B. Schrader (Ed.), *New directions for testing and measurement* (Vol. 5 pp. 1–10). San Francisco: Jossey-Bass.

Anastasi, A. (1981). Diverse effects of training on tests of academic intelligence. In B. F. Green (Ed.), *New directions for testing and measurement: Issues in testing— Coaching, disclosure, and ethnic bias* (Vol. 11, pp. 5–19). San Francisco: Jossey-Bass.

Anastasi, A. (1982a). *Contributions to differential psychology: Selected papers.* New York: Praeger.

Anastasi, A. (1982b). *Psychological testing* (5th ed.). New York: Macmillan.

Anderson, J. E. (1939). The limitations of infant and preschool tests in the measurement of intelligence. *Journal of Psychology, 8,* 351–379.

Atkin, R., Bray, R., Davison, M., Herzberger, S., Humphreys, L. G., & Selzer, U. (1977). Ability factor differentiation grades 5 through 11. *Applied Psychological Measurement, 1,* 65–76.

Bayley, N. (1970). Development of mental abilities. In P. H. Mussen (Ed.), *Carmichael's manual of child psychology* (3rd ed., pp. 1163–1209). New York: Wiley.

Berger, M. (1982). The 'scientific approach' to intelligence: An overview of its history with special reference to mental speed. In H. J. Eysenck (Ed.), *A model for intelligence* (pp. 13–43). Berlin and New York: Springer-Verlag.

Binet, A., & Simon, T. (1905). Méthodes nouvelles pour le diagnostic du niveau intellectuel des anormaux. *Année Psychologique, 11,* 191–336.

Birren, J. E., & Schaie, K. W. (Eds.). (1977). *Handbook of the psychology of aging.* New York: Van Nostrand Reinhold.

Birren, J. E., Woods, A. M., & Williams, M. V. (1980). Behavioral slowing with age: Causes, organization, and consequences. In L. W. Poon (Ed.), *Aging in the 1980s: Psychological issues* (pp. 293–308). Washington, DC: American Psychological Association.

Bisanz, J., Danner, F., & Resnick, L. B. (1979). Changes with age in measures of processing efficiency. *Child Development, 50,* 132–141.

Block, N. J., & Dworkin, G. (1976). IQ heritability and inequality. In N. J. Block & G. Dworkin (Eds.), *The IQ controversy: Critical readings* (pp. 410–542). New York: Pantheon.

Boehm, A. E., & Sandberg, B. R. (1982). Assessment of the preschool child. In C. R. Reynolds & T. B. Gutkin (Eds.), *Handbook of school psychology* (pp. 82–120). New York: Wiley.

Boring, E. G. (1923). Intelligence as the tests test it. *New Republic, 35,* 35–37.

Boring, E. G. (1957). *A history of experimental psychology* (2nd ed.). New York: Appleton-Century-Crofts.

Botwinick, J. (1977). Intellectual abilities. In J. E. Birren & K. W. Schaie (Eds.), *Handbook of the psychology of aging* (pp. 580–605). New York: Van Nostrand Reinhold.

Brody, E. B., & Brody, N. (1976). *Intelligence: Nature, determinants, and consequences.* New York: Academic Press.

Buros, O. K. (Ed.). (1953). *The fourth mental measurements yearbook.* Highland Park, NJ: Gryphon.

Buros, O. K. (Ed.). (1959). *The fifth mental measurements yearbook.* Highland Park, NJ: Gryphon.

Buros, O. K. (Ed.). (1965). *The sixth mental measurements yearbook.* Highland Park, NJ: Gryphon.

Buros, O. K. (Ed.). (1972). *The seventh mental measurements yearbook.* Highland Park, NJ: Gryphon.

Buros, O. K. (Ed.). (1975). *Intelligence tests and reviews: A monograph consisting of the intelligence sections of the seven Mental Measurements Yearbooks (1938–72) and Tests in Print II (1974).* Highland Park, NJ: Gryphon.

Buros, O. K. (Ed.). (1978). *The eighth mental measurements yearbook.* Highland Park, NJ: Gryphon.

Buss, A. R. (1973a). A conceptual framework for learning effecting the development of ability factors. *Human Development, 16,* 273–292.

Buss, A. R. (1973b). Learning, transfer, and changes in ability factors: A multivariate model. *Psychological Bulletin, 80,* 106–111.

Buss, A. R., & Royce, J. R. (1975). Ontogenetic changes in cognitive structure from a multivariate perspective. *Developmental Psychology, 11,* 87–101.

Butcher, H. J. (1968). *Human intelligence: Its nature and assessment.* London: Methuen.

Butterfield, E. C., Nielsen, D., Tangen, K. L., & Richardson, M. B. (1985). The-oretically based psychometric measures of inductive reasoning. In S. E. Embretson (Ed.), *Test design: Developments in psychology and psychometrics* (pp. 77–147). Or-lando, FL: Academic Press.

Campbell, A. C. (1961). Some determinants of the difficulty of non-verbal classifica-tion items. *Educational & Psychological Measurement, 21,* 899–913.

Carlson, J. S., & Jensen, C. M. (1980). The factorial structure of the Raven Coloured Progressive Matrices Test: A reanalysis. *Educational & Psychological Measurement, 40,* 1111–1116.

Carpenter, P. A., & Just, M. A. (1975). Sentence comprehension: A psycholinguistic processing model of verification. *Psychological Review, 82,* 45–73.

Carr, H. A., & Kingsbury, F. A. (1938). The concept of ability. *Psychological Review, 45,* 354–376.

Carroll, J. B. (1945). The effect of difficulty and chance success on correlations be-tween items or between tests. *Psychometrika, 10,* 1–19.

Carroll, J. B. (1961). The nature of the data, or how to choose a correlation coefficient. *Psychometrika, 26,* 347–372.

Carroll, J. B. (1974a). The aptitude-achievement distinction: The case of foreign lan-guage aptitude and proficiency. In D. R. Green (Ed.), *The aptitude-achievement distinction* (pp. 286–311). Monterey, CA: CTB/McGraw-Hill.

Carroll, J. B. (1974b). Fitting a model of school learning to aptitude and achievement data over grade levels. In D. R. Green (Ed.), *The aptitude-achievement distinction* (pp. 53–78). Monterey, CA: CTB/McGraw-Hill.

Carroll, J. B. (1976). Psychometric tests as cognitive tasks: A new "Structure of intel-lect." In L. Resnick (Ed.), *The nature of intelligence* (pp. 27–56). Hillsdale, NJ: Lawrence Erlbaum Associates.

Carroll, J. B. (1980a). *Individual difference relations in psychometric and experimental cognitive tasks.* Chapel Hill, NC: The L. L. Thurstone Psychometric Laboratory, University of North Carolina (Report No. 163), April [NTIS Document AD-A086 057.]

Carroll, J. B. (1980b). Measurement of abilities constructs. In U. S. Office of Personnel Management & Educational Testing Service, *Construct validity in psychological mea-surement* (pp. 23–41). Princeton, NJ: Educational Testing Service.

Carroll, J. B. (1980c). Remarks on Sternberg's "Factor theories of intelligence are all right almost." *Educational Researcher, 9*(8), 14–18.

Carroll, J. B. (1981). Ability and task difficulty in cognitive psychology. *Educational Researcher, 10*(1), 11–21.

Carroll, J. B. (1982a). The measurement of intelligence. In R. J. Sternberg (Ed.), *Hand-book of human intelligence* (pp. 29–120). Cambridge and New York: Cambridge University Press.

Carroll, J. B. (1982b). Review of Eysenck & Kamin's *The intelligence controversy. Applied Psychological Measurement, 6,* 241–244.

Carroll, J. B. (1983a). The difficulty of a test and its factor composition revisited. In H. Wainer & Samuel Messick (Eds.), *Principals of modern psychological measurement: A Festschrift in honor of Frederick M. Lord* (pp. 257–283). Hillsdale, NJ: Lawrence Erlbaum Associates.

Carroll, J. B. (1983b). Studying individual differences in cognitive abilities: Through and beyond factor analysis. In R. F. Dillon & R. R. Schmeck (Eds.), *Individual differences in cognition* (Vol. 1, pp. 1–33). New York: Academic Press.

Carroll, J. B. (1985). Exploratory factor analysis: A tutorial. In D. K. Detterman (Ed.), *Current topics in human intelligence, Vol. 1: Research Methodology* (pp. 25–88). Norwood, NJ: Ablex.

Carroll, J. B., Davies, P., & Richman, B. (1971). *The American Heritage word frequency book.* Boston: Houghton Mifflin.

Carroll, J. B., & Horn, J. L. (1981). On the scientific basis of ability testing. *American Psychologist, 36,* 1012–1020.

Carroll, J. B., & White, M. N. (1973). Age-of-acquisition norms for 220 picturable nouns. *Journal of Verbal Learning and Verbal Behavior, 12,* 563–576.

Caruso, D. R., Taylor, J. J., & Detterman, D. K. (1982). Intelligence research and intelligent policy. In D. K. Detterman & R. J. Sternberg (Eds.), *How and how much can intelligence be increased* (pp. 45–65). Norwood, NJ: Ablex.

Cattell, R. B. (1971). *Abilities: Their structure, growth, and action.* Boston: Houghton Mifflin.

Cattell, R. B. (1978). *The scientific use of factor analysis in behavioral and life sciences.* New York: Plenum.

Chiang, A., & Atkinson, R. C. (1976). Individual differences and interrelationships among a select set of cognitive skills. *Memory & Cognition, 4,* 661–672.

Clark, H. H., & Chase, W. G. (1972). On the process of comparing sentences against pictures. *Cognitive Psychology, 3,* 472–517.

Cohen, R. L., & Sandberg, T. (1980). Intelligence and short-term memory: A clandestine relationship. *Intelligence, 4,* 319–331.

Cooper, L. A. (1982). Strategies for visual comparison and representation: Individual differences. In R. J. Sternberg (Ed.), *Advances in the psychology of intelligence* (Vol. 1, pp. 77–124). Hillsdale, NJ: Lawrence Erlbaum Associates.

Cooper, L. A., & Regan, D. T. (1982). Attention, perception, and intelligence. In R. J. Sternberg (Ed.), *Handbook of human intelligence* (pp. 123–169). Cambridge and New York: Cambridge University Press.

Corman, L., & Budoff, M. (1974). Factor structures of retarded and nonretarded children on Raven's Progressive Matrices. *Educational & Psychological Measurement, 34,* 407–412.

Cunningham, W. R. (1980). Speed, age, and qualitative differences in cognitive functioning. In L. W. Poon (Ed.), *Aging in the 1980s: Psychological issues* (pp. 327–331). Washington, DC: American Psychological Association.

DeFries, J. C., & Plomin, R. (1978). Behavioral genetics. *Annual Review of Psychology, 29,* 473–515.

Detterman, D. K., & Sternberg, R. J. (Eds.). (1982). *How and how much can intelligence be increased.* Norwood, NJ: Ablex.

Egan, D. E. (1981). An analysis of spatial orientation test performance. *Intelligence, 5,* 85–100.

Ekstrom, R. B. (1979). Review of cognitive factors. *Multivariate Behavioral Research Monographs,* No. 79-2.

Ekstrom, R. B., French, J. W., & Harman, H. H. (1976). *Manual for kit of factor-referenced cognitive tests, 1976.* Princeton, NJ: Educational Testing Service.

Elliott, C., Murray, D. J., & Pearson, L. S. (1978–1982). *British Ability Scales—Manuals*. Windsor, England: National Foundation for Educational Research/NFER Publishing Co.

Engen, T. (1971). Psychophysics: I. Discrimination and detection. In J. W. Kling & L. A. Riggs (Eds.), *Woodworth & Schlosberg's experimental psychology* (3rd ed., pp. 11–46). New York: Holt, Rinehart & Winston.

Eysenck, H. J. (1979). *The structure and measurement of intelligence.* (With contributions by D. W. Fulker). New York: Springer-Verlag.

Eysenck, H. J. (1981). The nature of intelligence. In M. P. Friedman, J. P. Das, & N. O'Connor (Eds.), *Intelligence and learning* (pp. 67–85). New York and London: Plenum.

Eysenck, H. J., & Kamin, L. (1981). *The intelligence controversy.* New York: Wiley-Interscience.

Fagan, J. F., III, & McGrath, S. K. (1981). Infant recognition memory and later intelligence. *Intelligence, 5,* 121–130.

Ferguson, G. A. (1941). The factorial interpretation of test difficulty. *Psychometrika, 6,* 323–329.

Fischer, G. H. (1973). The linear logistic model as an instrument in educational research. *Acta Psychologica, 37,* 359–374.

Frederiksen, J. R. (1982). A componential theory of reading skills and their interactions. In R. J. Sternberg (Ed.), *Advances in the psychology of intelligence* (Vol. 1, pp. 125–180). Hillsdale, NJ: Lawrence Erlbaum Associates.

French, J. L. (Reviser) (1973). *The Henmon-Nelson Tests of Mental Ability.* Boston: Houghton Mifflin.

French, J. W. (1951). The description of aptitude and achievement tests in terms of rotated factors. *Psychometric Monographs,* No. 5.

Garrett, H. E. (1938). Differentiable mental traits. *Psychological Record, 2,* 259–298.

Garrett, H. E. (1946). A developmental theory of intelligence. *American Psychologist, 1,* 372–378.

Glaser, R. (1972). Individuals and learning: The new aptitudes. *Educational Researcher, 1*(6), 5–13.

Guilford, J. P. (1937). The psychophysics of mental test difficulty. *Psychometrika, 2,* 121–133.

Guilford, J. P. (1941). The difficulty of a test and its factor composition. *Psychometrika, 6,* 67–77.

Guilford, J. P. (1967). *The nature of human intelligence.* New York: McGraw-Hill.

Gustafsson, J-E. (1977). *The Rasch model for dichotomous items: Theory, applications, and a computer program* (Research Report No. 63). Mölndal, Sweden: University of Göteborg, Institute of Education.

Guttman, L. (1941). The quantification of a class of attributes: A theory and method for scale construction. In P. Horst et al., *The prediction of personal adjustment* (pp. 319–348). New York: Social Science Research Council.

Hakstian, A. R., & Cattell, R. B. (1976). *Comprehensive ability battery.* Champaign, IL: Institute for Personality and Ability Testing.

Hakstian, A. R., & Cattell, R. B. (1978). Higher-stratum ability structures on a basis of twenty primary abilities. *Journal of Educational Psychology, 70,* 657–669.

Hambleton, R. K. (1982). Advances in criterion-referenced testing technology. In C. R. Reynolds & T. B. Gutkin (Eds.), *Handbook of school psychology* (pp. 351–379). New York: Wiley.

Hearnshaw, L. S. (1980). Balance sheet on Burt. *Bulletin of the British Psychological Society, 33,* Supplement, 1–8.

Hindley, C. B. (1981). Individual difference in the patterning of curves of D. Q. and I. Q. scores from 6 months to 17 years. In M. P. Friedman, J. P. Das, & N. O'Connor (Eds.), *Intelligence and learning* (pp. 553–559). New York and London: Plenum.

Holzman, T. G., Glaser, R., & Pellegrino, J. W. (1976). Process training derived from a computer simulation theory. *Memory & Cognition, 4,* 349–356.

Holzman, T. G., Pellegrino, J. G., & Glaser, R. (1982). Cognitive dimensions of numerical rule induction. *Journal of Educational Psychology, 74,* 360–373.

Horn, J. L. (1978a). Human ability systems. In P. B. Baltes (Ed.), *Life-span development and behavior* (Vol. 1, pp. 211–256). New York: Academic Press.

Horn, J. L. (1978b). The nature and development of intellectual abilities. In R. T. Osborne, C. E. Noble, & N. Weyl (Eds.), *Human variation: The biopsychology of age, race, and sex* (pp. 107–136). New York: Academic Press.

Horn, J. L. (1980). Concepts of intellect in relation to learning and adult development. *Intelligence, 4,* 285–317.

Horn, J. L., & Cattell, R. B. (1966). Refinement of the theory of fluid and crystallized general intelligences. *Journal of Educational Psychology, 57,* 253–270.

Horn, J. L., & Stankov, L. (1982). Auditory and visual factors of intelligence. *Intelligence, 6,* 165–185.

Humphreys, L. G. (1979). The construct of general intelligence. *Intelligence, 3,* 105–120.

Hunt, E. B. (1974). Quote the Raven? Nevermore! In L. W. Gregg (Ed.), *Knowledge and cognition* (pp. 129–157). Hillsdale, NJ: Lawrence Erlbaum Associates.

Hunt, E. (1976). Varieties of cognitive power. In L. Resnick (Ed.), *The nature of intelligence* (pp. 237–259). Hillsdale, NJ: Lawrence Erlbaum Associates.

Hunt, E. (1978). Mechanics of verbal ability. *Psychological Review, 85,* 109–130.

Hunt, E., Frost, N., & Lunneborg, C. (1973). Individual differences in cognition: A new approach to intelligence. In G. Bower (Ed.), *The psychology of learning and motivation: Advances in research and theory* (Vol. 7, pp. 87–122). New York: Academic Press.

Hunt, E., & Lansman, M. (1982). Individual differences in attention. In R. J. Sternberg (Ed.), *Advances in the psychology of intelligence* (Vol. 1, pp. 207–254). Hillsdale, NJ: Lawrence Erlbaum Associates.

Hunt, E., Lunneborg, C., & Lewis, J. (1975). What does it mean to be high verbal? *Cognitive Psychology, 7,* 194–227.

Hunt, J. M. (1961). *Intelligence and experience.* New York: Ronald.

Hunt, J. M. (1981). Comments on "The modification of intelligence through early experience" by Ramey and Haskins. *Intelligence, 5,* 21–27.

Jackson, M. D., & McClelland, J. L. (1979). Processing determinants of reading speed. *Journal of Experimental Psychology: General, 108,* 151–181.

Jensen, A. R. (1972). *Genetics and education.* London: Methuen.

Jensen, A. R. (1980). *Bias in mental testing.* New York: The Free Press.

Jensen, A. R. (1981). *Straight talk about mental tests.* New York: The Free Press.

Jensen, A. R. (1982). The chronometry of intelligence. In R. J. Sternberg (Ed.), *Advances in the psychology of intelligence* (Vol. 1, pp. 255–310). Hillsdale, NJ: Lawrence Erlbaum Associates.

Jones, L. V. (1949). A factor analysis of the Stanford-Binet at four age levels. *Psychometrika, 14,* 299–331.

Jones, L. V. (1954). Primary abilities in the Stanford-Binet, age 13. *Journal of Genetic Psychology, 84,* 125–147.

Kaplan, R. M., & Saccuzzo, D. P. (1982). *Psychological testing: Principles, applications, and issues.* Monterey, CA: Brooks-Cole.

Kaufman, A. S. (1979). *Intelligence testing with the WISC-R.* New York: Wiley.

Kaufman, A. S. (1982). The impact of WISC-R research for school psychologists. In C. R. Reynolds & T. B. Gutkin (Eds.), *Handbook of school psychology* (pp. 156–177). New York: Wiley.

Keating, D. P. (1979). Toward a multivariate life-span theory of intelligence. *New Directions for Child Development, 5,* 69–84.

Keating, D. P., & Bobbitt, B. L. (1978). Individual and developmental differences in cognitive-processing components of mental ability. *Child Development, 49,* 155–167.

Kelley, T. L. (1927). *The interpretation of educational measurements.* Yonkers-on-Hudson, NY: World Book.

Kibby, M. W. (1981). Test review: The Degrees of Reading Power. *Journal of Reading, 24,* 416–427.

Knox, A. B. (1977). *Adult development and learning: A handbook on individual growth and competence in the adult years.* San Francisco: Jossey-Bass.

Kotovsky, K., & Simon, H. A. (1973). Empirical tests of a theory of human acquisition of concepts for sequential patterns. *Cognitive Psychology, 4,* 399–424.

Kucera, H., & Francis, W. N. (1967). *Computational analysis of present-day American English.* Providence, RI: Brown University Press.

Kuhlmann, F., & Anderson, R. G. (1963). *Kuhlmann-Anderson Intelligence Tests* (7th ed.). Princeton, NJ: Personnel Press.

Lansman, M. (1981). Ability factors and the speed of information processing. In M. P. Friedman, J. P. Das, & N. O'Connor (Eds.), *Intelligence and learning* (pp. 441–457). New York and London: Plenum.

Lewis, M., & Brooks-Gunn, J. (1981). Visual attention at three months as a predictor of cognitive functioning at two years of age. *Intelligence, 5,* 131–140.

Lohman, D. F. (1979). *Spatial ability: A review and reanalysis of the correlational literature.* Stanford, CA: Aptitude Research Project, School of Education, Stanford University (Tech. Report No. 8).

Lord, F. M., & Novick, M. R. (1968). *Statistical theories of mental test scores.* Reading, MA: Addison-Wesley.

Lutey, C., & Copeland, E. P. (1982). Cognitive assessments of the school-age child. In C. R. Reynolds & T. B. Gutkin (Eds.), *Handbook of school psychology* (pp. 121–155). New York: Wiley.

MacLeod, C. M., Hunt, E. B., & Mathews, N. N. (1978). Individual differences in the verification of sentence-picture relationships. *Journal of Verbal Learning and Verbal Behavior, 17,* 493–507.

Marshalek, B. (1981). *Trait and process aspects of vocabulary knowledge and verbal ability*. Stanford, CA: Aptitude Research Project, School of Education, Stanford University (Tech. Report No. 15).

Matarazzo, J. D. (1972). *Wechsler's measurement and appraisal of adult intelligence* (5th ed.). Baltimore, MD: Williams & Wilkins.

Mathews, N. N., Hunt, E. B., & MacLeod, C. M. (1980). Strategy choice and strategy training in sentence-picture verification. *Journal of Verbal Learning and Verbal Behavior, 19,* 531–548.

McCall, R. B. (1981). Early predictors of later IQ: The search continues. *Intelligence,* 1981, *5,* 141–147.

McNemar, Q. (1964). Lost: Our intelligence? Why? *American Psychologist, 19,* 871–882.

Metzler, J., & Shepard, R. N. (1974). Transformational studies of the internal representations of three-dimensional objects. In R. Solso (Ed.), *Theories in cognitive psychology: The Loyola Symposium* (pp. 147–201). Hillsdale, NJ: Lawrence Erlbaum Associates.

Mosier, C. I. (1940). Psychophysics and mental test theory: Fundamental postulates and elementary theorems. *Psychological Review, 47,* 355–366.

Mosier, C. I. (1941). Psychophysics and mental test theory. II. The constant process. *Psychological Review, 48,* 235–249.

Mulholland, T. M., Pellegrino, J. W., & Glaser, R. (1980). Components of geometric analogy solution. *Cognitive Psychology, 12,* 252–284.

Nährer, W. (1980). Zur Analyse von Matrizenaufgaben mit dem linearen logistischen Testmodell. *Zeitschrift für Experimentelle und Angewandte Psychologie, 27,* 553–564.

Neisser, U. (1979). The concept of intelligence. *Intelligence, 3,* 217–227.

Office of Strategic Services, Assessment Staff. (1948). *Assessment of men: Selection of personnel for the Office of Strategic Services.* New York: Rinehart.

Pellegrino, J. W., & Glaser, R. (1980). Components of inductive reasoning. In R. E. Snow, P-A. Federico, & W. E. Montague (Eds.), *Aptitude, learning and instruction. Vol. 1: Cognitive process analyses of aptitude* (pp. 177–217). Hillsdale, NJ: Lawrence Erlbaum Associates.

Pellegrino, J. W., & Kail, R., Jr. (1982). Process analyses of spatial aptitude. In R. J. Sternberg (Ed.), *Advances in the psychology of intelligence* (Vol. 1, pp. 311–365). Hillsdale, NJ: Lawrence Erlbaum Associates.

Pinneau, S. R. (1961). *Changes in intelligence quotient: Infancy to maturity.* Boston: Houghton Mifflin.

Poon, L. W. (Ed.). (1980). *Aging in the 1980s: Psychological issues.* Washington, DC: American Psychological Association.

Posner, M. I. (1978). *Chronometric explorations of mind.* Hillsdale, NJ: Lawrence Erlbaum Associates.

Posner, M. I., & Mitchell, R. (1967). Chronometric analysis of classification. *Psychological Review, 74,* 392–409.

Pyle, D. W. (1979). *Intelligence: An introduction.* London: Routledge & Kegan Paul.

Ramsey, P. H., & Vane, J. R. (1970). A factor analytic study of the Stanford-Binet with young children. *Journal of School Psychology, 8,* 278–284.

Rasch, G. (1980). *Probabilistic models for some intelligence and attainment tests* (expanded edition). Chicago: University of Chicago Press.

Raven, J. C. (1938–1965). *Progressive matrices.* New York: Psychological Corp., & London: H. K. Lewis.

Reinert, G. (1970). Comparative factor analytic studies of intelligence throughout the human life-span. In L. R. Goulet & P. B. Baltes (Eds.), *Life-span developmental psychology: Research and theory* (pp. 467–484). New York: Academic Press.

Rubin, D. C. (1980). 51 properties of 125 words: A unit analysis of verbal behavior. *Journal of Verbal Learning and Verbal Behavior, 19,* 736–755.

Salthouse, T. A. (1981). Converging evidence for information-processing stages: A comparative-influence stage-analysis method. *Acta Psychologica, 47,* 39–61.

Salthouse, T. A. (1982). *Adult cognition: An experimental psychology of human aging.* New York: Springer-Verlag.

Sanders, A. F. (1980). Stage analysis of reaction processes. In G. E. Stelmach & J. Requin (Eds.), *Tutorials in motor behavior* (pp. 331–354). Amsterdam: North-Holland.

Sattler, J. M. (1982). *Assessment of children's intelligence and special abilities* (2nd ed.). Boston: Allyn & Bacon.

Schaie, K. W. & Labouvie-Vief, G. (1974). Generational versus ontogenetic components of change in adult cognitive behavior: A fourteen-year cross-sequential study. *Developmental Psychology, 10,* 305–320.

Schmid, J., & Leiman, J. M. (1957). The development of hierarchical factor solutions. *Psychometrika, 22,* 53–61.

Seashore, C. E. (1919). *Manual of instructions and interpretations for Measures of Musical Talent.* Chicago: Stoelting.

Seashore, C. E., Lewis, D., & Saetveit, J. G. (1939). *Seashore Measures of Musical Talents* (rev. ed.). New York: Psychological Corp.

Siegler, R. S., & Richards, D. D. (1982). The development of intelligence. In R. J. Sternberg (Ed.), *Handbook of human intelligence* (pp. 897–971). Cambridge and New York: Cambridge University Press.

Simon, H., & Kotovsky, K. (1963). Human acquisition of concepts for sequential patterns. *Psychological Review, 70,* 534–546.

Snow, R. E. (1981). Toward a theory of aptitude for learning: I. Fluid and crystallized abilities and their correlates. In M. P. Friedman. J. P. Das, & N. O'Connor (Eds.), *Intelligence and learning* (pp. 345–362). New York and London: Plenum.

Spearman, C. (1904). "General intelligence", objectively determined and measured. *American Journal of Psychology, 15,* 201–293.

Spearman, C. (1923). *The nature of 'intelligence' and the principles of cognition.* London: Macmillan.

Spearman, C. (1927). *The abilities of man: Their nature and measurement.* New York: Macmillan.

Spiegel, M. R., & Bryant, N. D. (1978). Is speed of processing information related to intelligence and achievement? *Journal of Educational Psychology, 70,* 904–910.

Spreen, O., & Schulz, R. W. (1966). Parameters of abstraction, meaningfulness, and pronunciability for 329 nouns. *Journal of Verbal Learning and Verbal Behavior, 5,* 459–468.

Stankov, L., & Horn, J. L. (1980). Human abilities revealed through auditory tests. *Journal of Educational Psychology, 72,* 21–44.

Sternberg, R. J. (1977). *Intelligence, information processing, and analogical reasoning:*

The componential analysis of human abilities. Hillsdale, NJ: Lawrence Erlbaum Associates.

Sternberg, R. J. (1980a). A proposed resolution of curious conflicts in the literature on linear syllogisms. In R. S. Nickerson (Ed.), *Attention and performance VIII* (pp. 719–744). Hillsdale, NJ: Lawrence Erlbaum Associates.

Sternberg, R. J. (1980b). Sketch of a componential subtheory of human intelligence. *Behavioral & Brain Sciences, 3,* 573–614.

Sternberg, R. J. (1982a). A componential approach to intellectual development. In R. J. Sternberg (Ed.), *Advances in the psychology of intelligence,* (Vol. 1, pp. 413–463). Hillsdale, NJ: Lawrence Erlbaum Associates.

Sternberg, R. J. (Ed) (1982b). *Handbook of intelligence.* Cambridge and New York: Cambridge University Press.

Sternberg, R. J. (1982c). Reasoning, problem solving, and intelligence. In R. J. Sternberg (Ed.), *Handbook of human intelligence* (pp. 225–307). Cambridge and New York: Cambridge University Press.

Sternberg, R. J., Conway, B. E., Ketron, J. L., & Bernstein, M. (1981). People's conceptions of intelligence. *Journal of Personality and Social Psychology, 41,* 37–55.

Sternberg, S. (1969). Memory-scanning: Mental processes revealed by reaction-time experiments. *American Scientist, 57,* 421–457.

Sternberg, S. (1975). Memory scanning: New findings and current controversies. *Quarterly Journal of Experimental Psychology, 27,* 1–32.

Stormer, G. E. (1967). Dimensions of intellect unmeasured by the Stanford-Binet. (Unpublished doctoral dissertation, University of Illinois, 1966). *Dissertation Abstracts International, 27,* 2078A-2079A.

Sullivan, E. T., Clark, W. W., & Tiegs, E. W. (1963). *California Test of Mental Maturity* (1963 revision). Monterey, CA: CTB/McGraw-Hill.

Thorndike, E. L., & Lorge, I. (1944). *The teacher's word book of 30,000 words.* New York: Bureau of Publications, Teachers College, Columbia University.

Thorndike, R. L. (1966). Intellectual status and intellectual growth. *Journal of Educational Psychology, 57,* 121–127.

Thorndike, R. L., Hagen, E., & Lorge, I. (1954–1974). *Cognitive Abilities Test.* Boston: Houghton Mifflin.

Thurstone, L. L. (1938). Primary mental abilities. *Psychometric Monographs,* No. 1.

Thurstone, L. L. (1947). *Multiple factor analysis: A development and expansion of* "The vectors of mind." Chicago: University of Chicago Press.

Thurstone, L. L. (1955). *The differential growth of mental abilities.* Chapel Hill: Psychometric Laboratory (Report No. 14).

Thurstone, L. L., & Thurstone, T. G. (1946). *SRA Primary Mental Abilities,* 1962 edition. Chicago: Science Research Associates.

Tyler, L. E. (1978). *Individuality: Human possibilities and personal choice in the psychological development of men and women.* San Francisco: Jossey-Bass.

Undheim, J. O. (1978). Broad ability factors in 12- to 13-year-old children, the theory of fluid and crystallized intelligence, and the differentiation hypothesis. *Journal of Educational Psychology, 70,* 433–443.

Vernon, P. A. (1981). Reaction time and intelligence in the mentally retarded. *Intelligence, 5,* 345–355.

Vernon, P. A. (1983). Speed of information processing and general intelligence. *Intelligence, 7,* 53–70.

Vernon, P. E. (1961). *The structure of human abilities* (2nd ed.). London: Methuen.

Vernon, P. E. (1979). *Intelligence: Heredity and environment.* San Francisco: Freeman.

von Békésy, G. (1930). Über das Fechner'sche Gesetz und seine akustischen Beobachtungsfehler und die Theorie des Hörens. *Annalen der Physik, 7,* 329–359.

Walker, D. A. (1931, 1936, 1940). Answer pattern and score scatter in tests and examinations. *British Journal of Psychology, 22,* 73–86; *26,* 301–308; *30,* 248–260.

Wechsler, D. (1974). *Manual for the Wechsler Intelligence Scale for Children—Revised.* New York: Psychological Corp.

Wechsler, D. (1981). *Manual for the Wechsler Adult Intelligence Scale—Revised.* New York: Psychological Corp.

White, P. O. (1982). Some major components in general intelligence. In H. J. Eysenck (Ed.), *A model for intelligence* (pp. 44–90). Berlin: Springer-Verlag.

Whitely, S. E., & Schneider, L. M. (1981). Information structure for geometric analogies: A test theory approach. *Applied Psychological Measurement, 5,* 383–397.

Willerman, L. (1979). *The psychology of individual and group differences.* San Francisco: Freeman.

Willis, S. L., & Baltes, P. B. (1980). Intelligence in adulthood and aging: Contemporary issues. In L. W. Poon (Ed.), *Aging in the 1980s: Psychological issues* (pp. 260–272). Washington, DC: American Psychological Association.

Willis, S. L., Blieszner, R., & Baltes, P. B. (1981). Intellectual training research on aging: Modification of performance on the fluid ability of figural relations. *Journal of Educational Psychology, 73,* 41–50.

Wohlwill, J. F. (1973). *The study of behavioral development.* New York: Academic Press.

Wright, R. E. (1939). A factor analysis of the original Stanford-Binet scale. *Psychometrika, 4,* 209–220.

5

Learning Skills and the Acquisition of Knowledge

John D. Bransford
Nancy J. Vye
Lea T. Adams
Greg A. Perfetto
Vanderbilt University

In most educational settings, some people learn more readily than others. A major challenge for both practitioners and researchers is to understand why differences in learning occur and to devise procedures that can help less succesful students improve their abilities to learn.

In recent years, a number of researchers have explored questions about the relationship between skills for learning and the acquisition of knowledge. The major goal of this chapter is to provide an overview of this research. Our approach is to focus on the problem of learning new information and to ask whether existing research can help us understand why some people seem to learn more effectively than others. We also discuss the problem of helping less successful students improve their abilities to learn.

Mann (1979) in his book on the history of cognitive process training, noted that the goals of attempting to understand individual differences in learning and of helping people learn to learn represent old and well-established traditions. Mann's writings also illustrate how educators' approaches to these problems depended on tacit or explicit theories of the nature of thinking and learning. For example, a metaphor that seems to have reappeared throughout history involves the idea of "exercising the mind" in order to develop "mental muscle." This "theory" influenced the types of training provided as well as expectations about the kinds of effects to expect.

An experiment conducted recently by Ericsson, Chase, and Faloon (1980) yielded results that—at first glance—appear to be consistent with a "mental muscle" theory. Ericsson and his colleagues (1980) worked with an individual who spent 18 months practicing the memorization of random digit sequences. Given a sequence of numbers such as 74189426, for example, the task was to repeat the numbers in the exact order in which they were heard. Most adults can remember from six to nine numbers with little difficulty (e.g., Miller, 1956); the student who participated in the Ericsson et al. (1980) study was no exception to this pattern when he first began the experiment. By the end of the study, however, *the student's digit span had increased in length from 7 digits to 79 digits.* This represents an incredible improvement in performance.

Nevertheless, evidence shows clearly that the person's overall short-term memory "strength" or "capacity" was not increased. The critical data in the Ericsson et al. study involved the student's ability to remember *letter* strings rather than *number* strings. Although the student could remember strings of 79 numbers by the end of the experiment, he could remember only about 7 letters. This shows that his general capacity for holding information in short-term memory had not been increased. The reason for the student's dramatic improvement over the 18 month period was that he had learned to use his extensive knowledge of running (e.g., names and dates of races, ages of runners, running times, etc.) to chunk three or four numbers together to form a single functional unit. These chunks could then be grouped into higher order units for later recall. Because this strategy was impossible when letter strings were used as stimuli, the student's short-term memory for this information was no better than average (see also Chase & Simon, 1973; deGroot, 1965).

Results of the Ericsson et al. (1980) study are consistent with one of the major themes of this chapter: namely, that activities such as comprehending, remembering, inferencing, and problem solving are influenced in important ways by the nature and organization of people's knowledge. The first section of this chapter elaborates on the importance of previously acquired knowledge. We then consider the types of learning activities that seem necessary in order to acquire information that can be accessed when it is needed. Finally, we discuss the problem of helping people learn about themselves as learners so that they can become "intelligent novices" who are able to acquire new information on their own.

THE ROLE OF PREVIOUSLY
ACQUIRED KNOWLEDGE

Although we argue later that learning requires the use of effective strategies, it seems important to begin a discussion of learning by focusing on the role of the background knowledge available to learners. Sophisticated comprehension and learning strategies do little good if one lacks the knowledge necessary to comprehend.

Consider the following passage about Sally:

Sally first let loose a team of gophers. The plan backfired when a dog chased them away. She then threw a party but the guests failed to bring their motorcycles. Furthermore, her stereo system was not loud enough. Sally spent the next day looking for a "Peeping Tom" but was unable to find one in the yellow pages. Obscene phone calls gave her some hope until the number was changed. It was the installation of blinking neon lights across the street that finally did the trick. Sally framed the ad from the classified section and now has it hanging on her wall.

Most people have difficulty understanding the passage about Sally. This affects their ability to recall the information as well as their ability to answer inference questions such as "Where did Sally place the gophers?", "Whose number was changed?", "What did the ad say?". People's inabilities to comprehend do not stem from a lack of familiarity with the words in the passages; it does not contain highly technical vocabulary. Furthermore, each sentence in the passage conforms to basic rules of English syntax, so syntactic abnormalities are not responsible for the fact that the passage is difficult to comprehend. What is missing is information about Sally's intent or goal; the reader needs to know that she is attempting to force her neighbors to move. Given this information, the passage makes much more sense (read it again).

Most people note that information about Sally's goal allows them to make a number of inferences while reading or hearing the passage. For example, people frequently assume that the gophers were let out in the neighbor's yard, that the motorcycle and stereo noises were designed to bother the neighbor, that the Peeping Tom would have been hired to look in the neighbor's window, that the obscene phone calls were directed at the neighbor and that it was the latter's number that was changed, that the ad from the classified section said "House for Sale," and so forth. None of this information is supplied in the passage; it had to be supplied by the reader. For present purposes, the important point is that the ability to make these inferences does not only depend on general "inference skills"; it also depends on the activation of appropriate knowledge (i.e., on information about Sally's goal). For additional examples see Bransford and Johnson (1972, 1973), Bransford and McCarrell, (1974), Dooling and Lachman (1971), and Franks, Bransford, and Auble (1982).

The passage about Sally was written especially to illustrate how comprehension depends on the activation of general world knowledge. Similar processes seem to be involved in all instances of comprehension; people often are surprised when helped to notice the degree to which they spontaneously utilize previously acquired knowledge in order to comprehend. As an illustration, consider the following passage (cf. Mehan, 1977):

A thirsty ant went to a river. He became carried away by the rush of the stream and was about to drown. A dove was sitting in a tree overhanging the water. The dove plucked a leaf and let it fall. The leaf fell into the stream close to the ant and the ant climbed onto it. The ant floated safely to the bank. Shortly afterwards, a birdcatcher came and laid a trap in a tree. The ant saw his plan and stung him on the foot. In pain the birdcatcher threw down his trap. The noise made the bird fly away.

A number of assumptions are necessary in order to understand this story. For example, readers usually assume that the ant walked to the river and the dove flew to the tree, although this information was never explicitly presented. Similarly, readers realize that an ant might drown because it requires oxygen (it would be strange to worry about a fish drowning in a river), that the dove probably plucked the leaf with its beak, and so forth. Basic information about doves and ants therefore plays an important role in guiding the inferences that readers make.

Additional sets of inferences must also be drawn in order to understand the ant and dove story. One important set of inferences involves assumptions about the characters' goals. For example, most people assume that the dove plucked the leaf in order to save the ant, that the birdcatcher's plan was to trap the dove and that the ant bit the birdcatcher in order to repay the dove for its previous favor. Note that none of this information is stated in the story; in each case it is generated by the reader. The author of the passage did not need to explicitly present this information; it was assumed that readers would supply it. Indeed, communication would be extremely cumbersome if speakers and writers had to explicitly provide all the information necessary for comprehension. If people lack relevant background knowledge, however, they are unable to make the assumptions necessary to understand in ways that speakers and writers intend.

Differences in the Availability of Knowledge

The results of a number of studies illustrate how differences in previously acquired knowledge affect problem solving, learning, and memory. In a classic study by deGroot (1965), for example, an attempt was made to understand why chess masters were better at chess than were skilled yet less-accomplished players. One of deGroot's initial hypotheses was that masters could think of more possible moves than could novices. He also believed that masters could "think further ahead" than others and hence could calculate the strengths and weaknesses of various moves. deGroot explored these hypotheses by presenting masters and less-skilled players with examples from chess games and asking them to choose the next move; he also asked the participants to think aloud as they attempted to make their choice. Contrary to initial expectations, the masters did not think of a greater number of moves than did the novices, nor did the masters think further ahead (i.e., they did not choose a move and then consider its implications for the next 10 or so moves). Instead, the masters' initial choices of moves simply seemed to be qualitatively superior to those of the lesser experienced players.

These results suggested a second hypothesis to deGroot: Because of their experiences, chess masters may have developed a knowledge base that allows them to perceive the significance of various game positions and hence to generate qualitatively superior moves. As one test of this knowledge base hypothesis, deGroot presented masters and lesser experienced players with a view of a chess game for only 5 seconds and then asked them to reproduce the game (using new pieces and a new board) as accurately as they could. Results indicated that the chess masters were excellent at this short-term memory task whereas less-skilled players had considerable difficulty. Subsequent studies (Chase & Simon, 1973) demonstrated that the masters' superior performance was not due to a superior "short-term memory capacity." When supplied with chess pieces that were placed at random on a board, the chess masters were no better than others at remembering which piece went where, presumably because their knowledge base did not help them encode randomly placed pieces. When the chess configurations were meaningful, however, the experts were more readily able to perceive their significance than were the lesser experienced players.

deGroot (1966) argued as follows:

> We know that increasing experience and knowledge in a specific field (chess, for instance) has the effect that things (properties, etc.) which, at earlier stages, had to be abstracted, or even inferred are apt to be immediately perceived at later stages. To a rather large extent, *abstraction is replaced by perception,* but we do not know much about how this works, nor where the borderline lies. . . . As an effect of this replacement, a so-called 'given' problem situation is not really given since *it is seen differently* by an expert than it is perceived by an unexperienced person, but we do not know much about these differences. (deGroot, 1966, pp. 33-34)

For present purposes, the important point is that the expert performance of chess masters seems to heavily depend on the nature of the knowledge that they have acquired.

The results of many additional experiments illustrate how differences in previously acquired knowledge affect learning and memory (for reviews see Auble, 1982; Voss, Fincher, Greene, & Post, 1986). For example, a series of studies conducted by Voss and his colleagues (Spilich, Vesonder, Chiesi, & Voss, 1979) compared groups of college students who scored equivalently on tests of general reading comprehension but differed in their knowledge about the game of baseball. The students were asked to attempt a number of tasks, such as to recall as much as they could after hearing a play-by-play broadcast of one-half of an inning of baseball, to write a summary of the important events that occurred during portions of a baseball game, and so forth. In all cases, students who were "high knowledge" with respect to baseball performed considerably better than their low knowledge peers.

It is important to note that the low knowledge students in the preceding baseball studies were not completely ignorant about baseball. All students knew that the game involved a ball, bat, and gloves, that the object was to hit the ball in order to get runs and so forth. In short, the low knowledge individuals were not "no knowledge" individuals; the former simply knew less about baseball than did their high knowledge peers. In many task contexts, these differences in knowledge should have little or no effects. If the task were simply to differentiate the general sport of baseball from football, for example, even low knowledge individuals would have little difficulty; they would know that baseball involved bats and a round ball whereas football did not. In situations that require a more precisely defined knowledge base, however (e.g., situations such as the baseball studies just discussed), differences in previously acquired knowledge can have pervasive effects on people's abilities to understand and to remember what was seen or heard.

Interactions Between Knowledge and Strategies

Recent studies also indicate that the ability to use strategies depends on the knowledge available to the learner. As a simple illustration, consider the strategy of attempting to process information at a "deep," semantic level (e.g., deciding whether the word "dog" contains the letter "e," contains one or two syllables, and so forth). Results from a number of studies indicate that deep, semantic processing generally results in better memory than does shallow, superficial processing (e.g., Cermak & Craik, 1979; Craik & Lockhart, 1972; Hyde & Jenkins, 1969). Clearly, however, the ability to process at semantic levels presupposes a knowledge base that is adequate. If you do not know the meaning of a word such as "porbeagle," for example, attempts at deep or semantic processing do little good.

A number of theorists have argued that the general process of utilizing previously acquired knowledge in order to *elaborate* information is important for comprehension and memory (e.g., Anderson & Reder, 1979; Craik & Tulving, 1975; Rohwer, 1966, 1980). Once again, people's abilities to elaborate depend on the nature of their knowledge. Consider a statement such as "The discovery of a number of fossilized porbeagles in Kansas is intriguing" (cf. Adams & Bruce, in press, p. 8). Most people are much better able to elaborate the significance of this discovery when supplied with information about porbeagles; namely, that they were ocean-dwelling fish.

As another illustration of relationships between knowledge and elaboration, imagine that a biology novice is confronted with new facts such as "Arteries are thick, elastic, and have no valves." A biology novice who is familiar with the general terms "artery," "thick," "elastic," and "valves" could process this statement at a semantic level yet still be unable to elaborate on the statement. In contrast, a biology expert who processed the statement about arteries would undoubtedly create a memory representation that included a number of elaborations. For example, the expert would understand *why* arteries have particular properties and not others. Thus, the expert would realize that arteries need to be elastic in order to accommodate the spurts of blood that are pumped from the heart and that the elasticity can also serve the function of a one-way valve (see Bransford, Stein, Shelton, & Owings, 1981, for further discussion).

A simple way to illustrate how previously acquired knowledge facilitates elaboration and retention is as follows: Imagine trying to learn a list of 15 new facts such as *John flew the kite, Bill hid the axe, Jim hit his head on the ceiling, Ted walked on the roof, Mike built a boat,* and so forth. Each of these statements can be processed at a semantic level of analysis but it is still extremely difficult to remember who did what (e.g., to answer questions such as "What did Jim do?" or "Who built a boat?"). Contrast the preceding task with one in which different names are supplied—names that allow the activation of a rich knowledge base which in turn permits one to elaborate on each statement. Examples of this second set of sentences (plus some illustrations of possible elaborations) are as follows: *Benjamin Franklin flew the kite* (in order to explore the relationship between electricity and lightning), *George Washington hid the axe* (that he had used to chop down the cherry tree), *Wilt Chamberlain* (a tall basketball player) *hit his head on the ceiling* (because he is so tall), *Santa Claus walked on the roof* (to get to the chimney to deliver presents), *Noah built a boat* (to hold pairs of animals) and so forth. Given this second list, it is quite easy to answer questions such as "What did Santa Claus do?" or "Who hid the axe?" Analogously, imagine trying to remember statements such as *The pitcher intentionally walked the hitter with the .490 batting average, The pitcher struck out the opposing team's pitcher by throwing three straight strikes,* and so forth. Novices with respect to baseball may have difficulty remembering which person was walked versus which struck out because they lack the knowledge necessary to elaborate in a way that can make the information less arbitrary. In contrast, the baseball expert realizes that a .490 hitter is hitting very well and hence might be a likely candidate for an intentional walk, whereas pitchers are notoriously poor hitters and hence should be relatively easy to strike out.

In addition to elaboration, another important strategy for memory involves categorization. As an illustration, imagine that participants in a memory experiment hear 30 words that they know they will be asked to recall in any order that they choose. The words are potentially categorizable; thus, a list including *chair, boat, dog, car, table, cat,* and so forth can be divided into categories such as furniture, types of transportation and animals. If college students receive a list of words such as this they will generally categorize the information and hence will exhibit evidence of "clustering" (i.e., they will tend to recall furniture items together, transportation items together, etc., despite the fact that the items were originally presented in random order). Results from a number of studies indicated that categorization facilitates memory, in part because it helps individuals retrieve information that was stored (e.g., Bousfield, 1953; Bower, Clark, Lesgold, & Winzenz, 1969; Mandler, 1967; Tulving & Perlstone, 1966).

The imaginary experiment just described becomes more interesting if we assume that participants include a group of college students and a group of third graders. Not surprisingly, college students will recall a greater number of words than will the third graders; the former will also exhibit a much greater degree of clustering. Results such as these have often been used to support the notion that younger students (e.g., third graders) perform more poorly in memory tasks than do older students (e.g., college students) because the former are less likely to utilize strategies such as categorization. Until recently, however, few researchers have investigated the degree to which strategy utilization might be affected by the learner's knowledge base.

A study by Lindberg (1980) is especially informative in this context. In one condition of his experiment, Lindberg presented groups of third graders and college students with a 30-word list similar to the one just described and asked all participants to recall as many words as they could. The results were consistent with those previously described: The college students recalled more words and showed greater evidence of clustering. Are these results simply due to the fact that college students are likely to employ strategies such as categorization whereas third graders are not?

It is instructive to note that each of the words used by Lindberg was familiar to the third graders. Nevertheless, this does not guarantee that the third graders knew as much about each concept as did the college students (analogously, we noted earlier that people could be familiar with the general concept of baseball yet still lack the level of knowledge characteristic of a baseball expert). The third graders and college students almost undoubtedly differed in terms of their degree of knowledge about the concepts used in Lindberg's list.

In an attempt to turn the tables with respect to knowledge, Lindberg included a second condition in his experiment. In this condition, college students and third graders received a 30-word list comprised of items designed to be more familiar to the third graders than to the college students. Examples included names of Saturday morning TV shows, names of children's cartoon characters, and so forth. As in the previous condition, the words were presented in a random order because one of the goals of the study was to assess the amount of clustering that would occur. The results indicated that the third graders recalled more information than the college students *and* showed a greater amount of clustering (i.e., they tended to recall names of Saturday morning TV shows together, names of cartoon characters together and so forth). These results provide strong evidence that strategies such as categorization are influenced by the nature of the learner's knowledge base (see also Chi, 1978, 1981).

Processes such as reasoning, planning, and problem solving are also strongly influenced by the availability of relevant content knowledge (see also Greeno & Larkin, this volume). As an illustration of an effect on reasoning, imagine that people differ in their abilities to solve number analogy problems such as "2 is to 4 as 5 is to —." Even if we assume that all people in the study know something about numbers (just as everyone is previously mentioned studies knew something about baseball), their differences in performance could still be due to differences in the extent or organization of that knowledge.

A simple way to assess differences in number knowledge is to ask people to provide as many answers as possible to analogies such as "2 is to 4 as 5 is to —." Potential answers could include responses such as "7" (because both 4 and 7 are two more than their respective starting numbers); "10" (because 2 x 2 = 4 and 2 x 5 = 10), "25" (because the final number of each pair is the square of the initial number), "3" (because 4 and 2 are even numbers whereas 5 and 3 are odd numbers) and so forth. It seems clear that there are a large number of potential relationships among sets of numbers. Individuals may know something about numbers (they may be able to count, for example), yet lack the knowledge necessary for more sophisticated types of number tasks.

A study by Corsale and Gitomer (1979; cf. Glaser & Pellegrino, 1982) examined how differences in the knowledge base of elementary school students influenced the strategies they used to solve number analogy problems. Prior to having students solve the analogy problems, Corsale and Gitomer assessed how students' knowledge of numerical relationships was organized. This was done in two ways: (a) students were given a large set of numbers and asked to select groups of numbers that went together and tell why; and (b) students were presented with 20 pairs of numbers and asked to find as many relationships as they could for each pair.

Corsale and Gitomer were able to identify three dimensions that described the organization of students' knowledge of numerical relationships. The first dimension was the degree of abstractness found in the students' groupings and pair relationships (e.g., abstractness included the use of superordinate concepts such as the set of prime numbers or the use of exponential relationships such as one number being the square of another). The second factor involved the overall number of groupings and relationships generated without respect to how they were justified. The third factor involved the degree to which students' knowledge could be described in terms of bias toward either conceptual or computational justification of the groupings and pair relationships (e.g., "2 and 6 are even numbers" vs. "6 is 3 times 2"). Although students' knowledge could be described in terms of all three factors, results indicated that only the degree of abstractness was an important predictor of success in solving analogical number problems.

Protocols of students with the highest and lowest abilities provided additional evidence that the degree of abstractness was an important determinant of students' abilities to solve number analogies. The solutions of high ability students were based on more abstract reasoning. High ability students also showed a preference for abstract concepts over computational strategies. In part, the abstract nature of the strategies employed by high ability students enabled them to limit the range of possible solutions that they needed to consider. Low skill students, on the other hand, often engaged in computational strategies resulting in fewer constraints on the number of possible operations that could be used to solve the analogy.

Research by Goldman (1982) showed that the generation of plans for problem solving depends on the knowledge domain within which one is working. Goldman had children from the first, fourth, and seventh grades generate stories in which they were the protagonist attempting to satisfy a specific goal. The goals used in the study were drawn from familiar goal situations such as being friendly and getting a dog.

The content characteristics of the knowledge base used in generating these problem-solving stories were analyzed for each age group and each story. When children were asked to generate a story about getting a dog, no developmental differences were found between the three age groups. That is, even the younger children considered specific actions they would take, their own feelings about dogs, and the role of parents and family members. However, when the children generated stories about being friendly, large developmental differences were found. With an increase in age there was an increase in both the amount and the variety of information utilized in the stories. These results suggest that children's abilities to generate information about plans and strategies depends on the knowledge domain being considered. Similarly, children's abilities to *comprehend* stories that involve problem solving should depend on their familiarity with various knowledge domains (e.g., R.C. Anderson, 1984; Beck, 1984; Bruce, 1984).

Schema Theories

Much of the recent emphasis on the importance of previously acquired knowledge has come from the development of schema theories (for our purposes this includes frame and script theories; e.g., R.C. Anderson, 1977, in press; Brewer & Lichenstein, in press; Graessar & Nakamura, in press; Minsky, 1975; Rumelhart, 1980; Rumelhart & Ortony, 1977; C. Shank, 1980; Schank & Abelson, 1977; Spiro, Bruce, & Brewer, 1980). Schema theorists have attempted to characterize both the structure and function of knowledge. As an illustration, consider one's knowledge of a concept such as "restaurant." A very young child who hears this word may think only about eating. With experience, people develop what Schank and Abelson (1977) called a "restaurant script" (see also Bower, Black, & Turner, 1979). This includes information about the cast of characters who are involved in most restaurants (e.g., waiter or waitress, cook, cashier, customer) as well as information about typical types of activities (e.g., entering and being seated, ordering, eating, leaving a tip, paying the bill). Without this organized body of information many inferences would be impossible. For example, one needs a relatively sophisticated knowledge base in order to understand the significance of a statement such as "I left the waiter 5¢, which is more than he deserved."

Schemas (including scripts and frames) are assumed to fulfill a number of functions. Anderson (1984) lists six functions. He argues that they provide a basis for (a) assimilating information, (b) making inferential elaborations that fill in the gaps in messages, (c) allocating attention to important elements, (d) searching memory in an orderly fashion, (e) formulating a summary of information, and (f) making inferences that can enable one to reconstruct an original message despite having forgotten some of the details. It may be possible to add to this list of "schema functions," but the six just cited are sufficient to illustrate how the knowledge possessed by learners can have pervasive effects on performance. One clear implication of schema theory is that some students may appear to be poor learners *not* because they have some inherent comprehension or memory "deficits," but because they lack, or fail to activate, the background knowledge that was presupposed by a message or a text.

Research conducted during the past 10 years has provided information about different types of schemas that affect learning. A particularly important body of research involves the concept of "story grammars" and story schemas. A number of theorists argue that there are particular structures to stories and that people use their knowledge of these structures to comprehend narratives. A story grammar is an ordered description of the types of events and states contained in narratives. It has been suggested that "well-formed" stories consist of the following: an introduction to the main character, a description of his or her internal motivating states and goals, a description of attempts to reach a goal, and a description of the outcome of an attempt to reach the goal (Stein & Glenn, 1979).

Research suggests that people have knowledge of the structures or "story schemas" that are used to interpret narratives. For example, it has been shown that people are more likely to recall central story units than supporting content, that they tend to recall stories that are unusually ordered (as defined by a story grammar) in canonical form, that they take longer to read a unit when it is moved out of its normal place, and that they judge information within units as belonging together (e.g., Mandler & Goodman, 1982; Stein, 1979; Trabasso, Stein, & Johnson, 1981). Furthermore, effects of story schemas on learning have been observed with children across cultures (Mandler, Scribner, Cole, & DeForest, 1980) as well as with special populations of people (e.g., deaf, reading disabled) (Weaver, & Dickinson, 1982; Worden, Malmgren, & Gabourie, 1982). Several authors have also argued that some children lack adequate knowledge about basic story schemas and that this hurts their abilities to comprehend (e.g., Dickinson & Weaver, 1979).

Of course, the fact that children seem to possess knowledge about the "grammatical" structure of stories does not necessarily imply that they always comprehend story information in the same way as adults. Differences in more specific schemas may affect the kinds of elaborations and text-based inferences that children can make. As noted earlier, for example, children may lack knowledge of particular lexical items, or they may fail to understand more abstract concepts (e.g., "cooperation," "coincidence") that stories presuppose (e.g., Adams & Bruce, in press; Beck, 1984; Bruce, 1984). Similarly, adults may be familiar with the general structure of stories yet fail to understand because they lack more specific schemas. For example, Steffensen, Joag-Deci, and Anderson (1979) presented college students with stories about an American wedding versus a wedding involving natives of India. Americans misunderstood many aspects of the story about the Indian wedding and vice versa. Note that a story about an Indian wedding could be consistent with a person's overall story schema yet the person could still have difficulty because he or she lacked a "wedding schema" that was consistent with Indian culture (e.g., see R. C. Anderson, 1984; Kintsch & Greene, 1978). Many different sources of information therefore seem to be necessary in order to understand even relatively simple stories. For more complex domains, the need for multiple conceptual models or frameworks may be even more apparent.

THE ACQUISITION OF NEW KNOWLEDGE

Experiments discussed in the preceding section illustrate that differences in background knowledge can have powerful and pervasive effects on performance—powerful enough to allow third graders to exhibit better memory for a subject than college students, and pervasive enough to affect such activities as short-term retention, long-term retention, comprehension, reasoning, and problem solving. An obvious implication of these findings is that it is important to help people acquire new knowledge. This is hardly a revolutionary idea, of course; educators have been aware of the importance of teaching new information for centuries. Educators are also aware that effective learning is not equivalent to "rote memory"; the goal of education is not simply to memorize lists of facts. We assume that a major goal of education is to help people acquire knowledge that can provide a basis for subsequent learning (e.g., Bransford & Nitsch, 1978). We therefore focus on the degree to which new information may or may not be useful depending on how it is taught and learned.

Access and the Problem of Inert Knowledge

An important index of the usefulness of information is the degree to which it is activated when needed. The fact that people have acquired new information provides no guarantee that access will occur. As a simple illustration, consider the problem of comprehending statements such as "The haystack was important because the cloth ripped" and "The notes were sour because the seam split" (cf. Bransford & McCarrell, 1974). Most people have difficulty comprehending these statements, but not because they lack the knowledge necessary to do so. Instead, the problem is that they fail to activate relevant knowledge that they have already acquired. When provided with prompts that help them access relevant information (e.g., "parachute" and "bagpipes," respectively), the preceding statements become easy to comprehend.

The statements about the haystack and the notes are trick sentences, of course. An important component of the art of creating trick sentences and problems involves the ability to phrase things in a way that will cause otherwise competent people to fail to access information that they already know. We know of no educators who are so devious that all of their lectures and tests are composed of trick questions. Nevertheless, there appear to be many instances where students fail to access information that they have learned. Many years ago, Alfred Whitehead (1929) warned about the dangers of *inert knowledge*— knowledge that is accessed only in a restricted set of contexts even though it is applicable to a wide variety of domains. He also argued that traditional educational practice tended to produce knowledge that remained inert (see also Bereiter & Scardamalia, 1985; Brown, 1985; Brown & Campione, 1981; Scardamalia & Bereiter, 1985).

A study conducted by Gick and Holyoak (1980) provides an informative illustration of the problem of inert knowledge. They had college students memorize a story about a military campaign.

A general wishes to capture a fortress located in the center of a country. There are many roads radiating outward from the fortress. All have been mined so that while small groups of men can pass over the roads safely, a large force will detonate the mines. A full-scale direct attack is therefore impossible. The general's solution is to divide his army into small groups, send each group to the head of a different road, and have the groups converge simultaneously on the fortress. (Gick & Holyoak, 1980, p. 109)

After the students had successfully recalled the military problem and its solution, they were given Duncker's (1945) Radiation Problem to solve:

Suppose you are a doctor faced with a patient who had a malignant tumor in his stomach. It is impossible to operate on the patient, but unless the tumor is destroyed the patient will die. There is a kind of ray that may be used to destroy the tumor. If the rays reach the tumor all at once and with sufficiently high intensity, the tumor will be destroyed. At lower intensities the rays are harmless to healthy tissue, but they will not affect the tumor either. What type of procedure might be used to destroy the tumor with the rays, and at the same time avoid destroying the healthy tissue? (Gick & Holyoak, 1980, p. 308)

This problem can be solved in much the same way as the general solved the Military Problem. In particular, in the Radiation Problem many sources of less intense radiations could pass safely through the healthy tissue and converge on the tumor in sufficient intensity to destroy it.

Because subjects in the Gick and Holyoak study memorized the Military Problem, they presumably had knowledge that could be applied to the Radiation Problem. In fact, 90% of the students who received a hint that the military story was useful were able to use information from it to help solve the Radiation Problem. However, if no hint was given, only 20% of the subjects spontaneously used the military story. For those students who were not given a hint, the information they memorized in the context of the military story therefore remained inert.

Studies conducted by Perfetto, Bransford, and Franks (1983) provided additional evidence that relevant knowledge can remain inert even though it is potentially useful. They presented college students with a series of "insight" problems such as the following:

Uriah Fuller, the famous Israeli superpsychic, can tell you the score of any baseball game *before* the game starts. What is his secret?

A man living in a small town in the U.S. married twenty different women in the same town. All are still living and he has never divorced one of them. Yet, he has broken no law. Can you explain?

Most college students have difficulty answering these questions unless provided with hints or clues. Prior to solving the problems, some students were given clue information that was obviously relevant to each problem's solution. Thus, these students first received statements such as "Before it starts the score of any game is 0 to 0"; "A minister marries several people each week." The students were then presented with the problems and explicitly prompted to use the clue information (which was now stored in memory) to solve them: Their problem-solving performance was excellent. Other students were first presented with the clues and then given the problems but they were not explicitly prompted to use the clues for problem solution. Their problem-solving performance was very poor; in fact, it was no better than that of baseline students who never received any clues.

The Perfetto et al. results represent an especially strong demonstration of access failure (i.e., of inert knowledge) because the clues were constructed to be obviously relevant to problem solution. Indeed, the authors note that, before conducting the experiment, they expected even the uninformed students to spontaneously access the correct answers because of the obvious relationship between the problems and the clues. The failure of students to spontaneously activate relevant knowledge in new contexts is also well documented in other domains (e.g., Reed, Ernst, & Banerji, 1974; Weisberg, DiCamillo, & Phillips, 1978). A classic article by Solomon Asch (1969) provided an excellent discussion of the access problem (he notes that it was an issue emphasized by Hoffding in 1891). Asch described a paired-associate experiment which showed that an associative relationship (e.g., C–K) that was mastered on previous trials took just as many trials to learn as a entirely new association (e.g., X–M) if the former was not recognized as having been learned before (63% of the people in the experiment failed to recognize that the association was one they had just learned).

An emphasis on the problem of inert knowledge becomes especially important when theorists and educators begin to ask questions about factors that facilitate "learning." Many traditional modes of assessment provide misleading information about the degree to which various instructional procedures facilitate people's abilities to learn. As an illustration, consider the following pilot experiment carried out in our laboratories. Students in one group were told basic facts about the concept of attention and also given a memory aid to help them remember these facts. Students in a second group were provided with the same basic facts about attention but were prompted to notice that most of us waste a considerable amount of time by failing to adequately control our own attention (e.g., we often daydream). The purpose of the experiment was to assess whether one instructional condition produced better learning than the other.

A traditional way to address the preceding question is to ask students to remember the information they learned. Not surprisingly, the results of our pilot study indicated that instruction which emphasized memory aids resulted in better retention of facts about attention than did the instructional technique that prompted students to consider the importance of attentional control. These results, like numerous others that have been reported (e.g., see Bower, 1970; Bower & Clark, 1969; Paivio, 1971; Weinstein, 1978) suggest that the presentation of memory aids (some of these are discussed later) are an excellent way to help people learn.

The point we want to emphasize is that the "learning" assessment just described involves a *directed access* paradigm in which students are explicitly prompted to recall information about attention. An important issue that this paradigm fails to address involves the question of whether—once outside the particular testing context—students' knowledge about attention remains inert. One simple way to address this question is to call students back into the laboratory after a few days and ask them to estimate how many times they thought about the concept of attention outside the experimental context. When we used this procedure we found that students who had merely memorized facts about attention rarely thought about the concept of attention after they left the initial experiment. In contrast, students who were prompted to think about attention in the context of personal control over it thought about the concept quite frequently. For example, they indicated that they thought about it when trying to study, when becoming inattentive in lectures and so forth. The usefulness of this knowledge to the students—its noninert status—could not be assessed by many traditional measures. The latter generally indicate only *what* people know rather than whether they utilize what they know.

Some Reasons for Inert Knowledge

There are a number of reasons why knowledge may remain relatively inert and hence fail to be useful in many situations. As previously suggested, one is that students may be encouraged merely to memorize new information rather than be helped to understand the significance of the information. Another is that students may acquire concepts in a restricted context and hence fail to understand their applicability to a wider variety of domains. Students may also have acquired knowledge yet be unable to access it in an efficient manner that requires minimal attentional effort. Problems such as these are discussed more fully later.

Failure to Understand the Significance of New Facts

As one illustration of the problem of inert knowledge, recall our biology novice who was attempting to learn about veins and arteries (cf. Bransford et al., 1981). Assume that the novice reads a text stating that arteries are thick, elastic, and carry blood rich in oxygen from the heart; veins are thinner, less elastic, and carry blood rich in carbon dioxide back to the heart. To the novice, even this relatively simple set of facts can seem arbitrary and confusing. Was it veins or arteries that are thin? Was the thin one or the thick one elastic? Which one carries carbon dioxide from the heart (or was it to the heart)?

There are several ways to help students learn new factual content that initially seems unfamiliar and arbitrary. One is to prompt them to rehearse the facts until they are mastered; a more efficient approach is to teach them to use various mnemonic techniques. For example, the fact that arteries are thick could be remembered by forming an image of a thick, hollow tube that flashes "artery." The fact that arteries are elastic could be remembered by imagining that the tube is suspended by a rubber band that stretches and contracts, thereby causing the tube to move up and down. Students could also be prompted to embellish the image by having red liquid (blood) plus round (like an "o") bubbles (oxygen) pouring out of the tube, and these could be moving in a direction away from an image of a Valentine's Day heart. This composite image could serve as a basis for remembering that arteries are thick, elastic, and carry blood rich in oxygen away from the heart. An alternate technique is to suggest the use of verbal elaborations; for example, "*Art*(ery) was *thick* around the middle so he wore pants with an *elastic* waistband." There is a considerable amount of literature documenting the fact that the formation of images and linking sentences can facilitate retention (e.g., Bower, 1970; Bower & Clark, 1969; Paivio, 1971; Rohwer, 1966). Researchers have also explored the possibility of explicitly teaching various mnemonic techniques in order to improve people's abilities to learn (Weinstein, 1978).

It seems clear that mnemonic techniques can be very useful for helping people remember information (see Pressley, Levin, & Delaney, 1982). In order for that information to be useful in new contexts, however, it often is necessary for students to understand why certain relationships exist and to understand the functions they serve. For example, imagine that people remember "Arteries are elastic" either by thinking of a rubberband holding a tube or "*Art*(ery) and his *elastic* waistband." What if these people are confronted with the task of designing an artificial artery? Would it have to be elastic? What are the potential implications of hardening of the arteries? Would this have a serious impact on people's health? Learners who used the previously mentioned mnemonics to remember that arteries are elastic would have little basis for answering these questions. Indeed, the "rubberband" and "waistband" mnemonics could easily lead to misinterpretations: Perhaps hardening of the arteries affects people's abilities to stretch their arms and legs.

An alternative to encouraging students to memorize new facts is to help them understand the significance or relevance of new information. For example, the passage about veins and arteries stated that arteries are elastic. What is the significance of elasticity? How does this property relate to the functions that arteries perform? Certain types of information can help clarify this relationship. For example, our imaginary passage states that arteries carry blood from the heart—blood that is pumped in spurts. This provides one clue about the significance of elasticity—arteries may need to expand and contract to accommodate the pumping of blood. One can also ask why veins do *not* need to be elastic. Because veins carry blood back to the heart, perhaps they have less of a need to accommodate the large changes in pressure resulting from the heart pumping blood in spurts.

The process of supplying information that clarifies the significance of facts can be carried a step further. Because arteries carry blood *from* the heart there is a problem of directionality. Why doesn't the blood flow back into the heart? This will not be perceived as a problem if one assumes that arterial blood always flows downhill, but let us assume that our passage mentions that there are arteries in the neck and shoulder regions. Arterial blood must therefore flow uphill as well. This information might provide an additional clue about the significance of elasticity. If arteries expand from a spurt of blood and then contract, this might help the blood more in a particular direction. The elasticity of arteries might therefore serve the function of a one-way valve that enables blood to flow forward but not back. If one were to design an artificial artery it might therefore be possible to equip it with valves and hence make it nonelastic. However, this solution might work only if the spurts of blood did not cause too much pressure on the artificial artery. Our imaginary passage does not provide enough information about pressure requirements so a learner would have to look elsewhere for this information. In order to be useful, this new information would need to be presented in a way that helps learners to understand the significance of facts rather than merely to memorize the facts.

Students' abilities to comprehend the significance of new facts, rather than merely to memorize facts, is not simply a function of the degree to which teachers explicitly encourage the use of rote memory techniques. We suspect that a major reason why new information often remains unnecessarily inert is that teachers and authors frequently fail to realize that students lack the background knowledge necessary to understand the significance of information. For example, Cook and Mayer (1983) included a passage about the nitrogen cycle in their article about learning from prose. The passage includes information such as the following:

> The complex nitrogen cycle differs from the oxygen and carbon cycles in several ways. First, atmospheric nitrogen cannot be used directly by most green plants. It must be changed into a useable form—either ammonia or nitrate—before green plants can use it. Second, once nitrogen has been incorporated into nucleic acids and proteins, it can only be returned to inorganic forms through several steps, some of which require specialized types of bacteria. Third, most of these reactions occur in the soil, where availability of nitrogen is influenced by the solubility of inorganic nitrogen compounds.

As in the vein and artery example discussed earlier, it seems clear that there are important differences between simply memorizing the three ways that the nitrogen cycle differs from oxygen and carbon cycles and understanding the reasons for these differences. The Cook and Mayer passage provides no information that can help people understand reasons, hence the novice has little choice but to attempt to memorize a list of seemingly arbitrary facts.

An emphasis on the knowledge necessary to help people understand the significance of facts is important for analyzing the issue of what it means to "simplify" texts and lessons. The latter can be composed of relatively simple words and simple syntax yet still seem arbitrary. For example, Bransford (1979) discussed a passage written for elementary school children that focused on the topic of American Indian houses. It consisted of statements such as "The Indians of the Northwest Coast lived in slant-roofed houses made of cedar plank; some California Indian tribes lived in simple earth-covered or brush shelters; the Plains Indians lived mainly in tepees, etc." The story provided no information about why certain Indians chose certain houses. For example, it said nothing about the relationship between the type of house and the climate of the geographical area, nor about the ease of finding raw materials to build houses depending on the geographical area. Furthermore, the story said nothing about how the style of house was related to the lifestyle of the Indians (e.g., tepees are relatively portable). If students either did not know or failed to activate this extra information, the passage was essentially a list of seemingly arbitrary facts.

Note that passages such as the preceding ones about veins and arteries, nitrogen, and American Indian houses do not seem arbitrary to someone who has already developed expertise in these areas. The expert not only already knows the facts but also understands their significance or relevance. Experts who construct texts or lessons for novices are usually in a "schema activation" mode, but the learners are usually confronted with the problem of constructing new schemas or of developing more detailed schemas—they are in a "schema acquisition" mode. Failing to supply learners with information necessary for understanding can result in the acquisition of knowledge that remains unnecessarily inert because it cannot be used to solve new problems and to understand subsequent events.

Contextualized Knowledge

Another reason why knowledge may remain relatively inert is that is can be overly contextualized. As an illustration, consider a series of studies with college students conducted by Nitsch (1977). Students who participated in her experiments heard definitions of six new concepts (one example was "to minge": to gang up on a person or thing). The students were helped to understand the information rather than prompted merely to memorize the definition of each concept. For example, during a series of study trials, they were provided with four different examples of each concept. Students in one group, the *Same Context* group, learned the concepts in the same contexts; that is, each of the examples for a particular concept was drawn from a common context (all examples of "crinch" involved restaurants, examples of "minge" involved cowboys, etc.). Students in the second group, the *Varied Context* group, also learned the concept definitions, but they were presented in varied contexts (examples for "minge" might therefore range over restaurant contexts, cowboy contexts, and so forth).

Following acquisition, all participants received a test that asked them to identify novel examples of the concepts that they had learned. Students in the *Same Context* acquisition condition did very well at identifying novel examples of concepts that were from the same context as were the acquisition examples (i.e., they were able to identify novel examples of "crinch" that involved a restaurant context). However, these students performed quite poorly when presented with examples of concepts (e.g., crinch) that occurred in new contexts. In contrast, students who received varied context training were quite good at identifying concepts despite the fact that they were exemplified in new contexts. They were therefore able to apply their knowledge in a wider variety of domains.

Bransford (1979) provided an additional illustration of contextualized knowing. He describes the activities of a student preparing for an exam in statistics. The student could solve all the problems on the study sheets and hence felt prepared for the exam. A friend cut out the problems from each sheet, shuffled them, and asked the student to try again. This time the student failed miserably; he thought he had learned to solve the problems yet was inadvertently relying on chapter cues in order to choose the formulas and principles that were applicable to each problem. In order to perform effectively, the student needed to learn to recognize the applicability of various principles in a variety of contexts. Larkin (1979) noted that students learning physics are confronted by similar problems.

An obvious implication of discussions of the limitations of contextualized knowing is that concepts and principles should be exemplified in a variety of contexts in order to render the information less inert. Although this principle seems reasonable, it is important to note that the presentation of examples from a wide variety of contexts is not without its problems. In Nitsch's (1977) studies, for example, it was clear that students in the *Same Context* acquisition condition had a much easier time during initial learning than did students in the *Varied Context* acquisition group. Most students in the latter group experienced considerable difficulty and became confused during the initial learning trials.

In one of her experiments, Nitsch (1977) created a *Hybrid* group designed to facilitate initial learning as well as eventual transfer. Students in this group first received contextualized examples; this allowed them to become familiar with the concepts without becoming confused. When they then received several learning trials involving examples from varied contexts they had little trouble, because basic information had already been acquired. After training, students in this hybrid group also exhibited excellent transfer to novel contexts.

Overall, Nitsch's results illustrate that instructional procedures that facilitate initial learning do not necessarily facilitate flexibility of transfer. Furthermore, the results for her hybrid group suggest that the idea of developing instructional procedures that facilitate both acquisition and transfer is an important one to pursue.

Inefficiency of Access

A third reason why knowledge that is potentially useful can remain inert is that access to it may be inefficient and hence require a considerable amount of conscious attention; people's abilities to activate the information may not be automatized to a sufficient degree (e.g., see Hasher & Zacks, 1979; LaBerge & Samuels, 1974; Lesgold & Perfetti, 1978; Perfetti & Lesgold, 1977; Schneider & Shiffrin, 1977).

As a simple example of the importance of automaticity, imagine trying to comprehend the following hypothetical conversation between a person who has just presented a paper (Presenter) and a person from the audience (Questioner). Assume that you hear the conversation rather than having the opportunity to read it at a leisurely pace.

Questioner: "You claim that deep levels of processing lead to better recognition memory than shallow levels of processing but you have presented only hit rates and have said nothing about false positives."

Presenter: "I'm sorry, I forgot to mention that I used a forced choice procedure."

Questioner: "Oh, OK. Then what was the nature of your foils?"

The ability to understand this conversation—to decide whether the Presenter adequately addressed the Questioner's concerns about false positives, for example—requires knowledge about ways to measure recognition memory (which in turn requires knowledge of concepts such as hit rates, false positives, and forced choice procedures). People who have not yet acquired this information cannot hope to comprehend the preceding conversation. However, even people who have learned the meaning of these concepts can have great difficulty following the conversation. At Vanderbilt, for example, students in several of our courses learn about concepts such as those just mentioned. Nevertheless, it is not uncommon to find students who can provide accurate definitions for the concepts yet be unable to follow the preceding conversation. The reason is that effective comprehension of the conversation requires that relevant information be accessed quickly without too much strain on conscious attention (e.g., see Lesgold & Perfetti, 1978). Because many students have not automatized their abilities to access information about new concepts, their working memories become overtaxed and they are unable to follow what was said. (Note that students' access to information does not have to be as automatized in order to perform well on most nonspeeded college tests.)

A recent review conducted by Mezynski (1983) suggested that access problems similar to those in the example just described are not uncommon. Mezynski discussed a number of studies where researchers attempted to teach new vocabulary in order to improve reading comprehension. Each of the studies cited in her review was successful in increasing students' scores on vocabulary tests. In many studies, however, students who performed well on the vocabulary tests were nevertheless unable to use this new information under conditions where it needed to be accessed quickly; for example, their reading comprehension scores did not improve.

A study by Beck, Perfetti, and McKeown (1982) provided important information about instructional procedures that may be necessary in order to help students acquire knowledge that is easily accessible. Beck and her colleagues varied the amount of practice that students received on sets of vocabulary words that they were taught. The amount of practice had important effects on the speed and ease with which students could access what they had learned. It is important to note that the practice students received in the Beck et al. study was not simply drill such as mere rehearsal of definitions of words. Instead, Beck et al. prompted students to use new words in a variety of contexts. Given new vocabulary items such as "glutton" and "obese," for example, exercises devised by Beck et al. included questions such as "Would a glutton be likely to be obese?" (Students were encouraged to answer the questions as quickly as possible.) Activities such as these seem to be very important for helping students acquire knowledge that is easily accessed in a variety of domains.

Research also indicates that a person's mood or affective state has important effects on the speed and ease of access. If someone is in a sad or unpleasant mood, for example, it can be difficult to access information that was acquired while in a more positive affective state (e.g., Bower, 1981; Weingartner, Miller, & Murphy, 1977). Students who have a history of failure with various tasks (e.g., solving word problems, reading) may be in a relatively negative state when attempting to engage in such activities; they may therefore have difficulty accessing knowledge that was acquired under more positive affective circumstances. Negative feelings about tasks can also hamper access to the extent that people explicitly think about possible failures and hence use attentional resources that, ideally, should be devoted to the task at hand (e.g., Brown, Bransford, Ferrara, & Campione, 1983; Dweck, this volume).

Schema Theory and the Primacy of the Abstract

The reasons for inert knowledge that were just discussed (i.e., memorization rather than comprehension of the significance of information, contextualized knowledge, inefficiency of access) overlap considerably. In particular, they can be viewed as resulting from problems with the structure and organization of people's knowledge. As noted earlier, recent theories of the nature of knowledge emphasize the importance of organized bodies of knowledge called *schemas* (also frames and scripts). Schema theory provides a useful way of describing factors that may influence the degree to which new information remains inert.

As an illustration of how the problem of inert knowledge can be related to schema theory, consider once again the study by Gick and Holyoak (1980) indicating that college students who learned a solution to the fortress problem failed to apply this knowledge to the solution of an analogous problem (the x-ray problem) unless explicitly prompted to do so. A schema theorist might ask whether information about the fortress problem could be presented in a way that increased the probability that it would be utilized to solve the x-ray problem even under conditions where students were not explicitly prompted.

For example, the fortress problem could be introduced as one illustration of a more general class of problems that might be called "divide and conquer" problems. During instruction, additional illustrations of this type of problem (but not the x-ray problem) could be included as well. Given this type of instruction, students should be more likely to solve the x-ray problem because they have been helped to develop a schema that is richer and more general than the knowledge acquired by students who participated in the Gick and Holyoak (1980) study. Gick and Holyoak (1983) conducted a study such as this and found that spontaneous transfer did occur. Other discussions of schema acquisition can be found in J. R. Anderson (1981, 1982); Bransford and Nitsch (1978); Bransford, Nitsch, and Franks (1977); and Rumelhart and Norman (1978).

In general studies of schema acquisition suggest that it can be important to help people activate general knowledge that provides a "frame" for viewing particular sets of information as examples of more general principles. As an illustration, imagine presenting students with a passage about camels that includes facts such as "Camels have special eyelids that protect their eyes yet still let in light; Camels have coarse hair around their ear openings; Camels can close their nose passages." It is one thing to help students develop a "camel schema" that includes facts such as these; it is quite a different matter to help them view this information as an instance of the more general problem of survival. In particular, each of the camel's features represents an adaptation to desert sandstorms, and camels' adaptations to deserts represent just one of a number of possible illustrations of adaptation (e.g., see Bransford et al., 1982).

Note that attempts to provide more abstract "frames" for relatively concrete sets of facts such as the ones about camels will not necessarily result in better memory for the factual information. If one's major goal is memory for specific facts, it may be better to encourage students to spend their time explicitly practicing this information rather than ask them to do something else such as thinking about issues of adaptation. As noted earlier in our discussion of inert knowledge, however, directed memory tests are not the only way to assess the quality of learning; one may also want to assess the degree to which potentially useful information is activated in new contexts. For example, assume that students read a story about desert travelers who wear veils over their faces despite the fact that the desert is hot. Students who understand how various features of camels help them adapt to desert sandstorms should be more likely to spontaneously utilize this information in the context of understanding desert travelers than should people who merely memorized information about camels as sets of descriptive facts.

In addition to the benefits of incorporating specific instances into more general, abstract schemas, researchers have emphasized the importance of helping students see how various schemas are related to one another. An example from Lawler (1981) represents a case in point.

I asked Miriam [Lawler's 6-year-old daughter] 'How much is seventy-five plus twenty six?' She answered, 'Seventy, ninety, ninety-six, ninety-seven, ninety-eight, ninety-nine, one hundred, one-oh-one' (counting up the last five numbers on her fingers). I continued *immediately,* 'How much is seventy-five cents and twenty-six?' She replied 'That's three quarters, four and a penny, a dollar one.' (p. 4)

Lawler noted that Miriam did not apply the results of her first calculation to the second formulation of the problem; instead, she appeared to view the two problems as unrelated. Lawler argued that the knowledge structure (he called these structures "microworlds") activated for the "number addition" problem was different from the structure activated for the "money" problem. These structures must presumably be interrelated in order for someone to realize that the answers each provides can be the same.

Studies by Resnick (1981) provided strong evidence for the importance of helping students understand relationships among different schemas or representations. Resnick noted that elementary school children learning about arithmetic are frequently taught in two different ways: through the use of Dienes blocks and through the teaching of traditional algorithms for addition and subtraction. Resnick found that children often knew about Dienes blocks and about addition and subtraction algorithms yet behaved as if these were two separate systems that had no direct connection to one another. These results suggest that children need to learn to coordinate these two different modes of representation (i.e., to learn to move from one to the other) in order to understand elementary arithmetic. In the absence of explicit instructions to relate similar procedures, many children merely memorize the operations that are used in various contextual domains (e.g., in the domain of Dienes blocks and in typical "counting" domains) without understanding the relationship among these domains.

LEARNING TO LEARN

Discussion in the preceding sections emphasized two reasons why some students may learn more effectively than others. The first is that less successful students may lack the domain-specific knowledge or schemas necessary for learning; the second is that their knowledge may be in a form that renders it unnecessarily inert. Overall, the preceding discussion emphasized that people's lack of relevant content knowledge can *cause* many problems. However, lack of knowledge can also be viewed as a *symptom* of something else. Hypotheses about this "something else" can take a number of forms. Some people may know less than their peers simply because of a lack of exposure to relevant information. In other cases it is not uncommon to assume that a lack of age-appropriate knowledge is a symptom of something like "inferior intelligence."

This leads to questions about the nature of intelligence and whether it is something that can be improved. An examination of the issue of intelligence is beyond the scope of this paper (for excellent discussions see Baron, 1985; Brown & Campione, 1982; Pellegrino & Glaser, 1979, 1980; Pellegrino & Lyon, 1979; Resnick, 1976; Resnick & Glaser, 1976; Simon, 1976; Sternberg, 1977a, 1977b, 1978, 1981; Sternberg & Detterman, 1979). Rather than attempt to discuss the vast literature on intelligence, our approach in the remainder of this chapter is to review literature that suggests that a lack of knowledge can often be viewed as a symptom of a lack of general thinking and learning skills and, most importantly, that people can be helped to improve their abilities to think and learn.

Differences in the Utilization of Knowledge

A major reason for emphasizing the importance of helping people improve their abilities to think and learn is that many individuals fail to take effective approaches to tasks involving learning, remembering, and thinking. They frequently fail to rehearse information, for example, or to use strategies such as elaboration and categorization. We noted earlier that the use of strategies is strongly affected by the availability of relevant content knowledge (e.g., it is difficult to elaborate on a statement about porbeagles if one lacks knowledge of this concept). In this section we emphasize situations where all participants seem to have the necessary content knowledge yet they differ in their use of effective learning strategies. Our goal is to identify some of the strategies used by "intelligent novices" as they attempt to learn about new domains and to explore the conditions necessary to help people increase their abilities to learn.

Brown et al. (1983) provided an example of someone who might qualify as an "intelligent novice." They noted that one of them decided to learn about physics (the learner was a psychologist—not a physicist) and to keep a log of the experience. A physicist picked a particular topic and supplied relevant material to read. The psychologist found the task difficult but it seemed clear that there were many general skills and strategies that facilitated learning. These included (a) a general sense of what it meant to understand something rather than merely memorize it, (b) the ability to recognize that some texts were more advanced than others and that the advanced texts were not the place to begin, (c) the ability to recognize when certain technical terms were crucial and needed to be understood more adequately, (d) knowledge of the need to search for relevant examples of certain concepts and principles that were defined abstractly in a particular passage, (e) knowledge of the importance of removing examples and example problems from the text context, randomizing them, and seeing if one really understood them, (f) the ability and willingness to formulate questions to ask a physicist when the texts would not suffice, and (g) the ability to determine whether the physicist's answers to those questions made sense (to the learner, that is).

Brown et al. (1983) noted that the most important information available to the learner may have been that the texts were objectively difficult, hence fault did not rest with his learning potential but with inadequacies in his background knowledge. The learner was therefore willing to ask questions of the expert rather than give up for fear of seeming stupid. In general, the learner knew something about how to learn and hence was aware of the difficulties to be expected as well as some of the mistakes to avoid (merely memorizing rather than trying to understand, looking up each and every unknown word, placing equal weight on all concepts, for example).

In contrast to Brown et al.'s example, a number of studies illustrate ineffective approaches to learning tasks. For example, Turnure, Buium, and Thurlow (1976) presented educably retarded 7-year-olds (their IQ scores were around 70) with a list of 21 pairs of words such as "soap-jacket" and "nurse-toaster." After hearing all 21 pairs, the children were presented with the first member of each pair (e.g., soap) and asked to recall the second member (e.g., jacket). Their memory scores varied considerably depending on what they were prompted to do during acquisition. For example, performance was extremely poor (averaging only 2 of 21 correct) under conditions where children were prompted to merely repeat the words after the experimenter presented each one. In contrast, children remembered an average of 14 of 21 pairs when they were prompted to ask themselves questions such as "What is the soap doing under the jacket?" or "Why is the soap hiding under the jacket?"

Note that the preceding questions were designed to prompt the children to activate knowledge that provided elaborations of the relationships between word pairs. Under these conditions, the memory performance of the educably retarded children was as good as the performance of their same-age peers whose scores on IQ tests fell within the normal range. These results illustrate that the memory performance of educably retarded individuals (which is usually quite poor when they are not prompted to use appropriate strategies) is not due to some inherent "memory deficit." Instead, their poor performance stems, in part at least, from a failure to spontaneously elaborate the information to be learned.

A series of studies involving fifth graders who generally were either successful or less successful in school (all were in regular classrooms) provides further support for the hypothesis that less successful learners may be less likely to utilize appropriate knowledge even when it is potentially available (e.g., Bransford et al., 1982; Franks, Vye, Auble, Mezynski, Perfetto, Bransford, Stein, & Littlefield, 1982; Stein, Bransford, Franks, Vye, & Perfetto, 1982; Stein, Bransford, Franks, Owings, Vye, & McGraw, 1982). In one study, participants received either an *explicit* or *implicit* version of a passage about two different types of robots. The explicit version of the passage described the functions of each robot (to wash outside windows in tall, high-rise buildings versus washing outside windows in 2-story houses) plus a number of properties of each robot (e.g., one had suction cup feet, battery power, a parachute on its back, etc.; the other had spiked feet, an extendible stomach, a motor with an electric cord, etc.). The explicit version also included specific explanations or elaborations of each robot's properties. For example, the high-rise robot had suction cup feet to help it climb and a parachute in case it fell; the two-story robot had spiked feet that could stick into the ground for stability, an extendible stomach for raising it to the second story and so forth.

The implicit version of the robot passage was identical to the one just described except that no elaborations were provided for why each robot had particular properties. It was assumed that effective learners would supply these elaborations on their own. The passage was designed so that the properties assigned to each robot seemed arbitrary unless one understood why they were relevant, hence memory for which robot had which properties should be poor unless appropriate elaborations were made.

The results of the experiment were congruent with the hypothesis that less successful students may be less likely to utilize potentially available information unless explicitly prompted to do so. For the explicit version of the passage (which supplied reasons for each robot's properties), the memory performance of the successful and less successful students was comparable—both groups did very well. In contrast, there were large differences in performance given the implicit version of the passage. The successful students performed as well as their counterparts who had received the explicit version; the less-successful students performed quite poorly. These latter students failed to spontaneously use information about each robot's function to understand the reasons for its structure, hence they encountered the problem of attempting to remember a list of seemingly arbitrary facts (see also Franks, Vye, Auble, Mezynski, Perfetto, Bransford, Stein, & Littlefield, 1982).

Research conducted by Thorndyke and Stasz (1980) provided additional information about differences in approaches to learning. In one study, adults were asked to learn maps that contained both spatial and verbal information. Results indicated that good learners, unlike poor learners, formulated effective learning strategies. For example, good learners generally segmented the information into parts and then focused on each subset. In addition, a variety of techniques for encoding information were used (e.g., encoding of relations and patterns, use of imagery). Good learners also evaluated their learning progress and used this information to guide the strategies utilized on subsequent learning trials.

Learning as Problem Solving

The preceding discussion illustrates only a few of many studies that suggest that less mature learners frequently fail to utilize effective learning strategies (see also Adams, 1974; Bloom & Broder, 1950; Brown et al., 1983; Feuerstein,

Rand, & Hoffman, 1979; Feuerstein, Rand, Hoffman, & Miller, 1980; Hallahan, 1980; Wong, 1982). There appear to be a number of reasons why this pattern of behavior may occur. One is that less successful learners may have failed to acquire various strategies. Another is that they fail to recognize situations where various strategies are required.

The task of acquiring new information can be analyzed more explicitly by viewing learning as an instance of problem solving. A number of theorists argue that there is a variety of components of the problem solving process (e.g., Adams, 1974; Maier, 1930, 1931; Mayer, 1977; Newell & Simon, 1972; Sternberg, 1977a, 1978, 1981; Whimbey & Lochhead, 1980). For present purposes we emphasize five components: Identify, Define, Explore, Act, and Look and Learn. These form what Bransford and Stein (1984) called the IDEAL approach to problem solving.

As an illustration of a problem-solving approach to learning, imagine an effective learner who is reading a text and who encounters the statement "The notes were sour because the seam split." Unlike a less effective learner who may simply be going through the motions of reading while actually daydreaming, the effective learner will realize that a problem exists (i.e., he or she will *identify* the existence of a problem). Furthermore, the effective learner views the act of identifying problems as good rather than bad.

After the problem has been *identified* it must be *defined* more precisely. For example, a reader may assume that the "notes" sentence is incomprehensible because of a lack of information. The reader may also assume that her attention lapsed earlier and hence she missed crucial information in the text. This definition of the problem (or hypothesis) will lead to the *exploration* of possible solutions—an obvious one in this instance being to go back and re-read the previous text. The student must therefore *act* on this idea by actually re-reading and must then *look* at the effects of her activities; that is, she must evaluate whether it helped her solve the problem of understanding what the "notes" sentence means.

Assume that the act of re-reading does not solve the student's comprehension problem. To the extent that she realizes this she has again *identified* a problem but will now probably *define* it in a different way (e.g., perhaps the author left out important information). The point is that the effective learner will therefore re-enter the IDEAL cycle and remain in that cycle (each time defining the problem somewhat differently) until the problem is solved.

As an additional illustration of effective learning, consider the task of attempting to learn about the window-washing robots that were discussed earlier. However, assume that the passage describes only the properties of each robot: it says nothing about their functions nor about why each robot has the properties that it does.

Effective learners who read with the goal of understanding and remembering the information about the robots should be able to *identify* the existence of a problem; namely, that which robot has which properties seems arbitrary, hence the information can be difficult to remember. Furthermore, the effective learner realizes that the ability to remember (which could be due to rote memory strategies) does not guarantee that one understands the significance of various facts (i.e., that one understands why each robot has the properties that it does).

The learner who *identifies* the existence of a problem may then *define* it as involving a lack of information about why each robot has particular properties. This will lead to the *exploration* of various strategies such as (a) seeking particular types of information (e.g., what does the passage say about each robot's function?) or (b) generating hypotheses about what each robot's function must be. The effective learner will next *act* upon this information and then *look* at the effects of this activity. If the reader assumes that one robot plants flowers and the second paints houses, for example, he or she will have a difficult time solving the problem of understanding why each one has particular features. An alternative approach is to assume that one robot washes outside windows in two-story houses whereas the second washes windows in tall, high-rise buildings. As noted earlier, this approach works.

It would simplify matters if it were possible to identify the "stage" of problem solving that accounted for the difficulties experienced by less effective learners. We doubt that learning difficulties can be associated with only one or even two or three stages. Research suggests that less effective learners frequently experience difficulties at each of the junctions previously noted.

Consider first the process of problem *identification*. This is an especially important aspect of problem solving: if people do not realize that a problem exists one cannot expect them to look for a solution. Several researchers have found that less mature learners are less likely to notice problems. For example, they frequently fail to notice when texts contain incomplete or inconsistent information (Baker, 1979, 1982; Baker & Brown, 1984; Capelli & Markman, 1982; Markman, 1979, 1981). Less successful learners are also less likely to notice whether passages are easy or difficult to learn; hence they fail to vary their study time as a function of the difficulty of the task (e.g., Bransford et al., 1982; Owings, Peterson, Bransford, Morris, & Stein, 1980). At a global level, less successful learners are frequently unaware that they have failed to comprehend or master information, hence they do nothing to change their current state of affairs (e.g., see Bransford et al., 1981; Brown et al., 1983; Feuerstein et al., 1979; Feuerstein et al., 1980).

People can agree that a problem exists (problem *identification*) yet disagree about how it should be *defined* and represented. Problem definition is extremely important because if influences the types of solutions that will be considered (e.g., Maier, 1930, 1931; Newell & Simon, 1972). The results of several studies suggest that less successful students frequently have difficulty defining the source of learning problems. They may have difficulty determining whether a momentary lack of comprehension stems from problems at the word, sentence, or paragraph level, for example (Collins & Smith, 1980). Similarly, although less successful fifth graders may know that some things are easier to learn than others, they fail to realize that the arbitrariness of semantic relationships can be responsible for difficulties (e.g., Owings et al., 1980; Stein, Bransford, Franks, Owings, Vye, & McGraw, 1982; Stein, Bransford, Franks, Vye, & Perfetto, 1982).

As noted previously problem definition affects the *exploration* phase of problem solving because one's definition of problems constrains the search for solutions. Therefore, effective learners who can accurately define the source of comprehension failures should be more likely to choose the correct "repair" strategy (e.g., Collins & Smith, 1980), and learners who realize that they lack information necessary to make relationships less arbitrary should be more likely to search for relevant information that permits an understanding of the significance or relevance of the relationships to be learned (e.g., see Bransford et al., 1982; Stein, 1978; Stein & Bransford, 1979; Stein, Morris, & Bransford, 1978).

Problem definition and the exploration of possible strategies are also involved in students' attempts to anticipate the types of testing contexts in which information must eventually be utilized. Research indicates that particular learning activities may or may not be optimal depending on the testing context (e.g., Bransford, Franks, Morris, & Stein, 1977; Nitsch, 1977). Failures to define testing contexts with accuracy (these failures can be due either to the absence of planning or a lack of knowledge about different testing contexts) can therefore lead to the use of inappropriate strategies while attempting to learn. Similarly, the use of inappropriate test questions (e.g., those that emphasize rote memory rather than inferences) can affect the strategies that students use (e.g., see Hansen & Pearson, 1980; Pearson, 1984).

We noted earlier that the ability to solve problems often requires a number of passes through the IDEAL cycle; that is, people must *act* on hypotheses (which are influenced by their definition of a problem) and *look* at the effects of their activities in order to gather information about the most fruitful directions for change. A number of studies suggest that less successful learners are less likely than their more successful peers to revise current hypotheses and strategies. For example, poorer readers frequently fail to reevaluate their hypotheses about how to interpret materials that they are reading (e.g., Collins & Smith, 1980; MacGinitie, 1984). In addition, less mature learners seem less likely to use tests as sources of feedback that can guide their choice of strategies and hypotheses (e.g., Brown et al., 1983; Stein, Bransford, Franks, Vye, & Perfetto, 1982). Because it is relatively rare that anyone can always predict with accuracy the kinds of information that will be necessary in future situations, it seems extremely important to continually test one's current ideas and to look at the degree to which they are appropriate. Failures to do so could have pervasive effects on one's abilities to learn.

Attempts to Help People Learn to Learn

A major goal of research on differences in approaches to learning is to find ways to help people learn to learn more effectively. We noted at the beginning of this chapter that this goal has been acknowledged for centuries. It is to be hoped that current research provides information about ways to do this more effectively than has been done in the past.

Consider first the question of whether most of our current educational instruction emphasizes the skills and strategies necessary for effective learning and thinking. Even though the goal of helping students learn to learn has been prevalent for centuries, it does not necessarily follow that most instruction emphasizes this objective. Indeed, many educators argue that the opposite is true—that current educational practice tends to emphasize *what* to think and learn rather than *how* to think and learn (e.g., Lochhead & Clement, 1979).

Research by Durkin (1978–1979, 1984) is relevant in this context. She assessed third through sixth-grade teachers in 39 classrooms in 14 school systems. Each teacher was observed for 3 successive days while teaching either a reading or social studies class. Durkin's goal was to assess the amount of time spent teaching comprehension strategies—strategies that students could use to improve their abilities to derive meaning from text. The results were dramatic. The social studies teachers spent virtually *no* time on comprehension instruction. The reading teachers were only slightly better. Of the 11,587 minutes spent observing reading, only 45 minutes went to comprehension instruction. In this sample, at least, relevant strategies (as defined by Durkin) were rarely taught.

MacGinitie (1984) also argued that information about strategies is rarely taught in educational settings. One reason is that it is generally easier to teach content than to teach the processes or strategies necessary for the acquisition of content. If a child has misunderstood a text, for example, MacGinitie noted that teachers are much more likely to explain the correct interpretation than to help the child identify and practice the strategies necessary to derive meaning on his or her own. Cazden (1981) provided additional information about problems in teaching strategies. She noted that teachers often supply hints that help students improve their performance but that fail to help them develop important skills. For example, imagine a child who cannot identify the word "bus" on a word card. Cazden notes that a query such as "What do you ride to school?" can help the child produce a correct answer. Nevertheless, it fails to facilitate the development of word identification skills.

A major difficulty involved in teaching about strategies is that one must first analyze particular tasks in order to identify the strategies that are necessary (e.g., Brown & DeLoache, 1978; Resnick & Glaser, 1976). This can be extremely difficult, especially for complex tasks (e.g., reading comprehension). In addition, the explicitness of the instruction necessary for improvement depends on the skills and knowledge already available to the students. For example, Butterfield, Wambold, & Belmont (1973) discuss differences in the strategy instruction necessary for children whose IQ scores fell within the normal range versus those that were below average. The latter students needed much more explicit instruction in order to learn to use a strategy for performing a serial memory task (see also Brown, Campione, & Barclay, 1979; Case, 1978; Siegler, 1978).

An additional problem with many attempts to teach new strategies is that students often fail to use them spontaneously in new contexts. For example, students may learn a memory strategy involving categorization and use it during the experimental task to improve their memory performance. When confronted with similar tasks later, however, the students frequently fail to categorize in a systematic manner unless explicitly prompted to do so (e.g., Brown, Campione, & Day, 1981). Results such as these are similar to those discussed in the earlier section on access and the problem of inert knowledge; in the present case it is knowledge about strategies that remains inert rather than knowledge about factual content. It therefore seems insufficient simply to teach students to use particular strategies while they are performing particular tasks.

Learning and Metacognition

During recent years, a number of researchers have argued that one must take a "metacognitive" approach to teaching in order to provide a basis for transfer (e.g., Brown et al., 1981; Feuerstein et al., 1979; Feuerstein et al., 1980; Meichenbaum, 1985; Pressley, Borkowski, & O'Sullivan, 1983; Ryan, 1981). The overall goal is to teach students to select, refine, and hopefully even to invent new strategies by helping them acquire both *knowledge* about variables that affect their performance and *procedures* for monitoring and evaluating the efficacy of their current approach to various tasks (e.g., Brown & DeLoache, 1978; Feuerstein et al., 1979; Feuerstein et al., 1980; Flavell & Wellman, 1977; Hagen, Barclay, & Newman, 1982; Hallahan, 1980; Wong, 1982). An emphasis on metacognition is congruent with the assumption that learning can be viewed as an instance of problem solving and that a major goal of instruction is to help students improve their problem solving skills in a variety of content domains.

Brown et al. (1981) noted that many attempts to teach students new skills and strategies have not been conducted from a metacognitive perspective. In many cases, for example, students were taught strategies for a particular task yet received no information about why and when these were useful (Brown et al. referred to this as "blind" training). In these cases, students rarely used the strategies in new contexts unless explicitly reminded to do so.

Brown et al. contrasted "blind" training with "informed" training. In the latter, students learn about the significance of the strategies that they are taught. A study by Paris, Newman, and McVey (1982) represents an excellent example. They provided 7- and 8-year-olds with two different types of training for the task of remembering lists of 24 potentially categorizable pictures. During the third session of a total of five testing sessions, all students were taught to group related items, label them, rehearse the labels cumulatively, assess their readiness for a recall test and recall items by groups. Children in one training condition were merely taught the strategies; those in a second group were given a rationale for each strategy and provided with feedback about their performance after the recall trial. The data from the third session revealed improved performance on the part of both groups as compared to pre-training performance (sessions 1 and 2); the groups remembered more pictures and showed greater evidence of clustering (recall by groups). Furthermore, measures of overt study behavior showed that the children were more likely to use the strategies following training. They verbally rehearsed the pictures, sorted them into groups, and so forth, with greater frequency during the third than the first and second sessions.

Although the results from the training session suggest that the "blind" and "informed" groups profited equally from strategy instruction, the data from the fourth and fifth sessions demonstrate that "informed" children were more likely than "blind" to spontaneously use the acquired strategies in subsequent learning situations (although even the "informed" children did not employ all of the strategies later on). Children in the "informed" group maintained increased recall and clustering during the last sessions, whereas the "blind" group returned to pre-training performance levels. In addition, the "informed" children's overt study behavior showed greater evidence of strategy maintenance than the "blind" children's; in particular the former maintained sorting behavior. Data also indicated that, as a result of training, students in the "informed" group showed an increased awareness of the importance of memory strategies. Furthermore, degree of awareness correlated with strategy use as well as with the amount recalled on the memory test.

Although Paris et al.'s goal was not to study all possible ways of teaching strategies for learning, it is useful in this context to consider how strategy training for the problem of remembering categorizable lists could be extended. Assume that participants received additional training on coordinating the strategies and on the importance of monitoring the effects of these activities (children in Paris et al.'s study were not told about the interdependence and joint use of the strategies). For instance, children might be informed about the value of using the strategies in sequence (e.g., first, group related items, then label the groups, cumulatively rehearse the labels and items in each group and so forth). An important part of the training would be to help children self-check their readiness for a test and to use the information from the self-testing to pinpoint the items in need of further study, as well as to identify the particular strategies to use. Training that emphasizes monitoring and self-checking activities such as these has been called "self-control" training by Brown et al. (1981). Several studies suggest that "informed" plus "self-control" training results in better transfer than does "blind" or even "informed" training. For example, Brown et al. (1979) taught strategies for remembering lists of pictures to mildly mentally retarded students and found that, for the older ones at least (mental age = 8 years), self-control training resulted in greater transfer. Similarly, Brown et al. (1981) and Day (1980) found that "informed plus self-control" training was superior for a group of junior college students who were taught rules for summarizing texts. Direct training in self-control activities was most important for those students whose reading and writing skills were the weakest to begin with.

Like Brown et al. (1981), Pressley, Borkowski, and O'Sullivan (1983) also argue that different approaches to the teaching of skills and strategies have important effects of transfer. Pressley et al. refer to different teaching alternatives as (a) laissez-faire (similar to "blind" training); (b) explicit teaching of metamemory (similar to "informed training"), and (c) training of Metamemory Acquisition Procedures or MAPs (similar to self-control training). Pressley et al.'s discussion of MAPs is especially helpful because it focuses explicitly on the goal of helping students acquire procedures for continuing to learn about their own learning processes (see also Brown et al., 1983; Chi, 1987; Flavell, 1979). In addition, Pressley et al. discuss research that was designed to separate as much as possible the effects of "meta" instruction (instruction about MAPs) from the effects of specific strategy instruction per se.

A study by Lodico, Ghatala, Levin, Pressley, and Bell (1983) provided a nice example of research on MAPs. They trained 7- and 8-year-old children with tasks and materials that were quite different from the ones to be used on subsequent transfer tests. In one of the training tasks, children in the experimental group were prompted to use two different methods for drawing a circle: draw it freehand versus tracing around a cookie cutter. After training they were encouraged to evaluate which method was better and to explain why. The second training task involved memorization of a list of letters. The letters were first presented in random order; children studied them and then attempted to recall as many as they could. The children were then helped to see that, by rearranging groups of letters, they could create organized patterns such as the spelling of their own names (each child was given different sets of letters). After the letters (arranged into the child's name) were removed, children were again asked to recall. They were then asked to compare their two memory performances, explain how their performance was affected by the strategy used (rehearsal of random versus organized letter sequences), and state which strategy they might use later on.

Students in a control group received the same tasks (i.e., drawing a circle and remembering letters) and the same strategies (e.g., draw freehand versus trace around a cookie cutter, etc.). However, they received no instruction about the importance of monitoring their performance in order to see which strategies were the most effective for achieving particular goals.

Following training, all children received new tasks to perform that were dissimilar to the training tasks. They were also introduced to alternate strategies for performing each task. One task involved remembering a list composed of pairs of items, the second involved free recall of a list of individual items. For each task, students were first encouraged to learn a list by using one strategy (e.g., memorizing the pairs by elaborating on the relationship between each item) and then encouraged to learn a second list by using an alternate strategy (e.g., simply repeating each pair after it was presented). Students attempted to recall the items after each trial. Following recall of the second list, children were then asked to describe what their memory performance had been for each list and to explain why.

Nearly all children were able to state whether they had done well or poorly on particular lists. However, children who were members of the experimental group were much more likely than were members of the control group to explain their performance in terms of the effects of the strategies they had utilized. Furthermore, a higher percentage of children in the experimental group chose to use the more effective strategies when given a third learning trial, and these children were also able to justify their choices. Pressley et al. (1983) argue that, through MAP training, children developed a general procedure for monitoring their performance and hence were able to acquire new information about the effectiveness of strategies that differed considerably from those used during the initial training. As noted earlier in our discussion of learning as problem solving, the act of evaluating one's performance and learning from it can have pervasive effects on people's abilities to learn.

General Versus Specific Strategies and Skills

The experiments discussed in the preceding section provide important information about procedures necessary to help students improve their abilities to learn more effectively. A consistent finding is that people who are helped to understand why and when to use various strategies are more likely to utilize them appropriately in new contexts than are those who were merely told about each strategy. In addition, data suggest that training that emphasizes procedures for evaluating the relative efficiency of new strategies can increase the probability that students will continue to learn on their own.

Results such as those just described still leave open the question of which skills and strategies to teach in order to have the greatest impact on people's performance. Newell (1980) distinguished between general skills and strategies that operate across a wide variety of content domains and specific ones that are applicable only in a small set of contexts. Newell argued that there are fewer general than specific skills and strategies but that the former are relatively "weak" in that they do not provide detailed guidance. Suggestions such as "break problems into parts," "think before responding," and "be precise" are illustrations of strategies that have wide generality yet are weak. On the other hand, a strategy such as "create an image of a house filled with elephants in order to remember the pair 'house-elephant'" is quite specific yet limited in generality.

Many theorists argue that an emphasis on intermediate level skills and strategies is an effective approach for improving performance (e.g., Brown, 1985; Brown & Palincsar, 1982). Instruction in comprehension skills represents a case in point. As an illustration, consider a study by Short and Ryan (1982). They provided groups of fourth graders who were poor readers with "story grammar" training (see our earlier discussion of story grammars). Children in these groups were prompted to ask themselves questions that were derived from story grammars: Who is the main character? Where and when did the story take place? What did the main character do? How did the story end? How did the main character feel? Children were also helped to see why these questions were important to ask. The results indicated that, after several sessions of training, poor readers were able to recall as much information about new stories that they had read as were their more skilled peers.

Much to their credit, Short and Ryan also included a test asking students to detect errors in passages. Under these conditions, the poor readers who had received training performed somewhat better than untrained controls but their performance was still much poorer than that of their more skilled peers. Apparently, the "story grammar" approach needs to be extended in order to help students learn to detect errors in passages that they read.

Moldofsky (1983) advocated an approach to teaching reading comprehension that is similar to Short and Ryan's yet also different. Moldofsky noted that most stories revolve around a central problem and that students need to be helped to identify and define the central problem of each story. In "The Tortoise and the Hare," for example, Moldofsky noted that the central problem is that the hare *wants* to race a tortoise *but* the hare is too sure of himself.

Moldofsky first encourages children to look for the main character in each story and to think about what he or she needs, wants, feels, or thinks. Students are then encouraged to use this information to help them define the central story problem. Moldofsky argued that these activities are applicable to a wide range of materials and that they help students improve their abilities to comprehend and to learn.

Brown and Palincsar (1982) investigated the effectiveness of two self-questioning interventions, corrective feedback and strategy training, on reading comprehension. The authors conducted many intervention sessions with four seventh-grade problems readers. During these sessions (which were preceded and followed by baseline and maintenance sessions), two of the students received feedback followed by strategy training and the remaining two received the reverse sequence of interventions. During corrective feedback, students first read a passage and then attempted to answer comprehension questions. In the event of an incorrect response, students were provided with information about where in the passage the correct answer could be found. Strategy training consisted of an interactive learning game in which student and experimenter took turns leading a dialogue concerning a segment of the text: The dialogue leader would paraphrase the text, predict questions and remaining content and comment on any confusions and their resolutions. The results of the study indicated that the most successful training sequence was feedback followed by strategy training. The data also showed that by the end of the study, three of the four students had significantly improved their percentile rankings on a test of reading comprehension and all of the students showed evidence of maintenance 6 months after the intervention. These results (see also Palincsar, 1982) suggest that students can profit greatly from interventions designed to teach students self-questioning strategies that help them identify and understand central story events.

As a final illustration of the efficacy of teaching learning skills and strategies to improve reading comprehension, consider the approach taken by Paris and his research group (Cross, 1982; DeBritto, 1982; Jacobs, 1982; Lipson, 1982; Oka, 1982; Paris, 1982). These researchers report encouraging results from a large-scale intervention program designed to study the effects of cognitive strategy and metacognitive training on reading comprehension. Their training encompassed a range of strategies such as skimming to identify main ideas, notetaking, and procedures for summarizing texts, to name just a few. In addition, children in the study were given direct instruction on metacognitive components of reading. For example, they were presented with methods for evaluating their knowledge status and abilities, for identifying reading goals, for selecting strategies appropriate to these goals, and for monitoring the effectiveness of chosen strategies.

Experimental classes of third- and fifth-grade children were taught two classes per week for a period of 4 months (matched control classes were also included in the study). Although the story content and the strategy being trained varied from lesson-to-lesson, the instructional format consisted of a number of invariant features. During each lesson, a bulletin board containing a metaphor for the strategy to be taught was presented to the class. For example, the bulletin board for the module on planning for reading was entitled "Road Maps and Sign Posts for Reading," and depicted common road signs as metaphors for planful reading behaviors (i.e., a stop sign might mean "stop and evaluate what was read"). A set of goals and plans for each lesson and focal questions about the materials were explicitly presented to children. Other features of the instruction included direct instruction on the strategies ("informed" training), frequent and immediate feedback and practice opportunities, and emphasis on the application of previously learned knowledge and strategies.

Participants in the intervention program were given pre-, post- and follow-up (8 months after) tests on a variety of measures. A comprehensive review of the findings are not given here, but some of the more important results are highlighted. To assess whether trained children had in fact acquired the target strategies, a multiple-choice test designed to tap the content taught was administered at post- and follow-up testing. On this measure, third- and fifth-grade experimentals outperformed their controls.

Performance on measures of reading comprehension showed a similar advantage for trained over untrained children. On a posttest cloze task, both third-and fifth-grade experimental children scored higher than their controls. Another finding from the cloze task analysis was that poor and average readers in the experimental groups (as measured by the Gates–MacGinitie Reading Test) showed greater improvement on the posttest task than poor and average controls, whereas the good readers in the experimental group did not differ from the good controls at posttesting. Furthermore, among the poorer readers, the ones who learned the most during training were also the ones whose cloze scores improved the most. These findings point to the effectiveness of the interventions for those children who are in greatest need of remediation.

Because a primary purpose of the intervention was to investigate the extent to which strategy and metacognitive training mediated improvements in reading comprehension, assessments of children's awareness of these skills represent an important aspect of the data base. A variety of self-report measures were used: think-aloud, open-ended questions, and scaled questions. These were designed to assess children's knowledge of the importance of evaluation, planning and regulation, as well as more specific knowledge of comprehension strategies, task variables, and personal evaluations of reading abilities. For both third-and fifth-grade children, members of the experimental group showed greater pre- to posttest gains than controls on an empirically derived summary score of awareness and on subscale measures of planning and regulation. Overall, self-report and standard assessments of strategies and metacognitive knowledge indicate improvements as a function of training which in turn were associated with improvements on reading comprehension tests.

ISSUES FOR FUTURE RESEARCH

The studies described here show that it is possible to help students improve considerably their abilities to comprehend and remember information (see also Collins, Gentner, & Rubin, in press; Meichenbaum, 1985; Meyer, Brandt, & Bluth, 1980; Scardamalia & Bereiter, 1985; Wong, 1980). Clearly, this does not mean that effective training will necessarily eliminate all achievement differences among students (see especially Brown et al., 1983; Covington, 1985). However, the results do suggest that an explicit emphasis on how, when and why to use various strategies can help students reach levels of achievement that they otherwise might never have attained.

It is important to note that the comprehension-oriented training studies discussed previously illustrate only a subset of strategies that may be beneficial. A number of existing educational programs designed to improve thinking and learning emphasize skills and strategies that differ from those that we have discussed. For example, programs such as Feuerstein's Instrumental Enrichment (Feuerstein et al., 1980) use a large number of nonverbal exercises involving planning, strategy selection, evaluation, comparison and so forth. Lipman and colleagues' Philosophy for Children program (Lipman, 1985; Lipman & Sharp, 1978; Lipman, Sharp, & Oscanyan, 1980) emphasizes processes of formal and informal reasoning, and Whimbey and Lochhead's (1980) *Short Course in Analytical Reasoning* focuses on verbal and mathematical problems such as those found on the SAT and GRE. Still other programs focus more explicitly on memory strategies necessary to master information in order to prepare for formal tests (e.g., Dansereau, 1978; Weinstein, 1978). Each of these programs (plus others) is analyzed in considerable detail in a recent set of volumes (Chipman, Segal, & Glaser, 1985; Segal, Chipman, & Glaser, 1985), so we do not discuss them in this chapter. Instead, we consider an issue common to all attempts to help students improve their abilities to learn and to solve problems more effectively. The issue is: what kinds of results are reasonable to expect?

Assume that students receive instruction in thinking and learning strategies for approximately 1 hour per day during an academic year. Ideally, one would like to find relatively substantial gains in all areas of academic achievement (e.g., Math, Social Studies, Science, Reading) at the end of the year. However, based on our knowledge of the results of many educational assessments, results such as these are rare (e.g., Arbitman-Smith, Haywood, & Bransford, in press; Bransford, Stein, Arbitman-Smith, & Vye, 1985; Vye & Bransford, 1981). For example, Arbitman-Smith et al. report some gains in achievement (relative to a control group) following 2 years of training in Feuerstein's Instrumental Enrichment program. However, even these differences were modest rather than large.

Arbitman-Smith et al. note that they found much larger differences between the experimental and control groups on other tasks they administered. For example, students enrolled in Instrumental Enrichment were much better at planning, following complex instructions, explaining when and why they used various strategies and so forth. Arbitman-Smith et al. note that a major limiting factor on many tasks—on most of the items on the achievement tests, for example—was that students lacked the content knowledge necessary to perform the tasks successfully. The students had not been helped to systematically apply strategies while learning particular content areas; in addition, they had already missed a great deal of content knowledge that, instead of being taught explicitly in class, was often presupposed.

As noted in the first section of this chapter, the availability of strategies does little good if one lacks relevant knowledge or schemas. It seems clear that tasks such as organizing information for memory, comprehending texts, summarizing texts, solving problems, and so forth depend on the availability of relevant content knowledge. In most laboratory tests of the effects of skill training, researchers choose test materials that do not presuppose knowledge that students have not yet had a chance to learn (e.g., see the previous discussion of training studies). In everyday educational settings, however, progress is generally measured by more standardized assessments such as achievement tests. To the extent that the results of these tests depend on knowledge that students have not yet had an adequate chance to acquire, researchers may underestimate the potential importance of teaching thinking and learning skills.

Theory and research discussed in the present chapter suggest ways to increase the degree to which strategy training can produce gains in school achievement: students need to be helped to see how thinking and learning strategies apply to each content domain (e.g., Mathematics, History, Physics, etc.) that they are trying to learn. One advantage of offering instruction in each content area is that students would receive approximately 6 hours of "strategic thinking" practice per day as compared, say, to only one hour per day. Another advantage is that students could be helped to formulate *specific* learning and problem solving strategies that are relevant to particular content areas. This emphasis on specifics seems to be especially important. As noted earlier, for example, learning involves much more than the memorization of new facts and relationships; it requires activating knowledge that enables one to understand the significance or relevance of information (e.g., Bransford et al., 1981). In order to do so, people need exposure to core concepts that provide a basis for precise understanding of particular content domains. Generic training programs that emphasize only general and even intermediate level skills seem to be important and helpful; however, they rarely provide information about specific concepts, skills and strategies necessary to learn about particular content areas. Programs that help students develop specific as well as general skills seem to have the potential to produce powerful educational effects. Clearly, this is not the end.

ACKNOWLEDGMENT

Preparation of the chapter was supported in part by Grants NIE G-79-0117 and NIE G-80-0028. Opinions expressed herein are those of the authors and should not be attributed to NIE.

REFERENCES

Adams, J. L. (1974). *Conceptual blockbusting: A guide to better ideas.* New York: Norton.

Adams, M., & Bruce, B. (in press). Background knowledge and reading comprehension. In J. Langer & M. Smith-Burke (Eds.), *Reader meets author/bridging the gap: A psycholinguistic and sociolinguistic perspective.* Newark, DE: International Reading Association.

Anderson, J. R. (1981). *Cognitive skills and their acquisition.* Hillsdale, NJ: Lawrence Erlbaum Associates.

Anderson, J. R. (1982). Acquisition of cognitive skill. *Psychological Review, 89,* 369–406.

Anderson, J. R., & Reder, L. M. (1979). An elaborative processing explanation of depth of processing. In L. S. Cermak & F.I.M. Craik (Eds.), *Levels of processing and human memory* (pp. 385–403). Hillsdale, NJ: Lawrence Erlbaum Associates.

Anderson, R. C. (1977). The notion of schemata and the educational enterprise. In R. C. Anderson, R. J. Spiro, & W. E. Montague (Eds.), *Schooling and the acquisition of knowledge* (pp. 415–431). Hillsdale, NJ: Lawrence Erlbaum Associates.

Anderson, R. C. (1984). Role of reader's schema in comprehension, learning and memory. In R. Anderson, J. Osborn, & R. Tierney (Eds.), *Learning to read in American schools: Basal readers and content texts* (pp. 243–257). Hillsdale, NJ: Lawrence Erlbaum Associates.

Arbitman-Smith, R., Haywood, H. C., & Bransford, J. D. (1985). Assessing cognitive change. In C. M. McCauley, R. Sperber, & P. Brooks (Eds.), *Learning and cognition in the mentally retarded* (pp. 433–471). Baltimore, MD: University Park Press.

Asch, S. E. (1969). A reformulation of the problem of associations. *American Psychologist, 24,* 92–102.

Auble, P. M. (1982). *An examination of expertise.* Unpublished manuscript, Vanderbilt University.

Baker, L. (1979). Comprehension monitoring: Identifying and coping with text confusions. *Journal of Reading Behavior, 11,* 363–374.

Baker, L. (1982). An evaluation of the role of metacognitive deficits in learning disabilities. *Topics in Learning and Learning Disabilities, 2,* 27–35.

Baker, L., & Brown, A. L. (1984). Cognitive monitoring in reading. In J. Flood (Ed.), *Understanding reading comprehension* (pp. 21–44) Newark, DE: International Reading Association.

Baron, J. (1985). What kinds of intelligence components are fundamental? In S. Chipman, J. Segal, & R. Glaser (Eds.), *Thinking and learning skills* (Vol. 2, pp. 365–390). Hillsdale, NJ: Lawrence Erlbaum Associates.

Beck, I. L. (1984). Developing comprehension: The impact of the directed reading lesson. In R. Anderson, J. Osborne, & R. Tierny (Eds.), *Learning to read in American schools: Basal readers and content texts* Hillsdale, NJ: Lawrence Erlbaum Associates.

Beck, I. L., Perfetti, C. A., & McKeown, M. G. (1982). The effects of long-term vocabulary instruction on lexical access and reading comprehension. *Journal of Educational Psychology, 74,* 506–521.

Bereiter, C., & Scardamalia, M. (1985). Cognitive coping strategies and the problem of "inert knowledge." In S. Chipman, J. Segal, & R. Glaser (Eds.), *Thinking and learning skills* (Vol. 2, pp. 65–80). Hillsdale, NJ: Lawrence Erlbaum Associates.

Bloom, B. S., & Broder, L. (1950). *Problem-solving processes of college students.* Chicago: University of Chicago Press.

Bousfield, W. A. (1953). The occurrence of clustering in the recall of randomly arranged associates. *Journal of General Psychology, 49,* 229–240.

Bower, G. H. (1970). Analysis of a mnemonic device. *American Psychologist, 58,* 496–510.

Bower, G. H. (1981). Mood and memory. *American Psychologist, 36,* 129–148.

Bower, G. H., Black, J. B., & Turner, T. J. (1979). Scripts in memory for text. *Cognitive Psychology, 11,* 177–220.

Bower, G. H., & Clark, M. C. (1969). Narrative stories as mediators for serial learning. *Psychonomic Science, 14,* 181–182.

Bower, G. H., Clark, M. C., Lesgold, A. M., & Winzenz, D. (1969). Hierarchial retrieval schemes in recall of categorized word lists. *Journal of Verbal Learning and Verbal Behavior, 8,* 323–343.

Bransford, J. D. (1979). *Human cognition: Learning, understanding, and remembering.* Belmont, CA: Wadsworth.

Bransford, J. D., Franks, J. J., Morris, C. D., & Stein, B. S. (1979). Some general constraints on learning and memory research. In L. S. Cermak & F. I. M. Craik (Eds.), *Levels of processing and human memory* (pp. 331–354). Hillsdale, NJ: Lawrence Erlbaum Associates.

Bransford, J. D., & Johnson, M. K. (1972). Contextual prerequisites for understanding: Some investigations of comprehension and recall. *Journal of Verbal Learning and Verbal Behavior, 11,* 717–726.

Bransford, J. D., & Johnson, M. K. (1973). Considerations of some problems of comprehension. In W. Chase (Ed.), *Visual information processing* (pp. 383–438). New York: Academic Press.

Bransford, J. D., & McCarrell, N. S. (1974). A sketch of a cognitive approach to comprehension. In W. Weimer & D. Palermo (Eds.), *Cognition and the symbolic process* (pp. 189–229). Hillsdale, NJ: Lawrence Erlbaum Associates.

Bransford, J. D., & Nitsch, K. E. (1978). Coming to understand things we could not previously understand. In J. F. Kavanaugh & W. Strange (Eds.), *Speech and language in the laboratory, school and clinic* (pp. 267–307). Cambridge, MA: MIT Press.

Bransford, J. D., Nitsch, K. E., & Franks, J. J. (1977). Schooling and the facilitation of knowing. In R. C. Anderson, R. J. Spiro, & W. E. Montague (Eds.), *Schooling and the acquisition of knowledge* (pp. 31–55). Hillsdale, NJ: Lawrence Erlbaum Associates.

Bransford, J. D., & Stein, B. S. (1984). *The IDEAL problem solver.* NY: Freeman.

Bransford, J. D., Stein, B. S., Arbitman-Smith, R., & Vye, N. J. (1985). Three approaches to improving thinking and learning skills. In J. Segal, S. Chipman, & R. Glaser (Eds.), *Thinking and learning skills: Relating instruction to basic research* (Vol. 1, pp. 133–200). Hillsdale, NJ: Lawrence Erlbaum Associates.

Bransford, J. D., Stein, B. S., Shelton, T. S., & Owings, R. A. (1981). Cognition and adaptation: The importance of learning to learn. In J. Harvey (Ed.), *Cognition, social behavior and the environment* (pp. 93–110). Hillsdale, NJ: Lawrence Erlbaum Associates.

Bransford, J. D., Stein, B. S., Vye, N. J., Franks, J. J., Auble, P. M., Mezynski, K. J., & Perfetto, G. A. (1982). Differences in approaches to learning: An overview. *Journal of Experimental Psychology: General, 111,* 390–398.

Brewer, W. F., & Lichtenstein, E. H. (1981). Event schemas, story schemas, and story grammars. In A. Baddeley & J. Long (Eds.), *Attention and performance IX*. Hillsdale, NJ: Lawrence Erlbaum Associates.

Brown, A. L. (1985). Mental orthopedics, the training of cognitive skills: An interview with Alfred Binet. In S. Chipman, J. Segal, & R. Glaser (Eds.), *Thinking and learning skills: Current research and open questions* (Vol. 2, pp. 319–337). Hillsdale, NJ: Lawrence Erlbaum Associates.

Brown, A. L., Bransford, J. D., Ferrara, R. A., & Campione, J. C. (1983). Learning, remembering and understanding. In J. H. Flavell & E. M. Markman (Eds.), *Carmichael's manual of child psychology* (Vol. 1, pp. 77–166). New York: Wiley.

Brown, A. L., & Campione, J. C. (1981). Inducing flexible thinking: A problem of access. In M. Friedman, J. P. Das, & N. O'Connor (Eds.), *Intelligence and learning* (pp. 515–529). New York: Plenum.

Brown, A. L., & Campione, J. C. (1982). Modifying intelligence or modifying cognitive skills: More than a semantic quibble? In D. K. Detterman & R. J. Sternberg (Eds.), *How and how much can intelligence be increased?* Norwood, NJ: Ablex.

Brown, A. L., Campione, J. C., & Barclay, C. R. (1979). Training self-checking routines for estimating test readiness: Generalization from list learning to prose recall. *Child Development, 50,* 501–512.

Brown, A. L., Campione, J. C., & Day, J. D. (1981). Learning to learn: On training students to learn from texts. *Educational Researcher, 10,* 14–21.

Brown, A. L., & DeLoache, J. S. (1978). Skills, plans and self-regulation. In R. S. Siegler (Ed.), *Children's thinking: What develops?* (pp. 3–35). Hillsdale, NJ: Lawrence Erlbaum Associates.

Brown, A. L., & Palincsar, A. S. (1982). Inducing strategic learning from texts by means of informed, self-control training. *Topics in Learning and Learning Disabilities, 2,* 1–17.

Bruce, B. (1984). A new point of view on children's stories. In R. Anderson, J. Osborn, & R. Tierny (Eds.), *Learning to read in American schools: Basal readers and content texts.* Hillsdale, NJ: Lawrence Erlbaum Associates.

Butterfield, E. C., Wambold, C., & Belmont, J. M. (1973). On the theory and practice of improving short-term memory. *American Journal of Mental Deficiency, 77,* 654–669.

Capelli, C. A., & Markman, E. M. (1982). Suggestions for training comprehension monitoring. *Topics in Learning and Learning Disabilities, 2,* 87–96.

Case, R. (1978). A developmentally based theory and technology of instruction. *Review of Educational Research, 48,* 439–463.

Cazden, C. B. (1981). Performance before competence: Assistance to child discourse in the zone of proximal development. *The Quarterly Newsletter of the Laboratory of Comparative Human Cognition, 3,* 5–8.

Cermak, L. S., & Craik, F. I. M. (Eds.). (1979). *Levels of processing and human memory.* Hillsdale, NJ: Lawrence Erlbaum Associates.

Chase, W. G., & Simon, H. A. (1973). The mind's eye in chess. In W. Chase (Ed.), *Visual information processing* (pp. 215–281). New York: Academic Press.

Chi, M. T. H. (1978). Knowledge structures and memory development. In R. S. Siegler (Ed.), *Children's thinking: What develops?* (pp. 73–96). Hillsdale, NJ: Lawrence Erlbaum Associates.

Chi, M. T. H. (1981). Knowledge development and memory performance. In M. Friedman, J. P. Das, & N. O'Connor (Eds.), *Intelligence and learning* (pp. 221–229). New York: Plenum.

Chi, M. T. H. (1987). Representing knowledge and meta-knowledge: Implications for interpreting metamemory research. In F. E. Weinert & R. H. Kluwe (Eds.), *Metacognition, motivation, learning* (pp. 239–266). Hillsdale, NJ: Lawrence Erlbaum Associates.

Chipman, S., Segal, J., & Glaser, R. (Eds.). (1985). *Thinking and learning skills: Current research and open questions* (Vol. 2). Hillsdale, NJ: Lawrence Erlbaum Associates.

Collins, A., Gentner, D., & Rubin, A. (in press). Teaching study strategies. *Cognition & Instruction.*

Collins, A., & Smith, E. E. (1980). *Teaching the process of reading comprehension* (Tech. Rep. No. 182). Cambridge, MA: Bolt Beranek and Newman.

Cook, L. K., & Mayer, R. E. (1983). Reading strategies training for meaningful learning from prose. In M. Pressley & J. Levin (Eds.), *Cognitive strategies training and research.* New York: Springer-Verlag.

Corsale, K., & Gitomer, D. (1979, November). *Developmental and individual differences in mathematical aptitude.* Paper presented at the 20th annual meeting of the Psychonomic Society, Phoenix, AZ.

Covington, M. V. (1985). Strategic thinking and the fear of failure. In J. Segal, S. Chipman, & R. Glaser (Eds.), *Thinking and learning skills: Relating instruction to basic research* (Vol. 1, pp. 389–416). Hillsdale, NJ: Lawrence Erlbaum Associates.

Craik, F. I. M., & Lockhart, R. W. (1972). Levels of processing: A framework for memory research. *Journal of Verbal Learning and Verbal Behavior, 11,* 671–684.

Craik, F. I. M., & Tulving, E. (1975). Depth of processing and the retention of words in episodic memory. *Journal of Experimental Psychology: General, 104,* 268–294.

Cross, D. (1982, May). *Individual differences in the acquisition of reading skill.* Paper presented at the annual meeting of the International Reading Association, Chicago.

Dansereau, D. (1978). The development of a learning strategies curriculum. In H. F. O'Neil, Jr. (Ed.), *Learning strategies* (pp. 1–29). New York: Academic Press.

Day, J. D. (1980). *Training summarization skills: A comparison of teaching methods.* Unpublished doctoral dissertation, University of Illinois.

DeBritto, A. M. (1982, May). *Assessing comprehension with cloze tasks.* Paper presented at the annual meeting of the International Reading Association, Chicago.

deGroot, A. (1965). *Thought and choice in chess.* The Hague: Mouton.

deGroot, A. D. (1965). Perception and memory versus thinking. In B. Kleinmuntz (Ed.), *Problem solving* (pp. 19–50). New York: Wiley.

Dickinson, D. K., & Weaver, P. A. (1979, April). *Remembering and forgetting: Story recall abilities in dyslexic children.* Paper presented at the meeting of the American Educational Research Association, San Francisco.

Dooling, D. J., & Lachman, R. (1971). Effects of comprehension on retention of prose. *Journal of Experimental Psychology, 88,* 216–222.

Duncker, K. (1945). On problem-solving. *Psychological Monographs, 58,* (270).

Durkin, D. (1978–1979). What classroom observations reveal about reading comprehension. *Reading Research Quarterly, 14,* 481–533.

Durkin, D. (1984). Do basal reader manuals provide for reading comprehension instruction? In R. C. Anderson, J. Osborn, & R. J. Tierney (Eds.), *Learning to read in American schools: Basal readers and content texts.* Hillsdale, NJ: Lawrence Erlbaum Associates.

Ericsson, K., Chase, W., & Faloon, S. (1980). Acquisition of a memory skill. *Science, 208,* 1181–1182.

Feuerstein, R., Rand, Y., & Hoffman, M. B. (1979). *The dynamic assessment of retarded performers.* Baltimore, MD: University Park Press.

Feuerstein, R., Rand, Y., Hoffman, M. B., & Miller, R. (1980). *Instrumental enrichment.* Baltimore, MD: University Park Press.

Flavell, J. H. (1979). Metacognition and cognitive monitoring: A new area of cognitive-developmental inquiry. *American Psychologist, 34,* 906–911.

Flavell, J. H., & Wellman, H. M. (1977). Metamemory. In R. V. Hail, Jr. & J. W. Hagen (Eds.), *Perspectives on the development of memory and cognition* (pp. 3–33). Hillsdale, NJ: Lawrence Erlbaum Associates.

Franks, J. J., Bransford, J. D., & Auble, P. M. (1982). The activation and utilization of knowledge. In C. R. Puff (Ed.), *Handbook of research methods in human memory and cognition.* New York: Academic Press.

Franks, J. J., Vye, N. J., Auble, P. M., Mezynski, K. A., Perfetto, G. A., Bransford, J. D., Stein, B. S., & Littlefield, J. (1982). Learning from explicit versus implicit texts. *Journal of Experimental Psychology: General, 111,* 414–422.

Gick, M. L., & Holyoak, K. J. (1980). Analogical problem solving. *Cognitive Psychology, 12,* 306–355.

Gick, M. L., & Holyoak, K. J. (1983). Schema induction and analogical transfer. *Cognitive Psychology, 15,* 1–38.

Glaser, R., & Pellegrino, J. (1982). Improving the skills of learning. In D. K. Detterman (Ed.), *How and how much can intelligence be increased.* Norwood, NJ: Ablex.

Goldman, S. R. (1982). Knowledge systems for realistic goals. *Discourse Processes, 5,* 279–303.

Graessar, A. C., & Nakamura, G. V. (in press). The impact of a schema on comprehension and memory. In G. Bower (Ed.), *The psychology of learning and motivation.* New York: Academic Press.

Hagen, J. W., Barclay, C. R., & Newman, R. S. (1982). Metacognition, self-knowledge, and learning disabilities: Some thoughts on knowing and doing. *Topics in Learning and Learning Disabilities, 2,* 19–26.

Hallahan, D. P. (Ed.). (1980). Teaching exceptional children to use cognitive strategies. *Exceptional Education Quarterly, 1* (1).

Hansen, J., & Pearson, P. D. (1980). *The effects of inference training and practice on young children's comprehension* (Tech. Rep. No. 166). Urbana, IL: University of Illinois, Center for the Study of Reading, April 1980. (ERIC Document Reproduction Service No. ED 186–839).

Hasher, L., & Zacks, R. T. (1979). Automatic and effortful processes in memory. *Journal of Experimental Psychology: General, 108,* 356–388.

Hyde, T. S., & Jenkins, J. J. (1969). Differential effects of incidental tasks on the organization of recall of a list of highly associated words. *Journal of Experimental Psychology, 82,* 472–481.

Jacobs, J. (1982, May). *Children's reports about cognitive aspects of reading comprehension*. Paper presented at the annual meeting of the International Reading Association, Chicago.

Kintsch, W., & Greene, E. (1978). The role of culture-specific schemata in the comprehension and recall of stories. *Discourse Processes, 1,* 1–13.

LaBerge, D., & Samuels, S. J. (1974). Toward a theory of automatic information processing in reading. *Cognitive Psychology, 6,* 293–323.

Larkin, J. H. (1979). Information processing models and science instruction. In J. Lochhead & J. Clement (Eds.), *Cognitive process instruction: Research on teaching thinking skills* (pp. 109–118). Philadelphia: The Franklin Institute Press.

Lawler, R. W. (1981). The progressive construction of mind. *Cognitive Science, 5,* 1–30.

Lesgold, A. M., & Perfetti, C. A. (1978). Interactive processes in reading comprehension. *Discourse Processes, 1,* 323–326.

Lindberg, M. (1980). The role of knowledge structures in the ontogeny of learning. *Journal of Experimental Child Psychology, 30,* 401–410.

Lipman, M. (1985). Thinking skills fostered by Philosophy for Children. In J. Segal, S. Chipman, & R. Glaser (Eds.), *Thinking and learning skills: Relating instruction to basic research* (Vol. 1, pp. 83–108). Hillsdale, NJ: Lawrence Erlbaum Associates.

Lipman, M., & Sharp, A. M. (1978). *Growing up with philosophy*. Philadelphia: Temple University Press.

Lipman, M., Sharp, A. M., & Oscanyan, F. S. (1980). *Philosophy in the classroom*. Philadelphia: Temple University Press.

Lipson, M. Y. (1982, May). *Promoting children's metacognition about reading through direct instruction*. Paper presented at the annual meeting of the International Reading Association, Chicago.

Lochhead, J., & Clement, J. (1979). *Cognitive process instruction: Research on teaching thinking skills*. Philadelphia: The Franklin Institute Press.

Lodico, M. G., Ghatala, E., Levin, J. R., Pressley, M., & Bell, J. A. (1983). Effects of meta-memory training on children's use of effective memory strategies. *Journal of Experimental Child Psychology, 35,* 263–277.

MacGinitie, W. H. (1984). Readability as a solution adds to the problem. In R. Anderson, J. Osborn, & R. J. Tierney (Eds.), *Learning to read in American schools: Basal readers and content texts*. Hillsdale, NJ: Lawrence Erlbaum Associates.

Maier, N. R. F. (1930). Reasoning in humans: I. On direction. *Journal of Comparative Psychology, 10,* 115–143.

Maier, N. R. F. (1931). Reasoning in humans: II. The solution of a problem and its appearance in consciousness. *Journal of Comparative Psychology, 12,* 181–194.

Mandler, G. (1967). Organization and memory. In K. W. Spence & J. T. Spence (Eds.), *Psychology of learning and motivation* (Vol. 1, pp. 328–372). New York: Academic Press.

Mandler, J. M., & Goodman, M. (1982). On the psychological validity of story structure. *Journal of Verbal Learning and Verbal Behavior, 21,* 507–523.

Mandler, J. M., Scribner, S., Cole, M., & DeForest, M. (1980). Cross-cultural invariance in story recall. *Child Development, 51,* 19–26.

Mann, L. (1979). *On the trail of process: A historical perspective on cognitive processes and their training*. New York: Grune & Stratton.

Markman, E. M. (1979). Realizing that you don't understand: Elementary school children's awareness of inconsistencies. *Child Development, 50,* 643–655.

Markman, E. M. (1981). Comprehension monitoring. In W. P. Dickson (Ed.), *Children's oral communication skills* (pp. 61–84). New York: Academic Press.

Mayer, R. E. (1977). *Thinking and problem solving: An introduction to human cognition and learning.* Glenview, IL: Scott, Foresman.

Mehan, J. R. (1977). *Tale-spin, an interactive program that writes stories.* Proceedings from the Fifth International Joint Conference on Artificial Intelligence, 91–98.

Meichenbaum, D. (1985). Teaching thinking: A cognitive-behavioral perspective. In S. Chipman, J. Segal, & R. Glaser (Eds.), *Thinking and learning skills* (Vol. 2, pp. 407–426). Hillsdale, NJ: Lawrence Erlbaum Associates.

Meyer, B. J. F., Brandt, D. M., & Bluth, G. J. (1980). Use of top-level structure in text: Key for reading comprehension of ninth-grade students. *Reading Research Quarterly, 16,* 72–103.

Mezynski, K. (1983). Issues concerning knowledge acquisition: Effects of vocabulary instruction on reading comprehension. *Review of Educational Research, 53,* 253–279.

Miller, G. A. (1956). The magical number seven, plus or minus two: Some limits on our capacity for processing information. *Psychological Review, 63,* 81–97.

Minsky, M. (1975). A framework for representing knowledge. In P. H. Winston (Ed.), *The psychology of computer vision.* New York: McGraw-Hill.

Moldofsky, P. B. (1983, April). Teaching students to determine the central story problem: A practical application of schema theory. *The Reading Teacher,* 740–745.

Morris, C. D., Bransford, J. D., & Franks, J. J. (1977). Levels of processing versus transfer appropriate processing. *Journal of Verbal Learning and Verbal Behavior, 16,* 519–533.

Newell, A. (1980). One final word. In D. T. Tuma & F. Reif (Eds.), *Problem solving and education: Issues in teaching and research* (pp. 175–189). Hillsdale, NJ: Lawrence Erlbaum Associates.

Newell, A., & Simon, H. A. (1972). *Human problem solving.* Englewood Cliffs, NJ: Prentice-Hall.

Nitsch, K. E. (1977). *Structuring decontextualized forms of knowledge.* Unpublished doctoral dissertation, Vanderbilt University.

Oka, E. (1982, May). *Think aloud tasks as measures of reading behaviors and metacognition.* Paper presented at the annual meeting of the International Reading Association, Chicago.

Owings, R. A., Peterson, G. A., Bransford, J. D., Morris, C. D., & Stein, B. S. (1980). Spontaneous monitoring and regulation of learning: A comparison of successful and less successful fifth graders. *Journal of Educational Psychology, 72,* 250–276.

Paivio, A. (1971). *Imagery and verbal processes.* New York: Holt, Rinehart & Winston.

Palincsar, A. S. (1982). *Improving the reading comprehension of junior high students through the reciprocal teaching of comprehension-monitoring strategies.* Unpublished doctoral dissertation, University of Illinois.

Paris, S. G. (1982, May). *Combining research and instruction on reading comprehension in the classroom.* Paper presented at the annual meeting of the International Reading Association, Chicago.

Paris, S. G., Newman, R. S., & McVey, K. A. (1982). Learning the functional significance of mnemonic actions: A microgenic study of strategy acquisition. *Journal of
Experimental Child Psychology, 34,* 490–509.

Pearson, P. D. (1984). Guided reading: A response to Isabel Beck. In R. C. Anderson,
J. Osborn, & R. J. Tierney (Eds.), *Learning to read in American schools: Basal readers
and content texts.* Hillsdale, NJ: Lawrence Erlbaum Associates.

Pellegrino, J. W., & Glaser, R. (1979). Cognitive correlates and components in the
analysis of individual differences. *Intelligence, 3,* 187–214.

Pellegrino, J. W., & Glaser, R. (1980). Components of inductive reasoning. In R. E.
Snow, P. Frederico, & W. Montague (Eds.), *Aptitude, learning and instruction:
Cognitive process analysis* (pp. 177–217). Hillsdale, NJ: Lawrence Erlbaum
Associates.

Pellegrino, J. W., & Lyon, D. R. (1979). The components of componential analysis.
Intelligence, 3, 169–186.

Perfetti, C. A., & Lesgold, A. M. (1977). Discourse comprehension and sources of
individual differences. In M. Just & P. Carpenter (Eds.), *Cognitive processes in
comprehension* (pp. 141–183). Hillsdale, NJ: Lawrence Erlbaum Associates.

Perfetto, G. A., Bransford, J. D., & Franks, J. J. (1983). Constraints on access in a
problem solving context. *Memory & Cognition, 11,* 24–31.

Pressley, M., Borkowski, J. G., & O'Sullivan, J. (1983). *Memory strategies are made of
this: Metamemory and the teaching of study skills.* Submitted for publication.

Pressley, M., Levin, J. R., & Delaney, H. D. (1982). The mnemonic keyword method.
Review of Educational Research, 52, 61–91.

Reed, S. K., Ernst, G. W., & Banerji, R. (1974). The role of analogy in transfer between
similiar problem states. *Cognitive Psychology, 6,* 436–450.

Resnick, L. B. (Ed.). (1976). *The nature of intelligence.* Hillsdale, NJ: Lawrence
Erlbaum Associates.

Resnick, L. B. (1981). Syntax and semantics in learning to subtract. In T. Carpenter, T.
Moser, & G. Romberg (Eds.), *Addition and subtraction: Developmental perspectives*
(pp. 136–155). Hillsdale, NJ: Lawrence Erlbaum Associates.

Resnick, L. B., & Glaser, R. (1976). Problem solving and intelligence. In L. B. Resnick
(Ed.), *The nature of intelligence* (pp. 205–238). Hillsdale, NJ: Lawrence Erlbaum
Associates.

Rohwer, W. D., Jr. (1966). Constraints, syntax and meaning in paired-associate learning. *Journal of Verbal Learning and Verbal Behavior, 5,* 541–547.

Rohwer, W. D., Jr. (1980). An elaborative conception of learner differences. In R. E.
Snow, P. A. Frederico, & W. E. Montague (Eds.), *Aptitude, learning and instruction*
(pp. 23–46). Hillsdale, NJ: Lawrence Erlbaum Associates.

Rumelhart, D. E. (1980). Schemata: The building blocks of cognition. In R. J. Spiro, B.
C. Bruce, & W. F. Brewer (Eds.), *Theoretical issues in reading comprehension:
Perspectives from cognitive psychology, linguistics, artifical intelligence and education*
(pp. 33–58). Hillsdale, NJ: Lawrence Erlbaum Associates.

Rumelhart, D. E., & Norman, D. A. (1978). Accretion, tuning and restructuring:
Three modes of learning. In J. W. Cotton & R. L. Klatzky (Eds.), *Semantic factors in
cognition* (pp. 37–53). Hillsdale, NJ: Lawrence Erlbaum Associates.

Rumelhart, D. E., & Ortony, A. (1977). The representation of knowledge in memory.

In R. C. Anderson, R. J. Spiro, & W. E. Montague (Eds.), *Schooling and the acquisition of knowledge* (pp. 99–135). Hillsdale, NJ: Lawrence Erlbaum Associates.

Ryan, E. B. (1981). Identifying and remediating failures in reading comprehension: Towards an instructional approach for poor comprehenders. In T. Q. Waller & G. E. Mackinnon (Eds.), *Reading research: Advances in theory and practice.* New York: Academic Press.

Scardamalia, M., & Bereiter, C. (1985). Fostering the development of self-regulation in children's knowledge processing. In S. Chipman, J. Segal, & R. Glaser (Eds.), *Thinking and learning skills* (Vol. 2, pp. 563–577). Hillsdale, NJ: Lawrence Erlbaum Associates.

Schank, R. C. (1980). Language and memory. *Cognitive Science, 4,* 243–284.

Schank, R. C., & Abelson, R. P. (1977). *Scripts, plans, goals and understanding.* Hillsdale, NJ: Lawrence Erlbaum Associates.

Schneider, W., & Shiffrin, R. M. (1977). Controlled and automatic human information processing: I. Detection, search and attention. *Psychological Review, 84,* 1–66.

Segal, J., Chipman, S., & Glaser, R. (Eds.). (1985). *Thinking and learning skills: Relating instruction to basic research* (Vol. 1). Hillsdale, NJ: Lawrence Erlbaum Associates.

Short, E. J., & Ryan, E. B. (1982). *Metacognitive differences between skilled readers: Remediating deficits through story grammar.* Manuscript submitted for publication.

Siegler, R. S. (1978). The origins of scientific reasoning. In R. S. Siegler (Ed.), *Children's thinking: What develops?* (pp. 109–149). Hillsdale, NJ: Lawrence Erlbaum Associates.

Simon, H. A. (1976). Identifying basic abilities underlying intelligent performance of complex tasks. In L. Resnick (Ed.), *The nature of intelligence* (pp. 65–98). Hillsdale, NJ: Lawrence Erlbaum Associates.

Spilich, G. J., Vesonder, G. T., Chiesi, H. L., & Voss, J. F. (1979). Text processing of domain-related information for individuals with high and low domain knowledge. *Journal of Verbal Learning and Verbal Behavior, 18,* 275–290.

Spiro, R. J., Bruce, B. C., & Brewer, W. F. (1980). *Theoretical issues in reading comprehension: Perspectives from cognitive psychology, linguistics, artificial intelligence and education.* Hillsdale, NJ: Lawrence Erlbaum Associates.

Steffensen, M. S., Joag-Deci, C., & Anderson, R. C. (1979). A cross-cultural perspective on reading comprehension. *Reading Research Quarterly, 15,* 10–29.

Stein, B. S. (1978). Depth of processing reexamined: The effects of precision of encoding and test appropriateness. *Journal of Verbal Learning and Verbal Behavior, 17,* 165–174.

Stein, B. S., & Bransford, J. D. (1979). Constraints on effective elaboration: Effects of precision and self-generation. *Journal of Verbal Learning and Verbal Behavior, 18,* 769–777.

Stein, B. S. Bransford, J. D., Franks, J. J., Owings, R. A., Vye, N. J., & McGraw, W. (1982). Differences in the precision of self-generated elaborations. *Journal of Experimental Psychology: General, 111,* 399–405.

Stein, B. S., Bransford, J. D., Franks, J. J., Vye, N. J., & Perfetto, G. A. (1982). Differences in judgments of learning difficulty. *Journal of Experimental Psychology: General, 111,* 406–413.

Stein, B. S., Morris, C. D., & Bransford, J. D. (1978). Constraints of effective elaboration. *Journal of Verbal Learning and Verbal Behavior, 17,* 707–714.

Stein, N. L. (1979). How children understand stories. In L. Katz (Ed.), *Current topics in early childhood education* (Vol. 2). Norwood, NJ: Ablex.

Stein, N. L., & Glenn, C. G. (1979). An analysis of story comprehension in elementary school children. In R. Freedle (Ed.), *Advances in discourse processes* (Vol. 2). Norwood, NJ: Ablex.

Sternberg, R. J. (1977a). Component processes in analogical reasoning. *Psychological Review, 84,* 353–378.

Sternberg, R. J. (1977b). *Intelligence, information processing, and analogical reasoning: The componential analysis of human abilities.* Hillsdale, NJ: Lawrence Erlbaum Associates.

Sternberg, R. J. (1978). Isolating components of intelligence. *Intelligence, 2,* 117–128.

Sternberg, R. J. (1981). Intelligence as thinking and learning skills. *Educational Leadership, 39,* 18–20.

Sternberg, R. J., & Determan, D. (1979). *Human intelligence: Perspectives on its theory and measurement.* Norwood, NJ: Ablex.

Thorndyke, P., & Stasz, C. (1980). Individual differences in procedures for knowledge acquisition from maps. *Cognitive Psychology, 12,* 137–175.

Trabasso, T., Stein, N. L., & Johnson, L. (1981). Children's knowledge of events: A causal analysis of story structures. In G. Bower (Ed.), *Learning and motivation* (Vol. 15). New York: Academic Press.

Tulving, E., & Perlstone, Z. (1966). Availability versus accessibility of information in memory for words. *Journal of Verbal Learning and Verbal Behavior, 5,* 381–391.

Turnure, J. E., Buium, N., & Thurlow, M. L. (1976). The effectiveness of interrogatives for prompting verbal elaboration productivity in young children. *Child Development, 47,* 851–855.

Voss, J. F., Fincher, R. H., Greene, T. R., & Post, T. A. (1986). Individual differences in performance: The contrastive approach to knowledge. In R. J. Sternberg (Ed.), *Advances in the psychology of human intelligence.* (Vol. 3, pp 297–334). Hillsdale, NJ: Lawrence Erlbaum Associates.

Vye, N. J., & Bransford, J. D. (1981). Programs for teaching thinking. *Educational Leadership, 39,* 26–28.

Weaver, P. A., & Dickinson, D. K. (1982). Scratching below the surface structure: Exploring the usefulness of story grammars. *Discourse Processes, 5,* 225–243.

Weingartner, H., Miller, J., & Murphy, D. L. (1977). Mood-state-dependent retrieval of verbal associations. *Journal of Abnormal Psychology, 86,* 276–284.

Weinstein, C. E. (1978). Elaboration skills as a learning strategy. In H. F. O'Neil Jr. (Ed.), *Learning strategies* (pp. 31–55). New York: Academic Press.

Weisberg, R., DiCamillo, & Phillips, D. (1978). Transferring old associations to new situations: A nonautomatic process. *Journal of Verbal Learning and Verbal Behavior, 17,* 219–228.

Whimbey, A., & Lochhead, J. (1980). *Problem solving and comprehension: A short course in analytical reasoning.* Philadelphia: The Franklin Institute Press.

Whitehead, A. N. (1929). *The aims of education.* New York: Macmillan.

Wong, B. Y. L. (1980). Activating the inactive learner: Use of questions/prompts to enhance comprehension and retention of implied information in learning disabled children. *Learning Disability Quarterly, 3,* 29–37.

Wong, B. Y. L. (Ed.). (1982). Metacognition and learning disabilities. *Topics in Learning and Learning Disabilities, 2* (1).

Worden, P. M., Malmgren, I., & Gabourie, P. (1982). Memory for stories in learning disabled adults. *Journal of Learning Disabilities, 15,* 77–110.

6

Problem Solving and the Educational Process

James F. Voss
University of Pittsburgh

Problem solving has long been recognized as an important cognitive activity, important in relation to educational theory and practice as found in the classroom and important more generally to the issues that confront people in daily living (cf. Dewey, 1916). Thus, there are two, somewhat related ways in which problem solving has been viewed as critical to education. First, problem solving has been considered as part of the learning of subject matter, especially in mathematics and the physical sciences. Problem-solving exercises, moreover, have two functions. One is the testing function: problem solving is used to determine what the student has or has not learned. The other is the teaching function: working problems not only tells whether the student understands the subject matter, but also provides for a better understanding of that subject matter.

Second, problem solving has been viewed as critical in a way that transcends particular subject matters. The more general relationship of problem solving to education is that learning to solve problems is sometimes regarded as a goal of the schooling process. Thus, being also to solve problems is thought to be a characteristic of an "educated person." In this context, the formal education process is charged with providing the individual with the capability to cope with and solve life's problems, whatever they may be. This problem-solving goal of education assumes not only that general problem skills exist, but that they may be taught in the context of formal education. (Evidence related to this notion is considered later in the chapter.)

Problem solving and education thus have been related in two ways, in relation to subject matter learning, and in relation to the broader goals of the educational process. Quite importantly, each of these viewpoints suggests that problem solving is a critical component of the educational process, and further suggests that a better understanding of how problem solving takes place could improve the educational process. Furthermore, given its importance to the educational process, the study of problem solving should constitute one of the primary efforts of educational research.

Although the importance of problem solving to the educational process has been recognized for some time, the study of problem solving, until recently, has not been a primary area of psychological inquiry. Instead, explanations of how problem solving takes place typically have been derived from theories that had their bases in phenomena other than problem solving per se. Such theoretical viewpoints include Gestalt theory with its perceptual emphasis (e.g., Koffka, 1935), learning theories with an associationistic emphasis (e.g., Maltzman, 1955), and theories of cognitive development in which problem solving is used to monitor mental development (e.g., Piaget, 1926/1975). However, in recent years, problem solving has received increasing interest, a development due in large part to the growth of the theoretical approach termed *information processing*. Moreover, much of this research has been conducted within the context of particular academic disciplines. The remaining sections of this chapter survey research on problem solving in the light of this recent research. They consist of: (a) a brief discussion of some general conceptual issues; (b) a brief summary of more historical conceptions of the problem-solving process, followed by a description of the information processing model; (c) a summary of recent problem-solving research, especially as found in particular subject matter domains; (d) a summary of recent work on the effectiveness of problem-solving instruction; (e) a section on miscellaneous topics, presented in question–answer form; and (f) a concluding statement.

PROBLEM SOLVING: A FEW CONCEPTUAL ISSUES

The Nature of a Problem

Although what defines a problem has been the subject of debate (cf. Agre, 1982), there nevertheless has been general agreement among most investigators concerning this issue. A problem is said to exist when an individual in a particular situation has a goal but is unable to obtain the goal. In addition, it is frequently assumed that there is some type of obstacle or barrier that prevents the solver from reaching the goal (cf. Hayes, 1981; Johnson, 1955; Mayer, 1977; Wickelgren, 1974; Woodworth, 1938). (The obstacles that may exist must, of necessity, be broadly defined, and include such factors as lack of skill, lack of knowledge, failure to remember, etc.)

Defining a problem in terms of a situation, a goal, and an obstacle is reasonably straightforward, but a few elaborative comments are in order. First, it is assumed for the purposes of this chapter that having a goal entails being motivated to attain it. It is therefore unnecessary to state that the person has a goal "and is motivated to achieve it." On the other hand, the motivation to achieve a goal may of course vary from person to person or vary over time within one person. Second, if it is necessary to take a number of steps to reach a goal but taking these steps involves a routine execution, then there is no problem. In other words, if a goal cannot be achieved immediately, it does not necessarily mean there is a problem; a problem is presumed to exist when the steps needed to achieve the goal are not immediately apparent.[1] Third, for particular classes of problems, identifying a goal may be difficult and/or somewhat arbitrary. (This matter is considered later in the chapter.) Finally, no position is taken in this chapter regarding whether awareness is a necessary condition of having a problem. (In a research context, of course, the individual is almost always aware of the problem because it is presented as a problem statement.) In summary, what constitutes a problem is viewed in the present chapter in a traditional way, characterized by a solver who has a goal but cannot attain it because of some obstacle.

Early Conceptions of the Problem-Solving Process[2]

William James (1890) described solving a problem as a search that occurs when the means to an end does not occur simultaneously with the establishment of the end. Subsequently, a number of problem-solving analyses were developed, and for approximately the first half of the 20th century, the study of problem solving was dominated by four viewpoints. The first, here termed the *descriptive approach,* involved describing problem solving as a stepwise process. Dewey (1971), for example, spoke of five steps in the reflection process. The individual experiences a difficulty, the difficulty is defined, there is the generation of a possible solution, the implications of the solution are tested by reasoning, and the solution is verified. Similarly, Wallas (1926) described problem solving as a four-step process: preparation, incubation, illumination, and verification. *Preparation* consists of defining and studying a problem, *incubation* involves a relatively quiescent period in which the solver does not work on the problem, *illumination* consists of coming up with a possible solution, and *verification* of course involves the testing of the solution. Descriptions such as

---

[1]When one's goal is to obtain a tool from the basement, the fact that one cannot get it immediately because it takes a number of steps to get there does not in itself constitute a problem. The same for executing a well-known solution in a mathematics problem.

[2]Because the theoretical positions considered in this section have been discussed extensively in other published works and because the present chapter emphasizes an information processing approach, the treatment of these viewpoints in this chapter is brief. This brevity, however, is not meant to minimize the importance of this work.

these did not produce much theoretical advancement, but they did tend to bring the importance of problem solving into focus by pointing out that it is an integral facet of the thinking process and by arguing for its centrality in the processes of education.

A second approach to the study of problem solving was that developed by Piaget (e.g., 1926/1975, 1954). Concerned with issues of knowledge development, Piaget used problem solving as a means to study the processes involved in the mental growth of the child, arguing that problem-solving ability was related to the ontological development of particular mental structures. His theoretical notions have of course been widely discussed and have been quite influential in developmental psychology (cf. Flavell, 1963). More recently, Piaget's tasks have been reinterpreted in terms of other theoretical viewpoints, such as information processing (e.g., Klahr & Wallace, 1976) and a number of his theoretical assertions have been questioned (e.g., Bryant & Trabasso, 1971; Gelman & Gallistel, 1978; Siegler & Klahr, 1982; Trabasso, 1975). Nevertheless, his work has had a profound effect on the study of problem solving in children.

A third theoretical framework is that of Gestalt (e.g., Kohler, 1947; Koffka, 1935; Wertheimer, 1959) and neo-Gestalt psychology (e.g., Duncker, 1926, 1945; Katona, 1940; Maier, 1940). Gestalt psychology emphasized problem solving as a perceptual-like process, viewing the solution process as a restructuring of the solver's organization of the problem. Furthermore, such reconstruction typically was presumed to be accompanied by an experience of insight. Although it has been highly influential, the Gestalt approach has received its share of criticism (e.g., Bulbrook, 1932), and some of the findings employed to support the Gestalt position have been reinterpreted (e.g., Perfetto, Bransford, & Franks, 1983; Weisberg & Alba, 1981, 1982; but see Ellen, 1982). Nevertheless, the influence of the Gestalt and neo-Gestalt writers has been extensive, and the monographs by Duncker (1945) and by Wertheimer (1959) should be, in this writer's opinion, required reading for anyone interested in problem solving.

The fourth approach to problem solving was that of stimulus–response psychology. In one sense, Thorndike's (1898) research on problem solving by cats was a precursor to a more general stimulus–response model, for Thorndike emphasized the acquisition of responses in the particular stimulus situation that permitted the goal to be attained.

The stimulus–response view of problem solving, largely based on Hullian theory, was extensively developed by Maltzman (1955). This approach emphasized problem solving as the occurrence of a response that had an initially low probability of occurrence in a particular situation. Classes of responses were assumed to be organized in a hierarchical manner and the solution of a problem was achieved by selecting a response from the hierarchy until one was chosen that would enable the solver to obtain the goal or advance toward it.

In concluding the brief summary of these four approaches, two general observations should be made. First, the various viewpoints demonstrated that problem solving cannot be considered apart from other psychological processes. Phrased positively, problem solving is highly interrelated with those processes usually referred to as thinking, learning, memory, transfer, perception, and motivation. Also, although the various approaches to the study of problem solving were quite diverse, there have been attempts to integrate some of the viewpoints (e.g., Berlyne, 1965; Mowrer, 1960). Berlyne, for example, although maintaining the idea of a hierarchy of stimulus–response relations, also attempted to integrate this concept with that of Piagetian structures.

The Information-Processing Approach

As previously noted, over the last few decades, a substantial amount of problem-solving research has been conducted within a general framework called *information processing,* which, incidentally, is continuing to evolve. Selz (1922, 1964) is generally regarded as the intellectual forerunner of this view. (Also, see Humphrey, 1951, for a summary of Selz's position.) The more recent impetus has been largely provided by investigators who have had a strong affinity for the use of the computer simulation of problem solving, for example, Newell, Shaw, and Simon (1958) and Newell and Simon (1972), and Simon (1978). Furthermore, the development of the information-processing approach has involved not only psychologists but also individuals working in the field of computer science, especially in the area of artificial intelligence.

In order to describe the major components of the information-processing approach, the following example is presented. Assume a person is presented with a version of the missionaries and cannibal problem. (Sometimes the cast of characters consists instead of Hobbits and Orcs.) There are a number of missionaries and a equal number of cannibals who desire to cross a river. However, they have only one boat, and it holds a maximum of two people. Furthermore, at no time can there be more cannibals than missionaries on either side of the river. The problem is to determine how all individuals are able to get across the river. (A similar problem used frequently in research is the Tower of Hanoi. This problem consists of a number of pegs, for example, three, and a number of disks, for example, five. Each disk is of different size and all disks are initially placed upon one peg according to size, with the smallest at the top and largest at the bottom. The object is to move all the disks from one peg to another so that they end up in the same vertical order. However, only one disk may be moved at a time and at no time may a larger disk be placed upon a smaller disk.)

Considering now the information-processing jargon, the expression *task environment* is used to refer to the problem statement and its context. In the present case, the problem statement includes the description of an *initial state* of the problem (i.e., the missionaries and cannibals are on one side of the river and have one boat). The *goal state* of the problem is also defined, namely, all individuals are to reach the other side of the river. What the solver is asked to do is to show how the goal state may be achieved, given the initial state. Finally, in addition to the initial and goal states, the problem statement includes *constraints*. The constraints are the limiting conditions under which the problem is to be solved. In the present case they are the boat size (maximum of two people) and the restriction that at no time may there be more cannibals than missionaries on either side of the river.

How does the solver go about proposing a solution to the missionary–cannibal problem? To answer this question, further analysis is necessary. The steps necessary to solve the problem may be defined in terms of *states* and *operators*. The problem states consist of all possible arrangements of missionaries, cannibals, and boat that could exist (given the problem constraints). The operators consist of the actions that must be taken for the solution to move from one state to the next. Thus, in the present case, use of an operator could consist of taking away one missionary and one cannibal from the shore (subtraction) and placing them in the boat and moving them to the other side of the river. A state change would thus occur, with four missionaries and four cannibals now being on one side and one missionary and one cannibal of the other side. Then another operator is applied such as moving the missionary back to the side from which he started. Viewed in terms of states and operators, the solution thus involves going from the initial state, through a series of intervening states, and reaching the goal state, with each state-to-state transition occurring by the application of an operator. Moreover, because in this type of problem the solver is presumed to have knowledge of the possible states of the problem as well as knowledge of the operators, solving this problem may be viewed as a search process in which the solver looks for a path that goes from the initial state to goal.

A concept employed within the information-processing framework that is closely related to states and operators is the *problem space*. This term refers to the knowledge of the individual that is relevant to the problem interpretation and solution. For the missionary–cannibal problem, little interpretation of the problem is necessary because the initial state, goal, and constraints are clearly stated and there is essentially only one interpretation of the nature of the problem. With respect to problem-relevant knowledge, the problem space consists of the knowledge that all possible states that may occur and the means by which the solver may move from state to state (i.e., knowledge of the operators). Viewed another way, the problem space represents a demarcation of the information that the solver has that is of potential use to the solving of the problem. With is delineation, the solver does not need to search through large "areas" of memory, but only needs to search through a highly restricted space. Thus, finding the appropriate solution path may be regarded as a search through a relatively restricted problem space.[3]

The solver, in the initial state, must apply an operator and move to another state. On what basis does such move selection occur? The answer is that typically the solver uses a *strategy* (i.e., a reasonably systematic method that at least has the potential of leading to the solution of the problem). One of the most frequently used strategies in this type of problem has been termed *means–ends* analysis. Essentially, this consists of the solver considering the current state of the problem and the goal state, and selecting a move that will reduce the difference. The use of this strategy has been termed *working backwards* because move selection is based primarily upon the goal state as a means of selection. There are, of course, many other strategies, a number of which are discussed later in this chapter. Finally, the solver, in trying to select a move, may not be able to find a move that will place the solver closer to the goal. Under such conditions the solver may set up a subgoal and then select a move that advances the solution toward this subgoal.

On the spectrum of problems that have been employed in research, the missionary–cannibal problem is quite straightforward. It is what has been termed a *well-structured problem* (i.e., there is a clear exposition of the problem statement, its initial state, goal state, and constraints, and the problem space is well-defined). However, trying to understand how more complex problems are solved has led to development of additional concepts, and one of the most important of these is *problem representation.* Assume the problem under consideration is, "How may the crime rate in a particular community be reduced?" The initial state is given by the implicit assumption that the community has a high crime rate. The goal of the problem is to reduce the crime rate, although how much it should be reduced is unclear, which means that the goal that may be decided upon, such as, "Reduce major crime by 20%" is somewhat arbitrary. Also, the problem's constraints, which no doubt are numerous, are not presented in the problem statement. In this type of problem, which is ill structured as opposed to well structured (cf. Reitman, 1965; Simon, 1973), the solver usually will interpret the problem in terms of his or her own perception of the major causes or factors contributing to the problem, including the problem's constraints. This interpretive statement constitutes the representation of the problem.

In order to develop a representation, the solver typically must draw on his or her memory and/or possibly on other sources of information. What the individual knows about the problem, therefore, is quite important. But as is shown

---

[3]This discussion has not involved the concept of external memory. The solver, although not having information in memory, may know that the desired information may be obtained in for example, the library. The library source thus constitutes an "external" memory to which the solver has access.

later in this chapter, not only the person's knowledge, but also how that knowledge is organized, is important to the problem representation. Finally, it is noted that the nature of the representation that is developed is quite important not only because the solver is attempting to isolate the causal factors and constraints of the problem, but also because the solution that is proposed will be based on the particular representation that has been developed.

Another concept especially related to the solving of more complex problems is that of *planning*. This term refers to formulating a problem representation and including one or more possible strategies or plans that may be employed in the development of the solution. Sometimes a solution plan is completely worked out before the initial steps of the solution are actually executed. However, this is not always the case, because the solution plan may be changed while it is being executed. (The term *planning* is usually used in a more general sense than *strategy*, with strategy involving a well-defined sequence of actions, whereas planning includes considering and possibly evaluating the possible use of various strategies.)

In addition to the principles thus far considered, a number of theorists have incorporated into the information-processing framework ideas regarding how memory influences the problem-solving process. In particular, the role of working (or short-term) memory has been of concern. Often, it is assumed that working memory has a limited capacity and that at any given time, the working memory of the solver permits only a small amount of information to be processed. Hence, the solver typically knows the current state of the problem (how many missionaries and cannibals are on each side of the river and where the boat is) and may be considering which move to make next, but working memory may exclude most other information such as the state of the problem solution three steps back. Thus, the assumed capacity limitations of working memory imply that the solver is relatively limited in the number of moves that may be considered at any one time and in the ability to "backtrack." Within some theoretical positions, the solver is thus viewed as a *serial* processor (i.e., the solver considers moves in a step-by-step manner).

Armed with the rudiments of information processing concepts, some research findings are now considered. The results are organized in relation to specific subject matter domains.

RESEARCH FINDINGS: PROBLEM SOLVING IN PARTICULAR DOMAINS

Problem Solving in Chess

That complex processes such as problem solving should be studied in the context of games is not surprising; indeed, attempting to become reasonably skilled in card games such as poker and bridge and board games such as chess and Go constitutes a substantial challenge to one's problem-solving skills. Interestingly, the study of problem solving in the game context has generally not involved observation and analysis of the acutal play of the game. Instead, the most commonly used procedure, termed the *contrastive method,* has consisted of identifying individuals at various skill levels with respect to the play of a particular game and studying the performance of these individuals on tasks thought to be relevant to game performance. Thus, individuals who are experts or novices in chess may be given a memory task to determine whether experts are better able to remember a particular configuration of chess pieces. The basic assumption underlying the contrastive method is of course that we can approach the understanding of skill development within a particular domain (whether a game, an academic subject matter, or some other field) by determining what component processes characterize high level performance, and how these processes are similar to or different from processes characteristic of lower level performance. Furthermore, the contrastive method may supply information which suggests how a person with a low level of skill within a particular domain may develop into a highly skilled performer. Finally, it is acknowledged that the contrastive method is of course correlational and results must be interpreted with this in mind. (The reader may refer to Voss, Fincher-Kiefer, Greene, & Post, 1986, for a discussion of this methodology.)

Although the study of expert and novice performance is not new (cf. Binet, 1894; Bryan & Harter, 1897, 1899), recent interest in this approach was given impetus by research involving chess skill (Chase & Simon, 1973a, 1973b; de-Groot, 1965, 1966) and by research designed to assess how individuals who have high verbal or low verbal scores on tests such as the Scholastic Aptitude Test (e.g., Hunt, Frost, & Lunneborg, 1973; Hunt & Lansman, 1975) perform on different tasks. Because, within the game context, most of the research has employed the game of chess, it is this literature that is primarily considered.

One of the major findings with respect to chess skill is that experts surpass less skilled players in the ability to reproduce an array of pieces on a chess board when the pieces have been displayed in a game position. However, when the pieces are placed randomly on the board, the advantage disappears (Chase & Simon, 1973a, 1973b; deGroot, 1965, 1966). Pieces were presented in a particular array for 5 seconds and, with the board removed from view, the individual tried to place the pieces in the same positions in which they were on the board previously presented. An additional finding (Chase & Simon, 1973a) is that experts were not only better recalling the pattern of chess pieces at given points in the game, but they also were better at recalling the sequence of moves that occurred during the course of the game. Thus, expertise was found to be related to better recall of both spatial and temporal patterns, when such patterns were game-related.

These and other results led deGroot (1965, 1966) and Chase and Simon (1973a) to argue that chess skill includes a strong perceptual component, with

Chase and Simon stating that "All of our studies point to perceptual process-ing—the ability to perceive familiar patterns quickly—as the basic ability un-derlying chess skill" (p. 267). Similarly, these results also suggested a strong memory component, with the expert chess player presumed to have literally thousands of patterns stored in long-term memory (cf. Simon & Barenfeld, 1969; Simon & Gilmartin, 1973).

Chase and Simon (1973a) also considered chess skill in relation to short-term memory capacity. Assuming that short-term (or working) memory has a limited capacity consisting of seven bits of information (Miller, 1956), or fewer, see Simon (1974), Chase and Simon argued that expert chess players "chunked" more information per unit than did less skilled players. They studied chunking by presenting an individual with an array of chess pieces placed in a game position, asking the individual to reconstruct the pattern of pieces on another board. Chunk boundaries were assumed to be denoted when the individual glanced from the board on which the pattern was being reconstructed to the board on which the pieces were presented. It was then possible to determine how many pieces constituted a chunk and what relationship existed among the pieces within a chunk. It was found that the chunk of the expert was larger than that of the less skilled players and that the expert recalled more chunks, a finding not really expected because working memory capacity had been presumed to be equal for individuals, regardless of skill level. Chase and Simon suggested that for the expert, one chunk, in a sense, pointed to the next chunk, whereas for the less skillful player, the chunks were essentially independent. This notion was supported by research involving the game of Go (Reitman, 1976) in which it was found that chunks overlapped and experts thus could be more adept in taking advantage of the overlapping characteristics.

The interpretation of Chase and Simon (1973a) that chunks are developed to circumvent a limited working memory capacity has been questioned (e.g., Charness, 1976). In particular, Charness did not find interference effects that would be expected if information was being held in working memory, and Charness' interpretation more or less suggests direct access to long-term mem-ory without a working memory limitation (cf. Goldin, 1978b, Lane & Robert-son, 1979).

An important facet of chess skill is move selection, and as one would expect, the more skillful players select better moves than the less skillful (e.g., Holding & Reynolds, 1982). The question is on what basis the individual selects a particular move. deGroot (1966) found that, counter to intuition, experts do not search ahead, that is, explore the implication of potential moves, to any greater depth (number of subsequent moves) than do less skillful players. This result suggested, as did the findings of Chase and Simon (1973a), that move selection is primarily a function of pattern recognition (i.e., one recognizes a particular pattern of pieces and selects a move based on the particular config-uration). This interpretation, however, has been questioned. Using six groups of chess players that varied in level of expertise, Holding and Reynolds (1982) presented random patterns of chess pieces and had individuals both select moves and subsequently recall the array of pieces. They found that although recall did not vary with expertise, move selection did. Furthermore, they found that move selection was not necessarily based on the number of pieces remembered. Similarly, Charness (1981a), studying chess skill and aging, found that although memory performance was negatively related to age, skill in move selection and move evaluation was positively related. Finally, Charness (1981b) also, contrary to deGroot's results, found that the more skillful players do search more deeply when exploring potential moves (cf. Wagner & Scurrah, 1971). The data thus suggest that expert players do have a better memory for chess piece arrays that do less skilled players, but that among classes of experts such a difference is not found. Thus, chess expertise, in addition to the perceptual and memory component, involves another component related to the quality and evaluation of move selection.

One question that is raised by the expert–novice research is of course how an individual develops expertise (i.e., the question of learning). As noted previously, the contrastive method, basically cross-sectional, provides some idea about the process. However, the longitudinal study of expertise development would perhaps be a better way to study the issue, although this method also has shortcomings. Interestingly, some years ago Cleveland (1907) studied chess skill acquisition longitudinally and concluded that there are five stages involved in learning to play chess and reaching a high level of proficiency: (a) learning the names and moves of the pieces; (b) learning individual moves of offense and defense; (c) discovering the value of combinations of pieces; (d) becoming able to plan a game systematically in advance; and (e) acquiring "position sense" (i.e., a sense of strategic implications of a given position of chess pieces). Cleveland also discussed expert performance in relation to playing a number of games simultaneously and in the ability to play blindfolded. Although the delineation of these stages does not provide for determining the major factors contributing to expert performance, the research does support the importance of organization in the process of skill development (i.e., learning to play the game involves being able to utilize elements in constructing larger and larger complexes that constitute an understanding of the more abstract relations of the game).

It is of more than passing interest to note that Bryan and Harter (1897, 1899), in their classic work on the acquisition of telegraphy skill, reached conclusions quite similar to those stated by Cleveland (1907). Of particular interest is the finding that in learning to play chess as well as in sending and receiving telegraph messages, the individual acquires lower level skills from which higher level skills are generated and, most importantly, the individual cannot become highly skilled unless the lower level skills are highly practiced and mastered.

With regard to expertise development, an interesting question that has not been studied is whether experience per se necessarily produces expertise or whether some type of skill is required in order to take advantage of one's experience. It appears that the latter alternative may be the case, simply because there seem to be people who play games quite frequently but whose improvement is, at best, minimal. Furthermore, as Cleveland (1907) pointed out, acquiring knowledge of the patterns is an important process that takes place by combining elements into increasingly complex functional units, and these units seem to be well differentiated among experts. However, for whatever reason, some individuals may be less adept in developing the higher order units.

In conclusion, although the research surveyed with respect to chess skill has been only minimally concerned with the direct study of problem solving, the findings nevertheless point to some factors that are related to skillful problem solving in playing chess. First, experience provides an opportunity to learn and differentiate specific configurations of pieces, and knowledge of such patterns is of importance to move selection and evaluation. Second, individuals possessing a high level of skill are able to maintain a substantial amount of information in memory (possibly by a chunking process that circumvents a working memory capacity limitation or possibly by direct access to organized units in long-term memory). Third, the chess-related findings are in all likelihood not unique to the development of chess skill, since similar results have been obtained in studies involving skill in games such as Go (Reitman, 1976), and bridge (Charness, 1979, 1983; Engle & Bukstel, 1979).

Problem Solving in Physics and Mathematics

The question of how physics problems are solved has received considerable attention in recent years, and there also has been interest in how individuals solve algebra word problems, develop proofs in geometry, and construct computer programs. Much of this work has involved not only the contrastive method but also the collection of "think-aloud" protocols. In this procedure an individual is given a problem and asked to "think out loud" while solving the problem (i.e., say whatever comes to mind as he or she is going through the solution process). These accounts or protocols are then analyzed to determine the nature of processing that took place in the solving of the problem. (Ericsson & Simon, 1980, present a discussion of this procedure.)

The most important findings that have emerged from the research on physics problem solving are that: (a) problem representation is a critical component of the problem-solving process and (b) experts' knowledge is characteristically much more abstract than novices', and the experts use such knowledge in problem solving. Although these two issues are not independent, research showing the importance of the representation process is considered first.

Larkin (1979, 1981, 1983; Larkin, McDermott, Simon, & Simon, 1980) presented mechanics problems to experts and novices, collected and analyzed protocols, and found that the problem representation differed for the two classes of individuals. The expert, before developing any equations, often analyzed the problem by drawing a diagram (if one has not been given), and also studied the relations among the variables of the problem. Then, the expert would characterize the problem as belonging to a particular problem category (e.g., a "force" problem). Once the problem categorization was established, the expert proceeded to write down the appropriate equations that led to the solution of the problem. Larkin (1979, 1981) and Simon and Simon (1978) also showed that experts tended to work forward in solving problems (i.e., once the problem was classified, the expert was able to produce its solution without appealing to a strategy such as means–ends analysis).

That experts would attempt to classify problems is not surprising, yet it is of considerable importance to demonstrate that classification processes were used in the problem-solving activity. Indeed, Hinsley, Hayes, and Simon (1977), studying the solving of algebra word problems, also found that some mathematics graduate students were able to classify problems even before they completed reading the problem statement. (See also Paige & Simon, 1966.) Finally, Larkin (1979, 1981) and Simon and Simon (1978) also indicated that experts tend to apply equations in "bursts," an outcome interpreted as showing the equations were stored in functional units or "chunks." Larkin also showed that experts usually have sets of equations stored in relation to particular principles or laws.

The performance of novices, on the other hand, may be characterized as follows (Larkin, 1979, 1981). Novices attack the problem in a more piecemeal manner. For example, the novice may identify a parameter that is required for the solution and then select and apply an equation that contains that parameter. This procedure may then be followed until the solution is obtained. Thus, although the expert tends to form a representation of the problem, classify it, if possible, and then write the equations, the novice has a much less developed representation, focusing in on a variable or set of variables that is needed and employing a means–ends analysis strategy to work out the solution.

That the description just given of expert and novice problem-solving performance is to some extent an oversimplification is suggested by two additional findings. First, Larkin (1977), as well as Chi, Glaser, and Rees (1982), reported that when an expert is asked to solve a problem in an area of physics in which the expert's problem-solving experience has been limited, the expert's solving process looks more like that of the novice. Secondly, Chi, Glaser, and Rees (1982) reported that when a novice is familiar with a particular type of problem, the novice is able to develop a representation that cannot be distinguished from that of the expert.

Although protocol analysis has yielded findings which demonstrated differences between experts and novices in problem representation, a question of interest is what produces such differences. One way to try to provide an answer to this question is to determine how the knowledge structures of the expert and novice differ and how such differences may relate to problem solving. To address this issue, Chi, Feltovich, and Glaser (1981) and Chi, Glaser, and Rees (1982) conducted a series of studies that employed procedures other than protocol analysis. The methods included a sorting task in which experts and novices were asked to classify problems selected from a number of different chapters in a standard physics textbook and, in a second study, to sort the problems within each of the categories. In another study, individuals were asked to tell what they knew about the concepts that were mentioned as category labels in the problem-solving sorting task, and in yet another study, individuals were asked to describe their "basic approach" to the solution of a problem and to indicate what factors led them to that approach.

The results of these studies were reasonably consistent and may be summarized as follows. Individuals more knowledgeable in physics tended to sort problems in relation to abstract laws and principles whereas novices sorted problems in relation to surface structure (i.e., in terms of the concepts directly stated in the problem). Thus, although the expert may sort problems according to the Law of the Conservation of Energy, the novice may sort the problems in relation to a variable of the problem such as acceleration. Moreover, when the individuals were asked to sort the problems *within* each category, novices were not readily able to make fine discriminations, either sorting in a general way that was not especially relevant or making each problem a subcategory. On the other hand, experts sorted into reasonable subcategories, making distinctions that were to a large degree based upon the surface structure of the problem. Thus, the within-category sort of the experts highly resembled the initial category sort of the novices. This finding was interpreted as showing that the expert's knowledge is more abstract with problems classified according to higher level principles (the principles or laws were not stated in the problem), whereas novices categorized problems in relation to parameters that are lower ordered. Yet, experts performed a similar lower level sort when making within-category distinctions.

Two other tasks also demonstrated the more abstract organization of information by experts. During the previously mentioned category sorting task, the obtained categories were frequently given labels by the participants. In one task, individuals who did not serve in the sorting task were asked to tell what they thought of in relation to these labels. In a second, somewhat different task, individuals were asked to summarize the contents of individual chapters of a physics textbook. In both cases, experts generated more information regarding laws and principles than did novices. This finding is especially noteworthy in relation to text summaries because both experts and novices had access to the same information (i.e., the information presented in the text). The difference in expert and novice performance was thus taken to reflect what was of differential importance to the two groups. Also, the probability that experts' knowledge is stored with respect to higher level principles strongly suggests that experts exceed novices in "inference power" (i.e., experts are more able than novices to follow inference paths that relate high level laws and principles to other concepts; (cf. Larkin, 1983).

The results of the physics-related research thus indicate that information is differentially organized in experts and novices; experts organize information in relation to higher level laws and principles, over and above the lower, more surface-level organization of the novices. In addition, experts use this knowledge to classify and solve physics problems. Novices, on the other hand, tend to organize information at a lower level such as that of specific variables. Interestingly, Adelson (1981) has also shown that novice programmers tend to organize a random input of computer code according to program syntax, whereas experts organize the code hierarchically in relation to the function of the program.

The research described thus far attempted to measure the organization of physics information and the use of such information in solving problems. Other attempts to describe the structure of physics knowledge have also been employed which, in some ways, are less elaborate. Shavelson (1972, 1974), Shavelson and Stanton (1975), and Preece (1976) attempted to map cognitive structure by the use of tasks such as word association, the sorting of concepts, and the construction of a graph structure linking concepts in terms of similarity. High inter-correlational measures were generally obtained for the three methods. In addition, Shavelson (1972) found that over the period of an academic course, students' performance became increasingly like that of the generally agreed upon content structure of the domain (cf. Thro, 1978). This result would be expected, but it is of interest because the study was longitudinal in nature and it provided a relatively simple methodology that could be carried out in a classroom (cf. Loftus & Loftus, 1974).

As previously noted, studies of expert–novice differences have generally been cross-sectional in nature, and there is a need to study the development of problem-solving expertise in a longitudinal manner. Although not studying this issue empirically, Larkin (1981) developed a simulation model that provided for its analysis. Larkin called the naive solver the "Barely Able" model and, after substantial learning had occurred, the model was termed the "More Able" model. The Barely Able model holds a number of equations related to force and energy and, when a problem is presented, selects and applies the equations according to a means–ends analysis. Of particular interest is the mechanism employed to simulate the learning process: Whenever an equation is successfully applied, new information is stored that indicates upon what variables the new solution took place. (For example, assume a successful solution is generated for a particular set of three "given" variables, and this equation has not been previously stored. A statement is now stored that indicates that if the "givens" of a problem include this particular set of three variables, and the solution calls for determining a particular fourth variable, the solution for the fourth may be obtained). An outcome of this procedure is that as more and more equations are stored, the solving increasingly take place via a working forward rather than working backward (means–ends) strategy. In this way, the model does simulate one of the differences between novice and expert problem solving, although the model does not take into account the experts' reliance upon more abstract principles.

In addition to the research on physics problem solving thus far described, interest has recently developed in determining what naive concepts individuals have regarding physics phenomena and how these concepts may influence the solving of related physics problems. A similar approach has been employed by Brown and Burton (1978) in trying to determine why children made particular errors in learning to subtract. What this research has thus far indicated is that individuals often have naive concepts that are inconsistent with physics principles and, moreover, that these concepts are frequently quite difficult to displace (cf. Caramazza, McClosky, & Green, 1981; Champagne, Klopfer, & Anderson, 1980; diSessa, 1982, 1983; McCloskey, 1983; McCloskey & Kohl, 1983). That such misconceptions may influence the solving of problems has been demonstrated by White (1983). (See also Clement, 1979.) White gave 40 high school science majors a set of force and motion problems and, from an analysis of the errors, found that misconceptions were primarily of three types. One was related to real-world knowledge, which seems only to take into account observable entities, suggesting that individuals are frequently not aware of unseen forces that operate upon an object. A second was that problem examples done in physics class are only partially understood. A third was that individuals are not aware that knowledge of scalar arithmetic may not be appropriate for vector computations. Thus, the sources of the errors include both real-world knowledge and an inadequate understanding of physics concepts. Similarly, Larkin (1983) has argued that novices have a physics world-view that provides them with the ability to develop a representation, but when confronted with many physics problems, the representations they are able to develop are not sufficient to solve the problems. Naturally, reliance upon these naive knowledge structures, which may include misconceptions, may generate errors. Experts, on the other hand, have other schema or knowledge structures that are based upon their knowledge of physics, and are thus able to solve the problems.

In addition to the question of how misconceptions may prevent the successful solution of physics problems, two other issues have been raised that are somewhat tangential, yet of interest. First, Wiser and Carey (1983) raised the question of whether ontogeny recapitulates phylogeny in the development of physics concepts (i.e., does the individual's knowledge development with respect to physics concepts resemble the evolution of physics concepts that took place over the history of science?). Although the authors pointed out that the comparison may hold only with respect to particular topics, the issue is of interest because the historical analysis could lead to ideas suggesting how misconceptions could be overcome.

Another point related to the misconception work has been made by Clement (1983), who stated that "Attempts to 'cover' a very large syllabus, and to present physics primarily in a formal mathematical language, may preclude students from learning basic qualitative concepts that give them an intuitive understanding of the subject" (p. 335). Considered in problem-solving terms, this statement suggests that current emphasis in teaching physics rests upon learning to use appropriate solution methods without sufficient instruction concerning how to represent problems or how to determine when the particular solution methods should be applied. Simon (1980) also made essentially the same point in stating that "Generally speaking, textbooks are much more clear in enunciating the laws of mathematics or nature than in saying anything about when these laws may be useful in solving problems" (p. 92). Indeed, Larkin (1983) reported results that bear upon these comments. In studying the performance of one subject who solved problems that were stated at the end of a chapter, Larkin concluded that texts often do not describe the conditions under which equations should be applied. Furthermore, Larkin conducted a study in which one group received training regarding problem representation, whereas a second group received training in equation generation and the algebraic components of computation. The former performed better on the subsequent solution of problems.

Turning now to the topic of geometry, research in this area has emphasized two concepts that thus far have received little attention in this chapter, namely, planning and procedural knowledge. The idea that planning often may be an important phase of problem solving is intuitively appealing. However, incorporating planning into problem solving theory, demonstrating the existence of planning empirically, and instructing the solver to plan are in fact complex issues.

Assume that a student is presented with the task of proving a geometric theorem and that the statement has the usual form of "Givens" and "To prove." A model developed by Greeno (1978) and supported by the findings of Greeno, Magone, and Chaiklin (1979) suggested that individuals proceed to a large extent on the basis of pattern matching. The solver is presumed to consider the "givens" of the problem and to conduct a memory search regarding what is known about the relations of the givens as well as how such information may be related to the "to prove" statement. Furthermore, the individual may make inferences from such information in a way that moves the solver closer to a solution. In this context, the solver plans by establishing a particular series of steps that may lead to the goal (or to a subgoal that in turn should lead to the goal) and, in so doing, also evaluates the plan. Planning thus takes place by making inferences based on the "givens" and determining what steps are needed to reach a goal. Furthermore, Greeno (1978) noted that one of the difficulties of doing geometry proofs or making geometrical constructions is that, although the final goal is stated in the problem, what subgoals should be pursued is indefinite. Thus, the solver, in developing a plan, must establish a goal structure so that an appropriate plan may be executed. This process, in turn, is likely to involve pattern recognition. For example, if the solver stated, "If I could only show that $^*A$ and $^*D$ are equal, I could then show that the triangles are congruent," this statement includes the recognition that the problem may call for a particular way of showing that triangles are congruent. The planning process thus involved making inferences about what could be done, and establishing a subgoal. Incidentally, in an observation similar to Simon's and Clement's regarding physics textbooks, Greeno (1978) has pointed out that instruction in geometry typically has not included the ideas of planning and strategy usage.

Two other lines of research on the planning process demonstrate other types of planning (cf. Sacerdoti, 1977). One involves the research of Jeffries, Turner, Polson, and Atwood (1981), who studied computer programming by experts. Although the experts varied in the way in which they pursued a programming problem, they employed one strategy that is of general significance: "top-down, breadth-first" processing. This procedure consists of decomposing a problem into subproblems and then solving each subproblem (divide-and-conquer). Computer programming instruction tends to emphasize this strategy because complex programming problems lend themselves to this procedure. The process can become complicated, because sometimes solving a sub-problem cannot be completed without information from some other sub-problem solutions. Thus, the solution process may involve a shifting back and forth among subproblems.

Another type of planning (Hayes-Roth & Hayes-Roth, 1979) has been termed *opportunistic*. This form of planning refers to solving a particular problem by setting up a sequence of subgoals but, when the opportunity presents itself to obtain a particular subgoal during the course of attaining some other subgoal, the solver becomes opportunistic and attains the "off-hand" subgoal. Hayes-Roth and Hayes-Roth (1979) used shopping as a case to demonstrate the model.[4]

Turning to the issue of procedural knowledge, this concept was first em-

---

[4]The strategies described here only scratch the surface of the strategies that have been delineated, especially by members of the artificial intelligence community.

ployed by Ryle (1949) in his work *The Concept of Mind.* Ryle made the distinction between *declarative knowledge* and *procedural knowledge,* with the former referring to "knowing that" and the latter to "knowing how." When we say a person "knows something," we generally are referring to declarative knowledge (e.g., knowledge of academic subject matter). However, the expression "knowing how" is usually used in relation to a sequence of actions, as "knowing how" to ride a bike or "knowing how" to solve a particular type of algebra problem.

When problem-solving skill is viewed in the context of the distinction between declarative knowledge and procedural knowledge, at least three issues emerge. First, in the development of most skills, initial learning generally involves the acquisition of declarative knowledge (cf. Fitts, 1964; Fleischman, 1967). Second, knowledge development tends to proceed from a declarative to a procedural emphasis. Third, highly skilled performance usually involves extended practice, which in turn means refinement of procedural knowledge. How procedural knowledge emerges has been a question studied by Anderson and his colleagues (Anderson, 1982; Anderson, Kline, & Beasley, 1979) with further study done on the issue in the context of geometry (Anderson, Greeno, Kline, & Neves 1981; Neves & Anderson, 1981). The issue of primary interest is how the student learns to solve geometry problems, especially because, as previously noted, geometry textbooks typically do not provide instruction regarding what procedures to follow in proof generation.

Anderson et al. (1981) considered the idea that students may learn from the examples given in texts, a process the authors interpret as learning by analogy. This possibility, despite its intuitive appeal, was rejected for two reasons. First, to learn by analogy students would need to remember the solutions for many problems, and this does not seem reasonable; instead, students seem to quickly forget how to solve specific problems. Second, the authors also argued that learning by analogy is superficial, primarily because the analogy is likely to be based on the apparent similarity of problem statements and not on the solution procedures. Thus, as long as the statement of one problem overlaps with another in some way, the student may pursue a solution not germane to the problem at hand.

Rather than accepting analogy as the probable mode of acquisition, Anderson et al. developed a model that postulated that students acquire declarative knowledge and utilize such knowledge to develop procedures. The model essentially states that solving problems produces a higher level schema for classes of problems and that this takes place by establishing, for particular problems, how concepts are used in the solutions to particular problems. The development of procedural knowledge from declarative thus is assumed to occur when solutions are performed a number of times on the same type of problem. The model thus suggests that individuals learn to prove geometrical theorems in relation to problem classification, a result quite in keeping with other findings presented in this chapter.

Problem Solving in the Social Sciences

Turning now to social science problem solving, perhaps the most obvious thing about this research is the lack of it. There are probably at least three reasons for this lack of attention. First, in many ways, solving social science problems is not as essential a component of the social science curriculum as solving science or mathematics problems is of science and mathematics curricula. (An exception to this notion is the curriculum development that followed the ideas of John Dewey, e.g., Dewey, 1940.) Second, the math and science curricula at the elementary and secondary levels typically have involved instruction in concepts that subsequently are found in courses offered at the college and postcollege levels; however, the "social studies" curriculum of the elementary school and to some extent the secondary school have frequently had contents not basic to the college or postcollege social science subject matter. (Although history is an exception to this statement, areas such as economics, political science, psychology, and sociology are examples.) Third, science and mathematics have higher priority with respect to the technological emphasis of the society and especially with respect to government funding. In any event, some recent research in social science problem solving is now considered.

Using the contrastive method, Voss, Tyler, and Yengo (1983) and Voss, Greene, Post, and Penner (1983) presented social scientists who were experts on the Soviet Union with the question of how agricultural productivity in the USSR could be increased, given that the solver assumed he or she was the Head of the Ministry of Agriculture of the Soviet Union. A protocol was collected from each person and analyzed. In addition to the experts, a number of other individuals were given the same problem, including undergraduates who were beginning a course on Soviet Domestic Policy (novices), the same undergraduates when they were completing the course (postnovices), graduate students in political science whose field of concentration in some cases was the Soviet Union and in other cases was not, social science faculty whose field of expertise was not the Soviet Union, chemists, a State Department career officer, and an Eastern European scholar visiting the United States. Discussion of the findings is focused upon five issues: problem representation, problem solution, the delineation of a problem-solving control structure, the delineation of a reasoning structure, and more generally, the relation of social science problem solving to that of other disciplines.

As in the physics-related research, the social science work yielded a substantial difference between experts 'and novices' problem representation. Experts followed one of two procedures. The majority decomposed the problem into a number of subproblems that could somewhat loosely be termed the *major factors* (causes) related to the problem of low agricultural productivity. However, the experts did not simply "list" the subproblems but gave a relatively careful documentation of their analysis. Such an analysis often included an excursion into the history of the problem, pointing out previous attempts that had been tried and failed (e.g., Khruschev's land reform ideas). Such historical analysis sometimes even included a statement of the origins of the problem as found before the Bolshevik Revolution. Finally, experts often stated the problem constraints explicitly (e.g., climate, relatively little arable land, and the Socialist system). From such analysis an expert typically established a few subproblems that were taken to be critical, or the expert essentially placed the subproblems under an "umbrella" stating, for example, this is essentially a "political" problem. The second type of problem representation consisted of problem conversion. In this case the expert converted the problem into one that could conceivably be handled (e.g., the problem is one of inadequate technological modernization). Although this label is almost as general as "political," the difference was that the latter analysis did not involve decomposing the problem into a set of subproblems but instead converted the problem to one that could be addressed. When this procedure is used the converted problem is usually at a relatively abstract level.

The representation developed by novices was extremely simple. Essentially, novices considered the problem as involving a number of quite low level, concrete subproblems (e.g., there is a shortage of tractors, there is a shortage of repair parts, crop rotation is needed, etc.). Furtheremore, the novice often did not differentiate the subproblem from its solution as, for example, when stating "rotate crops," a statement constituting both a solution and, by implication, a subproblem. Finally, an interesting result was that the postnovices, who acquired information germane to the problem in the academic course, did virtually no better than the novices. This finding suggests that the postnovices might have stored the relevant declarative information while taking the course but were unable to utilize it in the problem context (i.e., the postnovices had not yet developed procedural knowledge from information they acquired in the course).

The representation developed by individuals other than the novices, postnovices, and experts varied somewhat between the novice and expert extremes. Three of four chemists gave novice-like protocols, whereas the fourth represented the problem as one of working in bureaucracy. Political science graduate students and social science faculty not having Soviet expertise usually attempted to develop a representation in a manner similar to the Soviet experts, but this attempt was usually not extensive, apparently because the individuals lacked knowledge of the USSR.

Before going on to the solution process, two additional points may be made regarding representation development. First, the need to develop a good problem representation is especially critical when the solver is confronted with ill-structured problems (cf. Reitman, 1965; Simon, 1973). This is because as previously noted, the representation involves establishing the major components of the problems (i.e., causal factors and constraints) and if they are not appropriately incorporated into the representation, the solution has little chance of succeeding. Second, in unpublished work, Voss and his colleagues found that affective components can also be incorporated in a representation. Thus, when given a problem involving United States–USSR relations, representation development is highly influenced by the individual's perception of the USSR (i.e., how aggressive, reactive, etc.).

With respect to problem solution, once the problem was represented, the experts provided one (or possibly two) abstract solutions to the problem. For example, an expert who delineated the problem as one of inadequate modernization proposed that the solution would consist of greater capital investment in agriculture. Another expert who had delineated three major subproblems provided a solution to each and then attempted to integrate these into a more abstract solution. Novice solutions again tended to be "lists" and, as previously noted, were often not differentiated from subproblems. The solutions offered by other participants again varied between the expert–novice extremes, and the solutions offered were typically related to the nature of the representation. One advanced graduate student whose field of specialization was Latin America represented the problem by stating that he did not know much about the Soviet Union, but that he imagined the problem in the USSR had some similarities to lack of agricultural productivity in Latin America, and upon briefly considering these, he proposed a solution that was based upon the analogy.

One of the most important findings of this research was that experts' statement of the problem solution involved three components. First, upon offering an abstract solution to the problem, the experts often told what subproblems that solution could solve, and, in so doing, the experts often mentioned those factors that the novices identified as subproblems. This finding is of course quite similar to the expert-novice performance differences on physics-related tasks in which the novice knowledge organization was a subcategory of that of the expert.

Second, the social science expert isolated subproblems that would need to be considered if indeed the more abstract solution was adopted. For example, the expert who gave the solution that more capital should be invested in agriculture pointed out that this solution would mean that the Head of the Ministry of Agriculture would need to contact and convince the heads of other ministries, would need to go to Gosplan (economic planning committee), and perhaps would even need to go to the Politboro to convince its members to decrease the emphasis upon heavy industrial development and provide more support for agricultural development. The expert then considered how he would try to convince these agencies (solve the subproblem). It is notable that only the experts examined their own solutions with respect to what subproblems could be encountered and how they might be handled.

The third factor of the experts' solution process consisted of evaluation of a solution in relation to a particular problem constraint. Thus, when a person would indicate that solving a subproblem could be accomplished by increasing the incentive of the peasants via an increase in wages, this solution would be evaluated and usually rejected because it was opposed to the system.

Turning now to the issue of control and reasoning structures, the idea of a problem-solving control structure is that a solver has a number of operations or strategies at his or her disposal and that in the course of solving a problem these operations are applied (cf. Newell & Simon, 1972). Analysis conducted on the social science protocols led to delineation of a set of basic operators, *State constraint, State subproblem,* and *State solution,* and of other operators, *Interpret problem statement, Provide support, Evaluate,* and *Summarize. Interpret problem statement* was applied during the development of a representation. *Provide support* was used when the solver was about to develop an argument supporting his position. *Evaluate* involved evaluating and accepting or rejecting a solution, usually in relation to some constraint. Finally, *Summarize* was applied when the solver provided a "wrap up" statement that, for the solver, usually served an integrating function.

In addition to the problem-solving control structure, Voss et al. (1983) found that an additional component, the reasoning structure, was needed for a complete description of the problem-solving process, primarily for the expert protocols. The reasons for this require discussion.

As the reader has quite probably ascertained from the discussion, the contents of expert protocols provided considerable justification or argumentation for the position the expert stated. Indeed, inspection of the professional papers published in virtually any social science area reinforces this notion. Thus, the experts used the reasoning structure in conjunction with the problem-solving structure, especially to provide arguments and support for the statements made in representing and solving the problem. The reasoning operators described by Voss et al. (1983) are as follows: State argument, state assertion, state fact, present specific case, state reason, state outcome, compare/or contrast, elaborate and/or clarify, state conclusion, and state qualifier. These generally can be understood at face value. An important point to note in relation to these operators, however, is that by their application the expert is able to develop lines of argument (not just one fact, for example, backing a statement). Moreover, it is experts that are especially adept in developing such lines of argument.

Considering now social science problem solving in comparison to that of other areas, and especially in relation to the research in physics described previously in this chapter, it may seem there is a fundamental difference between social science problem solving and that found in physics. However, although there are differences, care must be exercised in assessing what there is about the subject matter in these disciplines that produces the differences. The argument presented by Voss et al. (1983) is that the issue does not turn on the subject matter per se, but instead is a function of the relative difference in knowledge growth that has occurred in different fields and, to some degree, differences in the empirical procedures that have been established in the disciplines.

Tweney has been studying scientific hypothesis testing and has done extensive analysis on the detailed notebooks of Michael Faraday. One of Tweney's (1981) papers presented data that, although not the focus of Tweney's interest, is nevertheless germane to the present discussion. The data indicated that in trying to solve the problem of electromagnetic induction, Faraday had spent considerable study in developing a representation of the problem and subsequently had proposed one, or possibly two, relatively abstract solutions to the problem. He made deductions from these solutions and tested the deductions in his laboratory. He also tested solutions to subproblems that he encountered. The solution process of Faraday thus resembled the social science problem-solving results considered in this paper more than it resembled, for example, the results of Larkin (1979, 1981) and Chi, Glaser, and Rees (1982) of the problem solving by physics experts.

Why is this the case? The answer lies in the fact that the research on physics problem solving by experts has consisted almost exclusively of studying how the expert identifies and solves problems that have already been solved and with which the expert is familiar. Faraday, however, was working on a problem to which a solution was not known and, under such conditions, Faraday's solution process more closely resembled that of the social science experts working on an unsolved problem than that of the physics experts working on a previously solved problem. (One would expect, of course, that if a protocol were taken from a contemporary physicist working on a research problem, the protocol would also resemble that of Faraday.)

It is clear that within the social sciences, the number of problems that have solutions that are agreed upon by the experts in the field is not plentiful. Certainly it does not approach that of physical sciences and mathematics. Furthermore, the social sciences have the serious problem that empirical testing of the solutions proposed for particular problems or subproblems is extremely difficult and often, for practical or ethical reasons, virtually impossible. In place of such empirical testing, what has apparently happened is that the social sciences have evolved a problem solving style that heavily relies on verbal argumentation rather than experimental testing, with solution evaluation consisting of statements of why a solution is desirable, what subproblems may be encountered and how they may be solved, and how the solution stands up against problem constraints. Voss et al. (1983) thus concluded that social science problem solving is not intrinsically different from solving problems in other domains. Instead, the differences emerge primarily from the differences in the extent to which the fields of study are developed in the nature of testing the problem solutions.

The Information Processing Viewpoint
of Problem Solving Briefly Revisited

Earlier in this chapter the information-processing approach to problem solving was described. This approach is now reconsidered especially as it relates to the finding described in the previous section of this chapter.

One of the facts that emerges from the research is that the question of how people solve problems cannot be answered by the statement of a simple rule or principle. Instead, people solve problems in many different ways, depending on the nature of the problem, the solver's experience with the subject matter, and other factors. The advantage of the information processing approach is that it provides a reasonably broad framework in which to consider the processes of problem solving, even accommodating alternative strategies and a variety of general theoretical viewpoints. If one asks how this framework may be helpful to instruction, the answer is that while the viewpoint provides no precise formulas by which to teach problem solving, it nevertheless points to a number of factors that are involved in the solving of problems.

First, the solver needs to understand the problem (cf. Greeno, 1977; Simon & Hayes, 1976). Problem understanding must be considered in a broad context, consisting not only of comprehending the problem statement, but also developing a reasonable representation of the problem and, in so doing, defining an appropriate problem space. In other words, a student solving an algebra word problem needs to be able not only to comprehend the problem statement, in the sense of understanding the language, but also to extract from the problem statement information that enables him or her to classify the problem or, if not that advanced, to extract from the problem those components that are likely to be germane to the solution. Furthermore, the solver needs to know what to do with the classification or components selected and this requires a well-developed and accessible problem space. Given this analysis, a factor that seems to be especially important in developing problem-solving skill, as mentioned previously in this chapter, is that the solver should learn to conduct an analysis of a problem before jumping into a particular solution. The need for such an analysis, which often is qualitative in nature, seems especially important with problems that have the complexity of the Soviet agriculture problem previously presented, for it is with such analysis that the major factors and constraints operating in relation to the problem may be understood.

Second, developing problem-solving skill, especially as found in complex subject matter domains, is a gradual process; there are no rules or short-cuts that enable a person to become an effective problem solver. The individual must build up a knowledge base of both declarative and procedural knowledge germane to the problems at hand. Moreover, as such knowledge develops, the skill seems to move to the "front end" of the processing system, at least for problems with which the solver is familiar. In other words, the sophisticated problem solver is able to recognize many problem situations and propose solutions. It is important to emphasize that this skill may be perceptual, as in chess, may involve problem classification, as in algebra and physics, or may involve isolation of problem components that tend to occur in, for example, certain types of social problems.

Third, in virtually all of the domains considered, the results clearly show that more effective problem solving is related to the development of increasingly abstract knowledge structures. Indeed, the findings are quite consistent with the idea that acquisition of knowledge within a domain begins with an understanding of the elements of the domain and their relations, and the knowledge then evolves into more abstract, yet quite organized, structures. Moreover, and quite importantly, one's problem-solving ability within a particular domain is apparently constrained by the extent of the knowledge development. Incidentally, an interesting question which has not received much attention is the extent to which problem-solving activity facilitates knowledge development (cf. Schoenfeld & Herrmann, 1982).

The assertions just made are not meant to imply that the problem solver is solely at the mercy of domain-related knowledge. A person with minimal knowledge of a domain could possibly apply general problem-solving strategies, but it is reasonable to ask what the use of such strategies may accomplish. Furthermore, there is the question of whether such strategies may be taught. The next section is concerned with such issues.

INSTRUCTION IN PROBLEM SOLVING

It has been proposed that there are general problem-solving strategies (i.e., strategies applicable in a large number of contexts), and that such strategies should be taught in schools. Both these assertions have been questioned. If such strategies do not exist, then problem solving is presumed to be a function of the particular subject matter domains. If such strategies do exist, they may not be able to be taught effectively.

As to the existence of general strategies, Greeno (1978, 1980) for example, has argued that although no single set of problem-solving skills is applicable in all situations, some skills are relatively general, whereas others are applicable only within a particular domain. Newell (1980) has provided a list of such strategies, referring to them as *weak methods* of problem solving. The term *weak methods* was used because although they are applicable in a wide range of circumstances, they lack power. In other words, although they may be applied, they often do not provide for detailed solutions within a particular domain. Some of the methods Newell describes are: (a) *Generate and test*—this method involves generating a solution and testing to determine whether it is appropriate. (The reader may note the similarity of this method to the previously

mentioned descriptions of Dewey and Wallas.) (b) *Constraint satisfaction*—
this method consists of testing solutions by determining whether they satisfy
the conditions or constraints of the problem. (c) *Means–ends analysis*—as
previously described, this method involves determining the difference between
the present state and the goal, and selecting an action to reduce this difference.
(d) *Heuristic search*—a set of particular operators is used to produce a systematic search. (e) *Subgoal decomposition*—this is the method of decomposition
previously described in which a problem is decomposed into a number of
subproblems. (f) *Hill climbing*—in this method, one identifies a dimension as
an index to reaching a solution; then movement along the dimension constitutes an approach to the goal, and reaching the appropriate end of the
dimensions indicates reaching the solution. For example, if the goal were to get
to Hawaii from Harrisburg, Pennsylvania, and there were no flights directly to
Hawaii, the hill-climbing method might adopt Westward movement as an
index, and the solver would initially fly from Harrisburg to Pittsburgh.

In addition to the above methods, Newell (1980) also pointed out that
because people tend to interpret input in terms of what they know, the solver
may attempt to map the parameters of a problem onto a known type of problem. If the solver, moreover, is not familiar with a particular type of problem
but sees a relationship to some other type of problem, the mapping process
may involve analogy and metaphor. Finally, Newell noted that when none of
the methods seems to be applicable, the individual may need to learn a solution
process. Interestingly, learning thus constitutes a solution process "when all
else fails." This point is nontrivial, for it indicates that individuals are armed
with a number of problem solving strategies and will quite likely apply these
before trying to work out a new solution process.

Despite the range and variety of the weak methods, these strategies constitute only a small number of the strategies that most individuals are capable of
employing. The *strong methods* tend to be domain-specific and include, for
example, methods of doing subtraction problems, methods of transposing and
multiplying expressions in algebra, and so on.

Given the existence of general problem-solving skills, an important question
is to what extent such skills may be taught. The educational significance of this
question is obvious, for equipping students with a set of problem-solving skills
of wide applicability should enhance their subsequent problem solving (cf.
Dorner, 1978). At the present time, the best answer to whether general skills
are instructible is that although courses that have the objective of teaching such
skills are offered at various universities and are often popular and evaluated by
students as quite useful, little objective evidence exists that provides support
for the idea that the courses are successful in teaching skills that students do in
fact apply in a large number of situations (Larkin, 1980; Reif, 1980). Furthermore, the success that has been reported often seems to be the product of
enthusiastic teaching. Larkin (1980), in referring to such courses, stated that

"With all their strong points, however, these instructional programs in problem solving remain idiosyncratic products of enthusiastic individuals" (p. 113). Larkin (1980) further argued that teaching problem solving in the classroom suffers from three major difficulties. First, it is intrinsically difficult to teach. Second, educational research has not used methodologies that provide information about problem solving processes. Third, although some problem-solving instruction has yielded positive results, little is known regarding why the processes work. Larkin (1980) further mentioned that "What is needed, and is not available, is believable research that elucidates the mechanisms of problem solving at a level of detail useful for designing instruction" (p. 113).

One course designed to teach problem-solving skill has been described by Rubenstein (1980). The course has been taught for a number of years at UCLA and it is administered through the School of Engineering. Rubenstein pointed out that the course has been successful, at least in the extent to which students indicate they find it useful, and Rubenstein reported that "some of the principles have worked for him" (p. 37). Two of these are, "If you want your students to learn a concept, give them an opportunity to teach you, the teacher" and "Make explicit the connection between knowledge and its application whenever possible." Reif (1980), however, in commenting on Rubenstein's course, pointed to the need for an objective critical evaluation.

There is evidence that, at a more specific level, instruction in particular problem solving heuristics may be effective, for example, de Leeuw (1978), Hayes (1980), Polya (1957, 1968). In a course offered at Carnegie-Mellon University, Hayes (1980) has found that the "method of loci," in which an elaborated image of a physical place is memorized once to be used repeatedly as an armature to support various tasks of memorization, can be taught so that students are able to use is in new contexts, as can the keyword method in learning the vocabulary of a foreign language. Hayes also noted that the Carnegie-Mellon course has enrolled students in the humanities, social sciences, and the arts, and contains sections on information acquisition, decision making, problem solving, and creativity.

The teaching of heuristics has also been explored by Schoenfeld (1979, 1982). In an initial study, Schoenfeld trained students on five strategies such as "draw a diagram" and "argue by contradiction or contrapositive." The training was not successful unless the students were taught when to use the strategy. As Schoenfeld (1979) stated, "That students can master a problem solving technique is no guarantee that they will use it" (p. 185). In a subsequent study, Schoenfeld (1982) employed an experimental group that received problem-solving training while a control group received training in structured programming. Using problems that were related, somewhat related, and unrelated to the problems used in training, it was found that the experimental group was superior in using "plausible approaches" and "working toward the solution." These studies thus again point to a theme that has frequently emerged in this chapter, namely, if problem solving is to be taught, an important component is to teach under what conditions the particular solution processes may be applied.

Although the question of whether general solving strategies may be taught is yet to be answered, the question of whether domain-related problem-solving skills may be taught has received a clear-cut "yes." The question that exists is thus not whether domain-related strategies can be taught but what methods are most effective in teaching such skills.

That intensive problem-solving instruction in mathematics can facilitate problem representation has been demonstrated by Schoenfeld and Herrmann (1982). Students' perceptions of mathematical problems were ascertained by the use of sorting and clustering procedures, and initially the perceptions reflected the surface features of the problems. However, after an intensive course which included training in problem-solving heuristics and in developing a systematic approach to solving problems, the perceptions resembled those found in experts.

One of the most extensive series of studies on domain-related instruction has been conducted in solving problems involving primarily the binomial theorem (Egan & Greeno, 1973; Mayer, 1974, 1975, 1982a, 1982b; Mayer & Greeno, 1972; Mayer, Stiehl, & Greeno, 1975). Using such problems, Mayer and Greeno (1972) instructed subjects either by a rule instruction method that involved assigning values to variables or by a method that emphasized the relations of the variables. The data led the authors to conclude that the former method led to the understanding of intra-problem connectedness and the latter to relating concepts of the binominal theorem to other concepts. In a subsequent study, Mayer et al. (1975) studied training in relation to mathematical aptitude and found that those individuals having greater mathematical aptitude benefited more from the more conceptual training than did students of lower aptitude. From these findings, the authors suggest that mathematical instruction should not be aimed solely at performing specific tasks but should have as its objective the development of the student's aptitude for mathematics. This study is of interest, for not only does it suggest that students of different aptitude may profit optimally from different types of training, but that teaching to enhance a person's mathematical aptitude may lead in the long run to more transfer than training on particular skills.

Issues pertaining to student aptitude and performance in algebra problem solving have also been studied by Krutetskii (1976) and by Silver (1979). Krutetskii found that, in solving algebra word problems, high ability students were differentiated from low ability students in their ability to discriminate relevant data from contextual data or irrelevancies, to quickly and accurately perceive the correct structure of the problem, to generalize across a wider range of mathematical problems, and to remember longer the formal structure of the problem. Silver (1979) obtained similar results and also found the better students were more able to extract information from problems after solving them (i.e., information regarding the mathematical structure of the problems).

Within the domain of physics, Larkin and Reif (1976) were successful in teaching students strategies pertaining to how one should extract quantitative information from text. The training, which emphasized understanding of new relations, was maintained and, the authors indicated, made the students less dependent upon instruction.

While working not with mathematical concepts but instead with the question of how to use a camera, Bromage and Mayer (1981) conducted two interesting experiments on what they termed *creative problem solving*. While providing information to subjects regarding the structure and function of a 35mm. camera, Bromage and Mayer tested the subjects on a variety of tasks that included listing all variables that can influence the quality of the photograph, indicating the meaning of terms such as ASA and f-stop, and, most importantly, solving problems such as "How would you take a picture of a pole vaulter on a cloudy day?" The result of interest is that the quality of solution offered was related to the type of training. Specifically, when subjects received explanatory training (i.e., relations involving how things work and why) problem solving was better than when they received descriptive training (Cf. de-Kleer & Brown, 1983).

Research has also pointed to two factors that should be taken into account when instruction in problem solving is being considered. First, Clement (1982) gave six problems to freshman engineering students and collected protocols during their solving process. From analysis of the protocols, Clement delineated the schemas used in the solution process. The interesting finding is that contradictory schemas may reside in the individual, who may shift back and forth among schemas in developing a problem solution. This finding, of course, points to the complexities that exist in trying to determine how problems are solved; the solution path may not be straightforward. The second finding involves a solver's knowledge of his or her own solution. Koplowitz (1979) has found that poor problem solvers tend to be inappropriately satisfied with their own solutions, a result that suggests that problem solving includes a critical component that permits the individual to evaluate the quality of a solution, and good solvers are apparently better at self-criticism. This is a potentially important issue and certainly merits further study.

In summary then, research on problem-solving instruction suggests that: (a) While general problem solving strategies exist, the extent to which they may be formally taught and utilized is open to question; (b) Teaching individuals to solve problems within a particular domain is quite feasible, but how such problem solving is taught may readily influence the skills that are developed. Furthermore, the aptitude of the learner may interact with the method of teaching in such a way that students of different aptitude may optimally learn via the use of different methods; (c) There probably should be more instructional emphasis upon developing aptitude in addition to learning specific skills, although of course, this is a complex issue.

PROBLEM SOLVING AND THE EDUCATIONAL PROCESS: MISCELLANEOUS QUESTIONS

When a person learns how to solve problems, how readily does this knowledge transfer to the solving of other problems?

The work of Schoenfeld (1979, 1982) cited in the previous section as well as in other findings suggest that positive transfer is not readily obtained in problem solving. In addition, Reed, Ernst, and Banerji (1974) had subjects solve a missionary–cannibal problem and then had the subjects solve what was the same problem presented in a different context, the jealous husbands problem. (The two problems required the identical set of moves.) No transfer was obtained unless the specific relation between the two problems was pointed out to the subject. Thus, one may conclude that for transfer to occur, the solver must be able to determine that a second problem is equivalent to the first with respect to its class membership. Similarly, Scandura (1974, 1977) considers transfer in terms of rules and their application.

In a sense, pointing out class membership is what investigators do in instructing students when to use particular solutions. As an example, if a student in algebra learns to solve a "work" problem, the student must subsequently be able to identify that type of problem if the previously acquired solution is to be applied. Interestingly, students, especially when first learning how to solve a particular problem, often do not realize that two problems belong to the same class when the "givens" and the "unknown" are varied. For example, in a distance = rate X time problem, distance and rate may be given in one problem and rate and time in another, and beginning students often fail to realize these are two views of the same basic ralationship. The same phenomenon seems to occur in geometry, trigonometry, and other topics involving equations.

But if transfer in problem solving is difficult to obtain, would that not mean that solving by analogy is extremely difficult or even impossible?

Evidence indicates that although solving by analogy is quite difficult, it is possible. The problem with analogies is that they tend to appeal at superficial levels and break down in a more detailed analysis. Gentner (1983) and Gentner and Gentner (1983), within the domain of physics, have demonstrated that the use of different analogies in instruction produced differences in the type of understanding obtained. The authors taught the analogy of electrical current as water-flow or as a moving crowd and found that the former resulted in better understanding of batteries and the latter resulted in better understanding of resistors. Thus, each analogy was effective in producing a type of understanding. Whether using either analogy in instruction was better (or worse) than using no analogy with respect to the acquisition of the physics concept could not be answered in the context of this study (cf. Gick & Holyoak, 1980, 1983, Schustack & Anderson, 1979).

Although research on problem solving is providing an increasing understanding of the processes involved, is not the research oriented more toward how people find solutions rather than how problems occur in the first place?

The answer is affirmative. Problem-solving research has generally been concerned with how particular problems are solved. Little research has been done on how problems are identified in the first place: "problem finding" (cf. Getzels, 1979). Indeed, the steps involved in formulating, defining, and refining a problem are important issues in need of study.

Are problem-solving models "culturally bound" or would the processes involved in solving problems be expected to be essentially equivalent over all cultures?

This question has received little attention. However, the following answer may be offered. Societies that are developed technologically would be expected to produce physicists, engineers, and the like, that would, within their respective disciplines, solve problems in a highly similar manner. This is because the instruction in such disciplines is, by-and-large, reasonably similar. However, divergence in the problem-solving process would be expected to occur under at least two conditions. One is when the processes used in a relatively technically undeveloped society are compared to those employed in a technologically developed society. Indeed, in an interesting study (Hutchins, 1983), navigation by South Sea islanders was studied and, in the terms of this chapter, the problem representation and the related solution process of the islanders were quite different than those of Western navigators. Yet the islanders were quite capable of accurate navigation over considerable distances. A second way in which the problem-solving process would be expected to vary with culture is for problems in which the constraints vary from one society to another. Thus, how an economic problem is represented and solved could be quite different if the problem occurred within a controlled economy, as in a Socialist nation, or within a mixed economy, as in the United States.

In this chapter it was shown that problem solving has been studied within a number of subject matter contexts. Have there been other subject matter areas studied that have not been mentioned in the text?

Yes. One is medical diagnosis. Johnson et al. (1981) developed a computer simulation model that they related to diagnostic reasoning as found in experts, trainees, and students. Johnson et al. found that individuals at each level of expertise approached the diagnosis problem in the same way. However, experts were superior because of two factors, a better knowledge of the disease involved and superior skill in interpreting the cues given by the patient; errors made by the less experienced individuals were primarily attributable to an inappropriate interpretation of the cues. Medical diagnosis has also been studied by Connelly and Johnson (1980); Elstein, Loupe, and Erdmann (1971); Elstein, Shulman, and Sprafka (1978); Lesgold (1984); Medin, Altom, Edelson, and Freko (1982); and Miller, Pople, and Myers (1982).

Another area that has been analyzed in terms of problem solving is writing (i.e., how people compose a passage about a particular subject). This research has especially included study of the planning process (e.g., Burtis, Bereiter, Scardamalia, & Tetroe, in press; Flower & Hayes, 1981) via analysis of the processing demands placed on the individual during writing (Scardamalia, 1982). The influence of the point of view taken during composition has also been studied (Mosenthal, Davidson-Mosenthal, & Krieger, 1981). One of the more important issues considered in this line of research has involved the need of the writer to deal with various levels of exposition during the course of production. Scardamalia, Bereiter, and Goelman (1982), for example, suggest that individuals have multiple text representations and must move from one level to another, as for example when one has a *general representation content* and then must move to a sentence, clause, or word level. These authors discuss the fact that such movement involves substantial processing demands, especially for children, and suggest how such movement takes place (see also Bereiter & Scardamalia, 1982).

Interestingly, music has also been the object of study. Halpern and Bower (1982) for example, demonstrated that experts remembered "Good" musical sequences (temporal patterns) better than "Bad" or "Random" sequences, whereas nonexperts could not differentiate. This finding is of course quite similar to that obtained in the recall of an array of chess pieces.

Finally, the subject of teaching itself has been the object of analysis. In an interesting analysis Collins and Stevens (1982) evaluated tapes and films of a number of expert teachers. Their analysis suggested that effective teachers establish goals and subgoals, they are effective in using strategies to reach these goals, and they employ a control structure that permits them to select and pursue different subgoals as well as successfully allocate time to achieve the subgoals. The goals of the teachers are hierarchical, with the lowest being knowledge of facts, the next highest consisting of rules and theories, and the highest involving teaching students to derive their own rules or theories in the domain. Furthermore, teachers use many strategies in accomplishing these goals, and a number of these are aimed at developing the understanding of causal relations in the particular domain. Finally, effective teachers are quite good at choosing examples, taking those that are positive and negative, selecting ones that involve generalization and discrimination, and choosing cases that deal with misconceptions.

Little has been said in this chapter about motivation. Does this factor not influence problem solving?

Intuitively, it would seen that motivation should generally have a positive affect upon problem solving. Motivation apparently can affect goal-setting (i.e., a more strongly motivated individual may set a more demanding goal than a less motivated individual). Locke, Shaw, Saari, and Latham (1981), in reviewing the literature on goal-setting, concluded that setting specific and challenging goals is more effective than having no goals, weak goals, or the goal of "do your best." Locke et al. also argued that goals affect performance by directing attention, mobilizing effort, increasing persistence, and motivating strategy development. Thus, motivation may be viewed as a factor that will influence the extent to which a person will participate in the problem-solving process, via effort in strategy development, persistence in memory search, extent of evaluation, or some other aspect of the process. If this analysis holds, then motivation will influence the quality of problem solving in an indirect rather than a direct manner; motivation may produce superior solutions not because the person highly motivated is intrinsically more capable of generating quality solutions but because the motivation enhances problem-solving activity and this may lead to a better solution.

CONCLUDING STATEMENT

The contents of this chapter to a large degree constitute a progress report on problem-solving research. What does this research suggest regarding the development of a better understanding of the relation between problem solving and the educational process? In this writer's opinion, two conclusions are of interest. First, the empirical and conceptual scope of problem-solving research has increased and apparently is going to continue to increase. Relatively few studies of problem solving currently taking place involve use of such classics of early research as the procedures problem, the candle-box problem, the nine-dot problem, and anagram problems. Instead, problem-solving research has come to include the study of many more tasks, tasks that are both complex and are found professionally, in the classroom, in the context of business and the professions, and in other aspects of "real life." Moreover, such work is motivating theory development as well as the development of new empirical techniques. One would think that such growth in problem solving activity should produce a need for teachers and students alike to increase their familiarity with basic problem-solving concepts and for results and theory to find their way into the classroom.

The increase in problem-solving research that is occurring, however, constitutes no guarantee that such work will influence the educational process. The incorporation of research findings and theory into textbooks and into the working knowledge of teachers is a complex issue. Indeed, perhaps it should be analyzed. Nevertheless, there probably is a growing opportunity to utilize problem-solving concepts in the instruction of various subject matters, and one would hope the opportunity becomes a positive reality.

Within the context of classroom instruction, one thing that must be remembered is that a major characteristic of a good problem solver is flexibility. This flexibility, moreover, likely emerges from experience with a variety of problems, as well as with the ability to adapt strategies and to retrieve information in a number of problem contexts. One does not acquire problem-solving skill by learning to use Steps 1 to 4 (whatever they may be) whenever a problem arises. Problem solving in education was emphasized, at least in some schools, in a period in which Dewey's philosophy was applied and, on occasion, distorted. But this movement failed to take into account the importance of the knowledge base that individuals must have to solve problems effectively. Good problem solving does not emerge from knowledge of method or strategy per se; good performance in solving problems requires a substantial knowledge base integrated with knowing how to use such knowledge in a wide range of problem contexts.

Second, it would seem that instruction has not exploited, or has not even begun to exploit, the potential of problem solving *as a learning device.* In the natural sciences and in mathematics numerous comments have been made suggesting that textbooks do not instruct in strategy utilization or in procedural knowledge development. Such instruction is probably quite difficult. But the odds are reasonably good that such instruction, within the context of subject matter, could enhance problem-solving skill within the domains in question. Moreover, in a point developed more fully elsewhere (Voss, 1986), social science instruction could probably be enhanced with appropriate problem-solving training, because such training could develop skills in argument and criticism as well as enhancing the individual's knowledge and awareness of the sociocultural world.

ACKNOWLEDGMENTS

Preparation of this chapter was supported by the Learning Research and Development Center, supported in part as a research and development center by funds from the National Institute of Education (NIE). The opinions expressed do not necessarily reflect the position or policy of NIE and official endorsement should not be inferred. The author wishes to thank Terri Yousko and Lisa Mack for their help in preparation of this chapter.

REFERENCES

Adelson, B. (1981). Problem solving and the development of abstract categories in programming languages. *Memory & Cognition, 9,* 422–433.

Agre, G. P. (1982). The concept of problem. *Educational Studies, 13,* 121–142.

Anderson, J. R. (1982). Acquisition of cognitive skill. *Psychological Review, 89,* 369–406.

Anderson, J. R., Greeno, J. G., Kline, P. J., & Neves, D. M. (1981). Acquisition of problem solving skill. In J. R. Anderson (Ed.), *Cognitive skills and their acquisition* (pp. 191–230). Hillsdale, NJ: Lawrence Erlbaum Associates.

Anderson, J. R., Kline, P. J., Beasley, F. M., Jr. (1979). A general learning theory and its application to schema abstraction. In G. Bower (Ed.), *The psychology of learning and motivation* (Vol. 13, pp. 277–318). New York: Academic Press.

Bereiter, C., & Scardamalia, M. (1982). From conversation to composition: The role of instruction in a developmental process. In R. Glaser (Ed.), *Advances in instructional psychology* (Vol. 2, pp. 1–64). Hillsdale, NJ: Lawrence Erlbaum Associates.

Berlyne, D. E. (1965). *Structure and direction in thinking.* New York: Wiley.

Binet, A. (1894). *Psychologie des grands calculateurs et joueurs d'echecs.* Paris: Hachette.

Bromage, B. K., & Mayer, R. E. (1981). Relationship between what is remembered and creative problem-solving performance in science learning. *Journal of Educational Psychology, 73,* 451–461.

Brown, J. S., & Burton, R. R. (1978). Diagnostic models for procedural bugs in basic mathematical skills. *Cognitive Science, 2,* 155–192.

Bryan, W. L., & Harter, N. (1897). Studies in the physiology and psychology of the telegraphic language. *Psychological Review, 4,* 27–53.

Bryan, W. L., & Harter, N. (1899). Studies on the telegraphic language: The acquisition of a hierarchy of habits. *Psychological Review, 6,* 345–375.

Bryant, P. E., & Trabasso, T. R. (1971). Transitive inference and memory in young children. *Nature, 232,* 456–458.

Bulbrook, M. E. (1932). An experimental inquiry into the existence and nature of "insight." *American Journal of Psychology, 44,* 409–453.

Burtis, P. J., Bereiter, C., Scardamalia, M., & Tetroe, J. (in press). The development of planning in writing. In C. G. Wells & B. Kroll (Eds.), *Exploration of children's development in writing.* Chichester, England: Wiley.

Caramazza, A., McCloskey, M., & Green, B. (1981). Naive beliefs in "sophisticated" subjects: Misconceptions about trajectories of objects. *Cognition, 9,* 117–123.

Champagne, A. B., Klopfer, L. E., & Anderson, J. H. (1980). Factors influencing the learning of classical mechanics. *American Journal of Physics, 8,* 1074–1075.

Charness, N. (1976). Memory for chess positions: Resistance to interference. *Journal of Experimental Psychology: Human Learning and Memory, 2,* 641–653.

Charness, N. (1979). Components of skill in bridge. *Canadian Journal of Psychology, 33,* 1–50.

Charness, N. (1981a). Aging and skilled problem solving. *Journal of Experimental Psychology: General, 110,* 21–38.

Charness, N. (1981b). Search in chess: Age and skill differences. *Journal of Experimental Psychology: Human Perception and Performance, 7,* 467–476.

Charness, N. (1983). Age, skill, and bridge bidding: A chronometric analysis. *Journal of Verbal Learning and Verbal Behavior, 22,* 406–416.

Chase, W. G., & Simon, H. A. (1973a). Perception in chess. *Cognitive Psychology, 4,* 55–81.

Chase, W. G., & Simon, H. A. (1973b). The mind's eye in chess. In W. G. Chase (Ed.), *Visual information processing.* New York: Academic Press.

Chi, M. T. H., Feltovich, P., & Glaser, R. (1981). Categorization and representation of physics problems by experts and novices. *Cognitive Science, 5,* 121–152.

Chi, M. T. H., Glaser, R., & Rees, R. (1982). Expertise in problem solving. In R. Sternberg (Ed.), *Advances in the psychology of human intelligence* (pp. 7–75). Hillsdale, NJ: Lawrence Erlbaum Associates.

Clement, J. (1983). A conceptual model discussed by Galileo and used intuitively by physics students. In D. Gentner & A. L. Stevens (Eds.), *Mental Models* (pp. 325–340). Hillsdale, NJ: Lawrence Erlbaum Associates.

Clement, J. J. (1979). Mapping a student's causal conceptions from a problem-solving protocol. In J. Lochhead & J. Clement (Eds.), *Cognitive process instruction* (pp. 133–147). Philadelphia, PA: The Franklin Institute Press.

Clement, J. J. (1982). Algebra word problem solutions: Thought processes underlying a common misconception. *Journal of Research in Mathematics Education, 13,* 16–30.

Cleveland, A. A. (1907). The psychology of chess and of learning to play it. *American Journal of Psychology, 18,* 269–308.

Collins, A., & Stevens, A. L. (1982). Goals and strategies of inquiry teachers. In R. Glaser (Ed.), *Advances in instructional psychology* (pp. 65–119). Hillsdale, NJ: Lawrence Erlbaum Associates.

Connelly, D., & Johnson, P. E. (1980). The medical problem solving process. *Human Pathology, 11,* 412–419.

deGroot, A. D. (1965). *Thought and choice in chess.* The Hague, Holland: Mouton Press.

deGroot, A. D. (1966). Perception and memory versus thought: Some old ideas and recent findings. In B. Kleinmuntz (Ed.), *Problem solving: Research, method and theory* (pp. 19–50). New York: Wiley.

deKleer, J., & Brown, J. S. (1983). Assumptions and ambiguities in mechanistic mental models. In D. Gentner & A. L. Stevens (Eds.), *Mental models* (pp. 155–190). Hillsdale, NJ: Lawrence Erlbaum Associates.

deLeeuw, L. (1978). Teaching problem solving: The effect of algorithmic and heuristic problem-solving training in relation to task complexity and relevant aptitudes. In A. M. Lesgold, J. W. Pellegrino, S. D. Fokkema, & R. Glaser (Eds.), *Cognitive psychology and instruction* (pp. 269–276). New York: Plenum Press.

Dewey, J. (1916). *Democracy and education: An introduction to the philosophy of education.* New York: Macmillan.

Dewey, J. (1940). *Education today.* New York: Greenwood.

Dewey, J. (1971). *How we think.* Chicago: Henry Regnery.

diSessa, A. A. (1982). Unlearning Aristotelian physics: A study of knowledge-based learning. *Cognitive Science, 6,* 37–76.

diSessa, A. A. (1983). Phenomenology and the evolution of intuition. In D. Gentner & A. L. Stevens (Eds.), *Mental models* (pp. 15–34). Hillsdale, NJ: Lawrence Erlbaum Associates.

Dorner, D. (1978). Theoretical advances of cognitive psychology relevant to instruction. In A. M. Lesgold, J. W. Pellegrino, S. D. Fokkema, & R. Glaser (Eds.), *Cognitive Psychology and Instruction* (pp. 231–252). New York: Plenum Press.

Duncker, K. (1926). A qualitative (experimental and theoretical) study of productive thinking (solving of comprehensible problems). *Pedagogical Seminary, 33,* 642–708.

Duncker, K. (1945). On problem solving. *Psychological Monographs, 58,* (Whole No. 270).

Egan, D. E., & Greeno, J. G. (1973). Acquiring cognitive structure by discovery and rule learning. *Journal of Educational Psychology, 64,* 85–97.

Ellen, P. (1982). Direction, past experience, and hints in creative problem solving: A reply to Weisberg and Alba. *Journal of Experimental Psychology: General, 111,* 316–325.

Elstein, A. S., Loupe, M. J., & Erdmann, J. G. (1971). An experimental study of medical diagnostic thinking. *Journal of Structural Learning, 2,* 45–53.

Elstein, A. S., Shulman, L. S., & Sprafka, S. A. (1978). *Medical problem solving.* Cambridge, MA: Harvard University Press.

Engle, R. W., & Bukstel, L. (1979). Memory processes among bridge players of differing expertise. *American Journal of Psychology, 91,* 673–690.

Ericsson, K. A., & Simon, H. A. (1980). Verbal reports as data. *Psychological Review, 3,* 215–251.

Fitts, P. M. (1964). Perceptual-motor skill learning. In A. W. Melton (Ed.), *Categories of human learning* (pp. 243–285). New York: Academic Press.

Flavell, J. H. (1963). *The developmental psychology of Jean Piaget.* Princeton, NJ: Van Nostrand.

Fleischman, E. A. (1967). Individual differences and motor learning. In R. M. Gagne (Ed.), *Learning and individual differences* (pp. 165–191). Columbus, OH: Merrill.

Flower, L. & Hayes, J. R. (1981). The pregnant pause: An inquiry into the nature of planning. *Research in the teaching of English, 15,* 229–244.

Gelman, R., & Gallistel, G. R. (1978). *The child's understanding of number.* Cambridge, MA: Harvard University Press.

Gentner, D. (1983). Structure-mapping: A theoretical framework for analogy. *Cognitive Science, 7,* 155–170.

Gentner, D., & Gentner, D. R. (1983). Flowing waters or teeming crowds: Mental models of electricity. In D. Gentner & A. L. Stevens (Eds.), *Metal models* (pp. 99–130). Hillsdale, NJ: Lawrence Erlbaum Associates.

Getzels, J. W. (1979). Problem finding: A theoretical note. *Cognitive Science, 3,* 167–172.

Gick, M. L., & Holyoak, K. J. (1980). Analogical problem solving. *Cognitive Psychology, 12,* 306–355.

Gick, M. L., & Holyoak, K. J. (1983). Schema induction and analogical transfer. *Cognitive Psychology, 15,* 1–38.

Goldin, S. E. (1978a). Effects of orienting tasks on recognition of chess positions. *American Journal of Psychology, 91,* 659–672.

Goldin, S. E. (1978b). Memory for the ordinary: Typicality effects in chess memory. *Journal of Experimental Psychology: Human Learning and Memory, 104,* 605–611.

Greeno, J. G. (1977). Process of understanding in problem solving. In N. J. Castellan, D. B. Pisoni, & G. R. Potts (Eds.), *Cognitive theory* (Vol. 2, pp. 43–83). Hillsdale, NJ: Lawrence Erlbaum Associates.

Greeno, J. G. (1978). Nature of problem-solving abilities. In W. K. Estes (Ed.), *Handbook of learning and cognitive processes,* Vol. 5, *Human information processing* (pp. 239–270). Hillsdale, NJ: Lawrence Erlbaum Associates.

Greeno, J. G. (1980). Trends in the theory of knowledge for problem solving. In D. T. Tuma & F. Reif (Eds.), *Problem solving and education: Issues in teaching and research* (pp. 9–23). Hillsdale, NJ: Lawrence Erlbaum Associates.

Greeno, J. G., Magone, M. E., & Chaiklin, S. (1979). Theory of constructions and set in problem solving. *Memory and Cognition, 7,* 445–461.

Halpern, A. R., & Bower, G. H. (1982). Musical expertise and melodic structure in memory for musical notation. *American Journal of Psychology, 85,* 31–50.

Hayes, J. R. (1980). Teaching problem-solving mechanisms. In D. T. Tuma & F. Reif (Eds.), *Problem solving and education: Issues in teaching and research* (pp. 141–147). Hillsdale, NJ: Lawrence Erlbaum Associates.

Hayes, J. R. (1981). *The complete problem solver.* Philadelphia, PA: The Franklin Institute Press.

Hayes-Roth, B., & Hayes-Roth, F. (1979). A cognitive model of planning. *Cognitive Science, 3,* 275–310.

Hinsley, D. A., Hayes, J. R., & Simon, H. A. (1977). From words to equations: Meaning and representation in algebra word problems. In P. A. Carpenter & M. A. Just (Eds.), *Cognitive processes in comprehension* (pp. 89–108). Hillsdale, NJ: Lawrence Erlbaum Associates.

Holding, D. H., & Reynolds, R. I. (1982). Recall or evaluation of chess positions as determinants of chess skill. *Memory & Cognition, 10,* 237–242.

Humphrey, G. (1951). *Thinking: An introduction to its experimental psychology.* London: Methuen.

Hunt, E., Frost, N., & Lunneborg, C. E. (1973). Individual differences in cognition: A new approach to intelligence. In G. Bower (Ed.), *The psychology of learning and motivation: Advances in research and theory* (Vol. 7, pp. 87–122). New York: Academic Press.

Hunt, E., & Lansman, M. (1975). Cognitive theory applied to individual differences. In W. K. Estes (Ed.), *Handbook of learning and cognitive processes* (Vol. 1, pp. 81–110). Hillsdale, NJ: Lawrence Erlbaum Associates.

Hutchins, E. (1983). Understanding Micronesian navigation. In D. Gentner & A. L. Stevens (Eds.), *Mental models* (pp. 191–226). Hillsdale, NJ: Lawrence Erlbaum Associates.

James, W. (1890). *The principles of psychology.* New York: Dover.

Jeffries, R., Turner, A. A., Polson, P. G., & Atwood, M. E. (1981). The processes involved in designing software. In J. R. Anderson (Ed.), *Cognitive skills and their acquisition* (pp. 255–283). Hillsdale, NJ: Lawrence Erlbaum Associates.

Johnson, D. M. (1955). *The psychology of thought and judgment.* New York: Harper.

Johnson, P. E., Duran, A. S., Hassebrock, F., Moller, J., Prietula, M., Feltovich, P. H., & Swanson, D. B. (1981). Diagnostic reasoning. *Cognitive Science, 5,* 235–284.

Katona, G. (1940). *Organizing and memorizing.* New York: Columbia University Press.

Klahr, D., & Wallace, J. G. (1976). *Cognitive development: An information processing view.* Hillsdale, NJ: Lawrence Erlbaum Associates.

Koffka, K. (1935). *Principles of Gestalt psychology.* New York: Harcourt Brace.

Kohler, W. (1947). *Gestalt psychology.* New York: Liveright.

Koplowitz, H. (1979). The feeling of knowing when one has solved a problem. In J. Lochhead & J. Clement (Eds.), *Cognitive process instruction* (pp. 305–309). Philadelphia, PA: The Franklin Institute Press.

Krutetskii, V. A. (1976). In J. Kilpatrick & I. Wirszup (Eds.), *The psychology of mathematical abilities in school children* (pp. 365–399). Chicago: The University of Chicago Press.

Lane, D. M., & Robertson, L. (1979). The generality of levels of processing hypothesis: An application to memory for chess positions. *Memory & Cognition, 7,* 253–256.

Larkin, J. H. (1977). *Problem solving in physics.* Working paper from the group in Science and Mathematics Education, University of California, Berkeley.

Larkin, J. H. (1979). Information processing models and science instruction. In J. Lochhead & J. Clement (Eds.), *Cognitive process instruction* (pp. 109–119). Philadelphia, PA: The Franklin Institute Press.

Larkin, J. H. (1980). Teaching problem solving in physics: The psychological laboratory and the practical classroom. In D. T. Tuma & F. Reif (Eds.), *Problem solving and education: Issues in teaching and research* (pp. 111–125). Hillsdale, NJ: Lawrence Erlbaum Associates.

Larkin, J. H. (1981). Enriching formal knowledge: A model for learning to solve textbook physics problems. In J. Anderson (Ed.), *Cognitive skills and their acquisition* (pp. 311–334). Hillsdale, NJ: Lawrence Erlbaum Associates.

Larkin, J. H. (1983). The role of problem representation in physics. In D. Gentner & A. L. Stevens (Eds.), *Mental models* (pp. 75–98). Hillsdale, NJ: Lawrence Erlbaum Associates.

Larkin, J. H., McDermott, J., Simon, D. P., & Simon, H. A. (1980). Models of competence. *Cognitive Science, 4,* 317–345.

Larkin, J. H., & Reif, F. (1976). Analysis and teaching of a general skill for studying scientific text. *Journal of Educational Psychology, 68,* 431–440.

Lesgold, A. M. (1984). Acquiring expertise. In J. R. Anderson & S. M. Kosslyn (Eds.), *Tutorials in learning and memory: Essays in honor of Gordon Bower* (pp. 31–60). San Francisco: Freeman.

Locke, E. A., Shaw, K. N., Saari, L. M., & Latham, G. P. (1981). Goal setting and task performance: 1969–1980. *Psychological Bulletin, 90,* 125–152.

Loftus, G. R., & Loftus, E. F. (1974). The influence of one memory retrieval on a subsequent memory retrieval. *Memory & Cognition, 2,* 467–471.

Maier, N. R. F. (1940). The behavior mechanisms concerned with problem solving. *Psychological Review, 47,* 43–58.

Maltzman, I. (1955). Thinking: From a behavioristic point of view. *Psychological Review, 62,* 275–286.

Mayer, R. E. (1974). Acquisition processes and resilience under varying testing conditions for structurally different problem-solving procedures. *Journal of Educational Psychology, 66,* 644–656.

Mayer, R. E. (1975). Forward transfer of different reading strategies evoked by testlike events in mathematics text. *Journal of Educational Psychology, 67,* 165–169.

Mayer, R. E. (1977). *Thinking and problem solving: An introduction to human cognition and learning.* Glenview, IL: Scott, Foresman.

Mayer, R. E. (1982a). Different problem-solving strategies for algebra word and equation problems. *Journal of Experimental Psychology: Learning, Memory, and Cognition, 8,* 448–462.

Mayer, R. E. (1982b). Memory for algebra story problems. *Journal of Educational Psychology, 74,* 199–216.

Mayer, R. E., & Greeno, J. G. (1972). Structural differences between learning outcomes produced by different instructional methods. *Journal of Educational Psychology, 63,* 165–173.

Mayer, R. E., Stiehl, C. C., & Greeno, J. G. (1975). Acquisition of understanding and skill in relation to subject's preparation and meaningfulness of instruction. *Journal of Educational Psychology, 67,* 331–350.

McCloskey, M. (1983). Naive theories of motion. In D. Gentner & A. L. Stevens (Eds), *Mental models* (pp. 299–324). Hillsdale, NJ: Lawrence Erlbaum Associates.

McCloskey, M., & Kohl, D. (1983). Naive physics: The curvilinear impetus principle and its role in interactions with moving objects. *Journal of Experimental Psychology: Learning, Memory, and Cognition, 9,* 146–156.

Medin, D. L., Altom, M. W., Edelson, S. M., & Freko, D. (1982). Correlated symptoms and simulated medical classification. *Journal of Experimental Psychology: Learning, Memory, and Cognition, 8,* 37–50.

Miller, G. A. (1956). The magical number seven, plus or minus two: Some limits on our capacity for processing information. *Psychological Review, 63,* 81–97.

Miller, R. A., Pople, H. E., & Myers, J. D. (1982). INTERNIST-I, An experimental computer-based diagnostic consultant for general internal medicine. *New England Journal of Medicine, 307,* 468–476.

Mosenthal, P., Davidson-Mosenthal, R., & Krieger, V. (1981). How fourth graders develop points of view in classroom writing. *Research in the Teaching of English, 15,* 197–214.

Mowrer, O. H. (1960). *Learning theory and the symbolic processes.* New York: Wiley.

Neves, D. M., & Anderson, J. R. (1981). Knowledge compilation: Mechanisms for the automatization of cognitive skills. In J. R. Anderson (Ed.), *Cognitive skills and their acquisition* (pp. 57–84). Hillsdale, NJ: Lawrence Erlbaum Associates.

Newell, A. (1980). One final word. In D. T. Tuma & F. Reif (Eds.), *Problem solving and education: Issues in teaching and research* (pp. 175–189). Hillsdale, NJ: Lawrence Erlbaum Associates.

Newell, A., Shaw, J. C., & Simon, H. A. (1958). Elements of a theory of human problem solving. *Psychological Review, 65,* 151–169.

Newell, A., & Simon, H. (1972). *Human problem solving.* Englewood Cliffs, NJ: Prentice-Hall.

Paige, J. M., & Simon, H. A. (1966). Cognitive processes in algebra word problems. In B. Kleinmuntz (Ed.), *Problem solving* (pp. 51–119). New York: Wiley.

Perfetto, G. A., Bransford, J. D., & Franks, J. J. (1983). Constraints on access in a problem solving context. *Memory & Cognition, 11,* 24–31.

Piaget, J. (1975). *The child's conception of the world.* New York: Littlefield (originally published in 1926).

Piaget, J. (1954). *The construction of reality in the child.* New York: Basic Books.

Polya, G. (1957). *How to solve it: A new aspect of mathematical method* (2nd ed.). Garden City, NJ: Doubleday.

Polya, G. (1968). *Mathematical discovery: On understanding, learning, and teaching problem solving* (Vol. 2). New York: Wiley.

Preece, P. F. W. (1976). Mapping cognitive structure: A comparison of methods. *Journal of Educational Psychology, 68,* 1–8.

Reed, S. K., Ernst, G. W., & Banerji, R. (1974). The role of analogy in transfer between similar problem states. *Cognitive Psychology, 6,* 436–450.

Reif, F. (1980). Theoretical and educational concerns with problem solving: Bridging the gaps with human cognitive engineering. In D. T. Tuma & F. Reif (Eds.), *Problem solving and education: Issues in teaching and research* (pp. 39–50). Hillsdale, NJ: Lawrence Erlbaum Associates.

Reitman, J. S. (1976). Skilled perception in Go: Deducing memory structures from inter-response times. *Cognitive Psychology, 8,* 336–356.

Reitman, W. (1965). *Cognition and thought.* New York: Wiley.

Rubenstein, M. F. (1980). A decade of experience in teaching an interdisciplinary problem-solving course. In D. T. Tuma & F. Reif (Eds.), *Problem solving and education: Issues in teaching and research* (pp. 25–38). Hillsdale, NJ: Lawrence Erlbaum Associates.

Ryle, G. (1949). *The concept of mind.* London: Hutchinson.

Sacerdoti, E. D. (1977). *A structure for plans and behavior.* New York: Elsevier North-Holland.

Scandura, J. M. (1974). Role of higher order rules in problem solving. *Journal of Educational Psychology, 102,* 984–991.

Scandura, J. M. (Ed.) (1977). *Problem solving: A structural/process approach with instructional implications.* New York: Academic Press.

Scardamalia, M. (1982). How children cope with the cognitive demands of writing. In C. H. Frederiksen, M. F. Whiteman, & J. F. Dominic (Eds.), *Writing: The nature, development, and teaching of written communication.* Hillsdale, NJ: Lawrence Erlbaum Associates.

Scardamalia, M., Bereiter, C., & Goelman, H. (1982). The role of production factors in writing ability. In M. Mystrand (Ed.), *What writers know: The language, process and structure of written discourse.* New York: Academic Press.

Schoenfeld, A. H. (1979). Can heuristics be taught? In J. Lochhead & J. Clement (Eds.), *Cognitive process instruction* (pp. 315–338). Philadelphia, PA: The Franklin Institute Press.

Schoenfeld, A. H. (1982). Measures of problem solving performance and of problem solving instruction. *Journal for Research in Mathematics Education, 13,* 31–49.

Schoenfeld, A. H., & Herrmann, D. J. (1982). Problem perception and knowledge structure in expert and novice mathematical problem solvers. *Journal of Experimental Psychology: Learning, Memory, and Cognition, 8,* 484–494.

Schustack, M. W., & Anderson, J. R. (1979). Effects of analogy to prior knowledge on memory for new information. *Journal of Verbal Learning and Verbal Behavior, 18,* 565–583.

Selz, O. (1922). *Zur psychologie des produktiven Denkens.* Bonn: Cohen.

Selz, O. (1964). The revision of the fundamental conceptions of intellectual processes. In J. M. Mandler & G. Mandler (Eds.), *Thinking: From association to Gestalt* (pp. 225–236). New York: Wiley.

Shavelson, R. J. (1972). Some aspects of the correspondence between content structure and cognitive structure in physics instruction. *Journal of Educational Psychology, 63,* 225–234.

Shavelson, R. J. (1974). Methods for examining representations of a subject-matter structure in a student's memory. *Journal of Research in Science Teaching, 11,* 231–249.

Shavelson, R. J., & Stanton, G. C. (1975). Construct validation: Methodology and application of three measures of cognitive structure. *Journal of Educational Measurement, 12,* 67–85.

Siegler, R. S., & Klahr, D. (1982). When do children learn? The relationship between existing knowledge and the acquisition of new knowledge. In R. Glaser (Ed.), *Advances in instructional psychology* (pp. 121–211). Hillsdale, NJ: Lawrence Erlbaum Associates.

Silver, E. A. (1979). Student perceptions of relatedness among mathematical verbal problems. *Journal for Research in Mathematics Education, 10,* 195–210.

Simon, D. P., & Simon, H. A. (1978). Individual differences in solving physics problems. In R. S. Siegler (Ed.), *Children's thinking: What develops?* (pp. 325–348). Hillsdale, NJ: Lawrence Erlbaum Associates.

Simon, H. A. (1973). The structure of ill-structured problems. *Artificial Intelligence, 4,* 181–201.

Simon, H. A. (1974). How big is a chunk? *Science, 183,* 482–488.

Simon, H. A. (1978). Information-processing theory of human problem solving. In W. K. Estes (Ed.), *Handbook of learning and cognitive processes,* Vol. 5, *Human information processing* (pp. 271–296). Hillsdale, NJ: Lawrence Erlbaum Associates.

Simon, H. A. (1980). Problem solving and education. In D. T. Tuma & F. Reif (Eds.), *Problem solving and education: Issues in teaching and research* (pp. 81–96). Hillsdale, NJ: Lawrence Erlbaum Associates.

Simon, H. A., & Barenfeld, M. (1969). Information-processing analysis of perceptual processes in problem solving. *Psychological Review, 76,* 473–483.

Simon, H. A., & Gilmartin, K. (1973). A simulation of memory for chess positions. *Cognitive Psychology, 5,* 29–46.

Simon, H. A., & Hayes, J. R. (1976). Understanding complex task instructions. In D. Klahr (Ed.), *Cognition and instruction* (pp. 269–286). Hillsdale, NJ: Lawrence Erlbaum Associates.

Thorndike, E. L. (1898). Animal intelligence: An experimental study of the associative process in animals. *Psychological Review Monograph Supplement,* No. 8.

Thro, M. P. (1978). Relationships between associative and content structure of physics concepts. *Journal of Educational Psychology, 70,* 971–978.

Trabasso, T. R. (1975). Representation, memory and reasoning: How do we make transitive inferences? In A. D. Pick (Ed.), *Minnesota symposium on child psychology* (Vol. 9, pp. 135–172). Minneapolis: University of Minnesota Press.

Tweney, R. D. (1981, Nov.). *Confirmatory and disconfirmatory heuristics in Michael Faraday's scientific research.* Paper presented at Meeting of the Psychonomic Society, Philadelphia.

Voss, J. F. (1986). Social Studies. In R. F. Dillon & R. J. Sternberg (Eds.), *Cognition and instruction.* New York: Academic Press.

Voss, J. F., Fincher-Kiefer, R. H., Greene, T. R., & Post, T. A. (1986). Individual differences in performance: The contrastive approach to knowledge. In R. J. Sternberg (Ed.), *Advances in the psychology of human intelligence* (pp. 297–334). New York: Academic Press.

Voss, J. F., Greene, T. R., Post, T. A., & Penner, B. C. (1983). Problem solving skills in the social sciences. In G. Bower (Ed.), *The psychology of learning and motivation: Advances in research and theory* (Vol. 17, pp. 165–213). New York: Academic Press.

Voss, J. F., Tyler, S., & Yengo, L. A. (1983). Individual differences in the solving of social science problems. In R. F. Dillon & R. R. Schmeck (Eds.), *Individual differences in cognition* (pp. 205–232). New York: Academic Press.

Wagner, D. A., & Scurrah, M. J. (1971). Some characteristics of human problem solving in chess. *Cognitive Psychology, 2,* 454–478.

Wallas, G. (1926). *The art of thought.* New York: Harcourt, Brace.

Weisberg, R. W., & Alba, J. W. (1981). An examination of the alleged role of "Fixation" in the solution of several "Insight" problems. *Journal of Experimental Psychology: General, 110,* 169–192.

Weisberg, R. W., & Alba, J. W. (1982). Problem solving is not like perception: More on Gestalt theory. *Journal of Experimental Psychology: General, 111,* 326–330.

Wertheimer, M. (1959). *Productive thinking.* New York: Harper & Row.

White, B. Y. (1983). Sources of difficulty in understanding Newtonian dynamics. *Cognitive Science, 7,* 41–66.

Wickelgren, W. A. (1974). *How to solve problems.* San Francisco: Freeman.

Wiser, M., & Carey, S. (1983). When heat and temperature were one. In D. Gentner & A. L. Stevens (Eds.), *Mental models* (pp. 267–298). Hillsdale, NJ: Lawrence Erlbaum Associates.

Woodworth, R. S. (1938). *Experimental psychology.* New York: Henry Holt.

Author Index

295

Subject Index